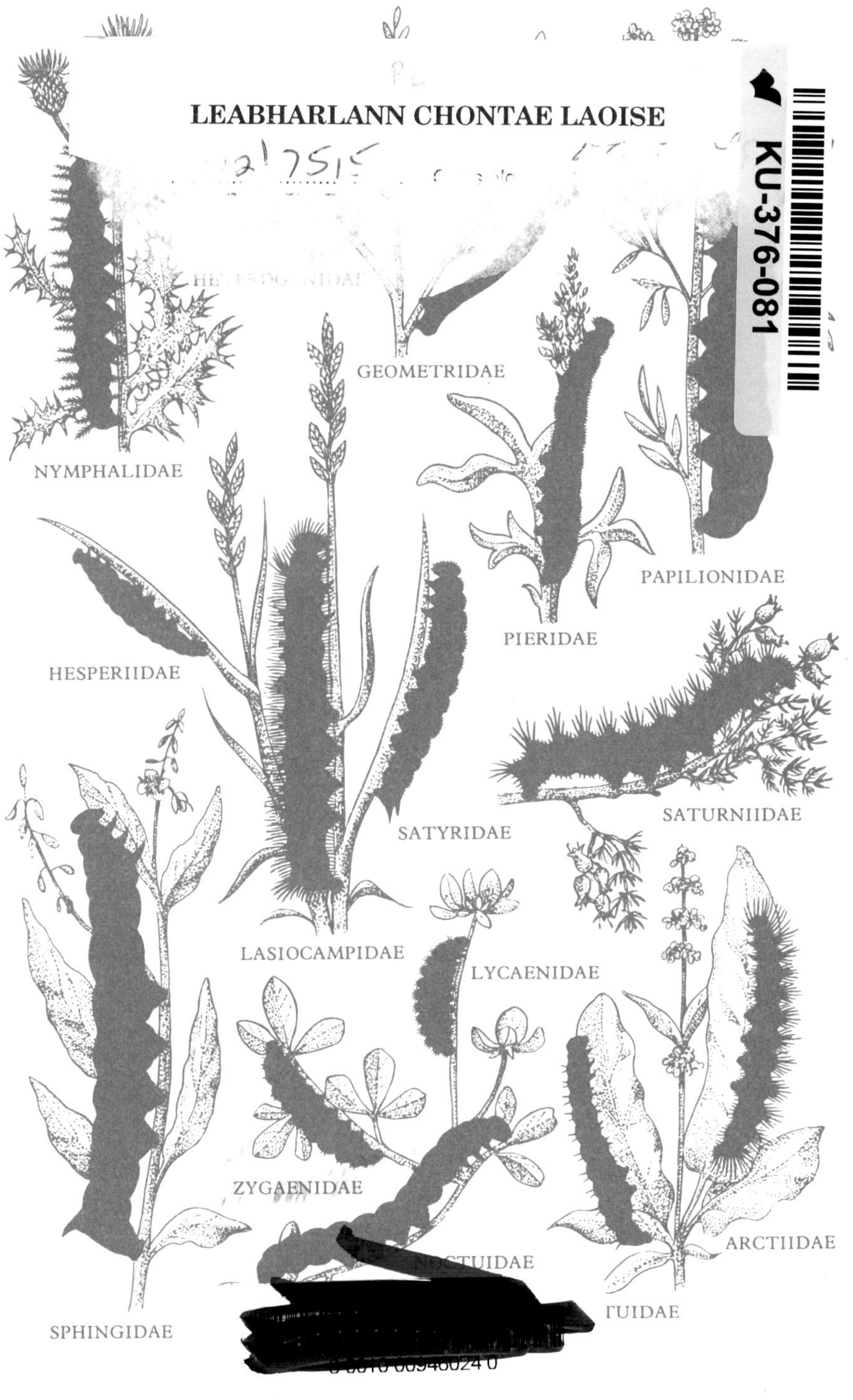
NYMPHALIDAE
GEOMETRIDAE
PAPILIONIDAE
PIERIDAE
HESPERIIDAE
SATURNIIDAE
SATYRIDAE
LASIOCAMPIDAE
LYCAENIDAE
ZYGAENIDAE
ARCTIIDAE
SPHINGIDAE

COLLINS FIELD GUIDE

# CATERPILLARS
## OF BRITAIN AND EUROPE

## Other titles in the *Collins Field Guide* series

Birds of Australia
***Graham Pizzey and Roy Doyle***

Birds of Britain and Europe, 5th edition
***Roger T Peterson, Guy Mountfort and P A D Hollom***

Birds of East Africa
***J G Williams and N Arlott***

Birds of Galapagos
***M Harris***

Birds of New Zealand
***R A Falla, R B Sibson and E S Turbott***

Birds of the Seychelles and Outlying Islands
***Malcolm Penny***

Birds of South-East Asia
***B King, M Woodcock and E Dickinson***

Birds of West Africa
***W Serle and G Morel***

Birds of the West Indies
***James Bond***

Butterflies of Britain and Europe
***L Higgins and N D Riley***

Grasshoppers and Crickets of Britain and Northern Europe
***Heiko Bellman***

Insects of Britain and Northern Europe, 3rd edition
***Michael Chinery***

Land Snails of Britain and Northern Europe
***M P Kerney, R A D Cameron, G Riley***

Larger Mammals of Africa
***Jean Dorst and Pierre Dandelot***

Mammals of Africa including Madagascar
***T Haltenorth and H Diller***

Mammals of Britain and Europe
***David Macdonald and Priscilla Barrett***

National Parks of East Africa
***John Williams and Norman Arlott***

Rare Birds of Britain and Europe
***P Alstrom, P Colston and I Lewington***

Reptiles and Amphibians of Britain and Europe
***E N Arnold, J A Burton and D W Ovenden***

Trees of Britain and Northern Europe
***Alan Mitchell***

Wildlife of the Falklands and South Georgia
***Ian Strange***

COLLINS FIELD GUIDE

# CATERPILLARS
# OF
# BRITAIN & EUROPE

DAVID J CARTER

Illustrated by

BRIAN HARGREAVES

HarperCollins*Publishers*

HarperCollins*Publishers*
77–85 Fulham Palace Road
London
W6 8JB

The HarperCollins website address is:

www.**fire**and**water**.com





ISBN 0 00 219080 X

First published 1986
Reprinted with corrections 1994

02 04 06 05 03 01

4 6 8 10 9 7 5 3

Colour reproduction by Alpha Reprographics, Harefield, Middlesex
Produced by Midas Printing Ltd.

# Contents

Preface 7

About this book 9

The anatomy of caterpillars 11

The life cycle 12

Caterpillar enemies 14

Caterpillar defences 15

How to find caterpillars 17

Rearing caterpillars 19

Study and conservation 21

HEPIALIDAE 23
COSSIDAE 24
ZYGAENIDAE 25
LIMACODIDAE 27
HETEROGYNIDAE 28
SESIIDAE 29
HESPERIIDAE 30
PAPILIONIDAE 33
PIERIDAE 36
LYCAENIDAE 41
RIODINIDAE 48
NYMPHALIDAE 48
SATYRIDAE 57
LASIOCAMPIDAE 61
SATURNIIDAE 65
BRAHMAEIDAE 67
ENDROMIDAE 67
DREPANIDAE 68
THYATIRIDAE 70
GEOMETRIDAE 73
SPHINGIDAE 116
NOTODONTIDAE 122
DILOBIDAE 128
THAUMETOPOEIDAE 201
LYMANTRIIDAE 202
ARCTIIDAE 207
CTENUCHIDAE 213
NOLIDAE 214
NOCTUIDAE 215

Bibliography 270

Foodplant tables 272

General index 287

Foodplant index 293

# The Colour Plates

The anatomy of a typical caterpillar 129

The life cycle of the Peacock Butterfly 130

The life cycle of the Emperor Moth 131

Caterpillars on their foodplants (Pls. 1–33) 132–197

Species often confused with caterpillars (Pl. 34) 198

Caterpillar enemies 200

# Preface

The aim of this book is to provide an identification guide to caterpillars that are likely to be encountered in gardens, parks and the countryside, and a useful reference work for students and ecologists interested in insect–plant relationships. While there are many books on British and European butterflies and moths, there are very few dealing specifically with caterpillars and most of these are long out of print.

It soon becomes apparent to the student of butterflies and moths that they are intimately linked with their foodplants, and the good lepidopterist learns to become a good botanist. By depicting caterpillars on their foodplants in the same arrangement as a flora, we hope that this book will have an equal appeal to entomologists and botanists as well as to gardeners, farmers, foresters and biology teachers.

Caterpillars have often been treated as the 'Cinderella' stage of butterflies and moths, and are frequently regarded as ugly or repulsive. It is hoped that the colour plates in this book will draw attention to the beauty of many of these fascinating creatures and promote an interest in their study. There is still much to learn about the life histories of even the more common species of European butterflies and moths, and there is plenty of opportunity for the keen amateur to make new discoveries.

We wish to acknowledge the Trustees of the British Museum (Natural History) for permission to use their extensive collections and other reference sources and to thank the Keeper of Entomology, Dr L. A. Mound, for his support and encouragement. Special thanks are due to the author's wife, Brenda Carter, for checking much of the manuscript and for assisting with research, and to the illustrator's wife, Joyce Hargreaves, for preparing the indexes.

*David Carter and Brian Hargreaves*
January 1986

# About this book

There are over five thousand different species of butterflies and moths in Britain and Europe and many of these are separated into numerous subspecies and races. The life histories of many species are still quite poorly known, and some caterpillars are so similar in appearance that they can only be distinguished by minute differences requiring the use of a microscope. Clearly, it is outside the scope of a book of this size to deal with the entire European fauna of these insects and so a selection of caterpillars of over five hundred species of butterflies and moths is described and figured, concentrating on those that are frequently encountered or of special interest.

The caterpillars represent the main feeding stage in the life cycle of butterflies and moths, and are usually found on their foodplants. Generally speaking, they are associated with distinct groups of foodplants, often closely related to each other. This relationship is so striking that it has been proposed that butterflies and moths reached the peak of their evolutionary development at the same time as the flowering plants and so to some degree have evolved in parallel, a fascinating case of coevolution. However, recent studies suggest that this may not be strictly true and that caterpillars may choose their foodplants on the basis of their chemical constitution. It seems that many caterpillars can distinguish between closely related organic chemicals, which either induce them to feed or act as repellents.

For whatever reason, caterpillars can often be grouped by their foodplants and this approach has been adopted in the arrangement of the colour plates in this book. Each plate illustrates the caterpillars feeding on a particular group of plants, the plants being arranged in roughly the same order as in *The Wild Flowers of Britain and Northern Europe* by Fitter, Fitter and Blamey (3rd edition). On the caption page facing each plate is a series of marginal colour illustrations of a selection of adult butterflies and moths, representing as far as possible a cross section of families and forms occurring on those particular foodplants. At the bottom of each caption page is a colour illustration of some aspect of the life history of one of the species figured.

It will become evident that it has not been possible to illustrate the caterpillars to the same scale as their foodplants, although, as far as possible, the caterpillars are roughly to scale with each other. Lengths of the caterpillars are given in the text but it must be remembered that these apply only to fully grown specimens. Most foodplants are figured with their flowers to facilitate identification but this does not necessarily mean that caterpillars will be found on the plants when they are in flower. Times of appearance are given in the text.

The text is arranged systematically, according to the order of Kloet and Hincks's revised *Check List of British Insects*, with additions from Leraut's *Liste Systématique et Synonymique des Lépidoptères de France, Belgique et Corse*. Butterfly nomenclature follows Higgins and Hargreaves's *Butterflies of Britain and Europe*.

In the text, emphasis is placed on foodplants in the British Isles, as these are generally better known and more reliably recorded than those in continental Europe. As many butterflies and moths are at the edge of their geographical range in the British Isles, it is not surprising that their foodplant range is often more restricted there than elsewhere. Wherever possible an indication is given when other foodplants are eaten in continental Europe. Scientific names of foodplants are placed in brackets after the common name. Where only a generic name is given (e.g. *Quercus*), this indicates that either a number of species are eaten or that the particular food-plant species is uncertain.

Accounts of biology also apply mainly to species in the British Isles unless otherwise stated. It would not be possible to record local variations in biology throughout Europe, even if these were fully known, but as a rule it can be assumed that northern localities will have fewer broods occurring later in the year, while southern regions will tend to have more broods, appearing earlier. Biology is also affected by such factors as altitude, availability of food and local temperature variations. Alpine races often have a similar biology to northern races. It should also be taken into account that caterpillars reared in captivity will often behave differently to those in the wild.

Although it is hoped that the arrangement and presentation of the plates will facilitate identifications, it is not possible to illustrate all hostplant–caterpillar associations without considerable repetition. If a caterpillar cannot be found illustrated on its foodplant, adjacent plates should first be examined. If this fails, the foodplant index should be consulted as well as the list of major foodplants in the appendix. This list includes polyphagous species, which feed on a wide range of plants, and should always be taken into account. After a time the common polyphagous species will be readily recognized and will cease to present difficulties in identification.

Many species of butterflies and moths have variable caterpillars, some displaying a wide range of different colour forms, and it has not proved practical to figure them all. The descriptive text deals with colour variation and also gives some indication if early instar caterpillars are substantially different to later instars. Some of the more striking examples of early instar caterpillars are figured in the plates.

Occasionally, caterpillars wander onto other plants when their own foodplant has become exhausted and these will inevitably cause problems of identification. This happens fairly frequently in the case of tree-feeding species, which may drop into the undergrowth. When caterpillars are found in such situations, a note should be made of the trees growing above.

# Introduction

## THE ANATOMY OF CATERPILLARS

(*See* page 129)
As the caterpillar is primarily a feeding machine, it is relatively simply constructed. It has a head, followed by thirteen body segments. The first three body segments comprise the thorax and the remaining segments the abdomen but for the purposes of description in this book, they are simply referred to as body segments 1 to 13.

The head is enclosed by a tough, sclerotized head capsule, which bears a number of important appendages and sensory structures. It is armed with a pair of stout jaws or mandibles, which are usually toothed but are sometimes modified into blunt grinding plates. The 'lips' above and below the mandibles are called the labrum and labium respectively. The labrum is a simple plate bearing a few sensory hairs but the labium is a much more complex structure, carrying the sensory labial palps and the spinneret. The spinneret is the outlet of the silk-producing glands. Silk is extruded as a liquid through an aperture at the tip of the spinneret and dries in the air to form fine but tough strands of silk. This silk serves a number of important functions: binding together leaves to form shelters and nests, spinning platforms on which to moult, providing escape lines and, ultimately, constructing the cocoon. On either side of the labium are the maxillary palps, another set of sensory organs responsible for testing food and guiding it towards the mouth. A further pair of sensory organs, the antennae, are situated on either side of the mandibles and behind these are the simple eyes or ocelli, usually six on each side, arranged roughly in a circle.

The three thoracic segments each carry a pair of segmented thoracic legs, terminating in simple claws. These legs are usually more important for holding the food than for walking. The abdominal segments do not carry true legs but body segments 6–9 and 13 usually bear pairs of simple, sucker-like, false legs known as prolegs. In certain groups, particularly in looper caterpillars of the family Geometridae, the number of prolegs is reduced. The prolegs bear circles or bands of small hooks called crochets, which enable them to maintain a secure grasp on the foodplant. These are so effective that in some cases it is practically impossible to remove a caterpillar from its foodplant without causing serious damage to the prolegs.

Sawfly caterpillars, which are very similar to those of butterflies and moths, may be distinguished by the presence of more than five pairs of prolegs on the body. In fact, many sawfly caterpillars appear to have legs along the entire length of the body.

The prolegs on segment 13 are often referred to as the claspers or anal claspers. In some species these claspers are modified to form long tails, a good example being the caterpillar of the Puss Moth (*Cerura vinula*).

Along the sides of the body are a series of oval or round spiracles, which are the external openings of an internal network of tubes called tracheae. These tubes distribute oxygen throughout the body. Spiracles are present on all body segments except 2, 3, 12 and 13. The size, shape and colour of the spiracles are often useful in identifying caterpillars. There is usually a stripe of colour along the side of the body following the line of the spiracles, which is called the spiracular line or band.

Each body segment has its own complement of hairs, often arising from small plates called pinacula. Some caterpillars are densely hairy, the hairs either being generally distributed or arranged in distinct tufts, sometimes arising from raised warts. These hairs are mainly sensory in function but can also serve to protect the caterpillar from parasites and predators. The hairs on some caterpillars are so small that they are hardly visible while others are long and may be barbed or plumed. Some may even carry poisons. The type and arrangement of body hairs is characteristic of particular groups of butterflies and moths and their study plays an important part in their classification.

Body segments 1 and 13 usually have a protective plate or shield on the back and the development and coloration of this structure often provides useful characters for identification.

The bodies of many caterpillars bear specialized glands. Many have a throat gland behind and beneath the head which, in some cases, is capable of squirting an offensive liquid such as formic acid. Others have a neck gland above and behind the head called an osmeterium, which emits a strong-smelling substance to repel predators. Caterpillars of the family Lymantriidae have small raised glands on the back, which probably produce poisonous substances for defence, while caterpillars of the butterfly family Lycaenidae have glands on the back that produce a sweet, liquid 'honeydew' to attract ants.

## THE LIFE CYCLE

(*See* pages 130–1)

The life cycle of butterflies and moths is divided into four distinct phases: egg, caterpillar, pupa and adult. Each phase is responsible for an important aspect of the insect's development. In the egg phase, the embryo develops into a minute caterpillar, which eventually bites its way out of the eggshell. The caterpillar represents the feeding and growth phase and moults several times to permit the body to expand. The stage between each moult is called an instar and most caterpillars go through four to six instars. The pupa represents a further developmental phase in which the body is extensively rearranged to form the adult butterfly or moth, which eventually emerges from the pupal shell and expands its wings before flying off. The word pupa derives from the Latin for a doll or puppet, and refers to the way in which the developing wings and other appendages are enclosed in a mummy-like case. The adult represents the breeding phase and is the most mobile of the four stages. It is thus able to seek a mate and distribute the species.

After hatching from the egg, many caterpillars consume the shell before searching for the foodplant. The first meal of eggshell often provides sufficient energy for the young caterpillar to travel some distance in search of its foodplant and it is probable that some go into hibernation having eaten only the eggshell.

Moulting is an important process. As the caterpillars are particularly vulnerable at this stage, they normally move to a place of concealment before spinning small mats of silk to which they attach themselves by their prolegs. Moulting commences as the front part of the body inflates to split the skin and the caterpillar gradually crawls forward, leaving the old skin still attached to the silken mat. In a similar way, the old head capsule splits open and is discarded. The caterpillar remains inactive for a time until the new skin has hardened and then resumes feeding.

When fully grown, the caterpillar becomes restless and wanders around to find a suitable pupation site, sometimes at some considerable distance from the foodplant. At this stage, it may change colour to merge with its new background. Just prior to pupation, many caterpillars become foreshortened and rather sluggish.

Most moth caterpillars construct some sort of protective cocoon in which to pupate. Some simply spin a few leaves together to form a rough shelter while others spin elaborate cocoons, sometimes incorporating leaves, bark or particles of soil and debris. Those that pupate below ground usually construct an earthen chamber, which is lined with silk. These cocoons protect the pupae and regulate the atmosphere inside so that they do not become too wet or dry. They also afford some protection from parasites and predators, particularly those that incorporate poisonous body hairs from the caterpillar.

Butterfly pupae, with the exception of the skippers, are not formed within cocoons but are mostly suspended from leaves and stems. The caterpillar spins a small pad of silk to which it clings with its hind claspers. The skin then splits at the head and the pupa gradually wriggles free, working the skin towards the tail. At the final critical point, the newly emerged pupa releases its tail from the old caterpillar skin and attaches itself to the silken pad by means of a hooked structure called the cremaster. The pupa being secured, the empty skin usually falls to the ground. Some species further support their pupae by means of a silken girdle spun around the middle of the body and attached to the leaf or stem.

As most butterfly pupae are not concealed in cocoons, they are often camouflaged by their shape or coloration. Small White butterfly (*Pieris rapae*) pupae are green when formed on the foodplant but grey or brown when formed on fences or similar surfaces. The golden coloration of some pupae gives rise to the popular term 'chrysalis' which is derived from the Greek word for gold. Many pupae resemble dead leaves and some even look like bird droppings.

Just before the adult butterfly or moth emerges from the pupa it darkens in colour, and it is often possible to detect the wing pattern through the pupa case. As the pupa skin splits open, the adult begins to emerge and swallows air to expand the body and further split the pupal case. It gradually frees the appendages and crawls away to a suitable resting site before pumping blood into the wings to expand them. Some female moths do not have functional wings and some do not even leave the cocoon, mating and laying eggs on the spot where they emerge.

The duration of each stage of the life cycle varies according to the species and sometimes to the conditions under which it is living. Many butterflies have only one generation at the northern limit of their distribution while in the south there may be three or more broods in a year. Eggs often hatch in one to four weeks, but some overwinter before producing young caterpillars in the following spring when there is a plentiful supply of fresh young foliage. Similarly, some caterpillars feed up rapidly and pupate within a few weeks while others overwinter before completing their growth. Others, particularly those feeding on wood and other foods of low nutritional value, take two or more years to complete their development. Even after spinning their cocoons, some caterpillars remain inside for several weeks or even months before pupating. The pupa is even more variable in duration, lasting from a few days to several years. Sometimes broods split with some pupae producing moths after a few weeks while the remainder do not emerge until the following year. Some have an extended emergence period so that adults may emerge over several months. Most adult butterflies do not live for more than a few weeks, but some hibernate before mating and laying eggs in the following year; butterflies such as the Brimstone (*Gonepteryx rhamni*) may live for as long as ten months. This amazing flexibility of the life cycle is one of the major factors contributing to the success of the butterflies and moths as a group and enables them to survive under a wide range of climatic conditions.

## CATERPILLAR ENEMIES

(*See* plate 35 on page 200)

Caterpillars are attacked by a wide range of predators and parasites and are subject to a number of sometimes quite devastating diseases. Predators range from spiders, mites and various carnivorous insects such as beetles, bugs, wasps, ants, earwigs and lacewing larvae, to reptiles, amphibians, birds and mammals. It is well known that small birds such as blue tits feed vast quantities of caterpillars to their young, and some foresters put up nesting boxes to encourage birds that can control the numbers of pest species in this way. Even such large birds as owls are known to hunt for caterpillars to supplement their diet. In the same way, mice and shrews are well-known predators of caterpillars, and a recent survey revealed that caterpillars also form a major part of the diet of some foxes, which forage on the ground for them.

Numerous different parasites attack caterpillars and will inevitably be encountered by anyone who attempts to rear butterflies and moths. Parasitic wasps are commonly referred to as 'ichneumons' but may belong to families other than the Ichneumonidae. Many have long ovipositors at the tip of the abdomen, enabling them to pierce the skin of caterpillars and to lay their eggs within. The parasitic grubs live and feed inside the caterpillar's body consuming all but the vital organs, so that for some time the caterpillar continues to feed and grow in the normal way. When the grubs are fully grown, they usually bore out through the caterpillar's skin to pupate and emerge as a new generation of wasps. One of the best known parasites to behave in this way is *Apanteles glomeratus* Linnaeus, belonging to the family Braconidae. It is a major parasite of the Large White butterfly (*Pieris brassicae*) and is often responsible for reducing the numbers of this important pest species. The grubs that emerge from the moribund caterpillar spin a distinctive mass of bright yellow cocoons alongside the body.

Some of the smaller parasitic wasps are unable to penetrate the skins of caterpillars and so adopt different strategies for gaining entrance. Some lay their eggs within the eggs of butterflies and moths, while others lay on the foodplant, where the eggs are ingested by the caterpillars during the normal course of feeding. Others lay their eggs on the caterpillar's body, where the grubs hatch and bore their way through the soft membranes situated between the segments. Some even remain as external parasites, attached to the skin.

Another group of parasites are flies of the family Tachinidae. Their methods of parasitizing butterflies and moths are very similar to those adopted by the parasitic wasps, although eggs are most commonly laid on the skin and grubs bore their way in. When fully grown, they bore their way out of the dying caterpillar and form their characteristic smooth, oval puparia nearby.

Fungi, mainly in the form of moulds, are serious enemies of eggs, caterpillars and pupae. One of the most interesting groups belongs to the genus *Cordyceps*. These fungi attack caterpillars living in the soil, particularly during hibernation. The fungal mycelia ramify throughout the body of the caterpillar, which dies and becomes 'mummified'. The mature fungus sends up a long stem, which bears a fruiting body above ground. The resulting 'vegetable caterpillars' are the subject of much interest in many parts of the world and in China they are ground up to make a tonic medicine.

Diseases of caterpillars fall into two categories, those caused by bacteria and those by viruses. Bacterial infections make the caterpillars lethargic and they cease to feed, emitting brown fluids from both ends of the body. The body contents liquefy and become foul smelling and the entire caterpillar blackens and dies. Caterpillars infected with viruses show certain different symptoms. The skin does not blacken and the dying caterpillars often remain hanging limply from the foodplant. There is no strong smell associated with freshly dead caterpillars that are the victims of virus disease. Caterpillars infected with one type of virus disease emit characteristic whitish pellets of frass.

Extensive research has been carried out on bacterial and viral diseases of insects to investigate the possibility of using them as agents of biological control. Both bacteria and viruses have been used with success in controlling outbreaks of pest caterpillars, particularly those of forest trees, using aerial sprays. The advantage of this type of germ warfare in comparison with other forms of insecticide is that in many cases only the pest species is killed and other insects remain unharmed. However, much further research is necessary before the extensive use of these sprays will be regarded as completely safe.

## CATERPILLAR DEFENCES

As the primary functions of caterpillars are to feed and grow, they are not adapted to be as mobile as adult butterflies and moths. For this reason, they are less able to escape from their enemies and so have adopted a number of different defence strategies. The most fleet-footed of caterpillars are probably those of tiger moths of the family Arctiidae, but even these feign death when first threatened, only later making a dash for freedom. Another escape method is to drop from the foodplant into the undergrowth and to crawl back when the danger is past. Some caterpillars improve on this method by dropping on a thread of silk and remaining suspended until it is safe to climb back up again. When suspended in mid-air they sometimes spin themselves around so rapidly that they become almost invisible.

Probably the most effective and universally adopted method of defence used by caterpillars is camouflage. Many caterpillars that feed on leaves are green, while those that tend to rest on stems are brown. Some caterpillars are even affected by the colour of their food, particularly if this happens to be flower petals. Young caterpillars of the Emperor Moth (*Saturnia pavonia*) are black, and rest on the stems of heather, where they are very difficult to detect. Fully grown caterpillars of this species are so large that they are unable to camouflage themselves on stems. Their bodies become green, banded with black, thus breaking up the body shape and making them quite difficult to detect when sitting amongst the foliage.

Many caterpillars are dark on the upper surface and light on the underside. This counter-shading effectively cancels out the shadows cast by the caterpillar's body and enables it to merge with the background. Another device that reduces shadow effects is a fringe of hairs low down along the sides of the body, which is pressed against the leaf or twig on which the caterpillar is resting. This method is further extended in the case of the Lappet Moth (*Gastropacha quercifolia*) and its relatives, which have a row of large, fleshy flaps along the sides of the body.

Grass-feeding and conifer-feeding caterpillars are mostly striped with green and white or yellow to blend with the narrow leaves of their foodplants. Many pine feeders have reddish-brown heads, which resemble small buds.

Looper caterpillars of the family Geometridae have the prolegs reduced to two functional pairs. This reduction of legs enables these mainly long and slender caterpillars to resemble twigs and stems, and for this reason they are sometimes called stick caterpillars. To heighten the effect, many species have swellings and markings on the body that resemble buds and leaf scars. The twig-like effect is further enhanced by the resting posture, with the body stretched out at an angle to the stem on which the caterpillar is resting. Caterpillars of the Essex Emerald (*Thetidia smaragdaria*) improve their camouflage by attaching small fragments of the foodplant to their bodies.

Many markings on caterpillars serve to disguise their shape and make them less conspicuous, but some species are distasteful to predators and so advertise their presence with striking body patterns of warning coloration. Caterpillars of the Cinnabar Moth (*Tyria jacobaeae*), which are distasteful to most birds, are brightly banded with orange and yellow and live and feed together in large groups, so that they are easily recognized and unlikely to be eaten accidentally. Caterpillars of the burnet moths (*Zygaena*) are boldly patterned with black and yellow, advertising the fact that they contain cyanide compounds and are highly poisonous.

The Puss Moth caterpillar (*Cerura vinula*) exploits a wide range of defence strategies. Its large, bright green body is effectively broken up by a blackish 'saddle' marking at the middle and so is well camouflaged. If threatened, however, it raises up the front half of the body to display a red ring around the head with two black 'eye spots'. At the same time it raises its two tails and extrudes a pair of lash-like, red filaments. In addition to this it is able to squirt a jet of formic acid from a gland in the throat.

The Elephant Hawk-moth (*Deilephila elpenor*) caterpillar does not possess any offensive weapons, normally relying on its camouflage pattern for protection but, when disturbed, it withdraws the head into the body, causing the front part to swell up and display a pair of large eye spots. The front half of the body is reared up and produces a remarkable snake-like appearance. Unlike most other hawk-moths, this species has the tail horn greatly reduced. This horn is almost certainly a defensive device in other hawk-moth caterpillars and remains effective in the early stages by being much larger in proportion to the body.

The Swallowtail (*Papilio machaon*) and many of its relatives have glands on the neck that emit a strong-smelling substance, which is apparently effective in deterring enemies.

Another protective device is the presence of dense hairs or large spines on the head and body. These effectively increase the caterpillar's size and make it difficult for small birds to swallow. However, cuckoos and other large birds are known to eat hairy caterpillars. The hairs probably also serve to deter some parasites from laying their eggs, although this is not always successful and some hairy caterpillars do become parasitized.

Although in many cases the hairs offer merely mechanical protection, a number of species have poisonous hairs. Many of these live communally to increase the effect of their poisonous nature, and caterpillars of the processionary moths (*Thaumetopoea*) move around in columns so that they are less likely to be attacked or eaten by mistake. The hairs of the Brown-tail Moth (*Euproctis chrysorrhoea*) caterpillar protect this insect throughout its life. Hairs from the body are incorporated into the cocoon at pupation and, on emergence, the female moth gathers some on the tip of her abdomen so that she can use them to cover her egg mass.

A number of species construct large communal nests of silk spun amongst the foliage, and only leave them at night when they come out to feed. Other caterpillars, such as those of many skipper butterflies, live in individual shelters constructed of rolled or folded leaves. Many caterpillars that do not have special shelters feed at night, hiding by day amongst debris on the ground, in crevices of bark or simply under leaves. Many cutworm caterpillars of the family Noctuidae live below ground by day, coming up to feed at the bases of the foodplants at dusk.

An interesting variation on the theme of camouflage may be found in those species that resemble bird droppings. Caterpillars of the Comma butterfly (*Polygonia c-album*) are excellent examples and even rest in a curved position to heighten the resemblance. Young caterpillars of the Alder Moth (*Acronicta alni*) are also excellent bird-dropping mimics but abandon this camouflage in the final instar, when they are boldly patterned with black and yellow and have large black paddle-shaped body hairs. This patterning suggests that the caterpillars are distasteful, but a display of warning coloration would probably be less effective than camouflage in the earlier stages.

A fascinating strategy of protective behaviour has been evolved in caterpillars of butterflies of the family Lycaenidae, where many have close associations with various species of ants. This is based on their ability to secrete a sugary fluid from glands situated on the back. This fluid is highly attractive to ants and they may be observed stroking the caterpillars' bodies to 'milk' them. In return for this reward, the ants do not attack the caterpillars and by their presence protect them from other predators. This is taken a stage further in species such as the Large Blue (*Maculinea arion*); the caterpillars are picked up by the ants and carried back to the nest, where they feed on ant larvae.

## HOW TO FIND CATERPILLARS

Caterpillars are often seen sitting on leaves and crawling across paths, but very many more remain concealed and seldom come to notice. However, it is often possible to find them by careful searching. When examining the foliage of trees and shrubs, particular attention should be paid to the undersides of leaves and to leaves that show signs of feeding. The presence of large caterpillars such as those of hawk-moths may be indicated by pellets of frass (droppings) on the ground beneath the foodplant. Leaves spun together with silk should also be examined, although the occupants will often prove to be caterpillars of the smaller moths not dealt with in this book. Nevertheless, they make a fascinating study in themselves and are well worth rearing.

Searching the foliage of low-growing plants is seldom as productive, but again the undersides of the leaves and the ground beneath should be examined. Perhaps the best time to look under sprawling, low-growing plants such as thyme (*Thymus*) and rock-rose (*Helianthemum*) is in the autumn and winter, when many hibernating caterpillars may be sheltering in the leaf litter.

Searching at night with a torch or lantern can be very productive, as many species are active at this time and may be seen feeding.

A simple way of obtaining quite large numbers of caterpillars is to use a beating tray. This may be a specially constructed piece of equipment made of canvas stretched over a wooden frame, or simply an inverted umbrella or a sheet spread out and placed beneath the branches of a tree or shrub. The branches are then sharply rapped with a stick to dislodge the caterpillars, which fall into the tray below. A warning should be given not to take the word 'beating' too literally as this will damage the foliage and probably kill many of the caterpillars. A sudden shock is more likely to dislodge caterpillars than a sustained onslaught, which will only make them cling on more tightly. Some large caterpillars such as those of the hawk-moths are seldom shaken out and must be searched for as already described. Beating is not very successful in windy weather as the caterpillars are already clinging tightly, and in wet weather the beating tray soon becomes waterlogged, to say nothing of the collector. After beating the branches the tray must be carefully examined for caterpillars, taking care not to miss some of the superb stick mimics. It is a good idea to allow the contents of the tray to settle for a short time to give the caterpillars a chance to regain their footing and move around. It is surprising how many caterpillars can be missed at a first examination.

A similar collecting method can be adopted for caterpillars on low-growing plants using a sweep net. This is a net with a stout metal frame which can be lightly but firmly swept through the foliage to dislodge the caterpillars feeding there. One of the main drawbacks of this method is that several different types of plant are often swept at the same time, and it is sometimes difficult to ascertain the correct foodplant for a particular caterpillar. This method is particularly successful on grasses at dusk when the caterpillars have just crawled up the stems to feed.

One of the fascinating aspects of sweeping and beating is that many different sorts of insects and spiders are dislodged, and the collector gains rewarding insights to the amazingly varied faunas of different plant communities. It is important to remember to return all unwanted insects to their foodplants without harming them.

Caterpillars with specialist feeding habits will have to be sought specially. Root feeders may be found by carefully digging up plants that are wilting or showing other symptoms of attack. However, this should never be done without the permission of the landowner, and it is now illegal to uproot certain plants from the countryside without a special permit. Wood borers are much more difficult to find and rear, but holes in tree trunks and branches containing wood particles and frass are a clear indication that caterpillars are present. It is sometimes possible to find wood borers in freshly felled trees but again permission should be sought before branches are cut.

When collecting, it is advisable to treat all hairy caterpillars with respect and to warn children not to handle them at all. Brown-tail (*Euproctis chrysorrhoea*) and processionary caterpillars (*Thaumetopoea*) can cause painful rashes on sensitive skin and serious damage to the sight can be caused if hairs penetrate the eye. Other caterpillars with irritant hairs include the Yellow-tail (*Euproctis similis*), the Vapourer (*Orgyia antiqua*) and the Fox Moth (*Macrothylacia rubi*). Even the hairs of the seemingly innocuous 'woolly bear' caterpillars of the Garden Tiger (*Arctia caja*) contain poisons although few people are affected by them. In the tropics, caterpillars of the moth family Limacodidae can cause extremely painful rashes and those of the saturniid moth *Lonomia achelous* from South America can cause dangerous bleeding from the mucous membranes.

## REARING CATERPILLARS

Caterpillars that have been collected must be kept in suitable containers with a supply of foodplant. Containers may range from glass or plastic tubes and boxes to old tobacco tins. The main points to observe are to avoid overcrowding, overheating, condensation and cannibalism. A plastic or glass container left in the sun for only a short time will become extremely hot inside and the occupants will soon die. If the container does not contain a small quantity of paper tissue or similar absorbent material, there is a danger that droplets of condensation will form in which small caterpillars can easily drown. Overcrowding will often lead to disease and cannibalism, particularly if insufficient foodplant is provided. A careful look-out should be maintained in the spring for caterpillars of the Dun-bar moth (*Cosmia trapezina*) as these are not only cannibalistic but will also kill and eat caterpillars of other species. They should be kept in individual tubes and reared separately. Young caterpillars of many butterflies of the family Lycaenidae show cannibalistic tendencies if they are confined together, and this also applies to caterpillars of the Orange-tip butterfly (*Anthocharis cardamines*).

When collecting caterpillars it is important to keep a careful record of their foodplants. A supply of foodplant sufficient for the first few days should also be collected but large quantities of foodplant will soon become stale and unpalatable. It is a good plan to ensure that an adequate supply of food is obtainable before collecting from a particular plant. Some keen collectors grow their own supply of foodplants in the garden or greenhouse, but it is often possible to gather a supply of common plants from nearby commons and waste ground. Where possible, plants growing on roadsides and those likely to have been sprayed with herbicides or insecticides should be avoided but, when in doubt, foodplants should be washed and carefully dried before use.

Where the original foodplant is not available, it is often possible to provide substitutes. It is best to try closely related plants first and if this is not possible a 'salad' of different leaves of similar size and texture to the original foodplant should be offered, careful note being taken of those leaves that are eaten. Where the species of caterpillar is known, its normal range of foodplants can be ascertained from this book. The most likely times for caterpillars to accept substitute foodplants are shortly after hatching and immediately after a moult. Some caterpillars that have starved for a few days will accept different foodplants, but this practice is not recommended and seldom leads to success. Even when a substitute foodplant is readily accepted, it does not necessarily mean that the caterpillars will successfully complete their development, so the correct foodplants should be used whenever possible.

Useful general purpose foodplants for caterpillars living on low-growing plants are dock (*Rumex*), dandelion (*Taraxacum*) and knotgrass (*Polygonum*). Lettuce (*Lactuca*) is frequently tried as a substitute food, but often proves to have too high a moisture content and sometimes causes diarrhoea. However, wilted lettuce leaves have been successfully used to feed caterpillars that normally eat lichens and algae. Caterpillars that feed on willow and sallow (*Salix*) can sometimes be persuaded to accept apple (*Malus*) leaves, and these may provide a useful substitute for the foliage of some other deciduous trees and shrubs. Garden pansies are frequently accepted by those species that normally feed on wild violets (*Viola*). At the end of the year, when foliage is scarce, bramble (*Rubus*) or privet (*Ligustrum*) may be tried as a last resort.

Rearing caterpillars is not only an interesting and rewarding pursuit but requires little or no expenditure on expensive equipment. Small caterpillars can be reared successfully in plastic sandwich boxes lined with absorbent paper tissue or newspaper and supplied frequently with fresh food. The boxes must be cleaned regularly to remove frass and stale foodplant and to dry condensation from the sides and lid. Care should be taken when handling caterpillars. It is usually better to allow them to wander on to fresh foodplant by themselves. A soft paintbrush is a good instrument for transferring small caterpillars, but attempting to remove large caterpillars from their foodplant by force will often cause fatal injuries. Similarly, caterpillars about to moult should never be disturbed. These can usually be recognized by the fact that they become immobile and slightly foreshortened, with the head rather prominent.

If eggs are obtained, they should be kept in small plastic boxes where they can be seen clearly. Newly hatched caterpillars should first be given the opportunity to eat their eggshells before transferring them to a small box containing foodplant. Foodplant should not be placed in the box containing eggs as this is liable to cause them to go mouldy.

It is often difficult to keep large caterpillars in plastic boxes although it is possible, provided that the boxes are large enough and that only a few are kept in each container. A more practical method is to use a rearing cage. This may be a commercially supplied perspex cylinder with a ventilated lid or a home-made wooden framed cage with sides of netting and glass. In these larger cages, sprays of foodplant can be fitted into a water container, making sure to plug the neck securely so that caterpillars cannot drown themselves. Alternatively, stems of foodplant can be pushed into the porous blocks used by florists for flower arranging. If potted foodplants are available, these are even better, although it should be borne in mind that large caterpillars eat an immense quantity of leaves and will soon defoliate a growing plant. Some caterpillars will not thrive on foodplants kept in water and so the above method is particularly suited to them.

Another method of providing fresh food is to 'sleeve' caterpillars on a growing branch out of doors. The sleeve consists of a tube of fine mesh netting, which is slipped over the branch and the ends tied off. The drawbacks of this method are that sleeves look rather unsightly in the garden and it is not possible to see the caterpillars clearly inside. As soon as the foliage has been eaten, the caterpillars must be transferred to a fresh branch. Although this method seems rather cumbersome, it has been successfully adopted by commercial butterfly breeders for many years. A similar method may be used with low-growing plants, covering them with hoops of wire over which netting is stretched and secured at the base. It is usually best to dig up the plants and place them in a tub or large bowl before doing this. One of the greatest drawbacks to this method is that it is virtually impossible to exclude spiders and other small predators.

Whatever method of rearing is adopted, the most important point to observe is cleanliness. Remnants of stale food and frass will soon become mouldy to the detriment of the caterpillars. It is impossible to exclude the viruses and bacteria that cause disease, but caterpillars will seldom be affected unless placed under undue stress. Such stresses are not fully understood but caterpillars that are overcrowded, poorly fed or kept in damp or dirty conditions are much more likely to fall victim. Prevention is the only successful treatment of disease, as infected caterpillars seldom recover. As soon as signs of disease are noticed, sick caterpillars should be removed and the remaining stock moved on to fresh food in a clean cage. Moulting and pupating caterpillars should not be mistaken for those with disease. The signs shown by moulting caterpillars have already been described, and pupating caterpillars only become foreshortened and start to change colour after a period of restless activity, usually having moved away from the feeding place.

After use, all rearing cages should be thoroughly disinfected. Plastic boxes and cages can be treated with a solution of proprietary disinfectant while wooden cages can be scrubbed with a strong solution of washing soda.

When caterpillars are fully grown, they should be provided with suitable pupation sites. Butterfly caterpillars should be given suitable stems and foliage from which to suspend their pupae, and moth caterpillars producing subterranean pupae should be placed in a box with a thick layer of slightly damp peat on the bottom. Other larvae should be provided with foliage, bark or soft cork, according to their requirements. Pupae formed in late spring or early summer will usually emerge within a few weeks and may be left in place until they do so. However, most pupae that are formed in the autumn overwinter and these will often dry out or become mouldy if neglected. They should be removed from the rearing cage and stored between layers of peat in small tins or other sealed containers that can be kept in a cool but frost-free place until the following spring. In spring the pupae can be transferred to a suitable emergence cage. This can be an ordinary rearing cage lined with a layer of peat or vermiculite in which the pupae are gently embedded. An alternative is to place pupae between the grooves of a sheet of corrugated cardboard placed on the bottom of the cage. Pupae can be lightly sprayed with water from a mist spray from time to time to induce emergence of the adults. It is not necessary or desirable to wet the pupae but simply to provide them with a humid atmosphere. When emergence is about to take place, suitable twigs and stems should be supplied for the newly emerged adults to crawl up before expanding and drying their wings. If suitable supports are not supplied at this stage, many deformed butterflies and moths will result.

When first attempting to rear caterpillars it is a good idea to collect them in the spring, as most will produce butterflies or moths during the summer and will not need to be overwintered. With experience, the more difficult species can be reared with success.

## STUDY AND CONSERVATION

The rewards of collecting and rearing caterpillars are much greater than those of simply collecting adult butterflies and moths, and are much more in keeping with modern attitudes towards conservation. Each female butterfly or moth lays a hundred or more eggs from which only one pair needs to survive to maintain the population. This is because a very large percentage will become the victims of predators or disease. When such a batch of eggs is carefully reared in captivity, it is possible to produce large numbers of butterflies or moths, from a single brood. By breeding and releasing suitable species, it is possible not only to have the joy of seeing these lovely creatures develop but also to reinforce the wild population by releasing them in a suitable habitat. While this may appeal to many naturalists, they should bear in mind a number of important guidelines. Firstly, reared butterflies and moths should only be returned to the place from which the eggs or caterpillars were originally taken, unless a suitable site is suggested by an experienced person from a body such as a county naturalist's trust. Secondly, if too many insects are reared and released in one place, there may be insufficient foodplants to support the caterpillars and the existing wild population may be damaged. The release of reared butterflies and moths at random is not recommended as these will seldom survive and may only confuse the records of local naturalists and ecologists.

Another way to increase the pleasures of rearing caterpillars is to keep a notebook of any interesting observations that you make. It is surprising how little we know about some relatively common butterflies and moths and detailed records of behaviour, numbers of instars, unusual foodplants, times of feeding, dates of pupation and emergence of adults are well worth keeping. Even a study of parasites and diseases could provide new information of value to those concerned with the preservation and study of our fauna. It is a good idea to join a local or national natural history or conservation society so that you can exchange ideas with others who have similar interests. Some of these societies publish their own journals and will welcome short notes on various aspects of the biology of butterflies and moths.

It is not recommended that a collection of caterpillars should be kept. It is difficult to preserve such soft-bodied creatures in a lifelike condition without the use of expensive and sophisticated equipment, and even then, results are not always satisfactory. A far better plan is to photograph the living caterpillars in their various stages of development. Although it will be necessary to master the techniques of close-up photography, the results will more than repay the effort. With the aid of modern automatic-exposure reflex cameras it is possible for the amateur to achieve results obtainable only by professionals a few years ago.

It has already been mentioned in this introduction that care should be taken to avoid damaging habitats and that permission should be sought before digging up plants. It should also be remembered that many areas of the countryside are controlled by naturalists' trusts, the National Trust and other such bodies who do not allow collecting on their property without special permission. Many European countries now impose severe restrictions on the unauthorised collecting of insects. Although this may be annoying, it is all part of a scheme to protect the wildlife of our countryside and should be respected as such.

# HEPIALIDAE

This family includes the swift moths and ghost moths. The caterpillars are mainly root feeders, although they sometimes sever plant stems at the base in the same way as cutworms of the family Noctuidae. They are rather slender, dirty whitish in colour and often have small, shining brown plates on the body. They feed on a wide range of low-growing plants.

**HEPIALUS HUMULI** Linnaeus *Ghost Moth* **Pl. 29**

**Distribution.** Widespread in northern and central Europe. Widely distributed and common throughout the British Isles.

**Description.** Length up to 40 mm; body shining white or greyish-white with distinct, greyish-brown spots; plate on segment 1 reddish-brown with an oblique black marking on either side; head shining reddish-brown.

**Habitat.** Meadows, downland, waste ground, gardens and other places where the foodplants grow.

**Foodplants.** A wide range of grasses and herbaceous plants, both wild and cultivated.

**Biology.** One generation a year. Eggs are laid in June. They are scattered at random by the female while in flight. Caterpillars hatch after about a fortnight and feed below ground on roots and tubers of various plants until the following May. Some caterpillars may take two years to complete their growth. Pupation occurs in the feeding place in May and moths emerge in the following month.

**HEPIALUS LUPULINUS** Linnaeus *Common Swift* **Pl. 27**

**Distribution.** Widespread throughout Europe. Widely distributed in the British Isles but most common in England and Wales; very local in Scotland.

**Description.** Length up to 38 mm; long and slender; body shining yellowish-white with indistinct, pale yellowish-brown spots; plates on segments 1 and 13 yellowish-brown; head shining reddish-brown.

**Habitat.** Meadows, agricultural land, gardens and other places where the foodplants grow.

**Foodplants.** A wide range of grasses and herbaceous plants, both wild and cultivated. Often a pest.

**Biology.** One generation a year. Eggs are laid in May or June. They are deposited at random by the female while in flight. Caterpillars hatch in about a fortnight and feed below ground on roots. They become fully grown by the following spring and pupate in the feeding place. Moths emerge in May and June. (The caterpillar figured on Plate 27 is not in a typical feeding position.)

# COSSIDAE

This family includes the Goat Moth (*Cossus cossus*) and the leopards. They are mostly wood borers, although the Reed Leopard (*Phragmataecia castanea*) feeds in reed stems. They are robust and smooth, without distinctive colour patterns.

**PHRAGMATAECIA CASTANEAE** Hübner *Reed Leopard* **Pl. 30**
**Distribution.** Widespread but local in central Europe. In the British Isles, confined to parts of eastern and southern England, where it is very local.
**Description.** Length up to 45 mm; skin wrinkled and glossy; body dirty yellowish-white with two pale purplish lines on the back; segment 1 with a large, yellowish-brown, toothed plate on the back; head flattened, yellowish-brown.
**Habitat.** Reed beds.
**Foodplant.** Reed (*Phragmites communis*).
**Biology.** One generation a year. Eggs are laid in clusters on reeds in July and hatch in the following month. The caterpillars feed low-down within the stems and overwinter twice before becoming fully grown in May of the third year. Pupation takes place within the stems and moths emerge in June.

**ZEUZERA PYRINA** Linnaeus *Leopard Moth* **Pl. 16**
**Distribution.** Widespread throughout Europe. In the British Isles, mainly confined to southern and central England and eastern Wales.
**Description.** Length up to 50 mm; body yellowish-white with blackish-brown spots; plates on segments 1 and 13 blackish-brown; head wedge-shaped, dark brown or black, shining.
**Habitat.** Woodland, wooded countryside, gardens, parks and orchards.
**Foodplants.** A wide range of deciduous trees and shrubs, including ornamental trees and fruit trees and bushes.
**Biology.** One generation a year. Eggs are laid singly or in batches in crevices of the bark in June and hatch in about three weeks. The caterpillars feed at first in young shoots or beneath the bark but later bore deeper into the wood. They take two or three years to complete their growth. Pupation takes place in May in cocoons of silk and wood particles within the caterpillars' tunnels. Moths emerge in the following month.

**COSSUS COSSUS** Linnaeus *Goat Moth* **Pl. 8**
**Distribution.** Widespread throughout Europe. Widely distributed in the British Isles but less common than it used to be; in some places very local and rather scarce.
**Description.** Length up to 65 mm; body yellowish-white, tinged with pink, with a broad band of dark purplish-red along the back; segment 1 with a black plate; head shining black, partly withdrawn into the body. These caterpillars have a characteristic, goat-like smell.
**Habitat.** Woodland, wooded countryside, gardens and orchards.
**Foodplants.** A wide range of deciduous trees, including fruit trees.
**Biology.** One generation a year. Eggs are laid in short rows or in small clusters in crevices of the bark in June. Caterpillars hatch in the following month and bore at

first between the bark and the wood. Later they penetrate into the heart wood, where they remain for 2–4 years before becoming fully grown. Pupation takes place in April in cocoons of silk and wood particles spun in the feeding tunnel or on the ground. Moths emerge in June.

# ZYGAENIDAE

The burnet moths and foresters belong to this family. The caterpillars are short and stout, tapering at the extremities, and bear tufts of short hairs, arising from small raised warts. The head is retracted into the body when at rest. Burnet moth caterpillars (*Zygaena*) are strongly patterned with green, yellow and black and many are known to contain cyanide compounds. They feed on the foliage of low-growing plants, particularly trefoils (*Lotus*) and clovers (*Trifolium*) and many construct spindle-shaped, papery cocoons.

**ADSCITA STATICES** Linnaeus *Forester* **Pl. 10**
**Distribution.** Widely distributed throughout Europe. Widespread but local in the British Isles.
**Description.** Length up to 12 mm; short and stout; body dull ochreous, minutely spotted with black, with small tufts of hairs arising from brownish or pinkish spots along the back and sides; head very small, dark brown, withdrawn into the body.
**Habitat.** Meadows, chalk downland, sea cliffs, heaths and woodland margins.
**Foodplants.** Common sorrel (*Rumex acetosa*) and sheep's sorrel (*R. acetosella*).
**Biology.** One generation a year. Eggs are laid in short rows on the foliage in June. The caterpillars feed from July until the autumn when they go into hibernation, completing their growth in the following spring. Pupation takes place at the end of April in silken cocoons under leaves or attached to stems of the foodplant. Moths emerge in June.

**ZYGAENA EXULANS** Hohenwarth *Scotch Burnet* **Pl. 25**
**Distribution.** Occurs in northern Europe and mountain regions of central Europe. In the British Isles, confined to a few mountain localities in Scotland.
**Description.** Length up to 20 mm; short and stout, abruptly tapered at the extremities; body dark greenish-grey with a line of yellow spots high up along each side; head black, withdrawn into the body.
**Habitat.** Mountains and upland moors.
**Foodplants.** Mainly crowberry (*Empetrum nigrum*) but also on bilberry (*Vaccinium myrtillus*) and cowberry (*V. vitis-idaea*).
**Biology.** One generation a year. Eggs are laid in July and caterpillars feed in the late summer before hibernating. They resume feeding in the following spring and either become full-grown by June or overwinter for a second year before completing their development. Pupation takes place in roundish, silvery-grey cocoons spun on low-growing vegetation or amongst rocks. Moths emerge in June or July.

**ZYGAENA FILIPENDULAE** Linnaeus *Six-spot Burnet* **Pl. 21**

**Distribution.** Widespread and common throughout Europe. Widely distributed in the British Isles, but in Scotland mainly confined to coastal regions.

**Description.** Length up to 22 mm; short and plump, tapering abruptly at the extremities; body greenish-yellow with a double line of black blotches on the back, on either side of which is a line of yellow markings; a further line of black markings usually extends along each side of the body but this is absent in pale forms; in some forms, the dark markings are greatly extended so that the caterpillar is practically black; head black, withdrawn into the body.

**Habitat.** Downland, meadows, sea cliffs, waste ground and woodland margins.

**Foodplant.** Birdsfoot trefoil (*Lotus corniculatus*).

**Biology.** One generation a year. Eggs are laid on the foodplant in July or August and caterpillars feed for a time in the autumn before going into hibernation. They resume feeding in the spring and are fully grown by the end of May. Some caterpillars overwinter for a second year. Pupation takes place in tough, elongate, pale straw-coloured, glossy cocoons attached to grass stems. Moths emerge in June or July.

**ZYGAENA TRIFOLII** Esper *Five-spot Burnet* **Pl. 21**

**Distribution.** Widely distributed in Europe. In the British Isles, confined to southern England and to Wales.

**Description.** Length up to 22 mm; very similar to *Z. filipendulae* but with body more bluish-green; less variable, without extremely light and dark forms.

**Habitat.** Damp meadows, marshy places and chalk downland.

**Foodplants.** In Britain the marshland race feeds on greater birdsfoot trefoil (*Lotus uliginosus*) and the downland race on birdsfoot trefoil (*L. corniculatus*).

**Biology.** One generation a year. Eggs are laid in small batches on the foodplant in June or July and caterpillars feed for a time before going into hibernation. They resume feeding in the following spring and are usually fully grown by the end of May or June, although some overwinter for a second year. Pupation takes place in elongate, glossy yellowish or whitish cocoons attached to grass stems or low down among the herbage. Moths emerge from May to July according to race.

**ZYGAENA LONICERAE** Scheven **Pl. 21**
*Narrow-bordered Five-spot Burnet*

**Distribution.** Widespread in Europe. Widely distributed in England, parts of Wales and the northern half of Ireland and also occurs on the island of Skye in Scotland.

**Description.** Length up to 22 mm; short and plump, very similar to *Z. filipendulae* and *trifolii* but more bluish and with distinctly longer hairs which show as a distinct blackish 'fuzz' around the body.

**Habitat.** Downland, grassy slopes, woodland margins, marshland and waste land.

**Foodplants.** Clover (*Trifolium*), trefoils (*Lotus*) and vetches (*Vicia*).

**Biology.** One generation a year. Eggs are laid on the foliage in July and caterpillars feed in late summer before going into hibernation. They resume feeding in the following spring and either become full-grown in May or overwinter for a second year. Pupation takes place in elongate, glossy, yellowish or whitish cocoons attached to grass stems. Moths emerge in June or July.

**ZYGAENA PURPURALIS** Brünnich *Transparent Burnet* **Pl. 26**

**Distribution.** Widespread in Europe. In the British Isles, restricted to Scotland, parts of western Ireland and one coastal locality in Wales.

**Description.** Length up to 20 mm; short and stout, tapering abruptly at the extremities; body dull yellowish-green, tinged with olive-green above; two lines of black spots extend along the back, on either side of which is a line of larger yellow spots; head blackish-brown, withdrawn into the body.

**Habitat.** Grassy slopes where the foodplant grows.

**Foodplant.** Wild thyme (*Thymus serpyllum*).

**Biology.** One generation a year. Eggs are laid in June and caterpillars feed in late summer before going into hibernation. They become active again in the following spring and are fully grown by the end of May. Some caterpillars overwinter for a second year before completing their development. Pupation takes place in roundish, silvery-grey silken cocoons spun on the ground or on rocks. Moths emerge in June.

**ZYGAENA TRANSALPINA** Esper **Pl. 19**

**Distribution.** Widespread in southern Europe.

**Description.** Length up to 20 mm; short and plump, tapering abruptly at the extremities; body greenish-yellow with a row of large black spots down the middle of the back, on either side of which is a line of rather indistinct yellow markings; a further line of black markings extends along each side of the body; head black, withdrawn into the body.

**Habitat.** Dry, warm grassland and scrub.

**Foodplants.** Crown vetch (*Coronilla varia*) and other *Coronilla* species, horseshoe vetch (*Hippocrepis comosa*), birdsfoot trefoil (*Lotus corniculatus*) and milk-vetches (*Astragalus*).

**Biology.** One generation a year. Eggs are laid in July and caterpillars hatch in August. After hibernation, they resume feeding in the spring and either pupate in June or overwinter for a second year before completing their development. Moths emerge in June or July.

# LIMACODIDAE

This mainly tropical family has only a few European representatives, including the Festoon (*Apoda limacodes*) and the Triangle (*Heterogenea asella*). The caterpillars are rather slug-like and to some extent resemble those of butterflies of the family Lycaenidae but do not have fully developed prolegs on the body. They feed on the foliage of trees. Tropical species often bear stinging hairs and are called nettle-grub moths.

**APODA LIMACODES** Hufnagel *Festoon* **Pl. 6**

**Distribution.** Widely distributed in central and southern Europe. In the British Isles, apparently confined to the southern half of England but may also occur in Ireland.

**Description.** Length up to 15 mm; strongly flattened and smooth; body green with indistinct whitish spots and two raised, longitudinal yellow ridges, along which are

series of bright pink markings; margins of body sometimes also marked by a yellow line, particularly above the head, which is retracted into the body and not usually visible.
**Habitat.** Woodland.
**Foodplants.** Oak (*Quercus*), beech (*Fagus sylvatica*) and, in continental Europe, also on other deciduous trees.
**Biology.** One generation a year. Eggs are laid in June or July and caterpillars feed from August to October. In autumn, the fully fed caterpillars construct cocoons, spun onto leaves, in which they remain until pupation in the spring. Moths emerge in June.

**HETEROGENEA ASELLA** Denis & Schiffermüller *Triangle* **Pl. 7**
**Distribution.** Widely distributed but very scarce in central Europe. In the British Isles, confined to a few localities in southern England, where it is very scarce.
**Description.** Length up to 12 mm; slug-like; body pale yellowish-green with a large, brown, saddle-shaped patch on the back; head retracted into the body.
**Habitat.** Woodland.
**Foodplants.** Oak (*Quercus*), beech (*Fagus sylvatica*) and poplar (*Populus*).
**Biology.** One generation a year. Eggs are laid singly on the foliage in July and caterpillars feed from August to October. In autumn, the fully grown caterpillars construct dark brown, gall-like cocoons on leaves and twigs, in which they remain through the winter before pupating in the spring. Moths emerge in June or July.

## HETEROGYNIDAE

Caterpillars of this family have medium-sized, shiny caterpillars, superficially similar to those of the burnet moths (Zygaenidae) but without hair tufts. They may be distinguished from other caterpillars by the presence of small, coronet-like rings of minute spines on the body between the usual hairs. They make characteristic, open network cocoons. They feed on the foliage of various plants of the family Leguminosae.

**HETEROGYNIS PENELLA** Hübner **Pl. 19**
**Distribution.** Widespread in southern Europe.
**Description.** Length up to 20 mm; body shining black, with bands of pale yellow along the back and sides; hairs fairly long and fine, yellowish-white; head shining black, often partly withdrawn into the body.
**Habitat.** Open country and hillsides where the foodplants grow.
**Foodplants.** Dyer's greenweed (*Genista tinctoria*) and other *Genista* species; also on broom (*Cytisus*).
**Biology.** One generation a year. Female moths of this species are wingless and mate and lay eggs without leaving the cocoon. The young caterpillars remain in the cocoon and devour the body of the dead female parent before leaving to live on the foodplants in May and June. Pupation takes place in loose, translucent cocoons attached to the herbage. Moths are on the wing in July and August.

# SESIIDAE

Moths of this family are called clearwings because their wings are largely devoid of scales. The small to medium-sized caterpillars bore in woody stems and branches and in the crowns and roots of low-growing plants. They are mostly whitish in colour and the body is usually slightly swollen behind the head.

**SYNANTHEDON TIPULIFORMOS** Clerck *Currant Clearwing* **Pl. 22**
**Distribution.** Widespread throughout Europe. Widely distributed in the British Isles but local and less common in Scotland and Ireland.
**Description.** Length up to 18 mm; body yellowish-white with shining yellowish-white spots from which arise short, reddish-brown hairs; plate on segments 1 and 13 yellowish-brown; spiracles small, with reddish-brown rims; head reddish-brown.
**Habitat.** Gardens, allotments and other places where the foodplants grow.
**Foodplants.** Redcurrant (*Ribes rubrum*), blackcurrant (*R. nigrum*) and gooseberry (*R. uva-crispa*).
**Biology.** One generation a year. Eggs are laid singly in cracks in the bark in June and hatch in about a fortnight. The caterpillars feed in the pith of the stem, causing the leaves to wilt. They overwinter in the stems before pupating in the following May, although some may overwinter for a second year. Moths emerge in June.

**SYNANTHEDON MYOPAEFORMIS** Borkhausen **Pl. 16**
*Red-belted Clearwing*
**Distribution.** Widespread in southern and central Europe, extending northwards to southern Scandinavia. In the British Isles, mainly confined to the southern half of England where it is locally common.
**Description.** Length up to 20 mm; body fairly plump, usually slightly swollen behind the head, white with inconspicuous, pale yellow spots; plates on segments 1 and 13 pale yellowish-brown; head reddish-brown, usually partly withdrawn into the body.
**Habitat.** Orchards, gardens and open woodland.
**Foodplants.** Apple (*Malus*), pear (*Pyrus*), rowan (*Sorbus aucuparia*), hawthorn (*Crataegus monogyna*) and various fruit and ornamental trees.
**Biology.** One generation a year. Eggs are laid in crevices of the bark in June or July and caterpillars hatch within a month. They feed for two years, boring between the bark and the wood, overwintering twice before pupating in May or June. The cocoons of silk and wood particles are spun within the burrow close to the exit hole which is only covered by a thin layer of bark. Moths emerge after about a fortnight.

**BEMBECIA SCOPIGERA** Scopoli *Six-belted Clearwing* **Pl. 20**
**Distribution.** Widely distributed but local in Europe. In the British Isles, confined to scattered localities in southern England and Wales. Length up to 13 mm; body slightly swollen behind the head, gradually tapering towards the tail; white, sometimes tinged with yellowish-pink; head pale brown with lighter mottling.
**Habitat.** Downland, fields, chalk quarries, gravel pits and sea cliffs.

**Foodplants.** Kidney vetch (*Anthyllis vulneraria*), birdsfoot trefoil (*Lotus corniculatus*) and horseshoe vetch (*Hippocrepis comosa*).
**Biology.** One generation a year. Eggs are laid on leaves, stems or exposed roots of the foodplant in July. Caterpillars hatch in July or August and feed on the roots until June of the following year. Pupation takes place in the feeding place at the end of June and moths emerge in the following month.

**BEMBECIA CHRYSIDIFORMIS** Esper *Fiery Clearwing* **Pl. 10**
**Distribution.** Occurs in central and southern Europe. In the British Isles, confined to a few localities in south-eastern England.
**Description.** Length up to 20 mm; body fairly plump, slightly swollen towards the head, shining brownish-white; plates on segments 1 and 13 pale yellowish-brown; head slightly flattened, reddish-brown.
**Habitat.** Chalky slopes, fields and woodland clearings.
**Foodplants.** Dock and sorrel (*Rumex*); in continental Europe, also recorded on *Artemisia* and related plants.
**Biology.** One generation a year. Eggs are laid near the roots of the foodplant in July. The caterpillars bore into the root-stocks in which they feed until the following May when they pupate in silken tubes spun in the feeding place. Some caterpillars overwinter twice before completing their growth. Moths emerge in June.

# HESPERIIDAE

Butterflies of this family are known as skippers. The smallish caterpillars can be readily recognized by their large heads and slightly constricted necks. Their bodies are covered with very short, fine hairs. Unlike most butterfly caterpillars, they live in the shelter of folded and spun leaves and pupate in slight silken cocoons.

**CARTEROCEPHALUS PALAEMON** Pallas *Chequered Skipper* **Pl. 32**
**Distribution.** Widespread but local in many parts of central and northern Europe. In the British Isles, now confined to parts of western Scotland, but formerly occurred in central and eastern counties of England.
**Description.** Length up to 23 mm; body green with dark green and white lines, becoming pale yellow before hibernation; after hibernation, body is pale brownish-white with pinkish-brown and white lines on the back and sides; head large, green, becoming pale brown.
**Habitat.** Open woodland and grassland with scrub.
**Foodplants.** Slender false-brome (*Brachypodium sylvaticum*) and purple moor-grass (*Molinia caerulea*); in continental Europe, also *Bromus* and other grasses.
**Biology.** One generation a year. Eggs are laid singly on grass blades in June and hatch in about ten days. The caterpillar lives within a tube-like shelter constructed from a spun grass blade, coming out to feed. When fully grown at the end of Septem-

ber, it constructs a shelter from spun blades of grass, in which it remains until the following spring. It emerges in March and rests on grasses for a time without feeding before pupating in a cocoon of dead grass blades. Butterflies emerge in late May.

### THYMELICUS SYLVESTRIS Poda *Small Skipper* **Pl. 31**

**Distribution.** Widespread and common in Europe except for the extreme north. In the British Isles, widely distributed and common in southern and central England and in Wales, becoming less common towards the north; absent from Scotland and Ireland.

**Description.** Length up to 21 mm; body fairly stout, tapering towards the extremities; green with a pale yellow margined, dark green line along the back, on either side of which is a band of yellowish-white; a further band of yellowish-white extends along each side below the level of the spiracles; head large, rounded, green.

**Habitat.** Meadows and other grassy places.

**Foodplants.** Yorkshire fog (*Holcus lanatus*), timothy grass (*Phleum pratense*) and other grasses.

**Biology.** One generation a year. Eggs are laid in rows within grass sheaths in July and hatch in about three weeks. After eating its eggshell, the young caterpillar spins a silken shelter in the leaf-sheath in which it remains through the winter. It becomes active again in the following April and starts feeding on young foliage, living in a folded grass blade. When fully grown in June, it pupates inside a coarse, open cocoon attached to a grass stem. The butterfly emerges in about three weeks.

### THYMELICUS ACTEON Rottemburg *Lulworth Skipper* **Pl. 32**

**Distribution.** Occurs locally in southern and central Europe. In the British Isles, confined to a few localities in Dorset and Devon.

**Description.** Length up to 24 mm; tapered towards the extremities; body green with a pale bordered, dark green line along the middle of the back, on either side of which is a pale greenish-yellow line; a pale greenish-yellow line extends through the spiracles, below which is a band of yellowish-white; head large, pale greenish-brown.

**Habitat.** Meadows, grassy banks and cliffs.

**Foodplant.** Heath false-brome (*Brachypodium pinnatum*).

**Biology.** One generation a year. Eggs are laid in rows in grass sheaths in July or August and hatch in about three weeks. The young caterpillar does not feed but constructs a silken shelter within the grass sheath where it remains through the winter. It emerges in April to feed on tender young foliage at night, hiding by day in a folded grass blade. In July, when fully grown, it pupates in a loose cocoon spun low down amongst the foodplant. The butterfly emerges in about a fortnight.

### HESPERIA COMMA Linnaeus *Silver-spotted Skipper* **Pl. 31**

**Distribution.** Widespread but local in Europe. In the British Isles, now confined to southern England where it is very local in occurrence.

**Description.** Length up to 26 mm; body rough-skinned, fairly stout, tapered towards the head; dull olive-green with a black collar behind the head; head large, black marked with brown.

**Habitat.** Downland and meadows on chalky soils.

**Foodplants.** Sheep's fescue (*Festuca ovina*).

**Biology.** One generation a year. Eggs are laid singly, low down on grass blades, in August but do not hatch until the following March or April. The caterpillar lives in a tent-like shelter of spun grass blades low down on the foodplant, coming out at night to feed. Pupation takes place in July in a tough cocoon spun amongst grass stems. The butterfly emerges in about ten days.

**OCHLODES VENATA** Bremer & Grey *Large Skipper* **Pl. 32**

**Distribution.** Widespread throughout Europe. Widely distributed and common in England and Wales and parts of southern Scotland; absent from northern parts of Scotland and from Ireland.

**Description.** Length up to 28 mm; fairly stout, tapering towards the extremities; body bluish-green with a dark line along the middle of the back and a yellowish line along the spiracles; head large, black, slightly marked with brown.

**Habitat.** Meadows, woodland margins, hedgerows, waste land and other rough grassland.

**Foodplants.** Cock's-foot (*Dactylis glomerata*) and slender false-brome (*Brachypodium sylvaticum*); in continental Europe, also on other grasses.

**Biology.** One generation a year. Eggs are laid singly on grass blades in June and hatch in 2–3 weeks. The caterpillar lives in a folded grass blade. It feeds until September, when it constructs a larger shelter of spun grass blades in which it overwinters. Feeding is resumed in the spring and the caterpillar is fully grown by the end of May. Pupation takes place in a silken cocoon spun amongst grass blades and the butterfly emerges in about three weeks.

**ERYNNIS TAGES** Linnaeus *Dingy Skipper* **Pl. 21**

**Distribution.** Widespread throughout central and southern Europe and many southern parts of northern Europe. Widely distributed in the British Isles but more common in southern England.

**Description.** Length up to 18 mm; fairly stout, tapered towards the extremities; body green, sometimes tinged with pale brown, with a dark green line along the middle of the back; head purplish-black.

**Habitat.** Downland, meadows, heaths, woodland margins and other places where the foodplant grows.

**Foodplants.** Birdsfoot trefoil (*Lotus corniculatus*); in continental Europe, also recorded on scorpion vetch (*Coronilla*), *Eryngium* and other plants.

**Biology.** One generation a year. Eggs are laid singly on the upper surfaces of leaves in May and hatch in about a fortnight. The caterpillar lives in a shelter of spun leaves, coming out at night to feed. It is fully grown by the beginning of August and constructs a large shelter of spun leaves in which it overwinters before pupating in the following spring without further feeding. The butterfly emerges in May.

**CARCHARODUS ALCEAE** Esper *Mallow Skipper* **Pl. 22**

**Distribution.** Widely distributed in central and southern Europe. Absent from the British Isles.

**Description:** Length up to 23 mm; fairly stout, tapered towards the extremities; body greyish-green, tinged with blue; collar behind head conspicuous, banded with black and yellow; spiracles yellow with black rims; head large, black.

**Habitat.** Hillsides where the foodplants grow.

**Foodplants.** Mallows (*Malva* and *Althaea*), *Hibiscus* and related plants.

**Biology.** One to three generations a year according to locality. Caterpillars live in shelters constructed from spun, folded leaves. Those of the last generation hibernate. First brood butterflies are on the wing in April and May and later broods occur throughout the summer.

**PYRGUS MALVAE** Linnaeus *Grizzled Skipper* **Pl. 15**

**Distribution.** Widespread throughout Europe, except for the extreme north. Widely distributed in southern and central England and in Wales, becoming scarce further north; absent from Scotland and Ireland.

**Description.** Length up to 19 mm; surface of skin rough; body green suffused with pale brown on the back, which is striped with darker olive-brown; head large, black.

**Habitat.** Downland, woodland margins and other coarse grassland.

**Foodplants.** Cinquefoil (*Potentilla*), wild strawberry (*Fragaria vesca*), bramble (*Rubus fruticosus*) and raspberry (*R. idaeus*).

**Biology.** One generation a year, occasionally with a second brood. Eggs are laid singly on leaves in May and hatch in about ten days. The young caterpillar lives at first under a silken web spun on the leaf but later lives in a folded leaf. It is fully grown by the middle of July and pupates in a loose cocoon spun among stems at the base of the foodplant. Butterflies usually emerge in the following April but in favourable years may emerge in August to produce a second brood of caterpillars in the autumn.

# PAPILIONIDAE

This family includes the swallowtails, festoons and apollo butterflies, each with a characteristic type of caterpillar. Apollo caterpillars are very hairy and predominantly black with red or yellow spots, while swallowtail caterpillars are smooth and mainly green in colour, with red and black markings. Festoon caterpillars are characterised by the presence of large, backward-directed spines along the back. A character shared by these groups is the forked gland or osmeterium on the neck. They feed on various herbaceous plants.

**PARNASSIUS APOLLO** Linnaeus *Apollo* **Pl. 13**

**Distribution:** Occurs in the mountains of central and southern Europe and at lower levels in Fennoscandia. Absent from the British Isles.

**Description.** Length up to 50 mm; body velvety black, covered with short black hairs arising from small raised warts; a line of large and small, rounded orange-red spots extends along each side above the level of the spiracles; head black.

**Habitat.** Mountain slopes, hillsides and other rocky places.

**Foodplants.** Stonecrop (*Sedum*) and houseleek (*Sempervivum*).

**Biology.** One generation a year. Eggs are laid singly near the foodplant in summer. Some hatch in the autumn but others overwinter, hatching in the following spring. The caterpillars only feed in sunshine and at other times hide under stones. They become fully grown in June. When disturbed, they are capable of extruding a scent-producing gland in the same way as the Swallowtail. Pupation takes place in loose cocoons spun under stones and moss and butterflies emerge in 2–4 weeks or more, according to weather conditions.

**PARNASSIUS PHOEBUS** Fabricius *Small Apollo* **Pl.** 14

**Distribution.** In Europe, confined to the Alps.

**Description.** Length up to 48 mm; velvety black, covered with short black hairs arising from small, raised warts, with a line of large and small red spots along each side above the level of the spiracles; very similar to the Apollo but smaller, with the small spots more equal in size and more reddish.

**Habitat.** Mountainsides in very wet situations.

**Foodplants.** Yellow saxifrage (*Saxifraga aizoides*) and mountain houseleek (*Sempervivum montanum*).

**Biology.** One generation a year. Caterpillars hibernate when very small among roots and become active in the following May. The pupae can withstand immersion in water for long periods. Butterflies are on the wing in July and August.

**PARNASSIUS MNEMOSYNE** Linnaeus *Clouded Apollo* **Pl. 12**

**Distribution.** Widely distributed in Europe, excluding the Iberian Peninsula and the British Isles.

**Description.** Length up to 42 mm; body velvety black, covered with black hairs arising from small black warts and with a line of orange-red spots along each side above the level of the spiracles. Similar to the Apollo but smaller, with the spots more triangular in shape.

**Habitat.** Wet, open woodland and meadows where the foodplant grows.

**Foodplant.** Corydalis (*Corydalis*).

**Biology.** One generation a year. Eggs are laid singly, often on wilted plants, in June but caterpillars do not hatch until the following April. Caterpillars feed only in sunshine, otherwise hiding under leaves and stones. If disturbed, they extrude a defensive gland in the same way as the Swallowtail. They become fully grown in May and pupate in cocoons spun among leaves. Butterflies are on the wing from late May to July.

**ARCHON APOLLINUS** Herbst *False Apollo* **Pl. 9**

**Distribution.** Occurs in south-eastern Europe and eastern Mediterranean countries.

**Description.** Length up to 40 mm; body velvety black, with two rows of roundish red spots along the back and a row of red spots along each side; sometimes also spotted with pale yellow or white; head black.

**Foodplant.** Birthwort (*Aristolochia*).

**Biology.** One generation a year. The pupae overwinter and butterflies are on the wing in March and April.

**ZERYNTHIA POLYXENA** Denis & Schiffermüller *Southern Festoon* **Pl. 9**

**Distribution.** Occurs locally in southern Europe but absent from the Iberian Peninsula, where it is replaced by the Spanish Festoon (*Zerynthia rumina* Linnaeus) which has a similar caterpillar.

**Description.** Length up to 35 mm; body pale brown or whitish, patterned with brown and spotted with black, with two rows of prominent, backward-pointing, pink or reddish, black-tipped spines; head brownish, sometimes withdrawn into the body.

**Habitat.** Rough, rocky places where the foodplant grows.

**Foodplant.** Birthwort (*Aristolochia*).

**Biology.** One generation a year. Eggs are laid singly or in small groups on the undersides of leaves in May and hatch in about a week. Caterpillars become fully grown in

4–5 weeks and the pupae overwinter, producing butterflies in the following April or May.

**PAPILIO ALEXANOR** Esper *Southern Swallowtail* **Pl. 24**

**Distribution.** Occurs locally in southern Europe but absent from the south-west.
**Description.** Length up to 65 mm; stout, tapering towards the head; body green with transverse black stripes along the back, broken by a series of orange spots; head black.
**Habitat.** Mountainsides.
**Foodplants.** *Trinia vulgaris, Seseli montanum, Ptychotis heterophylla* and other umbellifers.
**Biology.** One generation a year. The caterpillars feed in July. When disturbed, they can extrude a defensive gland from behind the head in the same way as the Swallowtail. The pupae overwinter and butterflies are on the wing from April to July.

**PAPILIO MACHAON** Linnaeus *Swallowtail* **Pl. 24**

**Distribution.** Widespread throughout Europe. In the British Isles, confined to the fens of eastern England.
**Description.** Length up to 41 mm; plump; body green, with transverse black bands, the central band of each segment broken by a series of red spots; head green with black markings. Young caterpillars are black with a white patch on the back.
**Habitat.** Fens and marshes; in continental Europe, also found in open countryside, often in sandy areas.
**Foodplants.** Milk parsley (*Peucedanum palustre*); in continental Europe, also on *Angelica*, fennel (*Foeniculum*), wild carrot (*Daucus carota*) and related plants.
**Biology.** One or two generations a year. Eggs are laid singly on leaflets of the food-plant in May or June and sometimes again in late summer. Caterpillars hatch after about a week and feed for about a month before becoming fully grown. They are active by day. When alarmed, they are capable of extruding a pair of orange-coloured, horn-like scent glands from behind the head. These emit a strong smell which is believed to repel predators. Pupae are attached to plant stems and either produce butterflies within three weeks or overwinter to produce butterflies in the following May or June. Pupae of the British subspecies can survive submersion in water for long periods.

**IPHICLIDES PODALIRIUS** Scopoli *Scarce Swallowtail* **Pl. 18**

**Distribution.** Widely distributed in central and southern Europe. Absent from the British Isles.
**Description.** Length up to 40 mm; very plump, tapering towards the extremities; body green with a yellowish line down the middle of the back, on either side of which is a series of oblique yellowish lines bearing small raised spots of red or yellow; head green, often withdrawn into the body.
**Habitat.** Open woodland, hedgerows and orchards.
**Foodplants.** Blackthorn (*Prunus spinosa*), hawthorn (*Crataegus monogyna*), cherry (*Prunus cerasus*) and other cultivated fruit trees.
**Biology.** One or two generations a year. Eggs are laid singly on the undersides of leaves of the foodplant. Caterpillars can be found from May to September, taking 1–2 months to complete their growth. Summer pupae are green and produce butter-flies in about a month, but autumn pupae are brown and overwinter before producing butterflies in the following spring.

# PIERIDAE

The whites and clouded yellows belong to this family of butterflies. The caterpillars are densely covered with short hairs, often with small, raised bases. They are predominantly green in colour, often with bands of yellow along the back and sides. They feed on the foliage of trees, shrubs and many low-growing plants. The whites feed mainly on plants of the family Cruciferae.

**LEPTIDEA SINAPIS** Linnaeus *Wood White* **Pl. 20**
**Distribution.** Widespread throughout Europe. Widely distributed but very local in the southern half of England and parts of south Wales; widespread in Ireland.
**Description.** Length up to 18 mm; body green with a dark line along the middle of the back and a yellow band, margined above with dark green, along the line of the spiracles; head green.
**Habitat.** Woodland and wooded countryside.
**Foodplants.** Meadow vetchling (*Lathyrus aphaca*), bitter vetchling (*L. montanus*), tuberous pea (*L. tuberosus*), birdsfoot trefoil (*Lotus corniculatus*) and related plants.
**Biology.** One generation a year, occasionally two. Eggs are laid singly on the undersides of leaves in May or June and hatch in about a week. Caterpillars feed mainly by day and are fully grown by the end of July. Pupae are attached to plant stems in July or August and usually produce butterflies in the following May, although they sometimes emerge early to produce a partial second brood in August.

**COLIAS PALAENO** Linnaeus *Moorland Clouded Yellow* **Pl. 25**
**Distribution.** Widely distributed in northern and parts of central Europe. Absent from the British Isles.
**Description.** Length up to 35 mm; body green, minutely spotted with black, with a yellow band along the spiracles on each side; head green.
**Habitat.** Boggy moorland, sometimes at high altitude.
**Foodplants.** Northern bilberry (*Vaccinium uliginosum*) and bilberry (*V. myrtillus*).
**Biology.** One generation a year. Eggs are laid singly on leaves of the foodplant, and hatch in about a week or overwinter to produce caterpillars in the following spring. Caterpillars are fully grown in May or June. The pupae are attached to low growing plants and produce butterflies in about a fortnight.

**COLIAS HYALE** Linnaeus *Pale Clouded Yellow* **Pl. 21**
**Distribution.** Widely distributed in southern and central Europe, regularly migrating further north. A scarce immigrant in the British Isles.
**Description.** Length up to 32 mm; body green, finely speckled with black; a white line extends along each side, marked with streaks of red and orange on either side of the spiracles; head green.
**Habitat.** Meadows, particularly lucerne fields. In the British Isles, usually in coastal regions.
**Foodplants.** Lucerne (*Medicago sativa*), vetch (*Vicia*), scorpion vetch (*Coronilla*) and other related plants.

**Biology.** Two generations a year in southern Europe. Eggs are laid singly on leaves, hatching in about ten days. Caterpillars of the first generation become fully grown in about a month but those of the second brood overwinter and do not complete their development until the following spring. The pupa is attached to a stem of the foodplant. Butterflies are on the wing from May to June and August to September.

**COLIAS AUSTRALIS** Verity *Berger's Clouded Yellow* **Pl. 19**

**Distribution.** Widely distributed in central and southern Europe, sometimes migrating further north. Occurs in the British Isles as a very scarce immigrant in southern England.

**Description.** Length up to 32 mm; body green, finely speckled with black; a yellow band extends along the middle of the back with a series of rectangular, black patches on either side; a similar yellow band extends along the spiracles, marked below with smaller black patches; head green.

**Habitat.** Downland and chalky grassland.

**Foodplants.** Crown vetch (*Coronilla varia*) and horseshoe vetch (*Hippocrepis comosa*).

**Biology.** Two or three generations a year in southern Europe. Eggs are laid singly on leaves of the foodplant. Caterpillars of the last brood overwinter, completing their growth in the following spring. Butterflies are on the wing from May to June and August to September.

**COLIAS CROCEUS** Geoffroy *Clouded Yellow* **Pl. 20**

**Distribution.** Widely distributed throughout southern and central Europe, regularly migrating further northwards. Occurs as an immigrant in many parts of the British Isles but particularly in southern England.

**Description.** Length up to 33 mm; body green, finely speckled with black; a yellowish-white line extends along each side, bearing a series of red and orange streaks on either side of the spiracles; below this line is a series of small, black patches, one to each segment; head green. Very similar to Berger's Clouded Yellow but with the fine body hairs a whitish colour.

**Habitat.** Downland, meadows and rough grassland.

**Foodplants.** Clover (*Trifolium*), lucerne (*Medicago sativa*) and various vetches and related plants.

**Biology.** Three or four generations a year in southern Europe. Eggs are laid singly on the upper surfaces of leaves and hatch in about a week. The caterpillars of summer broods become fully grown in about a month, but those of the final brood overwinter. Caterpillars are sometimes found in Britain in the summer months but they are not able to survive the winter. Pupae are attached to plant stems and produce butterflies in 2–3 weeks.

**COLIAS PHICOMONE** Esper *Mountain Clouded Yellow* **Pl. 20**

**Distribution.** Occurs in the Pyrenees, Asturias and Alps.

**Description.** Length up to 36 mm; body bluish-green, with short black hairs and a pale yellow stripe along the side of the body; head bluish-green.

**Habitat.** Grassy mountain slopes, often at high altitude.

**Foodplants.** Vetches (*Vicia*), lucerne (*Medicago sativa*) and related plants.

**Biology.** One generation a year. Eggs are laid singly on the upper surfaces of leaves of the foodplant. After their second moult, the caterpillars go into hibernation, resuming feeding in the following spring and becoming fully grown in May or June. Butterflies are on the wing from June to August according to locality and altitude.

**GONEPTERYX RHAMNI** Linnaeus *Brimstone* **Pl. 22**

**Distribution.** Widespread throughout Europe, except for the extreme north. Widely distributed in England, except for the extreme north, and in parts of Wales; rare in Scotland and rather local in Ireland.

**Description.** Length up to 33 mm; body green, finely speckled with black, becoming bluish-green on the sides above the white spiracular line; body below spiracles yellowish-green; head green, finely spotted with black.

**Habitat.** Open, damp woodland and scrub, particularly in chalk and limestone districts.

**Foodplants.** Buckthorn (*Rhamnus catharticus*), alder buckthorn (*Frangula alnus*).

**Biology.** One generation a year. Eggs are laid singly on the undersides of leaves or on shoots in May and hatch in about ten days. The caterpillar feeds for about a month, resting along the midrib of a leaf, where it is difficult to detect. Pupation takes place in July. Pupae are attached to stems of the foodplant and produce butterflies in about a fortnight. These butterflies do not mate and lay eggs until the following spring.

**APORIA CRATAEGI** Linnaeus *Black-veined White* **Pl. 17**

**Distribution.** Widely distributed in southern and central Europe, occurring as far north as Scandinavia. Extinct in the British Isles since 1925.

**Description.** Length up to 35 mm; body hairy, grey with a broad black band along the back, bearing two broad lines of orange-brown; spiracles black; hairs on the back reddish-brown, those on the sides pale grey; head black, hairy.

**Habitat.** Hedgerows, orchards and open countryside.

**Foodplants.** Hawthorn (*Crataegus monogyna*), blackthorn (*Prunus spinosa*), plum (*P. domestica*), apple (*Malus*) and other fruit trees.

**Biology.** One generation a year. Eggs are laid in batches on the undersides of leaves in May and hatch in about three weeks. The caterpillars live in a communal silken nest in which they remain throughout the winter. In the following spring, they come out to feed and may be seen basking on the outside of the web. They then split up into smaller groups and continue feeding until fully grown in May. Pupae are suspended from branches or plant stems and produce butterflies in June.

**PIERIS BRASSICAE** Linnaeus *Large White* **Pl. 13**

**Distribution.** Widespread throughout Europe. Widely distributed and often common in all parts of the British Isles.

**Description.** Length up to 40 mm; body pale green, heavily spotted with black on the back and less strongly marked with black on the sides; a yellow line extends along the middle of the back and there is a band of pale yellow along the spiracles; head greyish-green, marked with black.

**Habitat.** Fields, waste ground, gardens and places where suitable foodplants grow.

**Foodplants.** Cabbage (*Brassica oleracea*), nasturtium (*Tropaeolum*), wild mignonette (*Reseda lutea*) and other related plants, both wild and cultivated.

**Biology.** Two generations a year. Eggs are laid in batches on leaves in May and again in July. Caterpillars hatch in about a week and live and feed together, often reducing the foliage to skeletons. They have an unpleasant smell and their conspicuous markings probably advertise that they are distasteful to predators. Pupation takes place in about a month. The pupae are attached to fences, walls, tree trunks or even to the foodplant. First generation pupae produce butterflies in about a fortnight but second brood pupae overwinter to produce butterflies in the following spring.

**PIERIS RAPAE** Linnaeus *Small White* **Pl. 13**

**Distribution.** Widespread throughout Europe. Widely distributed and common in all parts of the British Isles except for the extreme north of Scotland, where it is rather scarce.

**Description.** Length up to 25 mm; body green, covered with fine short hairs, finely dotted with black, with a narrow yellow line along the middle of the back; a series of yellow markings extends along the line of the whitish, black-rimmed spiracles; head green.

**Habitat.** Fields, waste ground, gardens and other places where the foodplants grow.

**Foodplants.** Cabbage (*Brassica oleracea*), nasturtium (*Tropaeolum*), wild mignonette (*Reseda lutea*) and other related plants, both wild and cultivated.

**Biology.** Two generations a year. Eggs are laid singly on the undersides of leaves in April and again in July, hatching in about a week. The caterpillars are solitary and often feed in the hearts of cabbages rather than on the exposed leaves. They become fully grown within a month and attach their pupae to the foodplant or on fences or walls. First generation pupae produce butterflies in about three weeks but those of the final generation overwinter to produce butterflies in the following spring. Sometimes there is a third brood.

**PIERIS NAPI** Linnaeus *Green-veined White* **Pl. 13**

**Distribution.** Widespread throughout Europe. Widely distributed and common in all parts of the British Isles, except for the Shetlands.

**Description.** Length up to 25 mm; similar to the Small White but without a yellow line along the back and with black spiracles, each surrounded by a separate patch of yellow.

**Habitat.** Hedgerows, woodland margins, damp meadows and other open countryside where the foodplants grow.

**Foodplants.** Garlic mustard (*Alliaria petiolata*), cuckoo flower (*Cardamine pratensis*), hedge mustard (*Sisymbrium officinale*), charlock (*Sinapis arvensis*) and related plants.

**Biology.** Two generations a year. Eggs are laid singly on the undersides of leaves in May and again in July or August, hatching in about a week. The caterpillars feed on the foliage for about a month before pupating, attached to plant stems. First generation pupae produce butterflies within a fortnight but second brood pupae overwinter and produce butterflies in the following spring.

**PONTIA DAPLIDICE** Linnaeus *Bath White* **Pl. 13**

**Distribution.** Widespread in southern and central Europe, migrating further north and occasionally occurring in the British Isles.

**Description.** Length up to 25 mm; body bluish-grey with raised black dots; two yellow bands extend along the back and a broken line of yellow extends along the spiracles; head grey marked with yellow.

**Habitat.** Meadows, hedgerows and rough grassland, particularly on sandy soil.

**Foodplants.** Wild mignonette (*Reseda lutea*), mustard (*Sinapis*), rockcress (*Arabis*) and related plants.

**Biology.** Two or three generations a year. Eggs are laid singly on the undersides of leaves or on flowers and hatch in 7–10 days. Caterpillars become fully grown in about a month. Pupae of summer generations produce butterflies in about a fortnight but those of the last generation overwinter. Butterflies are on the wing from February to September in various broods, according to locality.

**PONTIA CALLIDICE** Hübner *Peak White* **Pl. 12**

**Distribution.** Occurs in the Pyrenees and Alps.

**Description.** Length up to 32 mm; body bluish-grey, with slightly raised black spots; two white bands extend along the back, marked with a series of yellow patches; a yellow band extends along the line of the spiracles on each side; head dark grey.

**Habitat.** Grassy mountain slopes at high altitude.

**Foodplants.** Dwarf treacle mustard (*Erysimum helveticum*), mignonette (*Reseda*) and related plants.

**Biology.** Usually one generation a year but sometimes two. Butterflies are on the wing in June and July and sometimes also in August. Caterpillars are usually found in August and September.

**ANTHOCHARIS CARDAMINES** Linnaeus *Orange-tip* **Pl. 12**

**Distribution.** Widespread throughout Europe, except for the extreme north. Widely distributed in the British Isles but more local in Scotland.

**Description.** Length up to 30 mm; body pale bluish- or greyish-green on the back, shading into white on the sides to below the level of the spiracles; underside dark green; body finely spotted with black; head coloured as body.

**Habitat.** Hedgerows, woodland margins and damp meadows.

**Foodplants.** Garlic mustard (*Alliaria petiolata*), hedge mustard (*Sisymbrium officinale*), cuckoo flower (*Cardamine pratensis*), charlock (*Sinapis arvensis*) and other related plants.

**Biology.** One generation a year. Eggs are laid singly in young flower heads in May or June and hatch in about a week. The caterpillars feed on the seedpods in June and July. Their resemblance to the pods on which they feed makes them very difficult to detect. Pupation takes place in July. The pupae are attached to various stems or twigs but seldom on the foodplant. Butterflies do not emerge until the following May.

**ANTHOCHARIS BELIA** Linnaeus *Morocco Orange-tip* **Pl. 12**

**Distribution.** Occurs in southern Europe, particularly Spain, Portugal and south-eastern France; also occurs in North Africa.

**Description.** Length up to 32 mm; body white, heavily spotted with black and with a broad yellow band extending along the middle of the back; head white, spotted with black.

**Habitat.** Open countryside and woodland margins, often in mountainous regions.

**Foodplants.** Buckler mustard (*Biscutella laevigata*) and hedge mustard (*Sisymbrium officinale*); also feeds on alison (*Alyssum*) in captivity.

**Biology.** One generation a year. The caterpillars feed on flowers and seedpods and the pupae overwinter, producing butterflies in the following spring. Butterflies are on the wing from May to July.

**EUCHLOE SIMPLONIA** Boisduval *Freyer's Dappled White* **Pl. 13**

**Distribution.** Occurs in many parts of Mediterranean Europe, including the Iberian Peninsula.

**Description.** Length up to 28 mm; body pale bluish-green, spotted with black, with a dark, greyish-green stripe along the middle of the back, bordered on either side by a band of pale yellow; a whitish line, edged below with yellow, extends along the line of the spiracles; head pale green spotted with black.

**Habitat.** Meadows and hillsides.

**Foodplants.** Candytuft (*Iberis*), buckler mustard (*Biscutella laevigata*), wild radish (*Raphanus raphanistrum*), rocket (*Sisymbrium*), wintercress (*Barbarea*) and other related plants.
**Biology.** Two generations a year, with butterflies on the wing from March to April and May to June. Second brood pupae overwinter.

# LYCAENIDAE

The small caterpillars of this butterfly family, which includes the blues, coppers and hairstreaks, are rather slug-like in shape, being short and stout and sometimes humped in the middle. They are usually covered with short, fine hairs. The head is withdrawn into the body when at rest. Caterpillars of the blues feed largely on plants of the family Leguminosae, hairstreaks on the foliage of trees and shrubs and coppers on docks (*Rumex*).

**CALLOPHRYS RUBI** Linnaeus *Green Hairstreak* **Pl. 19**
**Distribution.** Widespread and common throughout Europe. Widely distributed in the British Isles.
**Description.** Length up to 15 mm; body rather broad and plump, becoming flattened at the extremities, strongly indented between the segments; green with a dark line along the middle of the back from which radiates a series of oblique yellowish-white and dark green markings; a yellowish or whitish line extends along the spiracles; head brown, partly withdrawn into the body.
**Habitat.** Hedgerows, woodland margins, hillsides, moorland and other rough grassland.
**Foodplants.** Gorse (*Ulex europaeus*), broom (*Cytisus scoparius*), birdsfoot trefoil (*Lotus corniculatus*) and related plants; also on rock-rose (*Helianthemum*), bilberry (*Vaccinium myrtillus*), buckthorn (*Rhamnus*), bramble (*Rubus*) and other plants.
**Biology.** One generation a year. Eggs are laid singly on flowers or young shoots of the foodplant in May or June and hatch in about a week. The caterpillar feeds on the flowers, developing fruits and young leaves. Pupation takes place towards the end of July under leaf litter at the base of the foodplant. Butterflies emerge in May of the following year.

**THECLA BETULAE** Linnaeus *Brown Hairstreak* **Pl. 18**
**Distribution.** Widespread in Europe but more scarce in the south. Widely distributed but local in southern and central England and western Wales; in Ireland, apparently restricted to a small area in the west.
**Description.** Length up to 18 mm; rather broad and plump, becoming flattened at the extremities; strongly indented between segments; body green with whitish divisions between segments; two yellowish-white lines extend along the back, diverging towards the head; a series of oblique yellowish-white lines extends along each side; head blackish-brown, withdrawn into the body.

**Habitat.** Hedgerows, scrub and woodland margins.
**Foodplants.** Blackthorn (*Prunus spinosa*); in continental Europe, also recorded on other *Prunus* species and on birch (*Betula*) and beech (*Fagus*).
**Biology.** One generation a year. Eggs are laid singly on twigs, close to the buds, in late summer but do not hatch until the following spring. The caterpillars feed on the foliage from April to June. Pupae are attached to the undersides of leaves or hidden amongst leaf litter at the base of the foodplant. Butterflies emerge after about a month.

**QUERCUSIA QUERCUS** Linnaeus *Purple Hairstreak* **Pl. 6**
**Distribution.** Widespread throughout Europe. Widely distributed in the British Isles but most common in southern England, becoming increasingly rare towards the north; scarce in Ireland.
**Description.** Length up to 15 mm; broad and short, flattened towards the edges; body reddish-brown with a dark greyish-brown line along the middle of the back, bordered on either side by a series of oblique, dark brown markings; a whitish line extends along each side below the level of the spiracles; head small, dark brown, partly withdrawn into the body.
**Habitat.** Oak woodland.
**Foodplant.** Oak (*Quercus*).
**Biology.** One generation a year. Eggs are laid singly on twigs close to buds in July or August but do not hatch until the following spring. The caterpillars bore into the buds at first but later feed openly on the young foliage. They rest at the bases of opening buds, where they closely resemble the old scale leaves. Pupation takes place at the end of May in crevices of the bark or amongst moss and leaf litter on the ground. Butterflies emerge after about a month.

**STRYMONIDIA W-ALBUM** Knoch *White Letter Hairstreak* **Pl. 7**
**Distribution.** Widely distributed in Europe, although absent from much of the Iberian Peninsula. In the British Isles, largely confined to southern and central England and to Wales; rather local and becoming scarce.
**Description.** Length up to 15 mm; body rather short and broad, tapered at the extremities and flattened towards the sides; yellowish-green with a double line of dark green along the middle of the back, on either side of which is a series of dark green and pale yellowish-green diagonal markings; some specimens are marked with pink along the back and sides; head small, dark brown, partly withdrawn into the body.
**Habitat.** Woodland and hedgerows.
**Foodplants.** Wych elm (*Ulmus glabra*) and English elm (*U. procera*); in continental Europe, also on lime (*Tilia*) and other trees.
**Biology.** One generation a year. Eggs are laid singly in forks of twigs in July or August. Caterpillars hatch at the beginning of March of the following year and bore into flower buds. Later they also feed on the foliage. Pupation takes place on leaves or stems of the foodplant in May and butterflies emerge in about a month.

**STRYMONIDIA PRUNI** Linnaeus *Black Hairstreak* **Pl. 18**
**Distribution.** Widely distributed but local in Europe; absent from most of Italy and the Iberian Peninsula. In the British Isles, confined to a few localities in England between Oxford and Peterborough.
**Description.** Length up to 15 mm; short and broad, tapered at the extremities and

flattened towards the sides; body green with two rows of small, whitish humps marked with purplish-brown on the back; a series of pale yellowish oblique lines extends along either side, although these are sometimes indistinct; head pale brown, withdrawn into the body.
**Habitat.** Woodland and hedgerows.
**Foodplant.** Blackthorn (*Prunus spinosa*).
**Biology.** One generation a year. Eggs are laid singly in forks of small branches in August but do not hatch until the following spring. The caterpillars feed at first on opening buds and later on the young foliage. The black and white pupae resemble bird droppings and are attached to leaves and stems of the foodplant towards the end of May. Butterflies emerge in about three weeks.

**LYCAENA PHLAEAS** Linnaeus *Small Copper* **Pl. 10**
**Distribution.** Widespread and common throughout Europe. Widely distributed in the British Isles.
**Description.** Length up to 15 mm; short and stout, tapering towards the extremities; body green with a pinkish-purple line along the middle of the back and similar lines along each side below the level of the spiracles; the extent and depth of the pinkish markings is extremely variable; head brownish-green, retracted into body.
**Habitat.** Downland, pasture and other places where the foodplants grow.
**Foodplants.** Sorrel and dock (*Rumex*).
**Biology.** Two or three generations a year. Eggs are laid singly at the bases of leaves in May and July and sometimes again in the autumn. Caterpillars hatch in about a week and live and feed on the undersides of leaves. Summer caterpillars become fully grown in about a month but the last generation overwinters before completing its growth in the following spring. Pupae are attached to the undersides of leaves and to stems and produce butterflies within a month.

**LYCAENA DISPAR** Haworth *Large Copper* **Pl. 10**
**Distribution.** Widely distributed but very local in Europe. Extinct in the British Isles since about 1860.
**Description.** Length up to 21 mm; plump, tapering towards the extremities; body bright green, covered with small, white, raised dots; there are traces of a dark line along the middle of the back and dark, oblique stripes along the sides; head small, pale ochreous green, withdrawn into the body when at rest.
**Habitat.** Fens and other wet places.
**Foodplants.** Extinct British subspecies fed on water dock (*Rumex hydrolapathum*), but in continental Europe this species also feeds on other *Rumex* species.
**Biology.** One generation a year. Eggs are laid singly on leaves of the foodplant in August and hatch after about a fortnight. After the first moult, the caterpillars take on a pinkish tinge and go into hibernation. During this period they may be submerged in water for long periods. Feeding is resumed in the spring and caterpillars become fully grown in June. Pupation takes place on the foodplant and butterflies emerge in about a fortnight.

**CUPIDO MINIMUS** Fuessly *Small Blue* **Pl. 20**
**Distribution.** Widespread in Europe but absent from southern Spain and Portugal. Widely distributed but local in the British Isles, more common in southern England.
**Description.** Length up to 10 mm; short and stout, tapering towards the extremities; body pale ochreous, sometimes tinged with green, or pale yellow, with a dark

line down the middle of the back and a whitish line, sometimes tinged with pink at the margins, along each side below the level of the spiracles; head shining black, withdrawn into the body when at rest.

**Habitat.** Downland and grassy banks.

**Foodplants.** Kidney vetch (*Anthyllis vulneraria*); in continental Europe, also on other related plants.

**Biology.** One generation a year, with a partial second brood in southern localities. Eggs are laid singly amongst flower buds in June and hatch in about a week. The caterpillars bore into flowers to feed on the developing seeds and either hibernate when fully grown or pupate to produce second brood butterflies in late summer. Overwintering caterpillars pupate in the following spring and produce butterflies in May or June.

**EVERES ARGIADES** Pallas *Short-tailed Blue* **Pl. 21**

**Distribution.** Widely distributed in central and southern Europe but absent from the Iberian Peninsula. A rare migrant to the British Isles and parts of northern Europe.

**Description.** Length up to 10 mm; rather short and stout, tapering towards the extremities; body pale green with a dark line down the middle of the back, on either side of which is a series of pale, oblique stripes; head shining black, withdrawn into the body when at rest. Hibernating caterpillars are pale pinkish-brown with reddish-brown markings.

**Habitat.** Meadows, heathland and grassy forest clearings.

**Foodplants.** Birdsfoot trefoil (*Lotus corniculatus*), gorse (*Ulex europaeus*), medick (*Medicago*) and related plants.

**Biology.** Two or more generations a year. Eggs are laid singly at the bases of leaves and hatch in about a week. Caterpillars of the first generation become fully grown in 4–5 weeks, but those of the second or third brood overwinter when fully grown and pupate in the following spring. Pupae are attached to stems of the foodplant and produce butterflies in about a fortnight. First brood butterflies are on the wing in April and further broods appear during the summer.

**PLEBEJUS ARGUS** Linnaeus *Silver-studded Blue* **Pl. 19**

**Distribution.** Widely distributed throughout Europe, except for the extreme north. In the British Isles, this species now appears to be confined to southern and eastern England and west Wales.

**Description.** Length up to 13 mm; broad, tapering towards the extremities and flattened at the sides; body green with a white-bordered, blackish-brown stripe along the middle of the back and a white stripe along each side below the level of the spiracles; sides sometimes marked with brownish-green diagonal stripes; a reddish-brown form occurs, having a purple stripe along the back; head black, withdrawn into the body.

**Habitat.** Heathland, chalk and limestone grassland and coastal sand dunes.

**Foodplants.** Gorse (*Ulex europaeus*), birdsfoot trefoil (*Lotus corniculatus*), broom (*Cytisus scoparius*), bell heather (*Erica*) and related plants.

**Biology.** One generation a year. Eggs are laid singly on the undersides of leaves in summer but do not hatch until the following spring. When feeding on gorse, the caterpillars eat flowers, but on most other foodplants they eat foliage. They feed by day and night and become fully grown in three weeks. The pupae are formed on the ground at the base of the foodplant and produce butterflies within three weeks.

**ARICIA AGESTIS** Denis & Schiffermüller *Brown Argus* **Pl. 23**

**Distribution.** Widespread throughout Europe, except for the extreme north. In the British Isles, confined to southern and central England and Wales.

**Description.** Length up to 11 mm; fairly stout, tapering towards the extremities; body green with a purplish-green stripe along the middle of the back, on either side of which is a series of dark green, oblique lines; a pink-centred, purple stripe extends along each side below the level of the spiracles; head black, withdrawn into the body.

**Habitat.** Chalk and limestone downs, heaths and coastal sandhills.

**Foodplants.** Common rock-rose (*Helianthemum nummularium*), common storksbill (*Erodium cicutarium*), cranesbill (*Geranium*) and probably other related plants.

**Biology.** Two generations a year. Eggs are laid singly on the undersides of leaves in May or June and again in August, hatching in about a week. Caterpillars of the first generation become fully grown in about six weeks but those of the second brood hibernate when only partly grown, completing their feeding in the following spring. Pupation takes place at the base of the foodplant and butterflies emerge in about a fortnight.

**ARICIA ARTAXERXES** Fabricius *Northern Brown Argus* **Pl. 23**

**Distribution.** Widely distributed in northern Europe, also occurring in the mountains of central and southern Europe. In the British Isles, occurs in central and northern England and in Scotland.

**Description.** Length up to 13 mm; fairly stout, tapering towards the extremities; body green with a darker brownish-green line along the middle of the back, on either side of which is a series of dark green, oblique lines; a white stripe, bordered above with pink, extends along each side below the level of the spiracles; head black, withdrawn into the body.

**Habitat.** Grassy slopes and sheltered moorland.

**Foodplant.** Common rock-rose (*Helianthemum nummularium*).

**Biology.** One generation a year. Eggs are laid singly on the upper surfaces of leaves in July and hatch in about a week. The caterpillars hibernate when partly grown and complete their feeding in the following spring. Pupation takes place at the base of the foodplant in June and butterflies emerge in about three weeks.

**POLYOMMATUS ICARUS** Rottemburg *Common Blue* **Pl. 20**

**Distribution.** Widespread and common throughout Europe and the British Isles.

**Description.** Length up to 13 mm; fairly stout, tapering towards the extremities and flattened towards the sides; body green with a pale-bordered, dark green line along the middle of the back; a greenish-white line extends along each side below the level of the white spiracles; head shining black, withdrawn into the body.

**Habitat.** Downland, waste ground, sand dunes and other rough grassland.

**Foodplants.** Birdsfoot trefoil (*Lotus corniculatus*), rest-harrow (*Ononis*), clover (*Trifolium*) and other related plants.

**Biology.** Two generations a year, occasionally three. Eggs are laid singly on the upper surfaces of leaves in early and late summer, hatching in just over a week. Caterpillars of the first generation become fully grown in about six weeks but those of the second brood overwinter when partly grown, resuming feeding in the spring. Pupation takes place at the base of the foodplants in spring and summer and butterflies emerge in about a fortnight.

**LYSANDRA CORIDON** Poda *Chalkhill Blue* **Pl. 21**

**Distribution.** Widely distributed in central and southern Europe. In the British Isles, confined to southern England.

**Description.** Length up to 16 mm; fairly stout, tapered towards the extremities and flattened at the sides; body green with two yellow bands along the back and a double yellow stripe along each side below the level of the black spiracles; head shining black, withdrawn into the body.

**Habitat.** Chalk and limestone downland and hills.

**Foodplants.** Horseshoe vetch (*Hippocrepis comosa*); in continental Europe, also on other related plants.

**Biology.** One generation a year. Eggs are laid singly on leaves and stems in August but do not hatch until the following spring. The caterpillars feed on leaves and flowers, becoming fully grown in about ten weeks. Pupation takes place on the ground at the base of the foodplant and butterflies emerge in about a month.

**LYSANDRA BELLARGUS** Rottemburg *Adonis Blue* **Pl. 21**

**Distribution.** Widely distributed in southern and central Europe and in southern parts of northern Europe. In the British Isles, confined to a few restricted colonies in southern England.

**Description.** Length up to 16 mm; very similar in appearance to caterpillars of the Chalkhill Blue but darker green with darker body hairs.

**Habitat.** Chalk and limestone downland and hills.

**Foodplants.** Horseshoe vetch (*Hippocrepis comosa*); in continental Europe, also on scorpion vetch (*Coronilla*) and related plants.

**Biology.** Two generations a year. Eggs are laid singly on leaves and other parts of the foodplant in May or June and again in late summer, hatching in 2–3 weeks. First generation caterpillars become fully grown in just over a month but those of the second brood hibernate at the base of the foodplant when partly grown, completing their feeding in the following spring. Pupation takes place just below the surface of the soil or under leaf litter and butterflies emerge in about three weeks.

**CYANIRIS SEMIARGUS** Rottemburg *Mazarine Blue* **Pl. 20**

**Distribution.** Widely distributed throughout Europe. Extinct in the British Isles but may occur as an occasional migrant.

**Description.** Length up to 12 mm; short and stout, tapered at the extremities and flattened at the sides; body pale green, sometimes tinged with ochre, with a dark green line along the middle of the back and sometimes with further dark lines along the back and sides; head shining black, withdrawn into the body when at rest.

**Habitat.** Meadows, grassy slopes and other rough grassland.

**Foodplants.** Clover (*Trifolium*), kidney vetch (*Anthyllis*), melilot (*Melilotus*) and related plants.

**Biology.** One generation a year. Eggs are laid on flower heads in the summer and hatch in about ten days. The young caterpillars bore into the flower heads to feed on developing seeds but go into hibernation towards the end of the summer, becoming active again in the following spring, when they eat young shoots. When fully grown towards the end of spring, they pupate on stems and produce butterflies in about a fortnight.

**CELASTRINA ARGIOLUS** Linnaeus *Holly Blue* **Pl. 8**

**Distribution.** Widespread throughout Europe. Widely distributed in England, Wales and Ireland and also occurs in the extreme south of Scotland.

**Description.** Length up to 13 mm; fairly stout, tapering towards the extremities; body green or yellowish-green with a whitish line along each side below the level of the spiracles; some forms have a series of whitish, triangular patches along the back, through which extends a line of purplish or pinkish markings; sometimes the caterpillar is generally suffused with purplish-pink; head black, withdrawn into the body.

**Habitat.** Woodland, hedgerows and gardens.

**Foodplants.** Holly (*Ilex aquifolium*), ivy (*Hedera helix*), dogwood (*Cornus sanguinea*), spindle (*Euonymus*), alder buckthorn (*Frangula alnus*), snowberry (*Symphoricarpos*) and gorse (*Ulex europaeus*).

**Biology.** Two generations a year. Eggs are laid singly on buds of holly in spring and ivy in summer and hatch in about a week. The caterpillars feed on buds, flowers and developing berries and, when fully grown, attach their pupae to leaves. First generation pupae produce butterflies within three weeks but those of the second generation overwinter, producing butterflies in the following spring.

**MACULINEA ARION** Linnaeus *Large Blue* **Pl. 26**

**Distribution.** Widely distributed in Europe but absent from the extreme north and from southern parts of the Iberian Peninsula. Apparently extinct in the British Isles.

**Description.** Length up to 15 mm; stout, tapering gradually towards the tail and abruptly towards the head; body ochreous-white, sometimes tinged with purplish-pink; head black, withdrawn into the body when at rest. Young caterpillars are pink.

**Habitat.** Grassy hillsides with short turf and scrub.

**Foodplant.** Wild thyme (*Thymus serpyllum*); later feeding on ant grubs.

**Biology.** One generation a year. Eggs are laid singly on buds of thyme in July and hatch in about a week. The young caterpillars feed on the flowers and developing seeds until after their second moult, when they drop to the ground. At this stage, they are picked up by *Myrmica* ants, attracted by 'honeydew' secreted by glands on the caterpillars' backs, and carried back to the nest. There they feed on ant eggs and grubs, hibernating and becoming fully grown in the spring. Pupation takes place within the nest and, after about three weeks, the butterfly emerges and crawls out of the nest before expanding its wings.

# RIODINIDAE

The only European representative of this family, sometimes also called the Nemeobiidae, is the Duke of Burgundy Fritillary butterfly (*Hamearis lucina*). Its caterpillar is rather slug-like in appearance, resembling those of the family Lycaenidae, but is covered with fairly long, fine hairs and feeds on the foliage of *Primula* species.

**HAMEARIS LUCINA** Linnaeus *Duke of Burgundy Fritillary* **Pl. 25**
**Distribution.** Widely distributed in Europe, except for the extreme north and also southern Spain. In the British Isles, largely restricted to southern England, although also recorded from northern England.
**Description.** Length up to 15 mm; short, stout and hairy; body pale brown with a purplish- or greyish-brown band dotted with blackish-brown along the middle of the back, on either side of which is a further line of smaller, blackish spots; head yellowish-brown, partly withdrawn into the body.
**Habitat.** Woodland clearings and grassy slopes with scrub.
**Foodplants.** Cowslip (*Primula veris*) and primrose (*P. vulgaris*).
**Biology.** One generation a year. Eggs are laid singly or in small groups on the undersides of leaves in May and hatch in about a fortnight. Caterpillars feed for 5–6 weeks, hiding amongst dead leaves at the base of the plant when not active. Pupation takes place on the undersides of leaves in July but butterflies do not emerge until May of the following year.

# NYMPHALIDAE

This butterfly family includes the fritillaries and tortoiseshells. The caterpillars are medium-sized to large and usually have spines on the body and head. Those that do not have spines on the body, such as the Purple Emperor (*Apatura iris*) and the Two-tailed Pasha (*Charaxes jasius*), have particularly well-developed horns or prongs on the head. They feed on a wide range of trees, shrubs and low-growing plants.

**CHARAXES JASIUS** Linnaeus *Two-tailed Pasha* **Pl. 25**
**Distribution.** Widely distributed but local along the Mediterranean coasts of Europe.
**Description.** Length up to 60 mm; body plump, strongly tapered towards the two-pronged tail; green, finely spotted with yellowish-white; two blue-centred, yellow spots, ringed with black are present on the middle of the back; a yellow line runs along each side, extending along the prongs of the tail; head large, green marked with yellow, with four large, backward-pointing prongs, tipped with red.
**Habitat.** Warm coastal regions where the foodplant grows.

**Foodplant.** Strawberry tree (*Arbutus unedo*).
**Biology.** Two generations a year. Caterpillars feed from June to July and September to April. The pupae are suspended from the foodplant. Butterflies are on the wing from May to June and August to September.

**LADOGA CAMILLA** Linnaeus *White Admiral* **Pl. 28**
**Distribution.** Widespread in Europe but absent from the Iberian Peninsula and southern Italy. In the British Isles, confined to the southern half of England and a few localities in Wales, but more widespread than at the beginning of this century.
**Description.** Length up to 27 mm; body green with two rows of brown spines along the back; a whitish line extends along the spiracles, below which the body is purplish-brown in colour; head brown, spiny.
**Habitat.** Woodland.
**Foodplant.** Honeysuckle (*Lonicera periclymenum*).
**Biology.** One generation a year. Eggs are laid singly on the upper surfaces of leaves of the foodplant in June or July and hatch in about a week. After the second moult, the caterpillars go into hibernation, sheltering in curled leaves until the following spring when they resume feeding. In June, when fully grown, the caterpillars pupate, hanging from stems of the foodplant. The unusually shaped green and brown pupa resembles a dead honeysuckle leaf. Butterflies emerge in about a fortnight.

**LIMENITIS POPULI** Linnaeus *Poplar Admiral* **Pl. 3**
**Distribution.** Widely distributed in central Europe and parts of northern Europe but absent from the British Isles.
**Description.** Length up to 50 mm; body green, marked with purplish-brown along the back and sides and with an irregular ochreous band extending along the sides; segment 2 bears two large, spiny projections on the back; segment 3 and subsequent segments with smaller, spiny projections; head brown or blackish, with two blunt spines at the top.
**Habitat.** Damp, open woodland and forest clearings.
**Foodplants.** Aspen and poplar (*Populus*).
**Biology.** One generation a year. Eggs are laid on the upper surfaces of leaves in June or July. Young caterpillars overwinter while still small, completing their feeding in the following spring and becoming fully grown in May or June. Pupae are attached to leaves and produce butterflies in two to four weeks.

**APATURA IRIS** Linnaeus *Purple Emperor* **Pl. 2**
**Distribution.** Widely distributed in Europe but absent from Italy, southern Spain and southern France. In the British Isles, confined to southern England.
**Description.** Length up to 42 mm; plump, tapering strongly towards the extremities; body green, minutely spotted with yellowish-white, with a series of diagonal yellow stripes along each side; head green, with two long, red-tipped horns, each bearing a yellowish-white, longitudinal stripe.
**Habitat.** Woodland.
**Foodplants.** Goat willow (*Salix caprea*), grey sallow (*S. cinerea*) and, in continental Europe, also on other *Salix* species.
**Biology.** One generation a year. Eggs are laid singly on the upper surfaces of leaves in August and hatch in about a fortnight. In the autumn, after its second moult, the caterpillar goes into hibernation, sheltering in the fork of a twig or under a dead leaf spun to the stem. Feeding is resumed in the following March and the caterpillar

becomes fully grown towards the end of June. The leaf-like pupa is attached to a stem and produces a butterfly in about a fortnight.

**APATURA ILIA** Denis & Shiffermüller *Lesser Purple Emperor* **Pl. 3**

**Distribution.** Widely distributed in central and southern Europe but absent from much of the Iberian Peninsula and from the British Isles.

**Description.** Length up to 50 mm; body tapering towards the tail, which bears two small prongs, meeting to form a point; green with two red and yellow lines extending along the back from the head to the middle of the body; rear half with a series of diagonal, red and yellow stripes along the side; head green with two long, brown-striped horns which are forked at the tips.

**Habitat.** Open woodland, particularly in damp situations.

**Foodplants.** Aspen and poplar (*Populus*), sallow and willow (*Salix*).

**Biology.** One generation a year; two generations in some southern regions. The caterpillars hatch in August but overwinter on branches while still small. They resume feeding in the following spring and are fully grown by June. Butterflies are on the wing in July in the north and from May to June and August to September in the south.

**VANESSA ATALANTA** Linnaeus *Red Admiral* **Pl. 9**

**Distribution.** Widespread throughout Europe. This species has its breeding centre in southern Europe and North Africa but regularly migrates northwards to all parts of Europe, including the British Isles.

**Description.** Length up to 35 mm; occurs as several colour forms; the dark form is greyish-black with black spines ringed at the base with reddish-brown; a band of yellow patches extends along the sides; pale forms are greyish-green or ochreous-yellow, marked to varying extents with black, but with pale spines; head black.

**Habitat.** Hedgerows, woodland margins, gardens, waste ground and other places where the foodplant grows.

**Foodplants.** Stinging nettle (*Urtica dioica*) and related species; sometimes hop (*Humulus lupulus*) and pellitory of the wall (*Parietaria judaica*).

**Biology.** One or two generations a year. In Britain, the butterflies seldom survive the winter. Eggs are laid singly on the upper surfaces of leaves in June and sometimes again in late summer, hatching in about a week. Caterpillars feed in the shelter of curled leaves and become fully grown in about a month. The pupae are suspended within the feeding shelters and produce butterflies in 2–3 weeks.

**CYNTHIA CARDUI** Linnaeus *Painted Lady* **Pl. 29**

**Distribution.** Widespread throughout Europe. This species has its breeding centre in southern Europe and North Africa but regularly migrates northwards to all parts of Europe, including the British Isles.

**Description.** Length up to 28 mm; body black, finely dotted with white, with yellowish or black spines; an almost continuous yellow line extends along each side below the level of the spiracles; beneath this line, the body is marked with reddish-brown; head black.

**Habitat.** Rough meadows and other open countryside where the foodplants grow.

**Foodplants.** Thistles (*Carduus* and *Cirsium*), mallow (*Malva*), nettle (*Urtica*) and probably other plants, such as burdock (*Arctium*).

**Biology**. One or two generations a year. Eggs are laid singly on the upper surfaces of leaves in June and sometimes again in August, and hatch in about a week. The caterpillars feed within the shelter of spun leaves and become fully grown in about a month. Pupation takes place in shelters of spun leaves and butterflies emerge after a fortnight.

**AGLAIS URTICAE** Linnaeus *Small Tortoiseshell* **Pl. 9**

**Distribution.** Widespread throughout Europe. Widely distributed and common in the British Isles.

**Description.** Length up to 22 mm; body black, minutely dotted with white, with two broken bands of yellow along each side, below which the body is purplish-brown; sometimes there is a series of reddish-brown markings between the yellow lines; some forms are suffused with yellow; spines along the back and sides black or yellowish; head black.

**Habitat.** Hedgerows, gardens, parks, waste land and other places where the food-plant grows.

**Foodplant.** Stinging nettle (*Urtica dioica*).

**Biology.** Two generations a year. Eggs are laid in batches on the undersides of young leaves in May and again in July, and hatch in about ten days. The caterpillars live together in a communal web until after the final moult when they become solitary. They become fully fed within a month and suspend their pupae from plant stems. Butterflies emerge in about a fortnight. Second brood butterflies hibernate before mating and laying eggs in the following spring.

**NYMPHALIS POLYCHLOROS** Linnaeus *Large Tortoiseshell* **Pl. 7**

**Distribution.** Widespread throughout Europe. There are scattered records from various parts of southern Britain, but this species probably only occurs there now as an occasional migrant; absent from Ireland.

**Description.** Length up to 45 mm; body black, minutely spotted with white and marked with orange lines along the back and sides; spines orange-brown; head black.

**Habitat.** Woodland margins and wooded countryside.

**Foodplants.** Elm (*Ulmus*), sallow and willow (*Salix*), poplar and aspen (*Populus*), birch (*Betula*), cherry (*Prunus*) and pear (*Pyrus*).

**Biology.** One generation a year. Eggs are laid in batches encircling twigs in April and hatch in about three weeks. The caterpillars live together in a communal web at first, later leaving the web but remaining together. They become fully grown in June and pupate suspended from the foodplant. Butterflies emerge in about a fortnight but hibernate before mating and laying eggs in the following spring.

**NYMPHALIS ANTIOPA** Linnaeus *Camberwell Beauty* **Pl. 2**

**Distribution.** Widespread throughout Europe except for the southern half of the Iberian Peninsula. Occurs as an occasional immigrant in the British Isles, more usually along the eastern coasts of England.

**Description.** Length up to 54 mm; body black, finely spotted with white, with a series of reddish-brown patches along the back; spines long, black; prolegs reddish-brown; head shining black.

**Habitat.** Open woodland.

**Foodplants.** Sallow and willow (*Salix*), birch (*Betula*) and elm (*Ulmus*).

**Biology.** One generation a year. Eggs are laid in batches encircling twigs of the foodplant in the spring and hatch in 2–3 weeks. The caterpillars feed together in a communal web and remain together until fully grown in July. Pupae are suspended from the foodplant and produce butterflies in about three weeks. The butterflies hibernate before mating and laying eggs in the following spring but it is unlikely that butterflies would survive the winter in Britain.

**INACHIS IO** Hübner *Peacock* **Pl. 9**

**Distribution.** Widespread throughout Europe. Widely distributed in the British Isles but rather scarce in northern Scotland.

**Description.** Length up to 42 mm; body black, finely spotted with white, with long, black spines on the back and sides; prolegs yellowish-brown; head shining black.

**Habitat.** Woodland margins, hedgerows, gardens, parks and other places where the foodplant grows.

**Foodplant.** Stinging nettle (*Urtica dioica*).

**Biology.** One generation a year. Eggs are laid in batches on the undersides of nettle leaves in May and hatch in about a fortnight. The caterpillars live together in a communal web until after the final moult, when they leave the web and disperse. They become fully grown in about a month and suspend their pupae from plant stems. Butterflies emerge in about a fortnight but hibernate before mating and laying eggs in the following spring.

**POLYGONIA C-ALBUM** Linnaeus *Comma* **Pl. 9**

**Distribution.** Widespread throughout Europe. In the British Isles, confined to the southern half of England and to Wales but more widely distributed than formerly.

**Description.** Length up to 35 mm; body black, strongly banded with orange-brown, with a large patch of white extending along the back of the rear half of the body, including the spines; other spines pale orange-brown; head black, with two spined lobes.

**Habitat.** Woodland margins and hedgerows.

**Foodplants.** Stinging nettle (*Urtica dioica*), hop (*Humulus lupulus*), elm (*Ulmus*) and, in some regions, probably other trees such as willow (*Salix*).

**Biology.** Two generations a year. Eggs are laid singly or in small groups on the upper surfaces of leaves in May and again in July or August, hatching in two to three weeks. The caterpillars do not live in groups but rest singly on the undersides of leaves. The large white patch on the back gives the appearance of a bird dropping. Caterpillars are fully grown in about six weeks and suspend their pupae from stems of the foodplant. Butterflies emerge in 2–3 weeks. Those of the second generation hibernate before mating and laying eggs in the following spring.

**ARASCHNIA LEVANA** Linnaeus *European Map* **Pl. 9**

**Distribution.** Widespread in central and parts of southern Europe. Absent from the British Isles.

**Description.** Length up to 22 mm; body black, finely spotted with white, with broken yellowish-brown stripes along the back and sides; spines black or orange-yellow, bulbous at the bases; prolegs yellowish-brown; head black, with two spined lobes.

**Habitat.** Open woodland and woodland margins.

**Foodplant.** Stinging nettle (*Urtica dioica*).

**Biology.** Two generations, sometimes with a partial third brood. Eggs are laid in chains of 6–15, stacked one on top of another. Several chains may be suspended from the underside of one leaf. The caterpillars live together until after the final moult, when they disperse. Pupae are attached to leaf stems or twigs. Those of the final generation overwinter to produce butterflies in the following spring. Spring and summer broods of butterflies are quite different in pattern and coloration.

BOLORIA SELENE Denis & Schiffermuller **Pl. 23**
*Small Pearl-bordered Fritillary*
**Distribution.** Widespread throughout Europe but absent from Italy and southern Spain. Widely distributed in many parts of the British Isles but absent from Ireland.
**Description.** Length up to 22 mm; body pinkish-brown, marked with black and peppered with minute white spots; spines pinkish-yellow, with fine black hairs; the first pair of spines behind the head are long and look like horns; head black.
**Habitat.** Woodland clearings and margins, marshy moorland, hillsides and cliffs.
**Foodplants.** Dog violet (*Viola riviniana*), and in continental Europe, also on other *Viola* spp. and bilberry (*Vaccinium*). In captivity, will eat garden pansy.
**Biology.** One or two generations a year, normally single-brooded in Britain. Eggs are laid in June and hatch after about ten days. The caterpillar feeds on the foliage until the end of August, when it hibernates in a curled-up, dead leaf before completing its growth in the following spring. The pupa is formed in May, suspended from a pad of silk spun on a stem. The butterfly emerges after about a fortnight.

BOLORIA EUPHROSYNE Linnaeus *Pearl-bordered Fritillary* **Pl. 23**
**Distribution.** Widespread throughout Europe, except for the southern half of the Iberian Peninsula. Widely distributed in England, Wales and Scotland. In Ireland, confined to the Burren, Co. Clare.
**Description.** Length up to 25 mm; body black, with a row of white spots along the line of the spiracles; spines on the back vary in colour from black to yellow or white; head black.
**Habitat.** Woodland clearings and margins, particularly near streams and in other damp areas.
**Foodplants.** Dog violet (*Viola riviniana*), and in continental Europe, also on other *Viola* spp. In captivity, will feed on the foliage of garden pansy.
**Biology.** One or two generations a year, normally single-brooded in Britain. Eggs are laid on the foodplant in May or June, hatching in about a fortnight. The caterpillar feeds on the foliage until the end of July, when it enters hibernation, hidden in a dead, rolled violet leaf. Feeding is completed in the following spring and pupation takes place in May. The pupa is suspended from a pad of silk spun on a leaf or stem. The butterfly emerges after about ten days.

BOLORIA DIA Linnaeus *Violet Fritillary or Weaver's Fritillary* **Pl. 23**
**Distribution.** Widespread in temperate Europe but absent from the British Isles, Scandinavia and southern Spain and Italy.
**Description.** Length up to 22 mm; body dark grey with a broken, whitish streak along the back and reddish-yellow lines along the sides; spines yellowish, becoming whitish at the tips; head black.
**Habitats.** Grassy woodland clearings and hillsides.
**Foodplants.** Violets (*Viola*) and brambles (*Rubus*).

**Biology.** Two or three generations a year. Caterpillars may be found feeding on the foliage from April until September. Those of the second or third generation hibernate through the winter, completing their growth in the following spring. Butterflies are on the wing from April until October. This is one of the smallest European Fritillaries.

ARGYNNIS LATHONIA Linnaeus *Queen of Spain Fritillary* **Pl. 23**

**Distribution.** Widespread throughout Europe. Occurs as a scarce immigrant in the British Isles, more usually in south-eastern England.

**Description.** Length up to 35 mm; body black, finely spotted with white and marked with brown, with a double white line along the middle of the back; spines reddish-brown; prolegs yellowish-brown; head brown, marked with black.

**Habitat.** Rough grassland, heathland and other places where the foodplants grow.

**Foodplants.** Violet (*Viola*) and possibly on other plants.

**Biology.** Two generations a year, with an occasional third brood. Eggs are laid on the foodplant in May and August and hatch in about a week. Summer caterpillars become fully grown in about a month but those of the autumn generation usually hibernate. It is possible that some overwinter as pupae. The pupae are suspended from the foodplant and are said to resemble bird droppings. Butterflies are on the wing in various broods from February to October in continental Europe.

ARGYNNIS ADIPPE Denis & Schiffermuller **Pl. 23**
*High Brown Fritillary*

**Distribution.** Widespread in Europe. In the British Isles, largely confined to western England and parts of Wales. This butterfly was formerly more widespread and common in England but has suffered a recent decline and is now scarce.

**Description.** Length up to 38 mm; body reddish-brown or dark brown with a white line along the middle of the back, extending through a series of triangular, black markings; spines pale reddish-brown or pink; head reddish-brown.

**Habitat.** Woodland, open scrub and rough grassland.

**Foodplant.** Dog violet (*Viola riviniana*) and probably other species of *Viola*.

**Biology.** One generation a year. Eggs are laid singly on stems and leaves of the foodplant, or sometimes on other vegetation, in July but do not hatch until the following February. The caterpillars sometimes feed on the flowers at first but later eat the foliage. They feed by day, hiding among dead leaves under the foodplant at night. They become fully grown in 2–3 months and pupate in shelters of spun leaves, often at a distance from the foodplant. Butterflies hatch within a month.

ARGYNNIS AGLAJA Linnaeus *Dark Green Fritillary* **Pl. 23**

**Distribution.** Widespread throughout Europe. Widely distributed but local in the British Isles.

**Description.** Length up to 38 mm; body velvety-black, with black spines and a row of orange-red spots along each side below the level of the spiracles; head shining black.

**Habitat.** Grassland, moors and open woodland.

**Foodplants.** Violets (*Viola*).

**Biology.** One generation a year. Eggs are laid singly on stems or leaves of the foodplant and hatch in 2–3 weeks. After eating its eggshell, the young caterpillar goes into hibernation at the base of the foodplant, emerging in the following spring and feeding until June. It is active on sunny days, hiding beneath the foodplant when at rest. The pupa is suspended within a tent-like shelter of spun leaves and the butterfly emerges after about a month.

**ARGYNNIS PAPHIA** Linnaeus *Silver-washed Fritillary* **Pl. 23**

**Distribution.** Widespread in Europe but absent from southern Spain. Widely distributed in the southern half of Britain and in Ireland but declining in numbers and becoming scarce.
**Description.** Length up to 38 mm; body dark blackish-brown on the back, with two orange-yellow stripes; sides pale reddish-brown, lined and mottled with blackish-brown; spines reddish-brown with black tips, except for the first pair behind the head which are long, black and directed forward; head shining black.
**Habitat.** Woodland and woodland margins.
**Foodplants.** Dog violet (*Viola riviniana*) and other *Viola* species.
**Biology.** One generation a year. Eggs are laid singly in crevices of the bark of trees growing near the foodplant in July, hatching in about a fortnight. After eating its eggshell, the young caterpillar goes into hibernation on the tree trunk, becoming active again in the spring and descending to the ground to find its foodplant. It feeds by day and becomes fully grown towards the end of May. The pupa is suspended from the foodplant and produces a butterfly within 2–3 weeks.

**EURODRYAS AURINIA** Rottemburg *Marsh Fritillary* **Pl. 28**

**Distribution.** Widespread throughout Europe. Widely distributed in suitable localities in Ireland and western Britain but extinct in many eastern localities.
**Description.** Length up to 27 mm; body black, with bands of white speckling down the back and along the line of the spiracles; prolegs reddish-brown; spines and head black.
**Habitat.** Marshland and hillsides where the foodplants grow.
**Foodplants.** Devilsbit scabious (*Succisa pratensis*); in continental Europe, also on field scabious (*Knautia arvensis*), greater knapweed (*Centaurea scabiosa*), plantain (*Plantago*) and other plants.
**Biology.** One generation a year. Eggs are laid in batches on the undersides of leaves in June and hatch in about three weeks. The young caterpillars spin a web on the foodplant, under which they live and feed. After the third moult, they go into hibernation until the spring but emerge to bask on the outside of the web on sunny days in February and March. Caterpillars become fully grown by the end of April and disperse to pupate, attached to stems or foliage. Butterflies emerge in about a fortnight.

**MELITAEA DIAMINA** Lang *False Heath Fritillary* **Pl. 27**

**Distribution.** Widespread but local in Europe; absent from southern Italy and Spain and from the British Isles.
**Description.** Length up to 35 mm; body dark greyish-brown, with orange-yellow spines; head blackish-brown.
**Habitat.** Damp meadows and boggy grassland.
**Foodplants.** Common cow-wheat (*Melampyrum pratense*), plantain (*Plantago*), speedwell (*Veronica*) and other plants.
**Biology.** One generation a year, probably two broods in some southern localities. Caterpillars overwinter when partly grown, completing their feeding in the following spring. Butterflies are usually on the wing from June to July.

**MELITAEA DIDYMA** Esper *Spotted Fritillary* **Pl. 27**

**Distribution.** Widespread throughout central and southern Europe and some southern parts of northern Europe. Absent from the British Isles.

**Description.** Length up to 28 mm; body whitish, lined with black and with two rows of large, reddish-orange spots along the back, each surrounding a spine; other spines whitish, with fine black hairs; head reddish-brown.

**Habitat.** Meadows and hillsides where the foodplants grow.

**Foodplants.** Plantain (*Plantago*), speedwell (*Veronica*), toadflax (*Linaria*) and other plants.

**Biology.** One to three generations a year, with butterflies on the wing from May to August, according to locality and altitude. Caterpillars of the final generation overwinter and pupate in the following spring. Butterflies emerge in about a fortnight.

**MELITAEA PHOEBE** Denis & Schiffermüller *Knapweed Fritillary* **Pl. 29**

**Distribution.** Widespread throughout central and northern Europe. Absent from the British Isles.

**Description.** Length up to 30 mm; body blackish-grey, lined with black and finely dotted with white; a whitish band extends along the sides; spines orange-yellow; head black.

**Habitat.** Meadows and flowery slopes.

**Foodplants.** Knapweed (*Centaurea*) and sometimes plantain (*Plantago*).

**Biology.** One to three generations a year according to locality. Butterflies may be seen on the wing from April to August. Caterpillars of the final generation overwinter.

**MELITAEA CINXIA** Linnaeus *Glanville Fritillary* **Pl. 27**

**Distribution.** Widespread in Europe, except for the extreme north. In the British Isles, confined to the Isle of Wight and the Channel Islands.

**Description.** Length up to 25 mm; body black, with transverse bands of white spots; spines short, black; prolegs and head reddish-brown.

**Foodplants.** Ribwort plantain (*Plantago lanceolata*), sea plantain (*P. maritima*) and other *Plantago* species; in continental Europe, also on hawkweed (*Hieracium*) and knapweed (*Centaurea*).

**Biology.** One generation a year. Eggs are laid in batches on the undersides of leaves in June and hatch in about three weeks. The caterpillars live together in a communal web, going into hibernation after their fourth moult. Towards the end of February, they emerge to bask on the outside of the nest and soon resume feeding, becoming fully grown by the end of April. Pupae are attached to plant stems and butterflies emerge in about three weeks.

**MELLICTA ATHALIA** Rottemburg *Heath Fritillary* **Pl. 27**

**Distribution.** Widespread throughout Europe. In the British Isles, confined to south-western England and a restricted area of south-eastern England. This is a scarce species in England, where it is protected by law.

**Description.** Length up to 24 mm; body black, spotted with greyish-white; spines orange-yellow, tipped with white; prolegs greyish-white; head black, marked with white.

**Habitat.** Coppiced woodland, woodland clearings and woodland margins.

**Foodplants.** Common cow-wheat (*Melampyrum pratense*), plantain (*Plantago*),

foxglove (*Digitalis purpurea*), wood sage (*Teucrium scorodonia*) and other plants.
**Biology.** One generation a year. Eggs are laid in batches on the undersides of leaves in July and hatch in about a fortnight. The caterpillars live in webs spun on the undersides of leaves. They go into hibernation at the end of August, sheltering among dead leaves, but resume feeding in the following March and become fully grown in May. The pupae are attached to plant stems or foliage and produce butterflies in about a fortnight.

# SATYRIDAE

This family of butterflies includes the browns, heaths and graylings. The caterpillars are predominantly green or brown, with longitudinal lines and stripes, and bear a characteristic pair of points at the tail. They feed at night on grasses.

**PARARGE AEGERIA** Linnaeus *Speckled Wood* **Pl. 31**
**Distribution.** Widely distributed in Europe, except for the extreme north. Widespread throughout the British Isles but less common in northern England.
**Description.** Length up to 27 mm; body yellowish-green with a white-bordered, dark green stripe along the middle of the back and light and dark lines along the sides; two whitish points at the tail; head rounded, bluish-green.
**Habitat.** Woodland glades and margins, hedgerows and scrub.
**Foodplants.** Cock's-foot (*Dactylis glomerata*), couch-grass (*Agropyron repens*), annual meadow-grass (*Poa annua*) and other grasses.
**Biology.** Two generations a year; possibly a third. Eggs are laid singly on grass blades in April or May and again in the summer, hatching in about ten days. The caterpillars feed by night or day and those of the first brood become fully grown in a month. Late summer caterpillars may pupate in the autumn, or overwinter while small and complete their growth in the following spring. Pupae are suspended from plant stems and those which do not overwinter produce butterflies within a month.

**LASIOMMATA MEGERA** Linnaeus *Wall* **Pl. 31**
**Distribution.** Widespread throughout Europe, except for the extreme north. Widely distributed in the British Isles but, in Scotland, mainly confined to the southern coastal regions.
**Description.** Length up to 25 mm; body bluish-green, with white lines along the back and sides; two pale green, white-tipped points at the tail; head rounded, bluish-green.
**Habitat.** Hedgerows, woodland margins, scrub and open grassland.
**Foodplants.** A wide range of grasses.
**Biology.** Two generations a year. Eggs laid singly on grass blades or exposed roots in May or June and again in August, hatching in about ten days. The caterpillars feed mainly at night. Those of the first generation become fully grown in about a month but second brood caterpillars overwinter and pupate in the following spring. Pupae are attached to plant stems and produce butterflies in about a fortnight.

**EREBIA EPIPHRON** Knoch *Mountain Ringlet* **Pl. 32**

**Distribution.** Widely distributed in the mountains of Europe but absent from Fennoscandia. In the British Isles, confined to highland Scotland and the English Lake District.

**Description.** Length up to 19 mm; body green with two yellowish-white lines along the back and a broader yellowish-white stripe along each side below the level of the spiracles; two pale brown-tipped points at the tail; head rounded, bluish-green.

**Habitat.** Boggy upland moorland and mountainsides.

**Foodplant.** Mat-grass (*Nardus stricta*); in continental Europe, probably also on other grasses.

**Biology.** One generation a year. Eggs are laid singly on grass stems near the base of the plants in July and hatch in about three weeks. Young caterpillars go into hibernation at the end of August and resume feeding in the following March. At first they feed only at night but after the final moult, will also feed by day. They become fully grown in May and pupate in loose cocoons on the ground at the base of the foodplant. Butterflies emerge in about three weeks.

**EREBIA AETHIOPS** Esper *Scotch Argus* **Pl. 31**

**Distribution.** Widely distributed in central and south-eastern Europe. In the British Isles, confined to parts of northern England and to Scotland.

**Description.** Length up to 22 mm; body sparsely covered with short, stout bristles; ochreous, with two dark brown lines on the back and a whitish band along each side below the level of the spiracles; head rounded, reddish-brown.

**Habitat.** Damp grassland, open woodland and woodland margins.

**Foodplants.** Purple moor-grass (*Molinia caerulea*), blue moor-grass (*Sesleria caerulea*) and probably other grasses.

**Biology.** One generation a year. Eggs are laid singly on stems and blades of grasses in July and August, hatching in about a fortnight. Caterpillars feed until October, when they go into hibernation, hidden low down amongst the foodplants. Feeding is resumed in the following March and caterpillars are fully grown towards the end of June. They feed at night, hiding at the bases of grass stems by day. Pupae are formed in loose cocoons on the ground or low down among grass stems; butterflies emerge in about a fortnight.

**MELANARGIA GALATHEA** Linnaeus *Marbled White* **Pl. 32**

**Distribution.** Widespread throughout central and southern Europe. In the British Isles, mainly confined to southern England and parts of Wales but also occurs as far north as Yorkshire.

**Description.** Length up to 28 mm; body yellowish-green or pale brown with two dark lines along the back and a yellowish or whitish line along each side above the level of the spiracles; below the level of the spiracles is a less conspicuous pale line; tail with two pinkish-brown points; head reddish-brown.

**Habitat.** Downland, grassy slopes and other rough grassland.

**Foodplants.** Cat's-tail (*Phleum pratense*), cock's-foot (*Dactylis glomerata*), sheep's fescue (*Festuca ovina*) and other grasses.

**Biology.** One generation a year. Eggs are scattered at random over the foliage, often while the female is in flight. They are laid in July and August and hatch in about three weeks. Soon after hatching, the young caterpillars go into hibernation amongst dead grasses, becoming active again in early spring and feeding until the middle of June. They are active by day and if disturbed, roll into a ball and drop to the ground.

Pupation takes place on the ground beneath the foodplant and butterflies emerge in about three weeks.

**HIPPARCHIA SEMELE** Linnaeus *Grayling* **Pl. 32**

**Distribution.** Widespread throughout Europe, except for the extreme north. Widely distributed in the British Isles, especially in coastal localities.
**Description.** Length up to 30 mm; tapered towards the rear, body yellowish-white, with a brown line along the middle of the back and dark brown bands along each side above the level of the spiracles; an ochreous band extends along the spiracles; tail with two ochreous points; head brownish-white.
**Habitat.** Downland, heaths, sand dunes, cliffs and other dry grassland.
**Foodplants.** Various grasses.
**Biology.** One generation a year. Eggs are laid singly on grass blades or stems in July or August and hatch in 2–3 weeks. After the second moult, the caterpillars move to the base of the grasses where they overwinter, feeding during mild weather. They become active in the spring, feeding at night and hiding at the base of the foodplant by day. They are fully grown in June. Pupation takes place below the surface of the soil and butterflies emerge in July or August.

**HIPPARCHIA FAGI** Scopoli *Woodland Grayling* **Pl. 32**

**Distribution.** Widely distributed but local in central and southern Europe. Absent from much of the Iberian Peninsula and from the British Isles.
**Description.** Length up to 36 mm; tapering towards the tail, which bears two small points; body pale greyish-brown to yellowish-brown, with darker brown lines along the back and sides; a blackish-brown band extends along the middle of the back; head pale brown with four dark stripes.
**Habitat.** Open woodland and scrub.
**Foodplants.** Various soft grasses, such as *Holcus*, false-brome (*Brachypodium*) and fescues (*Festuca*).
**Biology.** One generation a year. The caterpillars overwinter and resume feeding in the following spring, becoming full-grown in May or June. Butterflies are on the wing in July and August.

**PYRONIA TITHONUS** Linnaeus *Gatekeeper* or *Hedge Brown* **Pl. 31**

**Distribution.** Widely distributed throughout central and southern Europe and also in southern parts of northern Europe. Widespread in southern England and in Wales, becoming less common and more coastal further north. Absent from Scotland. In Ireland, restricted to the south.
**Description.** Length up to 23 mm; tapered towards the rear; body ochreous-white, sometimes tinged with green, finely patterned with ochreous-brown markings; a dark brown line extends along the middle of the back and a dark-edged, white band extends along each side below the level of the spiracles; tail with two ochreous points; head pale brown.
**Habitat.** Hedgerows, woodland clearings and woodland margins.
**Foodplants.** Various grasses.
**Biology.** One generation a year. Eggs are laid singly on grass blades or stems in July and August, hatching in about three weeks. The caterpillars feed until October, when they go into hibernation, hiding low down amongst the grasses. They become active again in spring and are fully grown in June. Feeding takes place at night, the caterpillars resting at the base of the foodplant by day. Pupae are attached to grass stems and produce butterflies in about three weeks.

**MANIOLA JURTINA** Linnaeus *Meadow Brown* **Pl. 31**

**Distribution.** Widespread throughout Europe, except for the extreme north. Widely distributed and common in the British Isles.

**Description.** Length up to 25 mm; tapered towards the rear; body yellowish-green above, darker green below, covered with fairly long, white hairs; a yellowish-white line extends along each side below the level of the spiracles; tail with two whitish points; head rounded, bluish-green.

**Habitat.** Meadows, downland, heaths, open woodland and other grassland.

**Foodplants.** Various grasses, especially fine grasses such as meadow-grass (*Poa*) and bent-grass (*Agrostis*).

**Biology.** One generation a year. Eggs are laid singly on grass blades from July to September and hatch in about three weeks. The caterpillars feed throughout the winter in mild weather, hiding low down amongst the grasses when cold. They are mainly active at night, hiding at the base of the foodplant by day. Pupae are attached to grass stems in May and produce butterflies within a month.

**COENONYMPHA PAMPHILUS** Linnaeus *Small Heath* **Pl. 31**

**Distribution.** Widespread throughout Europe, except for the extreme north. Widely distributed and often common in the British Isles.

**Description.** Length up to 18 mm; body green, finely speckled with white, with a dark green line along the middle of the back, on either side of which is a dark-edged whitish line; a greenish-white line extends along either side below the level of the spiracles; tail with two pink-tipped, whitish points; head rounded, green.

**Habitat.** Downland, heaths, moorland, hedgerows and other grassy places.

**Foodplants.** Various grasses.

**Biology.** Two generations a year. Eggs are laid singly on grass blades near the ground in summer and again in autumn. Caterpillars of the first brood become fully grown in about five weeks but those of the second brood overwinter before completing their development in the following spring. They feed mainly at night. The pupae are suspended from grass stems and produce butterflies within a month.

**COENONYMPHA TULLIA** Müller *Large Heath* **Pl. 30**

**Distribution.** Widely distributed in central and northern Europe. Widespread but local in Scotland and Ireland and also occurs in parts of northern England and central Wales.

**Description.** Length up to 25 mm; body green with a yellow or white-edged, dark green line along the middle of the back, with two striking white bands along each side; tail with two pink-tipped, white points; head rounded, green.

**Habitat.** Boggy moorland and marshes.

**Foodplants.** White beak-sedge (*Rhynchospora alba*), sedge (*Carex*) and probably cotton-grass (*Eriophorum angustifolium*) and various grasses.

**Biology.** One generation a year. Eggs are laid singly on the foodplant in July and hatch in about a fortnight. Caterpillars go into hibernation in September, after their second moult, becoming active again in the following March. They feed mainly at night and become fully grown in May. Pupae are attached to stems of the foodplant close to the ground and produce butterflies in about three weeks.

**APHANTOPUS HYPERANTUS** Linnaeus *Ringlet* **Pl. 31**

**Distribution.** Widely distributed in Europe but absent from Italy and parts of

southern Spain. Widespread in the British Isles, except for Scotland and parts of central and northern England.
**Description.** Length up to 21 mm; rather stout, tapered towards the rear; body ochreous, covered with short, dark bristles, with a dark band along the middle of the back; a white band extends along each side below the level of the spiracles and below this is an irregular line of blackish-brown; head reddish-brown.
**Habitat.** Woodland clearings and rides, hedgerows and other damp, grassy places.
**Foodplants.** Various grasses.
**Biology.** One generation a year. Eggs are scattered amongst grasses in July and August, hatching in 2–3 weeks. The caterpillars overwinter, feeding in mild weather, and become fully grown in the following June. They are active at night, hiding at the base of the foodplant by day. Pupae are formed in open cocoons on the ground beneath the foodplant and produce butterflies in about a fortnight.

# LASIOCAMPIDAE

The eggars and lackeys belong to this family of moths. The caterpillars are medium-sized to large and are densely hairy on the body and head. Those of the Lappet (*Gastropacha quercifolia*) and its relatives have hair-covered, fleshy protuberances low down along the sides. They feed on a wide range of trees, shrubs and low-growing plants. The egg-shaped cocoons produced by some species give rise to the name 'eggar'.

**POECILOCAMPA POPULI** Linnaeus *December Moth* **Pl. 3**
**Distribution.** Widespread in central and northern Europe. Widely distributed throughout the British Isles.
**Description.** Length up to 50 mm; covered with short, fine grey hairs; body pale grey, densely marked with fine spots of dark grey or black; sometimes suffused with ochre on the back; plates on segments 1 and 13 strongly marked with reddish-brown; head pale grey with black spotting.
**Habitat.** Woodland and hedgerows.
**Foodplants.** Oak (*Quercus*), birch (*Betula*), poplar (*Populus*), hawthorn (*Crataegus monogyna*) and other deciduous trees and shrubs.
**Biology.** One generation a year. Eggs are laid singly or in small groups on the bark in late autumn or winter but do not hatch until the following spring. The caterpillars feed from April to June. They are very well camouflaged when at rest on branches and tree trunks, stretched out straight and clinging very closely to the surface. Pupation takes place in June in dark greyish cocoons under leaf litter or in the soil. Moths emerge in late autumn or winter.

**TRICHIURA CRATAEGI** Linnaeus *Pale Eggar* **Pl. 17**
**Distribution.** Widespread in Europe. Widely distributed throughout Britain but local in Ireland.
**Description.** Length up to 40 mm; body black, covered with short, fine, reddish

hairs on the back and yellowish-white hairs on the sides, with tufts of longer black hairs; variably patterned with red and white or yellow on the back and sides but always with a double row of red warts on the back; head shining black.
**Habitat.** Open woodland, hedgerows and heaths.
**Foodplants.** Blackthorn (*Prunus spinosa*), hawthorn (*Crataegus monogyna*), birch (*Betula*), sallow (*Salix*), oak (*Quercus*), hazel (*Corylus avellana*), bilberry (*Vaccinium myrtillus*), bramble (*Rubus fruticosus*) and heather (*Calluna* and *Erica*).
**Biology.** One generation a year. Eggs are laid in rows of about ten on twigs of the foodplant in September but do not hatch until the following spring. The caterpillars feed from April to June. Pupation takes place in cocoons spun on the ground and moths emerge in August.

**ERIOGASTER LANESTRIS** Linnaeus *Small Eggar* **Pl. 17**
**Distribution.** Widely distributed in central and northern Europe. In the British Isles, apparently now confined to a few scattered localities in England and Ireland.
**Description.** Length up to 45 mm; body black, covered with long, pale yellowish hairs and with two rows of patches of short, reddish-brown hairs on the back, framed by yellowish-white lines; head grey with black markings.
**Habitat.** Hedgerows and scrubland.
**Foodplants.** Blackthorn (*Prunus spinosa*), hawthorn (*Crataegus monogyna*), birch (*Betula*), sallow (*Salix*) and, in continental Europe, also on other deciduous trees and shrubs.
**Biology.** One generation a year. Eggs are laid in small groups on twigs of the foodplant in February and March. The caterpillars may be found from April to early July, living in a communal silken web which they leave at night to feed on the foliage. Pupation takes place in July in pale brown cocoons on the ground but moths do not emerge until the following February or March and may remain in the pupa state for several winters.

**MALACOSOMA NEUSTRIA** Linnaeus *Lackey* **Pl. 16**
**Distribution.** Widespread throughout Europe. Widely distributed in the southern half of England and in Wales and Ireland but absent from Scotland.
**Description.** Length up to 45 mm; body bright greyish-blue, covered with fine, reddish-brown hairs; a white line extends down the middle of the back, flanked by orange-red and black lines; a black-edged, orange-red line extends below the spiracles on each side; head bluish-grey with two large, black spots.
**Habitat.** Hedgerows, open woodland, gardens and orchards.
**Foodplants.** Hawthorn (*Crataegus monogyna*), blackthorn (*Prunus spinosa*), apple (*Malus*), sallow (*Salix*) and many other deciduous trees and shrubs.
**Biology.** One generation a year. Eggs are laid in August in a band encircling a twig. Caterpillars hatch in the following spring and feed from April to June. They live in a communal nest of silk spun over the foliage and may be seen basking on the outside on sunny days. Pupation takes place in July in silken cocoons spun between leaves or in leaf litter on the ground and moths emerge in a few weeks.

**LASIOCAMPA TRIFOLII** Denis & Schiffermüller *Grass Eggar* **Pl. 21**
**Distribution.** Widespread in Europe. In the British Isles, mainly confined to coastal regions of England but sometimes occurs inland.
**Description.** Length up to 60 mm; body black, covered with reddish-brown hairs on the back and greyish-white hairs on the sides; three lines of small, bluish-white

spots extend along the back; plates on segments 1 and 13 orange, marked with black; head black, marked with reddish-brown.
**Habitat.** Coastal sandhills, heathland and waste ground.
**Foodplants.** Broom (*Cytisus scoparius*), creeping sallow (*Salix repens*), marram grass (*Ammophila arenaria*) and other grasses, bramble (*Rubus fruticosus*), lucerne (*Medicago sativa*), birdsfoot (*Ornithopus perpusillus*) and various related plants.
**Biology.** One generation a year. Eggs are laid at random amongst the foliage in August but do not hatch until the following spring. The caterpillars feed from March to June and, when fully grown, pupate in brown, oval cocoons spun low down amongst the foodplants. Moths emerge in August.

**LASIOCAMPA QUERCUS** Linnaeus *Oak Eggar* **Pl. 15**
**Distribution.** Widespread throughout Europe. Widely distributed in the British Isles, represented by two subspecies with a different biology.
**Description.** Length up to 65 mm; body dark brown to black, covered with tufts of brownish hairs; a line of whitish markings extends along each side above the level of the spiracles and sometimes a line of reddish markings is present below the spiracles; head dark brown.
**Habitat.** Woodland, hedgerows, downland, heaths and moorland.
**Foodplants.** The southern subspecies *L.q. quercus* Linnaeus feeds on a wide range of trees and shrubs, including bramble (*Rubus fruticosus*), oak (*Quercus*), sallow (*Salix*) and hawthorn (*Crataegus monogyna*); the northern and western subspecies *L.q. callunae* Palmer feeds on heather (*Calluna vulgaris*) and bilberry (*Vaccinium myrtillus*).
**Biology.** One generation a year in the south, the northern subspecies taking two years to complete one generation. Eggs are dropped at random by the female while in flight. In southern England the caterpillars hatch in August and go into hibernation while quite small, completing their growth in the following spring, pupating in July and producing moths in August. In the north and west, caterpillars overwinter while small but do not complete their growth until the end of the following summer and pass a second winter in the pupa state, producing moths in the following May or June. Pupation takes place in large, oval cocoons spun on the ground or amongst twigs of the foodplant.

**MACROTHYLACIA RUBI** Linnaeus *Fox Moth* **Pl. 24**
**Distribution.** Widespread in Europe. Widely distributed throughout the British Isles.
**Description.** Length up to 65 mm; body velvety black, clothed with dense, reddish-brown hairs on the back and greyish hairs on the sides; head black with brownish hairs. The hairs can cause an irritating rash. Young caterpillars are blackish-brown with pale yellow bands across the back between the segments.
**Habitat.** Heaths, commons, moorland, downland and sandhills.
**Foodplants.** Heather (*Calluna vulgaris*), heath (*Erica*), bramble (*Rubus fruticosus*), bilberry (*Vaccinium myrtillus*) and other low-growing plants, including creeping sallow (*Salix repens*).
**Biology.** One generation a year. Eggs are laid in batches around stems of the foodplant in June and caterpillars hatch by the end of the month. They become fully grown by the autumn, when they go into hibernation. In the following spring, they become active again and may be found sunning themselves but do not feed. Pupation takes place in March or April in brown cocoons of silk mixed with body hairs, spun low down amongst the foodplant. Moths emerge in May.

**DENDROLIMUS PINI** Linnaeus *Pine-tree Lappet* **Pl. 1**

**Distribution.** Widely distributed throughout continental Europe, with the exception of Belgium. Absent from the British Isles.

**Description.** Length up to 75 mm; covered with fine, short, greyish hairs; body brown or greyish-brown with a fine pattern of yellowish-brown, marked with black on the back; two bands of dense, white, scale-like hairs extend along the back, joining together on the first three segments; segments 2 and 3 with bluish-black, transverse bands on the back; head brown with darker patterning.

**Habitat.** Forests.

**Foodplants.** Pine (*Pinus*), sitka spruce (*Picea sitchensis*), silver fir (*Abies alba*) and Douglas fir (*Pseudotsuga menziesii*).

**Biology.** One generation a year. Eggs are laid singly or in small groups on the needles in July or August and hatch in 2–3 weeks. The caterpillars overwinter on the ground, returning to the foodplants in spring to complete their feeding. In northern Europe, caterpillars may overwinter for a second year. They are fully grown by the end of June and pupate in large, brownish-yellow cocoons spun on twigs or amongst needles. Moths emerge in about a month.

**PHILUDORIA POTATORIA** Linnaeus *Drinker* **Pl. 32**

**Distribution.** Widely distributed throughout Europe. Widespread in the British Isles but most common in England and Wales.

**Description.** Length up to 75 mm; body bluish-grey on the back, black on the sides, covered with pale reddish-brown hairs; a double row of small tufts of black hairs extends along the back; segments 2 and 11 each with a large tuft of black hairs in the middle of the back; a broad band of orange-red markings extends along each side above the spiracles, and below the spiracles a series of tufts of white hairs is interspersed with reddish markings; head black, marked with reddish-brown.

**Habitat.** Open woodland, fens and wet moorland.

**Foodplants.** Cock's-foot (*Dactylis glomerata*), couch-grass (*Agropyron repens*) and various other grasses and reeds.

**Biology.** One generation a year. Eggs are laid in small clusters on grass stems in August and caterpillars hatch in the same month. They feed for a time before going into hibernation and complete their growth in the following spring. The caterpillars are reported to drink from drops of dew, thus giving rise to the name 'drinker'. Pupation takes place in June in boat-shaped, yellowish-white cocoons attached to the foodplant; moths emerge in July.

**PHYLLODESMA ILICIFOLIA** Linnaeus *Small Lappet* **Pl. 25**

**Distribution.** Occurs locally in central and northern Europe. Very local in various localities in England but not recorded in recent years.

**Description.** Length up to 60 mm; body reddish-brown to yellowish, covered with pale reddish-brown hairs; a series of transverse, bluish-grey and black bands extends across the back between the segments, these bands sometimes broken to form a double row of squarish markings; a row of bluish-grey markings extends along the spiracles on each side; head dark grey.

**Habitat.** Moorland and open woodland.

**Foodplants.** Bilberry (*Vaccinium myrtillus*); also on sallow (*Salix*) and other trees in continental Europe.

**Biology.** One generation a year. Eggs are laid in May and caterpillars feed from June to mid-August. Pupation takes place at the end of August in silken cocoons spun among foliage of the foodplant. Moths emerge the following April or May.

**GASTROPACHA QUERCIFOLIA** Linnaeus *Lappet* **Pl. 17**
**Distribution.** Widespread in Europe. In the British Isles, confined to southern Britain, where it is locally common.
**Description.** Length up to 80 mm; body grey, closely dotted with black and covered with fine blackish hair; segments 2 and 3 with a transverse, blue and black band on the back; segment 11 with a small, black hump; low down on the sides is a series of fleshy 'lappets', covered by long blackish hairs; head black with pale grey markings.
**Habitat.** Woodland, hedgerows and scrubland; sometimes in orchards.
**Foodplants.** Blackthorn (*Prunus spinosa*), hawthorn (*Crataegus monogyna*), sallow (*Salix*), apple (*Malus*) and other fruit trees.
**Biology.** One generation a year. Eggs are laid in small groups on twigs or leaves in July or early August. Caterpillars hatch in about a fortnight and feed for a few weeks before going into hibernation, low down on stems of the foodplant. Feeding is resumed in the spring and caterpillars are full-grown in May. Pupation takes place in June in long, greyish-brown cocoons of silk mixed with body hairs, spun low down on the foodplant. Moths emerge in late June or July.

# SATURNIIDAE

The emperor moths belong to this family. The caterpillars are large, with body hairs often arising from raised warts or humps. The rear claspers are very strongly developed and have a very powerful grasp. They feed on the foliage of various trees, shrubs and low-growing plants.

**AGLIA TAU** Linnaeus *Tau Emperor* **Pl. 7**
**Distribution.** Widespread in Europe, except for northern regions and most of the southern Mediterranean region. Absent from the British Isles.
**Description.** Length up to 50 mm; plump, with segments strongly indented, tapered towards the head; body yellowish-green above the spiracles, bluish-green below, with a series of white or pale yellow diagonal stripes; a white line extends along each side below the level of the spiracles; a black-centred, reddish marking is present on the side of segment 4; head green. Young caterpillars have striking, antler-like projections on the back.
**Habitat.** Woodland.
**Foodplants.** Primarily beech (*Fagus sylvatica*) but also on other trees, such as oak (*Quercus*), birch (*Betula*) and lime (*Tilia*).
**Biology.** One generation a year. Caterpillars feed from May to August and, when fully grown, pupate in large, rough cocoons constructed of leaves and silk. Moths emerge in the following spring or later.

**PAVONIA PAVONIA** Linnaeus *Emperor Moth* **Pl. 24**
**Distribution.** Widespread throughout Europe. Widely distributed and locally common in the British Isles.

**Description.** Length up to 60 mm; body dark green or yellowish-green with transverse bands of black, bearing raised warts which are yellow or pinkish-purple, and carry short black bristles; spiracles bright orange, rimmed with black; head small, green. The extent of the black banding is very variable, sometimes reduced to black spots and sometimes expanded so that the bands join together. Young caterpillars are black with a yellowish line along the sides.
**Habitat.** Heaths, moorland, mountainsides, open woodland and commonland.
**Foodplants.** Heather (*Erica* and *Calluna*), bramble (*Rubus fruticosus*), bilberry (*Vaccinium myrtillus*), blackthorn (*Prunus spinosa*), hawthorn (*Crataegus monogyna*), sallow (*Salix*), birch (*Betula*) and probably other trees and shrubs; also on purple loosestrife (*Lythrum salicaria*) and meadowsweet (*Filipendula ulmaria*).
**Biology.** One generation a year. Eggs are laid in batches around the stems and twigs of the foodplants in May. The caterpillars feed from May to August and are surprisingly well camouflaged, especially when on heather. Pupation takes place in early autumn within large, flask-shaped, fibrous cocoons, spun amongst the foodplant. Moths emerge in the following spring.

**SATURNIA PYRI** Denis & Schiffermüller *Great Peacock* **Pl. 33**
*Distribution.* Widespread in southern Europe, also occuring in southern central Europe. Absent from the British Isles.
**Description.** Length up to 120 mm; body bright yellowish-green with tufts of black bristles arising from raised, blue-tipped warts on the back and sides; a whitish line extends along each side below the level of the spiracles; legs brown; plate on segment 13 brown; head green with a black V-shaped marking. Young caterpillars are black with red warts.
**Habitat.** Open woodland, scrub and orchards.
**Foodplants.** Apple (*Malus*), pear (*Pyrus*), sallow (*Salix*), poplar (*Populus*) and various other trees.
**Biology.** One generation a year. Eggs are laid in May or June and hatch in about a fortnight. Caterpillars feed until August and pupate in large, brown, pear-shaped cocoons, often spun in the forks of branches. Moths emerge in April or May of the following year.

**GRAELLSIA ISABELLAE** Graëlls *Spanish Moon Moth* **Pl. 1**
**Distribution.** Occurs locally in mountain regions of central Spain, the Pyrenees and the southern Alps of France.
**Description.** Length up to 80 mm; body yellowish-green dotted with white, sparsely covered with long, fine, pale brown hairs; a broad, reddish-brown, white-margined band extends along the back; segments 4–11 each with a transverse band of reddish-brown, broken by a broad white streak above and below the spiracle; plate on segment 1 black; head brown, marked with black.
**Habitat.** Mature pine forests.
**Foodplants.** Pine (*Pinus laricio* and *P. sylvestris*).
**Biology.** One generation a year. Eggs are laid in the spring and hatch in about a fortnight. The caterpillars feed for about two months. They pupate in flimsy silken cocoons, incorporating pine needles, on the ground. Moths emerge in March of the following year. This species is protected by law in most parts of its range.

# BRAHMAEIDAE

The one European representative, Hartig's Brahmaea (*Acanthobrahmaea europaea*) has a large caterpillar bearing long filaments on its back, which are lost after the final moult. It is believed to feed on *Fraxinus*.

**ACANTHOBRAHMAEA EUROPAEA** Hartig *Hartig's Brahmaea* **Pl. 8**
**Distribution.** Occurs in one locality in Lucania, Italy, where it is protected by law.
**Description.** Length up to 80 mm; body shining black, lined and spotted with white on the back and sides above the level of the spiracles, except on segments 1–3 which are strongly marked with yellow; below the spiracles are a series of diagonal yellow markings; segments 2 and 3 each with a pair of long black, sturdy filaments; segment 11 with a similar but shorter single filament on the back; in the final instar, these filaments are lost; head shining black.
**Habitat.** Woodland on the shores of a volcanic lake at 250–350 m altitude.
**Foodplants.** Ash (*Fraxinus*); in captivity will feed on privet foliage (*Ligustrum*).
**Biology.** One generation a year. Eggs hatch in about two weeks in captivity and caterpillars become fully grown in 3–5 weeks. Moths are on the wing at the end of March and the beginning of April.

# ENDROMIDAE

The one European representative of this family, the Kentish Glory (*Endromis versicolora*) is recognisable by an almost horn-like hump on the rear of the caterpillar's body and by its characteristic resting position with the front of the body raised. It feeds on birch (*Betula*) and other trees.

**ENDROMIS VERSICOLORA** Linnaeus *Kentish Glory* **Pl. 4**
**Distribution.** Widely distributed but local in Europe. In the British Isles, now confined to parts of northern Scotland; formerly also in south-eastern England.
**Description.** Length up to 63 mm; body very plump, tapering strongly towards the head; segment 11 with a horn-like hump on the back; body green, whitish on the back and densely spotted with black on the sides; a dark green line extends along the middle of the back, flanked by a series of oblique white bands; a yellowish-white band extends along the sides of the first three body segments; head green with yellowish-white bands.
**Habitat.** Open woodland and wooded moorland.

**Foodplants.** Silver birch (*Betula pendula*) and sometimes alder (*Alnus glutinosa*); possibly also on other deciduous trees.
**Biology.** One generation a year. In April eggs are laid in rows, usually two deep, on twigs, and caterpillars feed from May to July. They are gregarious when young, clustering together on twigs or leaves with the front parts of their bodies raised in a characteristic posture. Pupation takes place in large brown cocoons spun on the ground or just below the surface of the soil. Moths do not emerge until the following spring.

# DREPANIDAE

Moths of this family are known as hook-tips. The smallish caterpillars taper strongly towards the tail and lack properly-developed rear claspers. They rest in a characteristic manner with the front and rear ends of the body raised. They feed on the foliage of trees and shrubs.

**FALCARIA LACERTINARIA** Linnaeus *Scalloped Hook-tip* **Pl. 4**
**Distribution.** Widespread in Europe. Widely distributed throughout the British Isles.
**Description.** Length up to 20 mm; fairly slender, tapered towards the spiked tail; body brown, sometimes with a purplish suffusion; a double row of dark brown, triangular markings is sometimes present on the back; segments 2 and 3 each with a pair of pointed warts on the back; head purplish-brown with whitish markings, slightly notched.
**Habitat.** Woodland and heaths.
**Foodplant.** Silver birch (*Betula pendula*).
**Biology.** Two generations a year. Eggs are laid in small groups on the undersides of leaves in May and August and caterpillars feed from June to July and August to September. It is said that the caterpillars resemble miniature lizards (*Lacerta*), from which the name *lacertinaria* derives. Pupation takes place within cocoons spun in folded leaves in July and October. Moths emerge in August and May respectively, but in Scotland there is only one generation of moths, flying in late May and June.

**DREPANA BINARIA** Hufnagel *Oak Hook-tip* **Pl. 6**
**Distribution.** Widespread in central and southern Europe. Widely distributed in Wales and England, becoming less common towards the north; absent from Scotland and Ireland.
**Description.** Length up to 24 mm; fairly slender, tapering towards the spiked tail; body pale brown with a fine network of dark brown or blackish lines; segments 5–10 with a yellowish, saddle-shaped marking on the back; segment 3 with a large, double-pointed wart on the back; head pale brown with darker freckling, notched.
**Habitat.** Woodland.

**Foodplants.** Oak (*Quercus*); in continental Europe, also on other deciduous trees such as beech (*Fagus*) and alder (*Alnus*).
**Biology.** Two generations a year. Eggs are laid on the edges of leaves in June and August and hatch in about ten days. The caterpillars feed from June to July and in September. Pupation takes place in July and October in cocoons spun within folded leaves, and moths emerge in August and May respectively.

**DREPANA CULTRARIA** Fabricius *Barred Hook-tip* **Pl. 7**
**Distribution.** Occurs in central and parts of southern Europe. In the British Isles, confined to Wales and the southern half of England.
**Description.** Length up to 20 mm; fairly slender, tapering towards the spiked tail; body reddish-brown with a brownish-white, saddle-shaped marking on the back of segments 5–10; segment 3 with a double-pointed wart on the back; underside yellowish-white; head pale reddish-brown with darker markings, notched.
**Habitat.** Woodland.
**Foodplant.** Beech (*Fagus sylvatica*).
**Biology.** Two generations a year. Eggs are laid in May and August and caterpillars feed from June to July and in September. Pupation takes place in July and October in cocoons spun within folded leaves, and moths emerge in August and May respectively.

**DREPANA FALCATARIA** Linnaeus *Pebble Hook-tip* **Pl. 4**
**Distribution.** Widespread in Europe. Widely distributed throughout the British Isles but local and rather scarce in Ireland.
**Description.** Length up to 25 mm; fairly plump, tapering quite strongly to the spiked tail; body bright green to bluish-green, with a broad band of yellowish-brown or purplish-brown on the back, fading towards the head; segments 2, 3 and 5 each with a pair of raised warts on the back; head brown with pale markings, notched.
**Habitat.** Woodland and heaths.
**Foodplants.** Silver birch (*Betula pendula*) and alder (*Alnus glutinosa*).
**Biology.** Two generations a year, only one in Scotland. Eggs are laid in short rows on the undersides of leaves in May and August and caterpillars feed from June to July and in September. When feeding openly on the foliage, they are very well camouflaged, resembling small, shrivelled leaves. Pupation takes place in July and September in cocoons spun within folded leaves and moths emerge in August and May respectively.

**SABRA HARPAGULA** Esper *Scarce Hook-tip* **Pl. 8**
**Distribution.** Occurs in parts of central and northern Europe. In the British Isles, occurs very locally in western England.
**Description.** Length up to 25 mm; fairly slender, tapering towards the pointed tail; body yellow on the back and parts of the sides except for the first three segments which are suffused with purplish-brown; rest of body reddish-brown or purplish-brown; segment 3 has two pointed warts on the back; head pinkish with dark brown markings, notched.
**Habitat.** Woodland.
**Foodplants.** Small-leaved lime (*Tilia cordata*); in continental Europe, also on other deciduous trees.
**Biology.** One generation a year. Eggs are laid on the edges of leaves in June and

hatch in about ten days. The caterpillars feed until September and pupate in the autumn in brown silken cocoons spun within folded leaves. Moths emerge in the following June.

**CILIX GLAUCATA** Scopoli *Chinese Character* **Pl. 17**

**Distribution.** Widespread in central and southern Europe. Widely distributed in the British Isles but less common in the north and absent from the greater part of Scotland.

**Description.** Length up to 12 mm; plump in the middle, tapering abruptly towards the head and gradually towards the black, spiked tail; body reddish-brown, finely marked with a network of dark brown or blackish lines; a dark brown line runs along the middle of the back, extending through a broad band of pale, whitish-brown towards the rear; body segments 2 and 3 swollen, each with a pair of small pointed warts on the back; head pale brown with blackish spotting.

**Habitat.** Hedgerows and woodland margins.

**Foodplants.** Hawthorn (*Crataegus monogyna*), blackthorn (*Prunus spinosa*), plum (*P. domestica*) and sometimes apple (*Malus*), pear (*Pyrus*), rowan (*Sorbus aucuparia*) and bramble (*Rubus fruticosus*).

**Biology.** Two generations a year. Eggs are laid in May and August and caterpillars feed from June to July and September to October. When young, they eat the upper surfaces of leaves only, making distinctive blotches. Later they feed in the usual way. Pupation takes place in August and October in tough brown cocoons spun among leaves or under loose bark. Moths emerge in August and May respectively.

# THYATIRIDAE

This family includes the lutestrings. The smooth caterpillars are rather similar to those of the family Noctuidae but are often tapered towards the rear and have characteristic markings. They mainly feed at night on the foliage of trees and shrubs.

**THYATIRA BATIS** Linnaeus *Peach Blossom* **Pl. 15**

**Distribution.** Widespread throughout Europe, except for the extreme north. Widely distributed in the British Isles.

**Description.** Length up to 35 mm; body expanded behind head, segment 2 bearing a prominent, forward-directed hump; segments strongly indented when viewed from above; colour pale reddish-brown or purplish-brown, with a series of pale, triangular-shaped markings on the back; segments 5–9 and 11 each with a small hump on the back; head pale brown with darker markings, slightly notched.

**Habitat.** Woodland.

**Foodplant.** Bramble (*Rubus fruticosus*).

**Biology.** One generation a year. Eggs are laid in small batches on the edges of bramble leaves in June or July and the caterpillars feed from July to September. Pupation takes place in the autumn in cocoons spun among leaves, but moths do not emerge until the following May or June.

**HABROSYNE PYRITOIDES** Hufnagel *Buff Arches* **Pl. 15**

**Distribution.** Widespread throughout Europe, except the extreme north. Widely distributed in England, Wales and Ireland.

**Description.** Length up to 40 mm; body chestnut-brown, patterned with a fine network of blackish-brown lines; rings between segments blackish; a black line extends along the middle of the back; segment 4 with a large white spot above the spiracle on each side; head reddish-brown.

**Habitat.** Open woodland and commonland.

**Foodplant.** Bramble (*Rubus fruticosus*).

**Biology.** One generation a year. Eggs are laid in small groups on bramble leaves in July and caterpillars feed from August to October. They are active at night, hiding under leaf litter on the ground by day. Pupation takes place in the autumn in subterranean cocoons, but moths do not emerge until the following June or July.

**TETHEA OCULARIS** Linnaeus *Figure of Eighty* **Pl. 3**

**Distribution.** Widespread in Europe. In the British Isles, confined to England, where it is widely distributed in the south and midlands but becomes less common further north.

**Description.** Length up to 37 mm; body pale yellow, suffused with greenish-grey; a line of clear yellow extends along the spiracles on each side; plate on segment 1 pale grey, shining; segments 1, 2, 3 and 11 with black spots on the sides; head yellowish-brown, marked with black at the front.

**Habitat.** Woodland, parks and wooded countryside.

**Foodplants.** Poplar and aspen (*Populus*).

**Biology.** One generation a year. Eggs are laid in July and hatch in the same month. Caterpillars feed until the end of August or September, hiding by day between spun leaves or in a curled-up dead leaf. Pupation takes place in September in cocoons spun between leaves which fall to the ground. Moths emerge the following May or June.

**TETHEA OR** Denis & Schiffermüller *Poplar Lutestring* **Pl. 3**

**Distribution.** Widespread throughout Europe. Widely distributed in the British Isles, where it occurs as three distinct races.

**Description.** Length up to 20 mm; body pale bluish-green or yellowish with a whitish line along the spiracles on each side; above the spiracles, there is sometimes a line of black dots with pale centres; head pale brownish-yellow marked with black at the front.

**Habitat.** Woodland and wooded countryside.

**Foodplants.** Aspen (*Populus tremula*) and black poplar (*P. nigra*); apparently also on sallow (*Salix*) in continental Europe.

**Biology.** One generation a year. Eggs are laid in July and the caterpillars feed until the autumn. They hide by day between spun leaves, leaving their shelters to feed at night. Pupation takes place in the autumn in brown cocoons spun between leaves but moths do not emerge until the following June or July.

**OCHROPACHA DUPLARIS** Linnaeus *Common Lutestring* **Pl. 5**

**Distribution.** Widespread in central and northern Europe. Widely distributed throughout the British Isles.

**Description.** Length up to 22 mm; body greenish or greyish-white, with a broad band of dark green or greyish-green on the back; segment 1 with a shining black plate; a series of dark green or blackish spots extends along each side below the level of the spiracles; head yellowish-brown.

**Habitat.** Woodland.

**Foodplants.** Silver birch (*Betula pendula*), alder (*Alnus glutinosa*), oak (*Quercus*), and probably hazel (*Corylus avellana*) and poplar (*Populus*) in continental Europe.

**Biology.** One generation a year. Eggs are laid in July and caterpillars may be found from August to early October. They hide by day within shelters of spun leaves, coming out at night to feed. Pupation takes place in October within slight silken cocoons spun between leaves of the foodplant but moths do not emerge until June or July of the following year.

**ACHLYA FLAVICORNIS** Linnaeus *Yellow Horned* **Pl. 4**

**Distribution.** Widely distributed in Europe. Widespread in the British Isles and often common.

**Description.** Length up to 33 mm; body pale greyish-green to white, sometimes strongly shaded on the back with dark greyish-green; a series of black and white dots extends over the back and sides; segment 1 with a blackish plate, divided by a central whitish line; head yellowish-brown to reddish-brown, sometimes shaded with black towards the front.

**Habitat.** Woodland, heaths and moorland.

**Foodplant.** Silver birch (*Betula pendula*).

**Biology.** One generation a year. Eggs are laid in small groups on twigs, close to buds, in March or April. The caterpillars feed from late May to July, hiding by day in spun leaves. Pupation takes place in July in frail cocoons spun among leaves of the foodplant or on the ground. Moths do not emerge until the following spring and sometimes remain in the pupa state for a second winter.

**POLYPLOCA RIDENS** Fabricius *Frosted Green* **Pl. 6**

**Distribution.** Widespread in central and southern Europe. In the British Isles, it is confined to Wales and England, where it is quite common in the south but becomes scarce further north.

**Description.** Length up to 33 mm; body pale yellow, suffused to a varying extent with greenish-grey, often in the form of broken lines; spots on the back whitish, partly ringed with black; a clear yellow line extends along the spiracles on each side; head pale reddish-brown.

**Habitat.** Woodland.

**Foodplant.** Oak (*Quercus*).

**Biology.** One generation a year. Eggs are laid singly on twigs, close to the buds, in April or May and caterpillars feed from May to mid-July. They are active at night, hiding in spun leaves by day. Pupation takes place at the end of July in cocoons spun on the leaves, which eventually fall to the ground. Moths do not emerge until the following spring and may remain in the pupa state for two or more winters.

# GEOMETRIDAE

Caterpillars of this family are the well-known loopers or stick caterpillars. The name 'Geometra' is derived from the Latin for earth-measurer, and this is reflected in the American names span-worm and inch-worm. They are distinguished by having only two pairs of functional prolegs. They are mostly long and slender and many are superb twig mimics. They feed on the foliage of trees, shrubs and low-growing plants. Caterpillars of certain groups, particularly pug moths of the genus *Eupithecia*, feed on the flowers and seeds of various herbaceous plants.

**ARCHIEARIS NOTHA** Hübner *Light Orange Underwing* **Pl. 3**

**Distribution.** Occurs in many parts of Central Europe. In the British Isles mainly confined to parts of eastern and western England although also recorded from Moray in Scotland.

**Description.** Length up to 28 mm; usually green with black longitudinal stripes and a yellowish-white line along the spiracles; head and first segment of the thorax strongly spotted with black. A dingy olive-brown variety exists with pale pinkish-grey longitudinal stripes. Unlike most caterpillars of the family Geometridae, this species has four pairs of prolegs on the abdomen in addition to the anal claspers, although the front two pairs are weakly developed. It walks in the characteristic 'looper' manner.

**Habitat.** Open woods and places with scattered aspen trees.

**Foodplant.** Aspen (*Populus tremula*).

**Biology.** One generation a year. Eggs are laid in April and hatch in May. The caterpillar feeds on the leaves, spinning them together surface to surface to form a shelter. If disturbed it drops on a silken thread and remains suspended until the danger is past. When fully grown it burrows into bark or decaying wood to make a pupation chamber. Pupation takes place in July and moths usually emerge in the following April, although some have been known to remain in the pupa stage for 2–3 years.

**ALSOPHILA AESCULARIA** Denis & Schiffermüller *March Moth* **Pl. 16**

**Distribution.** Common throughout Europe. Occurs throughout the British Isles with the exception of the extreme north of Scotland.

**Description.** Length up to 26 mm; bright green with a dark green line along the back and yellowish-white lines on either side. May be distinguished from similar 'looper' caterpillars by the presence of an extra pair of rudimentary prolegs on segment 8.

**Habitat.** Hedgerows, woodland, gardens and orchards.

**Foodplants.** Apple (*Malus*), plum and cherry (*Prunus*), hawthorn (*Crataegus monogyna*), rose (*Rosa*) and many other deciduous trees and shrubs. Also on privet (*Ligustrum*).

**Biology.** One generation a year. Eggs are laid in April in large numbers forming a bracelet around a twig. They are covered with scales from the tip of the female's abdomen. Caterpillars feed, mainly at night, from April to June; when fully grown they burrow into the ground at the base of the foodplant to pupate within cocoons of silk and earth. Moths emerge in March of the following year; the females are wingless.

**PSEUDOTERPNA PRUINATA** Hufnagel *Grass Emerald* **Pl. 19**

**Distribution.** Widely distributed in central and south-eastern Europe. Widespread in the British Isles with the exception of northern Scotland.

**Description.** Length up to 26 mm; body green with a dark green line along the back flanked by a white line on either side; a broad, pinkish-white line below the spiracles; head strongly notched to form two conical points; first segment of the body with two red-tipped points similar to those on the head.

**Habitat.** Heaths, moors, commons and open woodland.

**Foodplants.** Gorse (*Ulex europaeus*), broom (*Cytisus scoparius*) and petty whin (*Genista anglica*). Will eat *Laburnum* in captivity.

**Biology.** One generation a year. Eggs are laid in July and hatch in about fifteen days. The young caterpillars go into hibernation soon after hatching, remaining on the foodplant through the winter. In May and June of the following year they resume feeding on the fresh foliage, and it is at this stage that they are usually found. They feed at night and rest by day on the foodplant, held stiffly at an angle to the stem so that they resemble small twigs. Pupation takes place at the end of June in thin silken cocoons spun among leaf litter on the ground. Moths emerge in the following month.

**GEOMETRA PAPILIONARIA** Linnaeus *Large Emerald* **Pl. 4**

**Distribution.** Widespread in central and northern Europe. Occurs throughout the British Isles except for northern Scotland.

**Description.** Length up to 29 mm; body rough-skinned, yellowish-green, with a series of large, reddish-brown warts along the back; head notched, green tinged with reddish-brown. Young larvae are brown but become green after hibernation.

**Habitat.** Woodland, heaths, moors and fenland.

**Foodplants.** Silver birch (*Betula pendula*), beech (*Fagus sylvatica*), alder (*Alnus glutinosa*), hazel (*Corylus avellana*) and broom (*Cytisus scoparius*).

**Biology.** One generation a year. Eggs are usually laid singly on the foodplant in July and hatch in 1–2 weeks. The caterpillar feeds until leaf-fall in the autumn when it goes into hibernation, attached to a small pad of silk spun near a bud. The following spring it feeds on the newly developed foliage and becomes fully grown in June. Pupation takes place within a flimsy silken web spun among dead leaves on the ground or in moss on the tree trunk. Moths emerge within a month.

**THETIDIA SMARAGDARIA** Fabricius *Essex Emerald* **Pl. 28**

**Distribution.** Widespread but local in central, southern and eastern Europe. In Britain, confined to restricted coastal areas of Essex where it is protected by law.

**Description.** Length up to 23 mm; body greyish with darker longitudinal lines; skin very rough, covered with leaf fragments; head notched, brown.

**Habitat.** In Britain confined to salt marshes but in continental Europe also on rough slopes and plains and in open woodland.

**Foodplants.** In Britain only sea wormwood (*Artemisia maritima*) but in continental Europe also other *Artemisia* species, yarrow (*Achillea millefolium*), groundsel (*Senecio*) and tansy (*Tanacetum vulgare*).

**Biology.** One generation a year in Britain, two generations in southern Europe.

Eggs are laid on stems and leaves, usually high on the plant, in July and hatch in about a fortnight. The young caterpillar immediately covers itself with fragments of the foodplant which it attaches to its body. It feeds at night and can withstand submergence in sea water at high tide. After hibernation it resumes feeding in the spring, and becomes fully grown by the end of May. Pupation takes place in an open meshed cocoon covered with leaf fragments and attached to a stem of the foodplant. Moths emerge in June.

**HEMITHEA AESTIVARIA** Hübner *Common Emerald* **Pl. 14**

**Distribution.** Widespread in Europe. Occurs in England, Wales and Ireland but most common in the south of the British Isles.

**Description.** Length up to 23 mm; long and thin; body surface rough, yellowish-green ornamented with reddish-brown, with V-shaped markings along the back; first segment of the thorax with a pair of conical projections similar to those of the deeply notched head. A brown form exists with whitish markings on the back.

**Habitat.** Hedgerows and woodland borders.

**Foodplants.** Before hibernation: mugwort (*Artemisia vulgaris*), docks (*Rumex*), cinquefoils (*Potentilla*) and other low-growing plants. After hibernation: oak (*Quercus*), birch (*Betula*), rose (*Rosa*), hawthorn (*Crataegus monogyna*), blackthorn (*Prunus spinosa*) and other deciduous trees and shrubs.

**Biology.** One generation a year. Eggs are laid in July and hatch in August. The caterpillar feeds at night, resting by day stretched out at an angle to the twig with its head and thoracic legs pressed close together. After hibernation it resumes feeding and becomes fully grown in May or June. Pupation takes place in a loose silken cocoon spun among the foliage. Moths emerge in June.

**HEMISTOLA CHRYSOPRASARIA** Esper *Small Emerald* **Pl. 12**

**Distribution.** Widespread in central and southern Europe but absent from the Iberian Peninsula. Occurs in southern and eastern England and rarely in Ireland.

**Description.** Length up to 25 mm; skin granular; body green with minute white spots; a rigid fold of skin extends along each side like a keel; first segment of the body with two fine brown points like those of the deeply divided head, but longer; head purplish-brown. Hibernating caterpillars are brown, becoming green as foliage develops in the spring.

**Habitat.** Chalk and limestone areas where the foodplant flourishes.

**Foodplant.** Traveller's joy (*Clematis vitalba*).

**Biology.** One generation a year. Eggs are laid in a pile of twelve or more on the stem in July and hatch in a few days. After feeding for a short time the young caterpillar goes into hibernation. It becomes active again in the following spring when new foliage develops and is fully grown by the end of June. It pupates between leaves spun together with silk. Moths emerge in July.

**JODIS LACTEARIA** Linnaeus *Little Emerald* **Pl. 4**

**Distribution.** Widespread in central and southern Europe. Occurs throughout England, Wales and Ireland and locally in southern Scotland.

**Description.** Length up to 21 mm; body long and very thin, bright green, paler between segments, with reddish spots along the back; first segment of the thorax with two conical points similar to those of the strongly notched head.

**Habitat.** Woodland margins and clearings and hedgerows.

**Foodplants.** Oak (*Quercus*), birch (*Betula*), alder (*Alnus glutinosa*), blackthorn

(*Prunus spinosa*), hawthorn (*Crataegus monogyna*) and bilberry (*Vaccinium myrtillus*).
**Biology.** One generation a year. Eggs are laid in July and hatch in August. The caterpillar feeds on the foliage from August to September and, when fully grown in October, spins a flimsy silken cocoon among the foliage in which it pupates. Moths emerge in the following June.

**CYCLOPHORA ANNULATA** Schulze *Mocha* **Pl. 8**
**Distribution.** Widespread in central and southern Europe. In the British Isles, confined to England and most common in the south-east.
**Description.** Length up to 23 mm; body dark velvety-green, with paler yellowish-green between segments; a yellow line extends along the back with a waved yellow line on either side; head brown with paler markings. A pale brown form also occurs.
**Habitat.** Woodland, particularly beech woods with maple; hedgerows and chalk hills.
**Foodplants.** Field maple (*Acer campestre*), sycamore (*Acer pseudoplatanus*); also recorded on birch (*Betula*) and hornbeam (*Carpinus betulus*) in continental Europe.
**Biology.** One or two generations a year. First generation eggs are laid in May and hatch in June. The caterpillars are full-grown in July when they pupate on the undersides of leaves or among moss. Where a second generation occurs, moths emerge in July and lay eggs in August. Caterpillars of the second generation are full-grown by the end of September and pupate in October. Moths emerge the following May.

**CYCLOPHORA ALBIPUNCTATA** Hufnagel *Birch Mocha* **Pl. 4**
**Distribution.** Widespread in Europe. Occurs locally throughout the British Isles.
**Description.** Length up to 23 mm; body reddish-brown to greyish-purple, with pale grey longitudinal lines, or bright green with yellowish lines; head brown.
**Habitat.** Open woodland and wooded heaths where birch bushes are common.
**Foodplants.** Silver birch (*Betula pendula*). Will also eat alder (*Alnus glutinosa*) and oak (*Quercus*) in captivity.
**Biology.** One or two generations a year. Eggs of the first generation are laid in May and hatch in June. When at rest, young caterpillars hang from the edges or undersides of leaves with their bodies twisted spirally. They become fully grown by the beginning of July and pupate under leaves, attached by silk. Where a second generation occurs, moths emerge in August and lay eggs which produce caterpillars that become fully grown by the end of September and pupate in October. Moths emerge in May of the following year.

**TIMANDRA GRISEATA** Petersen *Blood-vein* **Pl. 10**
**Distribution.** Occurs throughout Europe. Widespread in England and Wales, most common in southern England. Occurs locally in southern Scotland and rarely in Ireland.
**Description.** Length up to 23 mm; body reddish-brown to grey with dark chevron-shaped markings on the back; body swollen behind the head to produce a cobra-like appearance when at rest; head brown.
**Habitat.** Lush grassland, damp waste ground, hedgerows and ditches.
**Foodplants.** Dock (*Rumex*), sorrel (*R. acetosa*), knotgrass (*Polygonum aviculare*), chickweed (*Stellaria media*), common orache (*Atriplex patula*).
**Biology.** One or two generations a year. Eggs are laid in July and hatch in about ten days. Caterpillars sometimes feed up rapidly to produce moths in late summer but

more usually become fully grown by the following May. Pupation takes place in a slight silken cocoon on the ground. Moths emerge in June.

**SCOPULA NIGROPUNCTATA** Hufnagel *Sub-angled Wave* **Pl. 12**
**Distribution.** Widespread in central and southern Europe. In the British Isles, apparently confined to the south-east.
**Description.** Length up to 30 mm; body slender, tapering slightly towards head; skin transversely ribbed, greenish-grey with small black markings along the back; underside pale grey with a very pale central stripe; head grey, mottled with brown.
**Habitat.** Hedgerows and other places where the foodplants grow.
**Foodplants.** Usually traveller's joy (*Clematis vitalba*) but also marjoram (*Origanum vulgare*), woundwort (*Stachys*) and plantain (*Plantago*). In captivity will eat the withered leaves of knotgrass (*Polygonum aviculare*) and dandelion (*Taraxacum*).
**Biology.** One generation a year. Eggs are laid in July and hatch in about eleven days. Caterpillars feed from August until the autumn, when they go into hibernation. They resume feeding in the spring and are full-grown by June, when they pupate in cocoons at the base of the foodplant. Moths emerge in June and July.

**SCOPULA RUBIGINATA** Hufnagel *Tawny Wave* **Pl. 21**
**Distribution.** Widespread throughout Europe except for the extreme north. Widespread but local in England, most common in the breck district of Norfolk.
**Description.** Length up to 24 mm; body slender, tapering towards head; skin transversely ribbed, grey or pale brown, sometimes tinged with green, with three dark lines along the back and sometimes a series of five dark, lozenge-shaped markings.
**Habitat.** Dry, rough fields, hillsides and heaths.
**Foodplants.** Clover (*Trifolium*), trefoils (*Lotus*), thyme (*Thymus*), knotgrass (*Polygonum aviculare*) and various other low-growing plants, particularly of the family Leguminosae.
**Biology.** One or two generations a year. Eggs are laid in July and hatch in about a week. The caterpillars hibernate and complete their growth by the following May. When disturbed they twist themselves into a characteristic double coil. Pupation takes place in June in cocoons spun on the ground, often under moss. Moths emerge in the same month. Sometimes second generation caterpillars may be found in June and July.

**IDAEA BISELATA** Hufnagel *Small Fan-footed Wave* **Pl. 15**
**Distribution.** Central and southern Europe. Widespread in the British Isles with the exception of northern Scotland.
**Description.** Length up to 22 mm; slender, tapering slightly towards head; transversely ribbed, grey or greyish-brown with darker V-shaped markings on the back; head notched. A pale yellowish-brown form with similar markings also occurs.
**Habitat.** Woodland margins and hedgerows.
**Foodplants.** Bramble (*Rubus fruticosus*), knotgrass (*Polygonum aviculare*) and dandelion (*Taraxacum*).
**Biology.** One generation a year. Eggs are laid in July and hatch in August. The caterpillars feed throughout the winter when conditions are warm enough and become fully grown by the end of April. They appear to prefer withered and decaying leaves. If disturbed they fall from the plant and remain curled in a hook-shape for some time. Pupation takes place below the surface of the soil in May. Moths emerge in June.

**IDAEA DIMIDIATA** Hufnagel *Single-dotted Wave* **Pl. 24**

**Distribution.** Widespread throughout Europe. Occurs throughout the British Isles.

**Description.** Length up to 20 mm; slender, transversely ribbed; pale brown with a double blackish line along the back becoming a single broad stripe towards the tail, a series of oblique lines on either side sometimes making a distinct arrow-like pattern; the spiracles are situated on a whitish ridge below which is a series of black markings; head grey, slightly notched.

**Habitat.** Woodland margins, hedgerows, field borders and gardens, often in damp situations.

**Foodplants.** Cow parsley (*Anthriscus sylvestris*), bur chervil (*Anthriscus caucalis*), burnet saxifrage (*Pimpinella saxifraga*) and hedge bedstraw (*Galium mollugo*). In captivity will also eat withered leaves of dandelion (*Taraxacum*) and knotgrass (*Polygonum aviculare*).

**Biology.** One generation a year. Eggs are laid in July and hatch in the same month. The caterpillars feed from August to May and may be found on flowers or foliage. They rest in a characteristic manner with the front part of the body bent downwards and the head thrown back. Pupation takes place in a flimsy cocoon on the ground in June. Moths emerge in the same month.

**IDAEA CONTIGUARIA** Hübner *Weaver's Wave* **Pl. 25**

**Distribution.** Occurs locally in central and southern Europe. In the British Isles it is confined to North Wales.

**Description.** Length up to 23 mm; pale brown with irregular dark brown lines along the back, sometimes forming diamond shapes; below the spiracles is a broad band of dark brown.

**Habitat.** Heather-covered mountains.

**Foodplants.** Crowberry (*Empetrum nigrum*), heather (*Calluna vulgaris*) and navelwort (*Umbilicus rupestris*). In captivity will feed on knotgrass (*Polygonum aviculare*), chickweed (*Stellaria media*) and various species of *Erica*.

**Biology.** One generation a year but may produce a second brood in captivity. Eggs are laid in July and the caterpillars feed from September to May. Pupation takes place within a loosely woven cocoon in the soil in June. Moths emerge in about a fortnight.

**IDAEA AVERSATA** Linnaeus *Riband Wave* **Pl. 16**

**Distribution.** Occurs throughout Europe, except for the extreme north. Widespread in the British Isles but apparently absent from northern Scotland.

**Description.** Length up to 25 mm; body strongly wrinkled, tapered towards head, greyish-brown becoming ochreous towards tail; a series of dark brown V-shaped markings extends along the back and an undulating pale ochreous line low down along the sides; sometimes a distinct white spot on the back of segment 8; head greyish with black markings.

**Habitat.** Hedgerows, woodland borders and gardens. In Scotland also in marshy woodland.

**Foodplants.** Dandelion (*Taraxacum*), primrose (*Primula vulgaris*), knotgrass (*Polygonum aviculare*), lady's bedstraw (*Galium verum*), herb bennet (*Geum urbanum*), water avens (*G. rivale*), chickweed (*Stellaria media*), dock (*Rumex*).

**Biology.** One generation a year. Eggs are laid in July and hatch in August. The caterpillars feed until they are about one third grown and then go into hibernation, completing their development in the following spring. They are very sluggish and feign death if disturbed. Pupation takes place in May on the surface of the ground and moths emerge in the same month.

**IDAEA STRAMINATA** Borkhausen *Plain Wave* **Pl. 15**

**Distribution.** Widespread in Europe. Widely distributed in England and southern Scotland, rare in Ireland, not recorded in Wales.

**Description.** Length up to 22 mm; body strongly wrinkled and finely ribbed, pale pinkish-brown suffused with grey along the back, greenish-grey below line of spiracles; a series of four X-shaped grey markings on the back and a short grey band extending to the tail; head pinkish-brown, marked with grey.

**Habitat.** Sandy districts near woods and on heaths.

**Foodplants.** Dock (*Rumex*), dandelion (*Taraxacum*), chickweed (*Stellaria media*), violet (*Viola*), bedstraws (*Galium*), loosestrifes (*Lysimacha*), bramble (*Rubus*), bilberry (*Vaccinium myrtillus*) and many other low-growing plants.

**Biology.** One generation a year. Eggs are laid in July in strings of 6–20 lightly attached to each other. The caterpillar feeds from August to June, hibernating through the winter. Pupation takes place in June in a light web spun amongst leaves of the foodplant. Moths emerge in July.

**RHODOMETRA SACRARIA** Linnaeus *Vestal* **Pl. 9**

**Distribution.** Common in southern Europe, migrating to central and northern Europe. Occasionally recorded from many parts of the British Isles but most frequent in southern England.

**Description.** Length up to 25 mm; rather long and thin; body pale brown or green, becoming whitish on the underside; pale yellowish-brown rings are sometimes present between the segments; green forms usually have a broad, pale brown band along the back; a white-centred dark brown line along the back becomes more intense towards the tail; head pale reddish-brown.

**Habitat.** Fields, waste ground and rocky hillsides.

**Foodplants.** Knotgrass (*Polygonum aviculare*) and chamomile (*Anthemis*). Will eat dock (*Rumex*) in captivity.

**Biology.** A succession of broods. Caterpillars feed up rapidly in warm weather and an entire life cycle may be completed within a month. Pupation takes place within a fine network cocoon of yellow silk attached to stems of the foodplant.

**ORTHONAMA OBSTIPATA** Fabricius *Gem* **Pl. 9**

**Distribution.** Widespread in central and southern Europe. Occurs in England, Wales and Ireland but most common in southern England.

**Description.** Length up to 23 mm; a very variable species with the ground colour ranging from greyish-brown to bright green with small white spots; sometimes heavily marked with reddish-brown or blackish-brown on the back or with reddish-brown bands between the segments; on dark specimens there is usually a conspicuous pale patch with dark X-shaped markings on the back towards the tail; other markings are very variable but there is usually a brown or blackish streak along the abdominal proleg; head pale brown or green with darker brown markings.

**Habitat.** Hedgerows, scrub and low-lying, swampy ground.

**Foodplants.** Knotgrass (*Polygonum aviculare*), redshank (*P. persicaria*), groundsel (*Senecio vulgaris*), ragwort (*S. jacobaea*), hemp agrimony (*Eupatorium cannabinum*), dock (*Rumex*), field bindweed (*Convolvulus arvensis*) and other herbaceous plants.

**Biology.** A succession of generations, caterpillars usually feeding up within a month and sometimes in as little as a fortnight. Eggs are laid from spring to autumn and hatch in from five days to three weeks. The caterpillars feed at night, resting on stems and the undersides of leaves by day. Pupation takes place within cocoons of earth and silk near the surface of the soil. Moths emerge after about a fortnight.

**XANTHORHOE MUNITATA** Hübner *Red Carpet* **Pl. 14**

**Distribution.** Central and northern Europe. Occurs in northern England, Wales, Scotland and Northern Ireland.

**Description.** Length up to 25 mm; body wrinkled, pale green with light orange-brown bands between the segments; a dark green band along the back and another along the spiracles, extending down the anal clasper; head pale green marked with dark green. Another form occurs which is wholly suffused with pale purplish-brown.

**Habitat.** Mountains, rocky hillsides, moorland, bogs and marshes.

**Foodplants.** Lady's mantle (*Alchemilla vulgaris*), alpine lady's mantle (*A. alpina*), yellow saxifrage (*Saxifraga aizoides*), chickweed (*Stellaria media*), groundsel (*Senecio vulgaris*) and daisy (*Bellis perennis*).

**Biology.** One generation a year. Eggs are laid in August and hatch in September. The caterpillars apparently feed in mild weather throughout the winter and are fully grown by May. Pupation takes place on the ground in June and moths emerge in the following month.

**XANTHORHOE FLUCTUATA** Linnaeus *Garden Carpet* **Pl. 13**

**Distribution.** Widespread in Europe. Common throughout the British Isles.

**Description.** Length up to 25 mm; colour very variable, ranging from grey through brown to green, paler below the line of spiracles, sometimes pinkish; a series of pale blotches along the back, sometimes tinged with pink or pale orange; head pale, spotted with black.

**Habitat.** Gardens, waste land, hedgerows and lowland woodland.

**Foodplants.** Cabbage (*Brassica oleracea*), rape (*B. napus*), horse-radish (*Armoracia rusticana*), wallflower (*Cheiranthus cheiri*), hedge mustard (*Sisymbrium officinale*) and other plants of the family Cruciferae.

**Biology.** Two or more generations a year. Eggs are laid from April to September and caterpillars may be found from May to October. Caterpillars feed at night. Pupation takes place in silken cocoons below ground. Pupae of the second generation generally overwinter to produce moths in the following spring. Moths are on the wing from April until October.

**SCOTOPTERYX BIPUNCTARIA** Denis & Schiffermüller **Pl. 21**
*Chalk Carpet*

**Distribution.** Occurs in central and southern Europe. In the British Isles, widespread and common in southern England and Wales but becoming more local further north; it is apparently absent from Scotland and Ireland.

**Description.** Length up to 25 mm; body pale yellowish-grey, sometimes tinged with green or pink, darker above the line of spiracles; a series of dark grey lines extends along the back and sides; head pale yellowish-brown with dark brown markings.

**Habitat.** Chalk downland and limestone hills.

**Foodplants.** Clover (*Trifolium*), birdsfoot trefoil (*Lotus corniculatus*) and related plants.

**Biology.** One generation a year. Eggs are laid in August and hatch in the following month. The caterpillars hibernate while quite small and resume feeding in the following spring, becoming fully grown in June. They are active at night, hiding among roots by day. Pupation takes place at the base of the foodplant and moths emerge in July.

**SCOTOPTERYX CHENOPODIATA** Linnaeus **Pl. 20**
*Shaded Broad-bar*
**Distribution.** Widespread in Europe. Widely distributed throughout the British Isles.
**Description.** Length up to 25 mm; body pinkish-grey, sometimes tinged with bluish-grey, with a dark grey central line along the back, on either side of which is a brown-edged, pale yellowish line; underside pale grey; dots and spiracles black; head pinkish-grey, slightly notched.
**Habitat.** Downland, sandhills, waste ground and other grassy places where the foodplants grow.
**Foodplants.** Clover (*Trifolium*), vetches (*Vicia*), grasses and other plants.
**Biology.** One generation a year. Eggs are laid in August and caterpillars hatch in the following month. They overwinter and complete their development in the following spring, becoming fully grown in June. Caterpillars feed at night. Moths emerge from the pupa in July.

**SCOTOPTERYX MUCRONATA** Scopoli *Lead Belle* **Pl. 19**
**Distribution.** Widespread in Europe. Occurs locally throughout the British Isles.
**Description.** Length up to 25 mm; body wrinkled and rather stout, pale ochreous, variably banded with greyish-brown above the spiracles, sometimes tinged with green; two dark bands along the underside; head slightly notched, pale ochreous mottled with dark grey. Northern forms of the caterpillar are apparently darker.
**Habitat.** Heaths, moors and open woodland.
**Foodplants.** Gorse (*Ulex europaeus*) and broom (*Cytisus scoparius*).
**Biology.** One generation a year. Eggs are laid in July and hatch in August. The caterpillars are probably fully grown by the time they go into hibernation and pupate without further feeding in the spring. Pupation takes place among debris on the ground in May and moths emerge in June.

**EPIRRHOE GALIATA** Denis & Schiffermüller *Galium Carpet* **Pl. 26**
**Distribution.** Widely distributed and common in Europe. Widespread in the British Isles, particularly in coastal regions and in the west, rather rare in Scotland.
**Description.** Length up to 25 mm; long and slender; body pale brown, dotted with black; a dark line runs along the back and a dark brown band along each side; sometimes with dark, V-shaped markings on the back of the last six segments; underside with a series of dark stripes; head light brown with a dark V-shaped marking.
**Habitat.** Chiefly chalk and limestone regions.
**Foodplants.** Lady's bedstraw (*Galium verum*), heath bedstraw (*G. saxatile*) and hedge bedstraw (*G. mollugo*).
**Biology.** Two generations a year, one in the north. Eggs are laid in June and August, hatching in 7–10 days. Caterpillars of the first generation feed up quickly and pupate in July to produce moths in August. Those of the second generation pupate in October and moths do not emerge until the following June. Pupation takes place within an earthen cocoon below ground.

**CAMPTOGRAMMA BILINEATA** Linnaeus *Yellow Shell* **Pl. 10**

**Distribution.** Common throughout Europe and the British Isles.

**Description.** Length up to 24 mm; very variable in colour, ranging from green to reddish-brown or grey, banded with yellow or pink between segments; one dark and two pale lines extend down the back; a broad pale band below the spiracles; head pale green, brown or grey with darker markings.

**Habitat.** Occurs almost everywhere, but particularly common in hedgerows, meadows and gardens.

**Foodplants.** Chickweed (*Stellaria media*), dock (*Rumex*), dandelion (*Taraxacum*), rest-harrow (*Ononis repens*), strawberry (*Fragaria vesca*) and other low-growing herbaceous plants and grasses.

**Biology.** One generation a year in Britain, two generations a year in parts of Europe. Eggs are laid loosely on the foliage in August and hatch in September. The caterpillar feeds at night and hides by day at the base of the foodplant or under stones. At rest, it often curls its body into a characteristic 'question mark' shape. When fully grown, the following May, it pupates in an earthen cocoon just below the surface of the soil. Moths emerge in June.

**ENTEPHRIA FLAVICINCTATA** Hübner *Yellow-ringed Carpet* **Pl. 14**

**Distribution.** Northern and central Europe and mountainous regions of southern Europe. In the British Isles, confined to northern England, Scotland and Northern Ireland.

**Description.** Length up to 23 mm; variable in colour from green to olive-green, purplish-grey or brown; a series of conspicuous whitish or pinkish triangular markings along the back separated by reddish-brown chevrons; head pale brown with darker markings.

**Habitat.** Rocky places on mountains, hillsides and moorlands.

**Foodplants.** Yellow saxifrage (*Saxifraga aizoides*), mossy saxifrage (*S. hypnoides*), meadow saxifrage (*S. granulata*), purple saxifrage (*S. oppositifolia*), biting stonecrop (*Sedum acre*).

**Biology.** One generation a year. Eggs are laid in July and hatch in August. The caterpillars hibernate and complete their growth in the following spring, becoming fully fed by the end of May. They are particularly fond of the flowers of the foodplant. Pupation takes place in earthen cocoons in June. Moths emerge in July.

**LARENTIA CLAVARIA** Haworth *Mallow* **Pl. 22**

**Distribution.** Occurs throughout Europe except for the extreme north and south. Widespread in the British Isles but most common in southern England.

**Description.** Length up to 32 mm; green, sometimes yellowish between segments, with whitish dots and black spiracles; a brown or pinkish line extends down the middle of the back and a dark line along each side; head whitish with grey-green markings.

**Habitat.** Hedgerows, waste ground, dunes, sea cliffs and other places where the foodplants grow.

**Foodplants.** Common mallow (*Malva sylvestris*) and hollyhock (*Alcea rosea*).

**Biology.** One generation a year. Eggs are laid in October and overwinter, hatching in the following March or April. The caterpillars become fully grown in June and pupate in the soil near the foodplant. When caterpillars are disturbed they drop to the ground, curled up to resemble mallow seeds. Moths emerge in September.

**ANTICLEA BADIATA** Denis & Schiffermüller *Shoulder Stripe* **Pl. 14**
**Distribution.** Widespread throughout Europe. Common in the British Isles except for northern Scotland.
**Description.** Length up to 26 mm; colour varying from yellowish-green to pink with a broad band of dark green or purplish-black along the back; spots white, except for a line of black spots below the spiracles; green forms are yellowish between segments; head round, reddish-brown, often with a large black spot on either side.
**Habitat.** Hedgerows and woodland margins.
**Foodplants.** Dog rose (*Rosa canina*) and burnet rose (*R. pimpinellifolia*).
**Biology.** One generation a year. Eggs are laid on buds and stems in April and hatch in about ten days. The caterpillars feed at night on the foliage and are fully grown by the end of June. Pupation takes place at the beginning of July in silken cocoons covered with earth below the surface of the soil. Pupae overwinter and moths emerge in March of the following year.

**ANTICLEA DERIVATA** Denis & Schiffermüller *Streamer* **Pl. 14**
**Distribution.** Widespread in Europe. Widely distributed through most of Britain except for northern Scotland; local in Ireland.
**Description.** Length up to 26 mm; body bright green with narrow yellow rings between segments; a broken stripe of purplish-red or brown extends down the back, linking with a cross-stripe of the same colour to form a T-shaped marking; head purplish-red, tinged with green.
**Habitat.** Hedgerows and woodland margins.
**Foodplants.** Dog rose (*Rosa canina*) and honeysuckle (*Lonicera periclymenum*).
**Biology.** One generation a year. Eggs are laid on buds and stems in April and hatch in May. The caterpillars feed mainly on the flowers and, when fully grown at the end of June, descend to the ground and pupate in cocoons of silk and earth below the surface of the soil. Moths emerge in the following April.

MESOLEUCA ALBICILLATA Linnaeus *Beautiful Carpet* **Pl. 15**
**Distribution.** Widespread in Europe. Widely distributed in England, Wales and Ireland, local in southern Scotland.
**Description.** Length up to 25 mm; body green with a white-bordered reddish-brown line along the side of the thorax and the last five segments of the body; a series of white or pink-centred, red, trapezium-shaped markings extends along the back; head green, freckled with brown.
**Habitat.** Open woodland and woodland margins.
**Foodplants.** Bramble (*Rubus fruticosus*), dewberry (*R. caesius*), raspberry (*R. idaeus*) and strawberry (*Fragaria vesca*).
**Biology.** One generation a year. Eggs are laid in July and hatch in the same month. The caterpillar feeds at night, resting by day on the underside of the midrib of a leaf. When disturbed, it curls the first segments of the body into a spiral. It becomes fully grown by the end of September and pupates in a cocoon below the surface of the soil. Moths emerge in the following June.

**PELURGA COMITATA** Linnaeus *Dark Spinach* **Pl. 11**
**Distribution.** Widespread in temperate Europe. Occurs throughout the British Isles.
**Description.** Length up to 23 mm; body rather stout, surface of skin roughened, colour pale ochre, sometimes tinged with pink, heavily marked with greyish-black

above the spiracles; a conspicuous pale zigzag line extends along each side and a series of dark chevrons down the back; head whitish, marked with dark brown.
**Habitat.** Hedgerows, gardens, waste ground, sandy places in coastal regions.
**Foodplants.** Stinking goosefoot (*Chenopodium vulvaria*), fat hen (*C. album*), good King Henry (*C. bonus-henricus*) and common orache (*Atriplex patula*).
**Biology.** One generation a year. Eggs are laid in July and hatch in August. The caterpillar feeds at night on flowers and seeds, remaining on the seed heads by day, curved in a figure 2 shape. It is fully grown by the end of September when it descends to the ground and pupates in a slight cocoon in loose, dry soil in a sheltered place. Pupae overwinter and moths emerge in the following July.

## EULITHIS POPULATA Linnaeus *Northern Spinach* Pl. 25

**Distribution.** Widespread throughout Europe. Common in many parts of the British Isles although generally less frequent in southern England.
**Description.** Length up to 26 mm; very variable in colour, ranging from pale brown or grey to reddish-brown or yellowish-green, sometimes banded with reddish-brown between segments; a series of triangular or X-shaped, pinkish-white-centred, reddish-brown or dark brown markings extends along the back; head reddish-brown or dark brown.
**Habitat.** Usually mountains and upland heaths and bogs, sometimes also lower-lying heathland and fens.
**Foodplants.** Bilberry (*Vaccinium myrtillus*), cowberry (*V. vitis-idaea*), grey sallow (*Salix cinerea*), goat willow (*S. caprea*); also on other *Salix* spp. in captivity.
**Biology.** One generation a year. Eggs are laid in August but do not hatch until April of the following year. The caterpillar feeds at night, resting by day on the foodplant with its body extended straight and rigid. It is usually fully grown by the end of May and pupates between spun leaves of the foodplant. Moths emerge in July.

## ECLIPTOPERA SILACEATA Denis & Schiffermüller Pl. 23
*Small Phoenix*

**Distribution.** Occurs throughout Europe. Widespread but local throughout most parts of the British Isles.
**Description.** Length up to 29 mm; long and slender; body bright green with narrow yellow bands between segments; a broken reddish-brown line along the back, more strongly marked near the head and tail, and a few reddish-brown spots along the sides; legs reddish-brown; anal claspers with a white stripe; head notched, green, strongly marked above with dark reddish-brown.
**Habitat.** Hedgerows, damp woods and woodland margins, waste ground and hill-sides where the foodplants grow.
**Foodplants.** Rosebay willowherb (*Epilobium angustifolium*), broad-leaved willow-herb (*E. montanum*) and enchanter's nightshade (*Circaea lutetiana*).
**Biology.** Two generations a year in southern England, one generation further north. Eggs are laid in May and caterpillars feed up rapidly to produce moths in July. Second generation caterpillars hatch in July and are fully grown by the end of September. The resulting pupae overwinter and moths hatch in the following May. The caterpillars feed principally at night, remaining rigidly extended on the food-plant by day and resembling seed vessels. Pupae are formed in small, loose cocoons among leaf litter on the ground.

**CHLOROCLYSTA CITRATA** Linnaeus *Dark Marbled Carpet* **Pl. 25**

**Distribution.** Common and widespread in central and northern Europe. Widely distributed throughout the British Isles.

**Description.** Length up to 27 mm; green with very narrow yellowish-green rings between segments; a dark green line along the middle of the back; sometimes with a white line along the spiracles; head brownish-green.

**Habitat.** Woodlands, moors, hillsides and mountains.

**Foodplants.** Strawberry (*Fragaria vesca*), bilberry (*Vaccinium myrtillus*), alpine lady's mantle (*Alchemilla alpina*), heather (*Calluna vulgaris*), silver birch (*Betula pendula*), sallow (*Salix*).

**Biology.** One generation a year in Britain, two generations in parts of Europe. Eggs are laid in August but do not hatch until March of the following year. The caterpillars become fully grown in June and pupate between spun leaves. Moths emerge in the following month.

**CHLOROCLYSTA TRUNCATA** Hufnagel **Pl. 25**

*Common Marbled Carpet*

**Distribution.** Widespread and common in Europe. Common throughout the British Isles.

**Description.** Length up to 24 mm; green with yellow bands between segments, sometimes with a broad reddish band or red streaks below the line of the spiracles. Unmarked caterpillars are very similar to those of the Dark Marbled Carpet but are more slender and have a prominent pair of points at the tail.

**Habitat.** Hedgerows and woodland, wooded hillsides.

**Foodplants.** Silver birch (*Betula pendula*), bilberry (*Vaccinium myrtillus*), sallow (*Salix*), hawthorn (*Crataegus monogyna*), heather (*Calluna vulgaris*), strawberry (*Fragaria vesca*).

**Biology.** Two generations a year. Eggs laid in June produce larvae that feed up rapidly and pupate at the end of July to give moths in August. Second generation eggs are laid in August and hatch in September. The resulting caterpillars feed in the autumn and then hibernate before completing their growth in the following spring and pupating in May. Moths emerge in the same month. Pupation takes place between spun leaves.

**CIDARIA FULVATA** Forster *Barred Yellow* **Pl. 14**

**Distribution.** Widespread in temperate Europe. Widely distributed throughout the British Isles.

**Description.** Length up to 19 mm; bluish-green or yellowish-green with yellow bands between segments; a dark green line with a pale, whitish line on either side extends down the middle of the back; sometimes a line of conspicuous reddish-brown blotches is present along the sides; head green, slightly notched above.

**Habitat.** Hedgerows, fields and gardens.

**Foodplants.** Dog rose (*Rosa canina*), burnet rose (*R. pimpinellifolia*) and garden rose.

**Biology.** One generation a year. Eggs are laid in August but do not hatch until May of the following year. Caterpillars feed at night and are fully grown by the end of June. Pupation is within folded leaves of the foodplant. Moths emerge in July.

**THERA FIRMATA** Hübner *Pine Carpet* **Pl. 1**

**Distribution.** Widespread in central and northern Europe. Widely distributed in the British Isles but scarce in Ireland.

**Description.** Length up to 24 mm; body green with narrow white or yellowish bands between segments; two yellowish or greenish-white lines extend down the back on either side of a central dark green band; a white band is present below the spiracles; segments 1–3 with a large patch of reddish-brown on the sides; thoracic legs reddish-brown; head reddish, marked with brown.

**Habitat.** Pine woods.

**Foodplant.** Scots pine (*Pinus sylvestris*).

**Biology.** One generation a year. Eggs are laid in July but apparently do not hatch until the following spring. The caterpillars feed up at varying rates so that moths may be produced as early as June or as late as October. The caterpillars are well camouflaged, the body resembling pine needles and the head a small reddish-brown bud. Pupation takes place in cocoons spun among pine needles on the ground.

**THERA JUNIPERATA** Linnaeus *Juniper Carpet* **Pl. 1**

**Distribution.** Common in northern and central Europe. Fairly widespread in Scotland but in England mainly confined to the south-east. Recorded locally in Wales and Ireland.

**Description.** Length up to 21 mm; body green; pale bluish-green on the back with two broad, yellowish-white stripes; a broad yellowish-white line, low down along the sides, is outlined above with red; legs pinkish-red; head very round, green.

**Habitat.** Chalkhills, mountain slopes and moorland.

**Foodplant.** Juniper (*Juniperus communis*).

**Biology.** One generation a year. Eggs are laid in October but do not hatch until April of the following year. The caterpillar is fully grown by the end of August. Pupation takes place in a loose cocoon spun among fallen leaves on the ground. Moths emerge in October.

EUSTROMA RETICULATA Denis & Schiffermuller **Pl. 22**
*Netted Carpet*

**Distribution.** Locally distributed in central and northern Europe. In the British Isles, confined to the Lake District of England and an isolated locality in Wales.

**Description.** Length up to 25 mm; body pale green; a broken reddish-brown line extends down the centre of the back with a broad whitish line on either side; a few reddish-brown markings along the line of the spiracles; head pale brown.

**Habitat.** Damp valleys, alongside streams and other waterside localities.

**Foodplant.** Touch-me-not balsam (*Impatiens noli-tangere*).

**Biology.** One generation a year. Eggs are laid singly on the undersides of leaves in August and hatch in about a week. The caterpillars feed on leaves at first but soon transfer to the flower heads where they feed on the developing seeds. They are fully grown by October and pupate in tough cocoons spun amongst leaf litter. Moths emerge in July and August of the following year.

**HYDRIOMENA FURCATA** Thunberg *July Highflyer* **Pl. 5**

**Distribution.** Widespread in central and northern Europe. Occurs throughout the British Isles.

**Description.** Length up to 20 mm; body dark reddish-brown to dark purplish-brown or blackish with two broad, irregular bands of white above the spiracles and

one white band immediately below; underside greenish, flushed with pink; head brown.
**Habitat.** Hedgerows, woods, fields, hillsides and mountain slopes.
**Foodplants.** Hazel (*Corylus avellana*), sallow (*Salix*), poplar (*Populus*), bilberry (*Vaccinium myrtillus*) and heather (*Calluna vulgaris*).
**Biology.** One brood a year. Eggs are laid in August but do not hatch until the following May. The caterpillars feed at night, remaining concealed among spun shoots or in catkins by day. They are fully grown in June and pupate among debris on the ground.

**HORISME VITALBATA** Denis & Schiffermüller **Pl. 12**
*Small Waved Umber*
**Distribution.** Widespread in Europe. In the British Isles, confined to southern England and Wales.
**Description.** Length up to 30 mm; body grey, variably suffused with brown; an irregular black line, bordered with white, extends along the back and across the greyish-white head; a pale ochreous line runs along the underside.
**Habitat.** Hedgerows in chalky districts where the foodplant grows.
**Foodplant.** Traveller's joy (*Clematis vitalba*).
**Biology.** Two generations a year. Eggs are laid in June and September. Caterpillars feed mainly at night. Those of the first generation are fully grown by the end of July and pupate to produce moths in August. Second generation caterpillars pupate in October, producing moths in the following May. Pupation takes place in a slight silken cocoon below the soil.

**HORISME TERSATA** Denis & Schiffermüller *Fern* **Pl. 12**
**Distribution.** Occurs in central and southern Europe. In the British Isles, confined to southern England and Wales.
**Description.** Length up to 30 mm; body pale brown; a dark brown or blackish stripe bordered with pale yellow extends along the back and across the head; two dark lines extend along the underside.
**Habitat.** Hedgerows, particularly in chalky districts where the foodplant flourishes.
**Foodplants.** Traveller's joy (*Clematis vitalba*) and also meadow buttercup (*Ranunculus acris*).
**Biology.** One generation a year. Eggs are laid in July and hatch in August. The caterpillars feed at night but remain on the foodplant by day. They are fully grown by the end of September and pupate in silken cocoons just below the surface of the soil. Moths emerge in June of the following year.

**MELANTHIA PROCELLATA** Denis & Schiffermüller **Pl. 12**
*Pretty Chalk Carpet*
**Distribution.** Widespread in central and southern Europe. In the British Isles, confined to southern England.
**Description.** Length up to 32 mm; pale ochreous-brown with three dark greyish-brown lines along the back, and a broad dark brown lateral line along the sides terminating at about three-quarters the length of the body so that the hind end appears pale; spiracles black; underside greyish-brown with a pale ochreous central line; head marked with dark reddish-brown.
**Habitat.** Sheltered hedgerows, damp woodlands and other places in chalky districts where the foodplant grows.

**Foodplant.** Traveller's joy (*Clematis vitalba*).

**Biology.** One generation a year in England, two generations in parts of Europe. Eggs are laid on the foliage at the end of July and caterpillars hatch in August. The caterpillar when at rest lies stretched out and closely pressed to the stem or the midrib of a leaf. It feeds up rapidly and by the middle of September constructs a cocoon of silk and earth in which it pupates. The pupa overwinters and the moth emerges in the following June.

**TRIPHOSA DUBITATA** Linnaeus *Tissue* **Pl. 18**

**Distribution.** Widespread in Europe. Widely distributed in England, Wales and Ireland; scarce in southern Scotland.

**Description.** Length up to 27 mm; body smooth and plump, tapering towards head, green with pale yellowish-green bands between segments; four fine, broken lines of yellow extend along the back, with a broad yellow line above the spiracles; head green, without markings. Another form exists with dark green lines along the back.

**Habitat.** Woodland and hedgerows.

**Foodplants.** Buckthorn (*Rhamnus catharticus*), alder buckthorn (*Frangula alnus*) and bird cherry (*Prunus padus*).

**Biology.** One generation a year. Eggs are laid in May and the caterpillars feed in June and July, concealing themselves between leaves spun together with silk. In August, when fully grown, the caterpillars pupate in cocoons of silk and earth in the ground. Moths emerge in the same month and are active in the autumn but do not lay eggs until the following June, after hibernation.

**PHILEREME TRANSVERSATA** Hufnagel *Dark Umber* **Pl. 22**

**Distribution.** Widespread in Europe. Widely distributed in England but less common in the north. Recorded from south Wales but not known in Scotland or Ireland.

**Description.** Length up to 24 mm; body green, with narrow, yellowish-green rings between segments; a dark green line extends along the back and a white line along each side of the abdomen; spiracles reddish-orange; a conspicuous patch of purplish-brown extends along the hind-most spiracles and anal claspers; head green. Another variety is greyish-white with a broad band of purplish-brown along the back, dark spots along the sides and greyish-brown on the underside; the head is black.

**Habitat.** Woodlands and hedgerows in chalky districts, also fenland carr.

**Foodplant.** Buckthorn (*Rhamnus catharticus*).

**Biology.** One generation a year. Eggs are laid in August but do not hatch until the following April or May. The caterpillar spins leaves together to make a shelter. It is fully grown by the beginning of June and constructs an elongate cocoon of silk and earth in the ground in which it pupates. The moth emerges in July.

**EPIRRITA DILUTATA** Denis & Schiffermüller *November Moth* **Pl. 7**

**Distribution.** Northern and Central Europe. Widespread throughout the British Isles.

**Description.** Length up to 26 mm; body green with narrow, yellowish-green rings between segments; underside whitish; a white line extends along each side; body variably marked with purplish-red, ranging from a narrow line along the back to a series of broad, transverse bands, one to each segment; some specimens have no purplish markings at all; head green, without markings.

**Habitat.** Woodlands and hedgerows.
**Foodplants.** Oak (*Quercus*), elm (*Ulmus campestris*), silver birch (*Betula pendula*), blackthorn (*Prunus spinosa*), hawthorn (*Crataegus monogyna*) and other deciduous trees and shrubs.
**Biology.** One generation a year. Eggs are laid in November but do not hatch until the following April. The caterpillar feeds mainly at night, remaining on the foodplant by day. It is fully grown by the end of June and pupates in a silken cocoon just below the surface of the soil. The moth emerges in October.

**EPIRRITA FILIGRAMMARIA** Herrich-Schaffer **Pl. 25**
*Small Autumnal Moth*
**Distribution.** Apparently confined to the British Isles, ranging from northern England to the Hebrides and Orkneys and also occurring in parts of Northern Ireland.
**Description.** Length up to 24 mm; body bluish-green; underside whitish; a dark green line extends along the back with two yellowish-white lines on either side; dots yellowish-white; a broad yellowish-white line extends along each side below the spiracles; head green with slight brown mottling.
**Habitat.** Moorland and hillsides.
**Foodplants.** Bilberry (*Vaccinium myrtillus*) and heather (*Calluna vulgaris*).
**Biology.** One generation a year. Eggs are laid in September but do not hatch until early in the following year. The caterpillar feeds in the spring and becomes fully grown in May when it pupates in the soil. The moth emerges in August.

**OPEROPHTERA BRUMATA** Linnaeus *Winter Moth* **Pl. 16**
**Distribution.** Widespread in central and northern Europe. Widely distributed and common throughout the British Isles.
**Description.** Length up to 20 mm; body bluish-green, yellowish-green or greenish-grey, usually with a dark line down the middle of the back with two yellowish-white lines on either side, the outer lines broken and irregular; a yellowish-white line extends along the spiracles or immediately below them; in many specimens there are narrow yellowish rings between the segments; head pale greenish-brown with dark brown markings.
**Habitat.** Orchards, woodlands, hedgerows, moorland.
**Foodplants.** Apple (*Malus*), pear (*Pyrus*), oak (*Quercus*), birch (*Betula*), hazel (*Corylus avellana*), blackthorn (*Prunus spinosa*), hawthorn (*Crataegus monogyna*) and many other deciduous trees and shrubs. On moorland, caterpillars will feed on heather (*Calluna vulgaris*).
**Biology.** One generation a year. Eggs are laid in crevices in bark in November and December but do not hatch until the beginning of April. The caterpillar spins leaves together to form a shelter. It feeds on young shoots and leaves and attacks the blossom of fruit trees, sometimes causing severe damage. It is fully grown by the end of May and descends to the ground to pupate in the soil. The moth emerges in the winter. Adult females have greatly reduced wings and are unable to fly.

**OPEROPHTERA FAGATA** Scharfenburg *Northern Winter Moth* **Pl. 4**
**Distribution.** Central and Northern Europe. Widespread in England and Scotland and recorded from parts of south Wales and Northern Ireland.
**Description.** Length up to 21 mm; body yellowish-green with a greyish stripe

along the back; a grey line, edged above with yellow, extends along the spiracles, which are black; head and thoracic legs black.

**Habitat.** Woodland, hedgerows, orchards and other places where the foodplants grow.

**Foodplants.** Silver birch (*Betula pendula*), beech (*Fagus sylvatica*), apple (*Malus*), hawthorn (*Crataegus monogyna*) and other deciduous trees and shrubs.

**Biology.** One generation a year. Eggs are laid in November but do not hatch until the following April. The caterpillar feeds in a similar manner to the Winter Moth, becoming fully grown by the end of June and descending to the ground to pupate in the soil. The moth emerges in October or November. Adult females have slightly larger wings than those of the Winter Moth but are also flightless.

**PERIZOMA DIDYMATA** Linnaeus *Twin-spot Carpet* **Pl. 25**

**Distribution.** Central and northern Europe. Common and widespread throughout the British Isles.

**Description.** Length up to 23 mm; body green with narrow yellowish rings between the segments; a dark green line along the back with two pale green lines on either side; a band of white extends along each side just below the line of the spiracles; head pale green, slightly marked with pale brown above.

**Habitat.** Heathland, moorland, woodland and waste ground.

**Foodplants.** Bilberry (*Vaccinium myrtillus*), primrose (*Primula vulgaris*), wood sage (*Teucrium scorodonia*), rough chervil (*Chaerophyllum temulentum*), wood anemone (*Anemone nemorosa*), lesser celandine (*Ranunculus ficaria*), chickweed (*Stellaria media*), red campion (*Silene dioica*) and other plants.

**Biology.** One generation a year. Eggs are laid in July but do not hatch until the following April. The caterpillar feeds on the foliage and flowers and becomes fully grown towards the end of May. Pupation takes place on the ground in a silken cocoon. The moth emerges in June.

**PERIZOMA SAGITTATA** Fabricius *Marsh Carpet* **Pl. 12**

**Distribution.** Central Europe. In the British Isles, apparently confined to the fenlands of eastern England although it is also recorded from Kent, Worcestershire and Warwickshire.

**Description.** Length up to 22 mm; body yellowish-green with broad transverse bands of dark green across the back; a broad, irregular band of pink extends along each side, bordered below with dark green or black; head green, marked with dark brown.

**Habitat.** Fenland.

**Foodplants.** Common meadow-rue (*Thalictrum flavum*) and lesser meadow-rue (*T. minus*).

**Biology.** One generation a year. Eggs are laid in July on stalks or in flowers. The caterpillar hatches in early August and feeds in the flowers and on the developing seeds. In September, when the caterpillar is fully grown, it either spins a cocoon amongst the flowers or descends to the ground to pupate at the base of the foodplant. The moth emerges in July of the following year.

**EUPITHECIA HAWORTHIATA** Doubleday *Haworth's Pug* **Pl. 12**

**Distribution.** Widely distributed in central Europe. Widespread in England and south Wales; locally common in Ireland, but not recorded from Scotland.

**Description.** Length up to 10 mm; short and stout; body dusky pink or yellowish-

green, usually with a dark grey band along the back and two grey lines along each side; head greenish-brown, marked with dark brown or black.
**Habitat.** Chalky districts where the foodplant grows.
**Foodplant.** Traveller's joy (*Clematis vitalba*).
**Biology.** One generation a year. Eggs are laid in July and hatch in the same month. The caterpillar feeds in the buds and may be detected by the presence of a blackish hole in the side of a bud. It later feeds on the stamens of open flowers and, when fully grown, at the end of August descends to pupate in the soil. It overwinters as a pupa and the moth emerges in the following June.

**EUPITHECIA ABIETARIA** Goeze *Cloaked Pug* **Pl. 1**
**Distribution.** Widespread in central and northern Europe. Local but widely distributed throughout the British Isles.
**Description.** Length approximately 18 mm; body dull pinkish-brown with small black spots on the back and a black plate on segment 1; head black.
**Habitat.** Conifer plantations.
**Foodplants.** In the British Isles, apparently confined to Norway spruce (*Picea abies*). In continental Europe, also on other species of spruce (*Picea*) and pine (*Pinus*).
**Biology.** One generation a year. Eggs are laid in June and the caterpillars feed on unripe seeds within the cones in July and August. Their presence may be detected by excrement exuding from holes bored in the cones. The fully grown caterpillars leave the cones and pupate in cocoons on the ground in September. Moths usually emerge in the following June but some remain in the pupa state for a second winter.

**EUPITHECIA LINARIATA** Denis & Schiffermüller *Toadflax Pug* **Pl. 27**
**Distribution.** Widespread in Europe. Widely distributed in Britain but more common in the south; there are a few doubtful records from Ireland.
**Description.** Length up to 16 mm; rather short and stout; body greenish-yellow to bluish-green, often with conspicuous blackish-brown transverse bands across the back but sometimes with pale markings or without markings; head pale reddish-brown.
**Habitat.** Fields, waste ground and roadsides.
**Foodplant.** Common toadflax (*Linaria vulgaris*).
**Biology.** One generation a year in the British Isles, two generations a year in parts of continental Europe. Eggs are laid in July and the caterpillars feed in flowers and seed capsules in August and September. The fully grown caterpillars pupate in earthen cocoons at the end of September to produce moths in June of the following year.

**EUPITHECIA PULCHELLATA** Stephens *Foxglove Pug* **Pl. 27**
**Distribution.** Central and western Europe. Widespread throughout the British Isles.
**Description.** Length up to 21 mm; body yellowish-green to greyish-green or dark grey with a dark band along the back and dark lines along the sides; head brown with darker markings.
**Habitat.** Woodland, waste ground and other places where the foodplant grows.
**Foodplant.** Foxglove (*Digitalis purpurea*).
**Biology.** One generation a year. Eggs are laid in June and the caterpillars feed in the flowers in July and August. They spin across the mouths of the flowers, making a closed compartment, and feed on the stamens and developing seeds within. When fully grown, they leave the flowers to pupate in the soil in September. Attacked

flowers usually remain on the plant long after the others have fallen. Moths emerge in May of the following year.

**EUPITHECIA PYGMAEATA** Hübner *Marsh Pug* **Pl. 11**

**Distribution.** Northern Europe. Widespread in Britain except for southern England; very local in Ireland.

**Description.** Length up to 14 mm; skin rather roughened; body dull yellowish-green with a band of olive-green along the back, sometimes broken into individual markings; on either side is a line of the same colour; head pale greenish-brown with darker brown markings.

**Habitat.** Marshy ground, sandhills and waste ground.

**Foodplants.** Field mouse-ear (*Cerastium arvense*), greater stitchwort (*Stellaria holostea*) and related plants.

**Biology.** One generation a year; possibly a partial second generation in some regions. Eggs are laid on the flowers in June and the caterpillars feed on the flowers and seedheads in July. When almost fully grown, the caterpillars feed with their rear ends protruding from the seed capsules. They pupate in cocoons spun among the foodplant in August. Moths emerge in May of the following year, although in northern regions some may remain in the pupa state for a second winter.

**EUPITHECIA CENTAUREATA** Denis & Schiffermüller **Pl. 28**
*Lime-speck Pug*

**Distribution.** Widespread and common throughout Europe. Widely distributed throughout the British Isles, with the exception of northern Scotland.

**Description.** Length up to 19 mm; deeply wrinkled; very variable in colour, ranging from yellow to green, brown or grey, usually with a dark line along the back and sometimes with distinct reddish-brown markings along the back and sides.

**Habitat.** Meadows, roadsides, woodland margins and other places where suitable foodplants grow.

**Foodplants.** Ragwort (*Senecio jacobaea*), yarrow (*Achillea millefolium*), hemp agrimony (*Eupatorium cannabinum*); golden rod (*Solidago virgaurea*), black knap-weed (*Centaurea nigra*) and many other plants.

**Biology.** Two generations a year, the broods overlapping so that moths may be found from May to October. Eggs are laid in June and the caterpillars feed on the flowers of various plants. While some feed up rapidly to produce a second generation, others produce overwintering pupae giving rise to moths in the following June.

**EUPITHECIA ABSINTHIATA** Clerck *Wormwood Pug* **Pl. 28**

**Distribution.** Widespread in central and northern Europe. Widely distributed and often common in the British Isles.

**Description.** Length up to 21 mm; very variable in colour, ranging from green to yellow, brown or ochreous-white, but usually with a series of brown or blackish arrow-shaped markings along the back; head brown.

**Habitat.** Woodland margins, hedgerows, waste ground and other places where the foodplants grow.

**Foodplants.** Wormwood (*Artemisia absinthium*), hemp agrimony (*Eupatorium cannabinum*), ragwort (*Senecio jacobaea*), yarrow (*Achillea millefolium*), golden rod (*Solidago virgaurea*) and many other plants.

**Biology.** One generation a year. Eggs are laid in July and the caterpillars feed on flowers and developing seeds in August and September. When fully grown they pupate in the soil in October. Moths emerge in June of the following year.

**EUPITHECIA GOOSSENSIATA** Mabille *Ling Pug* **Pl. 24**

**Distribution.** Central and northern Europe. Widespread and often common in the British Isles.

**Description.** Length up to 19 mm; body pink with dark pink or brown chevrons or triangles along the back and a whitish line below the spiracles; head pale ochre, marked with dark brown.

**Habitat.** Heathland and moorland.

**Foodplants.** Heather (*Calluna vulgaris*) and heath (*Erica*).

**Biology.** One generation a year. Eggs are laid in July and the caterpillars feed on flowers in August and September. Pupation takes place in the soil in October and moths do not emerge until June of the following year.

**EUPITHECIA ASSIMILATA** Doubleday *Currant Pug* **Pl. 22**

**Distribution.** Central and northern Europe. Widespread throughout the British Isles.

**Description.** Length up to 22 mm; body yellowish-green with yellowish rings between the segments and a dark line along the back, or greyish-green with a series of blackish, lozenge-shaped markings along the back, interspersed with narrow reddish-brown markings between the segments; head green, sometimes marked with black.

**Habitat.** Hedgerows and gardens.

**Foodplants.** Redcurrant (*Ribes rubrum*), blackcurrant (*R. nigrum*) and wild hop (*Humulus lupulus*).

**Biology.** Two generations a year. Eggs are laid in May and the caterpillars feed up rapidly in June to pupate and produce moths in July and August. Eggs of the second brood hatch at the end of August and the resulting caterpillars feed in September and pupate in October. These pupae overwinter and moths emerge in the following May. The caterpillars feed on the undersides of leaves, making many small, elongate holes. Pupation takes place in the soil.

**EUPITHECIA VULGATA** Haworth *Common Pug* **Pl. 15**

**Distribution.** Widespread throughout Europe. Widely distributed and common throughout the British Isles.

**Description.** Length up to 20 mm; slender; body varying in colour from pale brown to greenish-grey, sometimes with dark grey or greenish-grey diamond-shaped markings on the back and a band of similar colour below the spiracles; head pale ochre marked with brown or greyish-green.

**Habitat.** Hedgerows, waste ground, gardens and other places where the foodplants grow.

**Foodplants.** Hawthorn (*Crataegus monogyna*), bramble (*Rubus fruticosus*), ragwort (*Senecio jacobaea*), golden-rod (*Solidago virgaurea*), bilberry (*Vaccinium myrtillus*) and many other trees, shrubs and herbaceous plants.

**Biology.** Two generations a year. Eggs are laid in June and the caterpillars feed up rapidly in July to pupate and produce moths in August. These lay eggs which hatch to produce caterpillars in September. The second brood caterpillars pupate in October but do not produce moths until the following May. The caterpillars feed on foliage and pupate in the soil.

**EUPITHECIA TRIPUNCTARIA** Herrich-Schaffer **Pl. 24**
*White-spotted Pug*

**Distribution.** Central and northern Europe. Widely distributed in England, south Wales, southern Scotland and Ireland.

**Description.** Length up to 20 mm; body green or brown with whitish rings between segments, sometimes without markings but usually with a series of dark triangular patches along the back, and brownish markings along the sides; underside dark green or brown; head green or brown with darker markings.

**Habitat.** Hedgerows and other damp, shady places where the foodplants grow.

**Foodplants.** Hogweed (*Heracleum sphondylium*), angelica (*Angelica sylvestris*), wild parsnip (*Pastinaca sativa*) and related plants; also on golden-rod (*Solidago virgaurea*) and elder (*Sambucus nigra*).

**Biology.** One generation a year. Eggs are laid in June and the caterpillars feed on flowers and developing fruits from July to September. Pupation takes place in the soil at the end of September but moths do not emerge until the following May.

**EUPITHECIA SIMPLICIATA** Haworth *Plain Pug* **Pl. 11**

**Distribution.** Central Europe. Widely distributed and locally common in southern England; scarce in Ireland.

**Description.** Length up to 23 mm; body pale grey, green or brown with a series of dark arrowhead-like markings along the back; sometimes without distinct markings.

**Habitat.** Waste ground, river banks and salt marshes.

**Foodplants.** Fat hen (*Chenopodium album*), common orache (*Atriplex patula*) and related plants.

**Biology.** One generation a year. Eggs are laid in July and caterpillars may be found in August and September. They feed at night, at first on buds but later on flowers and developing seed-heads, resting by day low down on the foodplant. Pupation takes place in the soil in October but moths do not emerge until June of the following year.

**EUPITHECIA DISTINCTARIA** Herrich-Schaffer *Thyme Pug* **Pl. 26**

**Distribution.** Central and southern Europe. In the British Isles, occurs in southern and western England, Wales, western Scotland and Ireland.

**Description.** Length up to 16 mm; body green with a dark purplish-pink stripe down the back, or entirely purplish-pink; head and thoracic legs yellowish-brown.

**Habitat.** Rocky coasts and limestone cliffs and quarries.

**Foodplant.** Wild thyme (*Thymus serpyllum*).

**Biology.** One generation a year. Eggs are laid in July and the caterpillars feed at night on flowers in August and September. They pupate in the soil in October and moths emerge in June of the following year.

**EUPITHECIA PIMPINELLATA** Hübner *Pimpinel Pug* **Pl. 24**

**Distribution.** Widespread in Europe. Widely distributed in England but most common in the south; less common in Wales and Ireland; absent from Scotland.

**Description.** Length up to 25 mm; body green, purplish-brown or pinkish-brown; the green form has a purplish-brown line down the back; all forms with a broad pale band along the sides, sometimes less distinct in green forms; head pale brownish-green or brown.

**Habitat.** Hedgerows and grassland in chalky districts.

**Foodplant.** Burnet saxifrage (*Pimpinella saxifraga*).

**Biology.** One generation a year. Eggs are laid in July and caterpillars may be found from August to October, feeding at night on flowers and developing seed capsules. Pupation takes place in the soil in November and moths emerge the following June.

**EUPITHECIA FRAXINATA** Crewe *Ash Pug* **Pl. 8**

**Distribution.** Central and southern Europe. Widespread throughout the British Isles.

**Description.** Length up to 20 mm; slender; body green with a broad white band along the side, interrupted by small patches of reddish-brown; sometimes with brown markings on the back; a brown form also exists.

**Habitat.** Woodland, hedgerows, gardens and other places where ash grows. The race associated with sea buckthorn is confined to coastal sandhills.

**Foodplants.** Ash (*Fraxinus excelsior*) and sea buckthorn (*Hippophae rhamnoides*).

**Biology.** One generation a year, sometimes with a partial second brood. Eggs are laid in July and the caterpillars feed from August to September. Pupation takes place in a crevice of the bark, under moss or in the soil in September and moths emerge in the following May and June. Sometimes second brood moths appear in August and September.

**EUPITHECIA VIRGAUREATA** Doubleday *Golden-rod Pug* **Pl. 28**

**Distribution.** Central Europe. Widely distributed throughout the British Isles but rather local.

**Description.** Length up to 19 mm; body very variable in colour, ranging from yellow to pale brown or grey with a series of distinctive, arrowhead-shaped dark markings along the back and dark brown triangular markings along the sides; head brown.

**Habitat.** Woodland margins and other places where the foodplants abound.

**Foodplants.** Golden-rod (*Solidago virgaurea*), ragwort (*Senecio jacobaea*) and possibly on other plants.

**Biology.** The biology of this species in the wild is not fully known but in captivity it produces two generations a year. Caterpillars may be found in the autumn feeding on flowers, and pupate in the soil to produce moths in the following May and June. Further moths appear in August, presumably from a summer brood of caterpillars.

**EUPITHECIA PUSILLATA** Denis & Schiffermüller *Juniper Pug* **Pl. 1**

**Distribution.** Widely distributed in northern and central Europe, local in southern Europe. Widespread throughout the British Isles wherever the foodplant abounds.

**Description.** Length up to 18 mm; very variable in colour and markings; the ground colour ranges from green to reddish-brown; some forms have a central dark line and two narrow yellowish lines along the back, while others are marked on the back with reddish-brown rectangles or dark brown arrowhead-shaped markings and black lines; all forms have a broad yellowish-white stripe along the sides.

**Habitat.** Mountains, hillsides, chalk downland and gardens.

**Foodplant.** Juniper (*Juniperus communis*).

**Biology.** One generation a year. Eggs are laid on twigs of the foodplant in late summer but do not hatch until early the following year. The caterpillars may be found feeding from April until early June. Pupation takes place in the soil at the end of June. Moths emerge over an extended period from July to September.

**EUPITHECIA PHOENICEATA** Rambur *Cypress Pug* **Pl. 1**

**Distribution.** Southern Europe. Introduced to the British Isles, and largely confined to southern England but is gradually extending its range.

**Description.** Length up to 17 mm; body green or pale greyish-brown, intricately patterned with different shades of green or brown to produce a chain-like effect along the back and sides; head pale green or brown with darker brown markings.
**Habitat.** Parks, gardens and other places where the foodplant grows.
**Foodplants.** Monterey cypress (*Cupressus macrocarpa*) and Lawson's cypress (*Chamaecyparis lawsoniana*), plus related species and hybrids. In continental Europe, occurs naturally on the Mediterranean cypress (*Cupressus sempervirens*).
**Biology.** One generation a year. Caterpillars feed on buds of mature foliage in autumn and winter and pupate in January or February to produce moths from May to October, but most commonly in August and September.

**EUPITHECIA LARICIATA** Freyer *Larch Pug* **Pl. 1**
**Distribution.** Northern and central Europe. Widespread throughout the British Isles.
**Description.** Length up to 21 mm; body green or light reddish-brown with a dark central stripe and two yellowish lines down the back; a yellowish-white or pale yellowish-green band extends along the sides; brown forms sometimes have a broad band of dark brown below the line of the spiracles; head brown or greenish-brown.
**Habitat.** Larch plantations.
**Foodplant.** European larch (*Larix decidua*).
**Biology.** One generation a year. Eggs are laid on the foliage in June and the caterpillars feed from June to August. Pupation takes place in the soil in early autumn and moths emerge in May of the following year.

**CHLOROCLYSTIS V-ATA** Haworth *V-Pug* **Pl. 12**
**Distribution.** Local in central and southern Europe. Widely distributed in southern and central England, Wales and Ireland.
**Description.** Length up to 16 mm; rather variable in colour and patterning; the ground colour ranges from green to reddish-brown or grey, often with a line of blackish or reddish-brown triangular markings along the back and with dull reddish-purple diagonal markings along the sides.
**Habitat.** Hedgerows and woodland margins.
**Foodplants.** Traveller's joy (*Clematis vitalba*), golden-rod (*Solidago virgaurea*), hemp agrimony (*Eupatorium cannabinum*), purple loosestrife (*Lythrum salicaria*) and many other plants.
**Biology.** One generation a year in northern parts of its distribution but two overlapping broods further south. Eggs are laid in April, producing caterpillars in May which pupate in June and emerge as moths in July. Second brood eggs are laid in July and the caterpillars feed in August and September. Pupation takes place in late September but moths do not emerge until the following April. These times are very variable and, due to long emergence periods, moths may be found in any month from April to August or even later. The caterpillars feed on flowers and pupation takes place in the soil.

**CHLOROCLYSTIS RECTANGULATA** Linnaeus *Green Pug* **Pl. 16**
**Distribution.** Widely distributed throughout Europe. Widespread throughout the British Isles but most common in southern England and Wales.
**Description.** Length up to 15 mm; body pale yellowish or bluish-green, sometimes with a distinctive purplish-red or dark green line along the back, tapering towards the head; head brown.

**Habitat.** Orchards, gardens and hedgerows.
**Foodplants.** Apple (*Malus*), pear (*Pyrus*) and sometimes blackthorn (*Prunus spinosa*).
**Biology.** One generation a year. Eggs are laid on flower buds in June and July but do not hatch until the following April when the buds begin to open. The caterpillars feed on the flowers, spinning the petals together with silk. They are fully grown by the end of May and pupate under loose bark on the tree trunk or in the soil at its base. Moths emerge in the following month.

**CHLOROCLYSTIS DEBILIATA** Hübner *Bilberry Pug* **Pl. 25**
**Distribution.** Local in central and northern Europe. Locally common in England, Wales and Ireland but apparently absent from Scotland.
**Description.** Length up to 15 mm; body green with a dark green stripe along the back; head dark brown.
**Habitat.** Open woodland and sheltered hillsides and valleys where the foodplant abounds.
**Foodplant.** Bilberry (*Vaccinium myrtillus*).
**Biology.** One generation a year. Eggs are laid in July but do not hatch until April of the following year. The caterpillars feed on the foliage, spinning it together loosely to form a shelter. Pupation takes place in the soil at the end of May and moths emerge in the following month.

**GYMNOSCELIS RUFIFASCIATA** Haworth *Double-striped Pug* **Pl. 17**
**Distribution.** Central and southern Europe. Widely distributed throughout the British Isles.
**Description.** Length up to 17 mm; very variable, the ground colour ranging from whitish to yellowish-green, brown, red or purplish-pink, usually with a pale band down the back bearing a series of dark chevrons or triangles; head yellowish-brown.
**Habitat.** Heaths, moorland, waste ground and gardens.
**Foodplants.** Gorse (*Ulex europaeus*), broom (*Cytisus scoparius*), traveller's joy (*Clematis vitalba*), hawthorn (*Crataegus monogyna*), holly (*Ilex aquifolium*), heather (*Calluna vulgaris*) and many other shrubs and herbaceous plants.
**Biology.** Usually two generations a year but sometimes three. Eggs are laid in May and the caterpillars feed up rapidly and pupate by the end of June to produce moths in July. Second brood eggs are laid in August and the caterpillars feed in September. Pupation takes place in October but moths do not emerge until April of the following year. The caterpillars feed on various flowers according to the season and pupation takes place in the soil.

**CHESIAS LEGATELLA** Denis & Schiffermüller *Streak* **Pl. 19**
**Distribution.** Widespread in warmer regions of central and southern Europe. Widely distributed throughout the British Isles.
**Description.** Length up to 28 mm; body green or greenish-yellow, sometimes with bands of yellowish-green between the segments; three dark green lines along the back and a broad white or yellow stripe along the line of the spiracles; yellow forms may be without markings; head pale green or yellowish-brown with brown markings.
**Habitat.** Heathland, open pine forests and hillsides where the foodplant abounds.
**Foodplant.** Broom (*Cytisus scoparius*).
**Biology.** One generation a year. Eggs are laid in October but do not hatch until the following spring. The caterpillars feed on the foliage, resting with their bodies held

at an angle to the stem so that they resemble small twiglets. They become fully grown by the end of June and pupate in the soil. Moths emerge in September.

**CHESIAS RUFATA** Fabricius *Broom-tip* **Pl. 19**

**Distribution.** Widely distributed in central and southern Europe. Widespread but more local than *C. legatella* in Britain; absent from Ireland.

**Description.** Length up to 27 mm; body bluish-green with pale yellowish-green bands between the segments; a dark green line and two yellowish or whitish lines along the back and a broad white stripe along the line of the spiracles; head yellowish-green.

**Habitat.** Heathland and other places where the foodplant is common.

**Foodplant.** Broom (*Cytisus scoparius*).

**Biology.** One generation a year. Eggs are laid in June and July and hatch within a month. The caterpillars feed from June to September, resting in a similar way to those of *C. legatella*. Pupation takes place in the soil in October but moths do not emerge until the following May or June. Some remain in the pupa state for a second winter before emerging.

**LITHOSTEGE GRISEATA** Denis & Schiffermüller *Grey Carpet* **Pl. 12**

**Distribution.** Central and southern Europe. In the British Isles, confined to the Breck district of eastern England.

**Description.** Length up to 22 mm; body green or olive-green with three dark green lines along the back, sometimes overlaid by dark wedge-shaped markings; a yellow stripe along the spiracles is sometimes marked above and below with blotches of purplish-brown; head green.

**Habitat.** Open sandy fields.

**Foodplant.** Flixweed (*Descurainia sophia*) and also treacle mustard (*Erysimum cheiranthoides*).

**Biology.** One generation a year. Eggs are laid in June and the caterpillars may be found in July and August. They bear a strong resemblance to the seed pods on which they feed. Pupation takes place in the soil in September but moths do not emerge until the following June and sometimes remain in the pupa state for a second winter.

**VENUSIA CAMBRICA** Curtis *Welsh Wave* **Pl. 16**

**Distribution.** Northern and alpine Europe. Widely distributed in the British Isles, occurring locally in upland regions of northern and western England, Wales, Scotland and Ireland.

**Description.** Length up to 21 mm; body yellowish-green with a faint yellowish line down the back, marked to a variable extent with irregular blotches of reddish-brown, particularly in the middle and at the extremities of the body; head green.

**Habitat.** Uplands, hillsides and mountains.

**Foodplant.** Rowan (*Sorbus aucuparia*).

**Biology.** One generation a year. Eggs are laid in July and the caterpillars feed up rapidly in August, pupating at the end of the month. Pupation takes place in the soil. Moths do not emerge until June of the following year.

**MINOA MURINATA** Scopoli *Drab Looper* **Pl. 22**

**Distribution.** Central and southern Europe. In the British Isles, confined to southern England and Wales.

**Description.** Length up to 13 mm; body greyish-pink, marked to a variable extent with black; pale pink warts; grey underside; an irregular orange or yellowish-pink stripe below the spiracles on either side; head brown, marked with black.

**Habitat.** Open woodland.

**Foodplants.** Wood spurge (*Euphorbia amygdaloides*) and other *Euphorbia* species.

**Biology.** Usually one generation a year in Britain but two generations a year in continental Europe. Eggs are laid in June and the caterpillars feed from July to September. Pupation takes place in the soil and moths emerge in the following May and June.

**LOBOPHORA HALTERATA** Hufnagel *Seraphim* **Pl. 3**

**Distribution.** Central and northern Europe. Widespread in England but more common in the south; also occurs in south Wales, northern Scotland and locally in Ireland.

**Description.** Length up to 18 mm; body green with slightly darker bands between the segments; an indistinct dark green line along the middle of the back; sometimes a yellowish line along the sides; anal segment with two distinct points; head green.

**Habitat.** Woodland.

**Foodplants.** Aspen (*Populus tremula*) and other *Populus* and *Salix* species.

**Biology.** One generation a year. Eggs are laid in June and the caterpillars may be found in June and July. They feed at night, resting by day stretched flat among the leaves. Pupation takes place on the ground in August but moths do not emerge until May of the following year.

**TRICHOPTERYX CARPINATA** Borkhausen *Early Tooth-striped* **Pl. 5**

**Distribution.** Central and northern Europe. Widely distributed throughout the British Isles.

**Description.** Length up to 23 mm; body bluish-green with narrow whitish rings between segments; a broad cream-coloured stripe extends along each side below the line of the spiracles; anal points prominent, also cream-coloured; head greyish-green.

**Habitat.** Open woodland and wooded heaths.

**Foodplants.** Silver birch (*Betula pendula*), alder (*Alnus glutinosa*), goat willow (*Salix caprea*) and honeysuckle (*Lonicera periclymenum*).

**Biology.** One generation a year. Eggs are laid singly on twigs in May and the caterpillars feed from June to July or August. Pupation takes place in the autumn on or below the soil in a slight silken cocoon attached to a stone or root. Moths emerge in the following April.

**ACASIS VIRETATA** Hübner *Yellow-barred Brindle* **Pl. 23**

**Distribution.** Central Europe. Widespread but local throughout England, Wales and Ireland. Recorded from a few localities in southern Scotland.

**Description.** Length up to 17 mm; body pale green, sometimes tinged with pink; three broken pink lines along the back sometimes strongly expanded to form a series of purplish-pink wedge-shaped markings; head brown, sometimes marked with purplish-pink.

**Habitat.** Open woodland, hedgerows, wooded heaths and commons.

**Foodplants.** Holly (*Ilex aquifolium*), ivy (*Hedera helix*), privet (*Ligustrum*), dogwood (*Cornus sanguinea*), guelder rose (*Viburnum opulus*), rowan (*Sorbus aucuparia*) and other plants.

**Biology.** One generation a year, sometimes two. Eggs are laid in June and the caterpillars feed in June and July. The caterpillars feed at first on flowers and later on leaves, spinning silken threads across the blossom and foliage. Pupation takes place at the end of July in the soil. Moths usually emerge in May of the following year, but in warm regions emerge in August and September to produce second brood caterpillars which feed in the autumn.

**ABRAXAS GROSSULARIATA** Linnaeus *Magpie Moth* **Pl. 17**
**Distribution.** Widespread but local in continental Europe, most common in warmer central regions. Widespread throughout the British Isles but sporadic in appearance, sometimes very common in gardens.
**Description.** Length up to 32 mm; body pale yellowish-white marked extensively with black blotches which sometimes coalesce to produce an almost entirely black caterpillar; a broad orange-red line extends along the spiracles; segments 1–3 sometimes suffused with pale red; head shining black.
**Habitat.** Gardens, hedgerows and woodland margins.
**Foodplants.** Currants and gooseberry (*Ribes*), hawthorn (*Crataegus monogyna*), euonymus (*Euonymus japonicus*), blackthorn (*Prunus spinosa*), orpine (*Sedum telephium*), heather (*Calluna vulgaris*) and other plants.
**Biology.** One generation a year. Eggs are laid in batches on the undersides of leaves in August. The caterpillars feed from August to May although some do not hibernate but become fully grown and produce moths in the autumn. Pupation usually takes place in May in open-weave silken cocoons on the foodplant. Moths normally emerge in July. The caterpillars of this species are sometimes fruit pests.

**ABRAXAS SYLVATA** Scopoli *Clouded Magpie* **Pl. 7**
**Distribution.** Central Europe. Widely distributed in the British Isles but more common in Wales and western England.
**Description.** Length up to 29 mm; body creamy white with black longitudinal stripes, a broken band of pale yellow down the back and a continuous broad, pale yellow line along the spiracles; head and thoracic legs shining black.
**Habitat.** Damp woodland.
**Foodplants.** Wych elm (*Ulmus glabra*) and other *Ulmus* species; beech (*Fagus sylvatica*).
**Biology.** One generation a year. Eggs are laid in June and the caterpillars feed from July to September or October. Pupation takes place in the soil in the autumn and moths emerge in the following May.

**LOMASPILIS MARGINATA** Linnaeus *Clouded Border* **Pl. 2**
**Distribution.** Widespread in Europe. Widely distributed in the British Isles, except for northern Scotland.
**Description.** Length up to 21 mm; body bluish-green, becoming yellowish-green between segments; four dark green lines along the back and a brown plate on the last segment; dots black; spiracles black with white centres; head green with two broad bands of purplish-brown.
**Habitat.** Woodlands, fens and other damp places.
**Foodplants.** Various species of willows and sallows (*Salix*), aspen (*Populus tremula*), black poplar (*Populus nigra*) and hazel (*Corylus avellana*).
**Biology.** Apparently only one generation a year in Britain but two generations in parts of continental Europe. Eggs are laid in June and July and caterpillars may be

found from June until September. It is possible that some of these feed up rapidly to produce a second generation. They feed by night, hiding during the day on the undersides of leaves. Pupation takes place in the soil in autumn and moths normally emerge in the following May or June, although some may remain in the pupa state for 2–3 years.

## SEMIOTHISA NOTATA Linnaeus *Peacock Moth* Pl. 4

**Distribution.** Central and northern Europe. Widespread but very local in southern England. Recorded in the past from Wales and Scotland; rare in Ireland.
**Description.** Length up to 24 mm; body olive-green with brown markings on the back and sides, or brown with dark markings along the back and green below the spiracles; head usually dark brown, sometimes green.
**Habitat.** Heath-carpeted woodland.
**Foodplants.** Silver birch (*Betula pendula*), goat willow (*Salix caprea*) and grey willow (*S. cinerea*).
**Biology.** Two generations a year. Eggs are laid in June and the caterpillars feed up rapidly to pupate and produce moths in July and August. Second brood eggs are laid in August and the caterpillars feed up in September, pupating in October to produce moths in the following May and June. Pupation takes place in the soil.

## SEMIOTHISA ALTERNARIA Hübner *Sharp-angled Peacock* Pl. 18

**Distribution.** Widespread throughout Europe. Occurs locally in Britain but most frequently in southern England.
**Description.** Length up to 24 mm; very variable in coloration, ranging from yellowish-green to brown or grey; grey and brown forms have fine, irregular dark lines along the back and sides; green forms variably marked with reddish-brown blotches on the back and sides; head brown.
**Habitat.** Open woodland.
**Foodplants.** Blackthorn (*Prunus spinosa*), alder (*Alnus glutinosa*) and goat willow (*Salix caprea*).
**Biology.** Two generations a year. Eggs are laid in May and the resulting caterpillars feed up rapidly in June to pupate and produce moths in July. Second brood caterpillars feed in August and September and pupate in October. Pupation takes place in the soil. Moths emerge in May of the following year.

## SEMIOTHISA CLATHRATA Linnaeus *Latticed Heath* Pl. 21

**Distribution.** Widespread and common in Europe. Occurs throughout the British Isles but most common in southern and eastern England.
**Description.** Length up to 22 mm; body green with white lines on the back and a broad white line along the small black spiracles; underside with fine, dark longitudinal lines; head slightly notched, green with brown mouthparts.
**Habitat.** Fields, heathland and downland.
**Foodplants.** Clover (*Trifolium*), black medick (*Medicago lupulina*) and related plants.
**Biology.** Two generations a year. Eggs are laid in May and the caterpillars feed up rapidly in the following month to produce moths in July. The second generation eggs produce caterpillars in August, and these feed up and pupate in the soil in the autumn. Moths emerge in the following April or May.

**SEMIOTHISA CARBONARIA** Clerck *Netted Mountain Carpet* **Pl. 25**

**Distribution.** Central and northern Europe. In the British Isles, confined to highland Scotland.

**Description.** Length up to 22 mm; body dingy ochreous-brown or brownish-white with dark, wavy, longitudinal stripes; spiracles black with white centres; head brown.

**Habitat.** Mountainsides.

**Foodplants.** Alpine bearberry (*Arctostaphylos uva-ursi*), silver birch (*Betula pendula*) and sallow (*Salix*).

**Biology.** One generation a year. Eggs are laid in May and the caterpillars may be found from June to August. They feed at night, hiding under leaves by day. Pupation takes place among dead leaves on the ground in August or September and moths emerge in April of the following year.

**SEMIOTHISA WAUARIA** Linnaeus *V-moth* **Pl. 22**

**Distribution.** Widespread and common in Europe. Widely distributed in England, Wales and Scotland but very local in Ireland.

**Description.** Length up to 25 mm; body green or brown with prominent black spots; four white or yellowish-white wavy lines along the back and a broad band of yellow along the line of the black spiracles; head green or brown with black dots.

**Habitat.** Gardens and orchards.

**Foodplants.** Redcurrant (*Ribes rubrum*), blackcurrant (*R. nigrum*) and gooseberry (*R. uva-crispa*).

**Biology.** One generation a year. Eggs are laid in August but do not hatch until the following April. The caterpillars may be found from April until June. They feed at night on young shoots, hiding under the foliage by day. When fully grown at the end of June they pupate in open network cocoons spun amongst the foliage. Moths emerge in July.

**ISTURGIA LIMBARIA** Fabricius *Frosted Yellow* **Pl. 19**

**Distribution.** Central Europe. Very local in eastern England.

**Description.** Length up to 24 mm; body green or brown with a dark line down the middle of the back, flanked by pale lines and a black-edged yellow line along the spiracles; head green or brown.

**Foodplant.** Broom (*Cytisus scoparius*).

**Biology.** Two generations a year. Eggs are laid in June, and the resulting caterpillars feed up rapidly in June and July to pupate and produce moths in July and August. Second brood caterpillars feed in September and pupate in October, producing moths in the following May and June. Some remain in the pupa state for up to four years. Pupation takes place in the soil.

**PLAGODIS DOLABRARIA** Linnaeus *Scorched Wing* **Pl. 2**

**Distribution.** Widespread in Europe. Widely distributed throughout the British Isles but less common in the north.

**Description.** Length up to 40 mm; body dark greyish-brown, suffused with reddish-brown on the back and with reddish-brown triangular markings low down on the sides; front segments are swollen and body segment 8 has a prominent hump; head pale brown with dark brown markings.

**Habitat.** Woods and woodland margins.

**Foodplants.** Oak (*Quercus*), silver birch (*Betula pendula*) and sallow (*Salix*).

**Biology.** One generation a year. Eggs are laid in June and the caterpillars feed from July until October. They are very well camouflaged and resemble twigs when at rest. Pupation takes place at the foot of the tree under moss in October but moths do not emerge until the following June.

**OPISTHOGRAPTIS LUTEOLATA** Linnaeus *Brimstone Moth* **Pl. 17**

**Distribution.** Widespread and common in Europe. Widely distributed and often common in the British Isles.

**Description.** Length up to 33 mm; body greyish-brown to reddish-brown, sometimes greenish, mottled with various shades of green and brown; sixth body segment with a prominent, double-pointed hump; head brown. Unlike most geometrid caterpillars, this species has two extra pairs of small prolegs on the abdomen.

**Habitat.** Woodland, hedgerows, parks and gardens.

**Foodplants.** Hawthorn (*Crataegus monogyna*), blackthorn (*Prunus spinosa*), apple (*Malus*) and other related trees.

**Biology.** Two generations a year. Moths may be found in any month from April to August, and so eggs are laid throughout the spring and summer. First generation caterpillars feed in the spring, pupating in June and July to produce moths in midsummer. Second generation caterpillars pupate in the autumn. Pupation takes place in a thick silken cocoon constructed on or near the ground.

**EPIONE REPANDARIA** Hufnagel *Bordered Beauty* **Pl. 2**

**Distribution.** Widespread in central and southern Europe. Widely distributed throughout the British Isles.

**Description.** Length up to 28 mm; body brown or grey with pale ochreous triangular patches and paired white spots along the back; a broad, pale ochreous band below the spiracles on either side; segment 5 has a small, double pointed hump on the back; head greyish-brown above, ochreous below.

**Habitat.** Woodland and woodland margins.

**Foodplants.** Willow and sallow (*Salix*), alder (*Alnus glutinosa*) and black poplar (*Populus nigra*).

**Biology.** Usually one generation a year in Britain but two generations in parts of continental Europe. Eggs are laid on the foodplant in July and August but do not hatch until the following spring. The caterpillars feed from April to June and when fully grown pupate to produce moths in July.

**APEIRA SYRINGARIA** Linnaeus *Lilac Beauty* **Pl. 26**

**Distribution.** Widespread in Europe. Widely distributed in the British Isles, particularly in southern England and Wales, but absent from Scotland.

**Description.** Length up to 30 mm; body stout, tapered strongly towards the head and tail, with a distinctive pair of curved projections on the back of segment 8 and smaller paired humps on segments 6 and 7; pale ochre marked with dark olive-brown or purplish-brown; head greyish-brown.

**Habitat.** Hedgerows and woodland margins.

**Foodplants.** Privet (*Ligustrum vulgare*), honeysuckle (*Lonicera periclymenum*) and lilac (*Syringa vulgaris*).

**Biology.** One generation a year in Britain but sometimes a second brood in captivity. Eggs are laid in July and hatch in August, the young caterpillars going into hibernation and completing their development in the following May and June. They feed at night, remaining on the foodplant by day when they resemble dead leaves. Pupation takes place in flimsy cocoons attached to twigs in June and moths emerge in July.

**ENNOMOS AUTUMNARIA** Werneberg *Large Thorn* **Pl. 4**

**Distribution.** Widespread throughout Europe. Very local in England, recorded once from Ireland.

**Description.** Length up to 55 mm; very slender, tapering towards head; brown or greenish-brown patterned with ochreous-brown, glossy; body segments 5, 6 and 8 have swellings, giving a twig-like appearance; head rather square in outline, greyish-brown marked with ochre.

**Habitat.** Woodlands.

**Foodplants.** Silver birch (*Betula pendula*), alder (*Alnus glutinosa*), blackthorn (*Prunus spinosa*), hawthorn (*Crataegus monogyna*) and other deciduous trees and shrubs.

**Biology.** One generation a year. Eggs are laid in the autumn but do not hatch until the following spring. Caterpillars may be found from May to August, feeding on the foliage at night and stretched out stiffly among twigs by day. Pupation takes place between leaves in August and moths emerge in the following month.

**ENNOMOS QUERCINARIA** Hufnagel *August Thorn* **Pl. 6**

**Distribution.** Common in central Europe. Widespread in England, particularly in the south, and recorded from parts of Wales and Scotland; widely distributed in Ireland.

**Description.** Length up to 47 mm; body varying in colour from brown to green with ochreous and blackish markings along the back and sides; body segments 5, 6, 8 and 11 with humps or swellings, giving the appearance of a twig; head greenish or greyish-brown, sometimes marked with ochre.

**Habitat.** Woodland.

**Foodplants.** Oak (*Quercus*), lime (*Tilia vulgaris*), silver birch (*Betula pendula*), hawthorn (*Crataegus monogyna*) and other deciduous trees and shrubs.

**Biology.** One generation a year. Eggs are laid in rows on the undersides of leaves in the autumn but do not hatch until the following spring. Caterpillars may be found in the summer months, feeding at night and resting among twigs by day. Pupation takes place in cocoons spun between leaves in July and moths emerge in the following month.

**ENNOMOS ALNIARIA** Linnaeus *Canary-shouldered Thorn* **Pl. 5**

**Distribution.** Widespread in Europe. Widely distributed throughout the British Isles.

**Description.** Length up to 50 mm; fairly slender, tapering towards the head; body reddish-brown marked with dark purplish-brown on the back and sides and sometimes tinged with green below; body segment 5 has a distinct raised swelling on the back; head brown.

**Habitat.** Marshy places and damp woodland margins.

**Foodplants.** Silver birch (*Betula pendula*), alder (*Alnus glutinosa*), sallow (*Salix*), elm (*Ulmus procera*), lime (*Tilia*) and other deciduous trees.

**Biology.** One generation a year. Eggs are laid in the autumn but do not hatch until the following May. Caterpillars may be found from May to July, feeding at night but remaining on the foodplant by day, when they resemble twigs. Pupation takes place towards the end of July in cocoons among foliage or under moss at the base of the tree. Moths emerge in the autumn.

**ENNOMOS FUSCANTARIA** Haworth *Dusky Thorn* **Pl. 8**

**Distribution.** Central Europe and southern parts of northern Europe. In the British Isles, most widely distributed in southern England but also recorded from south Wales and parts of central and northern England.

**Description.** Length up to 40 mm; slender, yellowish-green with yellowish rings between the segments; sometimes marked on the back and sides with reddish-brown; body segments 5, 6, 8 and 11 have slight projections on the back. Young caterpillars are a much darker green.

**Habitat.** Woodlands, hedgerows and other places where the foodplant grows.

**Foodplants.** Ash (*Fraxinus excelsior*). Also feeds on privet (*Ligustrum*) in captivity.

**Biology.** One generation a year. Eggs are laid close together near the tips of the twigs in the autumn but do not hatch until the following spring. The caterpillars feed at night from May to July, often eating circular holes in the leaves. They remain stretched out stiffly on the stalks by day. Pupation takes place in late summer between spun and twisted leaves. Moths emerge in August and September.

**ENNOMOS EROSARIA** Denis & Schiffermüller *September Thorn* **Pl. 8**

**Distribution.** Widespread throughout Europe. Widely distributed in southern England and Wales, becoming more scarce further north. Recorded from southern Scotland and as a rarity in Ireland.

**Description.** Length up to 40 mm; body grey or greyish-brown, sometimes tinged with purplish-pink or bluish-green; brown, bud-like swellings on body segments 2, 5, 6, 8 and 11 give a twig-like appearance; head grey or brown.

**Habitat.** Woodlands and hedgerows.

**Foodplants.** Oak (*Quercus*), silver birch (*Betula pendula*), lime (*Tilia vulgaris*) and beech (*Fagus sylvatica*).

**Biology.** One generation a year. Eggs are laid in the autumn but do not hatch until May of the following year. Caterpillars can be found from May to July. They feed at night, remaining stretched out on twigs of the foodplant by day. Pupation takes place in early August in an open web spun among the foliage, and moths emerge towards the end of the month.

**SELENIA DENTARIA** Fabricius *Early Thorn* **Pl. 4**

**Distribution.** Widespread throughout Europe. Widely distributed in the British Isles but most common in southern England.

**Description.** Length up to 38 mm; body yellowish-brown to brown, variably marked with reddish-brown and dark purplish-brown; third pair of thoracic legs swollen, resembling buds of a twig; body segments 7 and 8 swollen, with paired conical warts on the back; head brown or greyish-brown marked with white.

**Habitat.** Woodland margins and hedgerows.

**Foodplants.** Silver birch (*Betula pendula*), alder (*Alnus glutinosa*), blackthorn (*Prunus spinosa*), hawthorn (*Crataegus monogyna*), sallow (*Salix*) and many other deciduous trees and shrubs.

**Biology.** Two generations a year; one generation in Scotland. Eggs are laid in April and July and caterpillars can be found from May to June and August to September. They feed mainly at night, remaining on the foodplant by day where they resemble short twigs. Pupation takes place in June and October between spun leaves, pupae of the second generation remaining among leaf litter on the ground until the following spring. Moths are on the wing from March to April and July to August.

**SELENIA LUNULARIA** Hübner *Lunar Thorn* **Pl. 18**

**Distribution.** Widespread in Europe. Locally distributed throughout the British Isles.

**Description.** Length up to 38 mm; body varying in colour from dark greyish-brown to greenish-brown or light reddish-brown; third pair of thoracic legs swollen and bud-like; body segments 5 and 8 with paired, wart-like projections on the back; head black or brown, rather square and flattened in appearance.

**Habitat.** Hedgerows and woodland margins.

**Foodplants.** Blackthorn (*Prunus spinosa*), wild plum (*P. domestica*), oak (*Quercus*), silver birch (*Betula pendula*), ash (*Fraxinus excelsior*), dog rose (*Rosa canina*) and other deciduous trees and shrubs.

**Biology.** One generation a year. Eggs are laid in June and caterpillars may be found from July to September. They feed mainly at night, resting among twigs by day, when they are well camouflaged. Pupation takes place in October in flimsy silken cocoons spun between dead leaves or under moss, but moths do not emerge until May of the following year.

**SELENIA TETRALUNARIA** Hufnagel *Purple Thorn* **Pl. 5**

**Distribution.** Widespread throughout Europe. Occurs locally in many parts of the British Isles, particularly in southern England, but not known in Ireland.

**Description.** Length up to 38 mm; body varying in colour from dark greyish-brown to light reddish-brown; third pair of thoracic legs swollen like the buds of a twig; body segments 4, 5, 7 and 8 swollen; head brown or blackish-brown.

**Habitat.** Woodland and wooded heaths.

**Foodplants.** Silver birch (*Betula pendula*), alder (*Alnus glutinosa*), oak (*Quercus*), sallow (*Salix*) and many other deciduous trees.

**Biology.** Two generations a year. Eggs are laid in May and August and caterpillars may be found in June and September. They feed mainly at night, resting among twigs by day. Pupation takes place between folded leaves or under moss on the ground in July and at the end of September. First generation pupae hatch in July but those of the second generation remain among leaf litter through the winter, producing moths in the following spring.

**ODONTOPERA BIDENTATA** Clerck *Scalloped Hazel* **Pl. 18**

**Distribution.** Widespread and common in Europe. Widely distributed throughout the British Isles.

**Description.** Length up to 48 mm; body varying in colour from pale greyish-brown to purplish-brown or greyish-green, with a series of dark, lozenge-shaped markings and two rows of black spots along the back; body segment 11 has a slight, black-edged hump on the back; head pale brown or green marked with blackish-brown, slightly notched.

**Habitat.** Woodland and hedgerows.

**Foodplants.** Oak (*Quercus*), silver birch (*Betula pendula*), wild plum (*Prunus domestica*), blackthorn (*P. spinosa*), hawthorn (*Crataegus monogyna*) and other deciduous trees and shrubs.

**Biology.** One generation a year. Eggs are laid close together, usually around a twig of the foodplant, in June. The caterpillars grow very slowly and may be found from

July to October. They feed at night, resting by day on the foodplant. In the autumn fully grown caterpillars descend to the ground and pupate under moss or leaf litter at the foot of the tree. Moths emerge in the following May.

**CROCALLIS ELINGUARIA** Linnaeus *Scalloped Oak* **Pl. 18**

**Distribution.** Widespread throughout Europe. Widely distributed in the British Isles.

**Description.** Length up to 43 mm; body varying in colour from pale greyish-brown to reddish-brown or dark purplish-brown, sometimes with a series of dark, diamond-shaped markings along the back; body segment 11 has a slight, black-edged hump on the back; head pale or dark brown.

**Habitat.** Hedgerows, commonland, moorland.

**Foodplants.** Blackthorn (*Prunus spinosa*), wild plum (*P. domestica*), wild apple (*Malus sylvestris*), honeysuckle (*Lonicera periclymenum*) and many other deciduous trees and shrubs.

**Biology.** One generation a year. Eggs are laid in August but do not hatch until early spring of the following year. Caterpillars may be found from March to May. They feed at night, resting on the foodplant by day. Greyish-green forms are most commonly found in lichen-encrusted trees, where they are well camouflaged. Pupation takes place in June between leaves or under moss on the ground. Moths emerge in the following month.

**OURAPTERYX SAMBUCARIA** Linnaeus *Swallow-tailed Moth* **Pl. 23**

**Distribution.** Common and widespread in lowland Europe. Widespread throughout the British Isles.

**Description.** Length up to 50 mm; long and slender, tapering towards the head; body varying in colour from yellowish-brown to reddish-brown or olive-green with indistinct pale stripes along the sides; head brown, rectangular and flattened.

**Habitat.** Woodland and hedgerows.

**Foodplants.** Hawthorn (*Crataegus monogyna*), blackthorn (*Prunus spinosa*), elder (*Sambucus nigra*), privet (*Ligustrum*), ivy (*Hedera helix*) and many other trees and shrubs.

**Biology.** One generation a year. Eggs are laid in batches on the undersides of leaves in July and caterpillars hatch in the following month. After feeding in the summer, the caterpillars hibernate on the foodplant, often in crevices of bark, becoming active again in the spring. They rest by day with their bodies held straight and rigid at an angle to the twig and are very difficult to detect. They are fully grown by the beginning of June and pupate in cocoons of silk mixed with leaf fragments, suspended from the undersides of twigs. Moths emerge in July.

**COLOTOIS PENNARIA** Hübner *Feathered Thorn* **Pl. 2**

**Distribution.** Widespread and common throughout Europe. Widely distributed in the British Isles but most common in southern England and Wales.

**Description.** Length up to 50 mm; body grey, sometimes tinged with purple, with a series of ochreous or yellow markings along the back and sides; segment 12 with a pair of conical warts on the back; head reddish-brown with paler markings.

**Habitat.** Woodland.

**Foodplants.** Oak (*Quercus*), silver birch (*Betula pendula*), sallow (*Salix*), blackthorn (*Prunus spinosa*), hawthorn (*Crataegus monogyna*), poplar (*Populus*) and many other deciduous trees and shrubs.

**Biology.** One generation a year. Eggs are laid on twigs in November but do not hatch until the following spring. Caterpillars may be found from April to June. They feed mainly at night, remaining on the foodplant by day. In June the caterpillars descend to the ground to pupate beneath the soil. Moths emerge in October.

**ANGERONA PRUNARIA** Linnaeus *Orange Moth* **Pl. 18**

**Distribution.** Widespread throughout temperate Europe. Widely distributed in England but most common in the south. Occurs locally in southern and western Ireland.

**Description.** Length up to 50 mm; body varying in colour from pale yellowish-brown to greyish-brown or reddish-brown, sometimes with a series of blackish lines and dots along the back and sides; body segment 5 with a pair of small humps on the back; segment 9 with a prominent pair of long, pointed projections on the back; head brown.

**Habitat.** Woodland and hedgerows.

**Foodplants.** Blackthorn (*Prunus spinosa*), wild plum (*P. domestica*), hawthorn (*Crataegus monogyna*), silver birch (*Betula pendula*), traveller's joy (*Clematis vitalba*), broom (*Cytisus scoparius*) and many other trees and shrubs.

**Biology.** One generation a year. Eggs are laid in July and caterpillars hatch in August. They feed until September or October when they go into hibernation before completing their growth in the following spring. They are fully grown by May or June, when they pupate between spun leaves of the foodplant. Moths emerge in June or July.

**APOCHEIMA PILOSARIA** Denis & Schiffermüller **Pl. 18**
*Pale Brindled Beauty*

**Distribution.** Widespread and common in temperate Europe. Widely distributed throughout the British Isles but scarce in Ireland.

**Description.** Length up to 38 mm; stout, tapering towards the head; body greyish-brown or greenish-brown marked with reddish-brown; back and sides with small conical warts from which arise the body hairs, these warts being most prominent on segments 5, 6, 7 and 12; head greyish or greenish-brown.

**Habitat.** Woodland and hedgerows.

**Foodplants.** Blackthorn (*Prunus spinosa*), wild plum (*P. domestica*), hawthorn (*Crataegus monogyna*), silver birch (*Betula pendula*), oak (*Quercus*), lime (*Tilia vulgaris*), elm (*Ulmus procera*), sallow (*Salix*), poplar (*Populus*) and many other deciduous trees and shrubs.

**Biology.** One generation a year. Eggs are laid in March and caterpillars may be found from April to June. They feed at first on unopened leaf buds and later on the foliage. They are mainly active at night, resting on twigs of the foodplant by day. When fully grown at the end of June, they descend to the foot of the tree and pupate beneath the soil. Moths do not usually emerge until January or February of the following year. The females are wingless.

**APOCHEIMA ALPINA** Sulzer **Pl. 28**

**Distribution.** Occurs in the Alps but is apparently absent from other parts of Europe.

**Description.** Length up to 40 mm; body yellowish-white, strongly dotted and streaked with black; a broad yellow line runs along the middle of the back and a stripe of bright yellow extends along each side below the level of the spiracles; head yellow, spotted with black.

**Habitat.** Mountainsides.

**Foodplants.** Clover (*Trifolium*), daisy (*Bellis perennis*), yarrow (*Achillea millefolium*) and other plants.

**Biology.** One generation a year. Caterpillars feed from June to July. The pupae overwinter for one or two years before producing moths in March or April.

**LYCIA HIRTARIA** Clerck *Brindled Beauty* **Pl. 7**

**Distribution.** Widespread throughout temperate Europe. Widely distributed in the British Isles but most common in southern England.

**Description.** Length up to 55 mm; body reddish-brown, purplish-grey or greenish-grey, finely lined and speckled with black and spotted with yellow; first segment of body with a strong yellow band behind the head; head pale reddish-brown, freckled with black.

**Habitat.** Woodland, hedgerows, parks and roadside trees.

**Foodplants.** Lime (*Tilia vulgaris*), elm (*Ulmus procera*), willow (*Salix*), apple (*Malus domestica*), plum (*Prunus domestica*), pear (*Pyrus communis*) and almost any other deciduous tree or shrub.

**Biology.** One generation a year. Eggs are laid in April and caterpillars can be found from May to July. They feed at night, resting on twigs or branches of the foodplant by day. When fully grown at the end of July, they descend to the ground to pupate in the soil. Moths emerge in the following spring.

**BISTON STRATARIA** Hufnagel *Oak Beauty* **Pl. 6**

**Distribution.** Widespread but local in central and southern Europe. Widely distributed in England and Wales and recorded locally in Scotland. Widespread but scarce in Ireland.

**Description.** Length up to 55 mm; body varying in colour from greyish-brown to purplish-brown with two reddish-brown humps on the back and three smaller humps on the underside; sometimes a series of dark, diamond-shaped markings along the back; head reddish-brown, strongly notched.

**Habitat.** Woodland.

**Foodplants.** Oak (*Quercus*), silver birch (*Betula pendula*), elm (*Ulmus procera*), blackthorn (*Prunus spinosa*), rose (*Rosa*), and many other deciduous trees and shrubs.

**Biology.** One generation a year. Eggs are laid in April and caterpillars can be found from May to July. They feed at night, remaining on a branch or twig of the foodplant by day. When fully grown at the end of July, they descend to the ground and pupate beneath the soil. Moths do not emerge until February or March of the following year.

**BISTON BETULARIA** Linnaeus *Peppered Moth* **Pl. 6**

**Distribution.** Widespread in Europe. Widely distributed throughout the British Isles and sometimes common.

**Description.** Length up to 60 mm; body purplish-brown, brownish-green or green with a purplish line along the back; body segment 8 with a pair of prominent knob-like swellings; head brown, deeply notched.

**Habitat.** Woodland and hedgerows.

**Foodplants.** Oak (*Quercus*), silver birch (*Betula pendula*), elm (*Ulmus procera*), beech (*Fagus sylvatica*), sallow (*Salix*), wild plum (*Prunus domestica*) and many other deciduous trees and shrubs.

**Biology.** One generation a year. Eggs are laid in June and caterpillars may be found from July to September. They feed at night but remain on the foodplant by day, where they are well camouflaged. When fully grown in the autumn they descend to the ground and pupate in the soil at the foot of the tree. Moths do not emerge until May of the following year.

## AGRIOPIS AURANTIARIA Hübner *Scarce Umber* Pl. 4

**Distribution.** Widespread in Europe. Widely distributed and sometimes common in England and Wales but rare in Scotland and Ireland.

**Description.** Length up to 30 mm; body yellowish- or reddish-brown, strongly patterned with fine purplish-brown lines and often with a broad, dark brown band along either side; underside dark purplish-brown with yellow stripes; head reddish-brown.

**Habitat.** Woodland.

**Foodplants.** Silver birch (*Betula pendula*), hornbeam (*Carpinus betulus*), oak (*Quercus*), hawthorn (*Crataegus monogyna*), blackthorn (*Prunus spinosa*) and other trees and shrubs.

**Biology.** One generation a year. Eggs are laid in November but do not hatch until the following spring. Caterpillars may be found from April to June. They feed mainly at night but remain on the foliage by day. They descend to the ground when fully grown at the end of June and pupate in frail silken cocoons among leaf litter. Moths emerge in October.

## AGRIOPIS MARGINARIA Fabricius *Dotted Border* Pl. 5

**Distribution.** Widespread in Europe. Widely distributed and often common throughout the British Isles with the exception of northern Scotland.

**Description.** Length up to 29 mm; body very variable in colour, ranging from dull yellow to olive-green, reddish-brown or purplish-brown, with blackish markings along the back, sometimes forming a series of X-shapes; sometimes with a dark stripe above the white spiracles; head brown.

**Habitat.** Woodland and hedgerows.

**Foodplants.** Blackthorn (*Prunus spinosa*), hawthorn (*Crataegus monogyna*), oak (*Quercus*), silver birch (*Betula pendula*), hornbeam (*Carpinus betulus*), sallow (*Salix*) and other deciduous trees and shrubs.

**Biology.** One generation a year. Eggs are laid in April and the caterpillars feed from April until June. Fully grown caterpillars descend to the ground in June and pupate just below the surface of the soil at the foot of the tree. Moths do not emerge until February or March of the following year.

## ERANNIS DEFOLIARIA Clerck *Mottled Umber* Pl. 5

**Distribution.** Widespread throughout Europe. Widely distributed and often common throughout the British Isles although less common in northern Scotland.

**Description.** Length up to 32 mm; body reddish- or yellowish-brown with a black line above the spiracles; below this line, the body is yellow or ochreous, sometimes with patches of reddish-brown around the spiracles; head reddish-brown, notched.

**Habitat.** Woodland and hedgerows.

**Foodplants.** Oak (*Quercus*), silver birch (*Betula pendula*), hazel (*Corylus avellana*), blackthorn (*Prunus spinosa*), hawthorn (*Crataegus monogyna*), rose (*Rosa*), honey-

suckle (*Lonicera perclymenum*) and many other deciduous trees and shrubs.
**Biology.** One generation a year. Eggs are laid in the winter and caterpillars may be found from March to June, although the most usual months are April and May. When a caterpillar is disturbed, it drops from the leaf and remains suspended from a silken thread until the danger is past. In June, the fully grown caterpillars descend to the ground where they pupate. Moths emerge in late autumn and early winter.

**MENOPHRA ABRUPTARIA** Thunberg *Waved Umber* **Pl. 26**
**Distribution.** Widespread in central and southern Europe. Widely distributed in England and Wales but more common in the south. Rare in Scotland and Ireland.
**Description.** Length up to 40 mm; body greyish-brown, sometimes suffused with green or almost black, with pinkish or purplish-brown blotches and dark lines and bands along the back; also with three small, black-edged humps on the back; head greyish-brown, deeply notched.
**Habitat.** Hedgerows, gardens, parks and roadsides.
**Foodplants.** Privet (*Ligustrum*), lilac (*Syringa vulgaris*) and redcurrant (*Ribes rubrum*).
**Biology.** One generation a year. Eggs are laid in May and caterpillars may be found feeding from May to August. Pupation takes place in August in silken cocoons spun on twigs of the foodplant. Moths emerge in April of the following year.

**PERIBATODES RHOMBOIDARIA** Denis & Schiffermüller **Pl. 17**
*Willow Beauty*
**Distribution.** Widespread in Europe. Widely distributed throughout the British Isles.
**Description.** Length up to 40 mm; body varying in colour from greyish-brown to reddish-brown, sometimes mottled with yellowish-brown and with dark markings on the back, sometimes forming a series of diamond-shapes; head brown.
**Habitat.** Woodland and hedgerows.
**Foodplants.** Hawthorn (*Crataegus monogyna*), silver birch (*Betula pendula*), ivy (*Hedera helix*), privet (*Ligustrum*), lilac (*Syringa vulgaris*) and many other trees and shrubs.
**Biology.** One generation a year; occasionally a second brood of moths in September. Eggs are laid in August and caterpillars hatch in the early autumn, feeding for a time before going into hibernation. In the following spring they recommence feeding and become fully grown towards the end of May. Pupation takes place in June in silken cocoons attached to twigs of the foodplant. Moths emerge in July.

**ALCIS REPANDATA** Linnaeus *Mottled Beauty* **Pl. 7**
**Distribution.** Widespread throughout Europe except for the extreme south. Widely distributed and often common in the British Isles.
**Description.** Length up to 40 mm; very variable in colour, ranging from pale greyish-brown to yellowish-brown, dark reddish-brown or blackish-brown; pale forms have a dark brown line down the back and a series of diamond-shaped markings and black dots; head brown.
**Habitat.** Woodland, hedgerows, heaths and moorland.
**Foodplants.** Silver birch (*Betula pendula*), elm (*Ulmus procera*), hazel (*Corylus avellana*), hawthorn (*Crataegus monogyna*), bilberry (*Vaccinium myrtillus*), heather (*Calluna vulgaris*) and a wide range of other trees and shrubs.
**Biology.** One generation a year; occasionally a second brood of moths in September.

Eggs are laid in July and caterpillars hatch in the same month. They feed during the summer months but then go into hibernation before completing their growth in the following spring. When fully grown in May, they descend to the ground and pupate in the soil. Moths emerge in June.

HYPOMECIS ROBORARIA Denis & Schiffermuller *Great Oak Beauty* **Pl. 6**

**Distribution.** Widespread throughout Europe except for the extreme south. Locally distributed in England but most common in the New Forest in Hampshire. Absent from other parts of the British Isles.

**Description.** Length up to 50 mm; rather stout; body reddish-brown, sometimes marked with ochreous-brown; body segments 5 and 11 with greyish humps on the back; segment 6 with a swelling on the underside; head brown, notched.

**Habitat.** Woodland.

**Foodplants.** Oak (*Quercus*) and occasionally silver birch (*Betula pendula*). In continental Europe, this species may also feed on other deciduous trees.

**Biology.** One generation a year. Eggs are laid in July and caterpillars hatch in late summer. They feed in the autumn and then hibernate before completing their development in the following spring. When at rest on branches of the foodplant, they strongly resemble small twigs. They are fully grown by the end of May and descend to the ground where they pupate in slight silken cocoons just beneath the surface of the soil at the foot of the tree. Moths emerge in the following month.

**SERRACA PUNCTINALIS** Scopoli *Pale Oak Beauty* **Pl. 6**

**Distribution.** Widespread in central and southern Europe. In the British Isles, mainly confined to southern England although this species also occurs locally in southern Ireland.

**Description.** Length up to 45 mm; body varying in colour from brown to greenish-grey, often marked with reddish-brown; body segment 5 swollen, with a pair of wart-like projections on the back; head brown or greenish-grey, slightly notched.

**Habitat.** Woodland.

**Foodplants.** Oak (*Quercus*), silver birch (*Betula pendula*), and occasionally sallow (*Salix*). In continental Europe this species feeds on a wide range of deciduous trees and shrubs.

**Biology.** One generation a year; moths occurring occasionally in September may be of a second brood. Eggs are laid in June and caterpillars may be found in July and August. At the end of August, the fully grown caterpillars descend to the ground and pupate just below the surface of the soil. Moths do not emerge until June of the following year.

**CLEORODES LICHENARIA** Hufnagel *Brussels Lace* **Pl. 32**

**Distribution.** Occurs locally in central and southern Europe. Widely distributed in England, becoming less common towards the north. Occurs in parts of Wales and southern Scotland and is widespread and locally common in Ireland.

**Description.** Length up to 25 mm; body green or greyish-green, occasionally yellowish, mottled with black, with small, paired warts along the back; head pale reddish-brown.

**Habitat.** Damp woodland, hedgerows and roadsides.

**Foodplants.** Lichens growing on tree trunks, branches, wooden fences and posts.

**Biology.** One generation a year. Eggs are laid in July and caterpillars hatch in the following month. They feed in late summer and hibernate before completing their development in the following spring. Caterpillars are most frequently found in May and June when almost fully grown but they are extremely well camouflaged and difficult to detect. Pupation takes place in June in cocoons concealed among mosses and lichens. Moths emerge in the following month.

**EMATURGA ATOMARIA** Linnaeus *Common Heath* **Pl. 24**

**Distribution.** Widespread in Europe. Widely distributed throughout the British Isles.

**Description.** Length up to 30 mm; body very variable in colour, ranging from green to greyish-brown, ochreous or purplish-brown, often with pale, diamond-shaped markings and white spots along the back and with broken blackish lines along the sides; head brown or greenish, freckled with reddish-brown.

**Habitat.** Heaths and moorland.

**Foodplants.** Heather (*Calluna vulgaris*), bell heather (*Erica cinerea*), cross-leaved heath (*E. tetralix*), bog myrtle (*Myrica gale*) and other low-growing plants in similar habitats.

**Biology.** One generation a year. Eggs are laid in June, and caterpillars may be found feeding on foliage from July to September. Pupation takes place in the earth in Autumn but moths do not emerge until May of the following year.

**BUPALUS PINIARIA** Linnaeus *Bordered White* **Pl. 1**

**Distribution.** Widespread and common throughout Europe except for the extreme north. Widely distributed and often common in England, Wales and Scotland, but local in Ireland.

**Description.** Length up to 30 mm; body bright green with a broad, black-edged white line along the back and a yellow line bordered with dark green along each side; head green.

**Habitat.** Coniferous woodland.

**Foodplants.** Scots pine (*Pinus sylvestris*), Norway spruce (*Picea abies*), silver fir (*Abies alba*), European larch (*Larix decidua*) and other coniferous trees.

**Biology.** One generation a year. Eggs are laid in rows on the needles in June and caterpillars feed from July to September. They are often serious forest pests and are known as 'pine loopers'. Fully grown caterpillars descend to the ground in the autumn and pupate beneath the soil. Moths do not emerge until May or June of the following year.

**LOMOGRAPHA TEMERATA** Denis & Schiffermüller **Pl. 18**
*Clouded Silver*

**Distribution.** Widespread throughout Europe. Widely distributed in England and Wales but most common in the south. Rare in Scotland and locally common in Ireland.

**Description.** Length up to 26 mm; body bluish-green above, whitish-green below, usually with a row of brown-bordered reddish spots along the back, although these are sometimes replaced by a broken reddish-brown line with white spots on either side; head green with two reddish-brown spots.

**Habitat.** Hedgerows.

**Foodplants.** Blackthorn (*Prunus spinosa*), wild plum (*P. domestica*) and bird cherry (*P. padus*). In continental Europe, this species feeds on a wide range of deciduous trees and shrubs.

**Biology.** One generation a year. Eggs are laid in crevices of the bark or on twigs near leaf axils in May and June. Caterpillars hatch after about a fortnight and may be found feeding until August or September. Pupation takes place in slight cocoons spun beneath the soil in the autumn but moths do not emerge until the following spring.

**ALEUCIS DISTINCTATA** Herrich-Schaffer *Sloe Carpet* **Pl. 18**
**Distribution.** Occurs in western Europe. Locally common in parts of southern England but not known in other regions of the British Isles.
**Description.** Length up to 25 mm; body green or dark greyish-brown with blackish V-shaped markings along the back and conspicuous patches of white or green on body segments 7 and 8; head green or brown.
**Habitat.** Hillsides, heaths and hedgerows.
**Foodplant.** Blackthorn (*Prunus spinosa*).
**Biology.** One generation a year. Eggs are laid in August and caterpillars can be found from May to July. They feed at night and remain on the foodplant by day. When fully grown at the end of July, they descend to the ground and pupate in the soil. Moths do not emerge until the following spring.

**THERIA PRIMARIA** Haworth *Early Moth* **Pl. 17**
**Distribution.** Probably widespread in central Europe but distribution is uncertain due to confusion with other closely-related species. Widespread and often common in the British Isles with the exception of Scotland.
**Description.** Length up to 24 mm; body whitish-green to dark greyish-green with white lines along the back and sides; sometimes with blackish bands and spots on the back; head greyish-green.
**Habitat.** Hedgerows and heaths.
**Foodplants.** Hawthorn (*Crataegus monogyna*), blackthorn (*Prunus spinosa*), wild plum (*P. domestica*) and bilberry (*Vaccinium myrtillus*).
**Biology.** One generation a year. Eggs are laid in February in large batches on trunks and twigs of the foodplant, lightly covered with fragments of bark and other debris. Caterpillars hatch in early spring and feed until May. They descend from the foodplant at the end of May and pupate in flimsy silken cocoons on the ground. Moths emerge in January or February of the following year.

**CAMPAEA MARGARITATA** Linnaeus *Light Emerald* **Pl. 7**
**Distribution.** Widespread and common in Europe. Widely distributed throughout the British Isles.
**Description.** Length up to 37 mm; rather stout, tapering towards the head; underside flattened; body varying in colour from greenish or yellowish-brown to purplish-brown, with a fringe of hair-like filaments low down along either side; body segment 8 has a pair of extra prolegs; head greyish-brown with darker freckling.
**Habitat.** Woodland and hedgerows.
**Foodplants.** Oak (*Quercus*), beech (*Fagus sylvatica*), silver birch (*Betula pendula*), elm (*Ulmus procera*), hawthorn (*Crataegus monogyna*), blackthorn (*Prunus spinosa*) and other deciduous trees and shrubs.
**Biology.** One generation a year. Eggs are laid in July and caterpillars hatch in the following month. They feed in late summer and early autumn before hibernation, completing their growth in the following spring. Fully grown caterpillars descend to the ground at the end of May to pupate on the surface of the earth. Moths emerge in June.

GNOPHOS OBFUSCATA Denis & Schiffermuller *Scotch Annulet* **Pl. 19**

**Distribution.** Widespread and locally common throughout Europe. In the British Isles, mainly confined to highland Scotland but also occurs as a rarity in Ireland.

**Description.** Length up to 24 mm; body grey or greyish-brown sometimes with dark lines and V-shaped markings on the back, with a dark grey stripe along the spiracles, below which the body is paler; head greyish-brown.

**Habitat.** Heaths, moorland and mountain-sides.

**Foodplants.** Heather (*Calluna vulgaris*), bell heather (*Erica cinerea*), cross-leaved heath (*E. tetralix*), dyer's greenweed (*Genista tinctoria*), petty whin (*G. anglica*) and broom (*Cytisus scoparius*).

**Biology.** One generation a year. Eggs are laid in small groups on the foliage in July and caterpillars hatch in the following month. They feed for a time before going into hibernation and completing their development in the following spring. Pupation takes place in the soil in June and moths emerge in the following month.

GNOPHOS OBSCURATA Denis & Schiffermuller *Annulet* **Pl. 14**

**Distribution.** Widespread in central and southern Europe. Widespread in England occurring locally in Wales, Scotland and Ireland, mainly confined to coastal areas.

**Description.** Length up to 20 mm; rough-skinned; body greyish-brown tinged with purple or green, sometimes with white spots and a series of pale triangular markings along the back; body segment 12 has a pair of raised, black-streaked, whitish warts on the back; head greyish-brown.

**Habitat.** Chalk hills and cliffs, heaths and mountain sides.

**Foodplants.** Rock-rose (*Helianthemum nummularium*), creeping cinquefoil (*Potentilla reptans*), salad burnet (*Sanguisorba minor*), thyme (*Thymus serpyllum*), thrift (*Armeria maritima*), shining cranesbill (*Geranium lucidum*), wild strawberry (*Fragaria vesca*) and heather (*Calluna vulgaris*).

**Biology.** One generation a year. Eggs are laid in August and hatch in September. Caterpillars feed for a time before hibernating, and complete their growth in the following spring. They feed at night, hiding by day under stones or among roots. When fully grown at the end of May, they pupate among leaf litter on the ground. Moths emerge in July.

GNOPHOS GLAUCINARIA Hübner **Pl. 13**

**Distribution.** Occurs in upland regions of central and southern Europe. Absent from the British Isles.

**Description.** Length up to 25 mm; body grey to yellowish-grey with brown, angular spots on the back and a yellowish-white line along each side below the level of the spiracles; head whitish, freckled with dark grey.

**Habitat.** Mountains.

**Foodplants.** Stonecrop (*Sedum*), bistort (*Polygonum bistorta*), germander (*Teucrium*) and dandelion (*Taraxacum*).

**Biology.** Two generations a year in warmer regions; one generation at higher altitudes and further north. Caterpillars feed from September to May and July to August in southern Europe. In central Europe, moths are usually on the wing in July.

**ASPITATES GILVARIA** Denis & Schiffermüller *Straw Belle* **Pl. 16**

**Distribution.** Occurs locally in central and south-eastern Europe. In the British Isles it is confined to a few localities in southern England and restricted areas of Ireland where it is very local.

**Description.** Length up to 32 mm; greyish-brown to ochreous, sometimes tinged with pink along the sides; a broad pale stripe with a dark central line extends along the back: further pale and dark lines extend along the sides; many of these markings are continuous on the head, which is of a similar colour to the body; a pair of long conical points project from the rear end of the body.
**Habitat.** Chalk downland and other dry hillsides and fields.
**Foodplants.** Wild thyme (*Thymus serpyllum*), creeping cinquefoil (*Potentilla reptans*), yarrow (*Achillea millefolium*), black medick (*Medicago lupulina*), birdsfoot trefoil (*Lotus corniculatus*), thyme-leaved speedwell (*Veronica serpyllifolia*) and knotgrass (*Polygonum aviculare*).
**Biology.** One generation a year. Eggs are laid in rows on the foliage in July and caterpillars hatch in the following month. They feed for a time before going into hibernation and completing their growth in the following spring. Caterpillars are fully grown in June and pupate in flimsy webs spun on the foodplant. Moths emerge in July.

**PERCONIA STRIGILLARIA** Hübner *Grass Wave* **Pl. 19**
**Distribution.** Widespread in Europe. Widely distributed throughout the British Isles but most common in the south.
**Description.** Length up to 38 mm; body varying in colour from dark purplish-grey to ochreous or yellowish-brown, with a pair of dark lines down the back and further dark lines along the sides; body segments 5, 6 and 7 have pairs of warts on the back; head yellowish- or greyish-brown.
**Habitat.** Heaths and moorlands.
**Foodplants.** Heather (*Calluna vulgaris*), bell heather (*Erica cinerea*), gorse (*Ulex europaeus*) and broom (*Cytisus scoparius*).
**Biology.** One generation a year. Eggs are laid in July and caterpillars hatch in the following month. They feed for a time before going into hibernation and completing their growth in the following spring. When on gorse, they feed on the flowers. Pupation takes place in May in cocoons spun among twigs of the foodplant. Moths emerge in June.

# SPHINGIDAE

Moths of this family are the well known hawk-moths. The large caterpillars are mostly distinguished by the presence of a large horn on the back of body segment 11. The name Sphingidae refers to the sphinx-like attitude that some caterpillars adopt, with the head and thorax reared up. The skin is often rough and warty but body hairs are reduced to microscopic bristles. They feed on the foliage of trees, shrubs and low-growing plants.

**AGRIUS CONVOLVULI** Linnaeus *Convolvulus Hawk-moth* **Pl. 26**
**Distribution.** Widespread in southern Europe, migrating from Africa northwards to many parts of Europe, including the British Isles, where it occurs regularly, if not commonly.

**Description.** Length up to 110 mm; very variable in markings and coloration but may be divided into green and brown forms; green form has bright green body with brownish or blackish oblique stripes along the sides above the spiracles; brown forms have blackish- or purplish-brown body with pale brown or pinkish oblique stripes; spiracles black; horn on segment 11 red or yellowish, tipped with black; head reddish-brown or pale ochre, striped with black.
**Habitat.** Fields, waste ground and other places where the foodplants grow.
**Foodplants.** Field bindweed (*Convolvulus arvensis*) and other *Convolvulus* species.
**Biology.** Two or more generations a year in warm climates. Migrants may produce a summer brood in central Europe but this species does not breed in Britain. Eggs are laid singly on the foliage of bindweed and hatch in about a fortnight. Caterpillars are occasionally found in Britain in late summer but seldom reach maturity. Pupation takes place in large, fragile, subterranean cocoons. Moths are on the wing in central Europe from May to June and August to September.

**ACHERONTIA ATROPOS** Linnaeus *Death's Head Hawk-moth* **Pl. 27**
**Distribution.** Migrates to various parts of Europe from Africa each year. A regular but seldom common immigrant in the British Isles, most frequent in southern England.
**Description.** Length up to 130 mm; very variable in coloration and pattern, with brown, yellowish and green forms. Most caterpillars found in Europe are of the yellowish form, which has purplish-black spots on the back, and is diagonally striped with dark blue or purplish-brown; the horn on the back of segment 11 is rough in texture and bent into an 'S'-shape; yellow head with two broad, black stripes.
**Habitat.** Fields, gardens and other places where suitable foodplants grow.
**Foodplants.** Mainly on potato (*Solanum tuberosum*) and related plants but will eat a wide range of other plants and is often fed on garden privet (*Ligustrum ovalifolium*) in captivity.
**Biology.** In Africa, two or three generations a year. A summer brood is produced in some parts of Europe. Eggs are laid singly on upper surfaces of leaves. Caterpillars are sometimes found in southern England in late summer or autumn. Pupation takes place in large, fragile, subterranean cocoons. In southern parts of Europe, moths may emerge in the autumn but pupae seldom survive the winter.

**SPHINX LIGUSTRI** Linnaeus *Privet Hawk-moth* **Pl. 26**
**Distribution.** Widespread throughout Europe. Widely distributed in the southern half of Britain, occasionally occurring further north; absent from Ireland.
**Description.** Length up to 100 mm; body bright green, with seven diagonal, purple-edged, white stripes along each side; horn on the back of segment 11 shining black, sharply pointed; head yellowish-green with two broad black stripes.
**Habitat.** Parks, gardens and hedgerows.
**Foodplants.** Privet (*Ligustrum*), lilac (*Syringa vulgaris*) and ash (*Fraxinus excelsior*); in continental Europe, also on other plants, including guelder rose (*Viburnum*) and elder (*Sambucus*).
**Biology.** One generation a year. Eggs are laid singly on leaves or stems in June or July and hatch in about a fortnight. The caterpillars feed in July and August. They are mainly active at night but remain on the foodplant by day, when they are very well camouflaged and difficult to detect. Pupation takes place deep in the soil at the end of August and moths emerge in June of the following year. Sometimes pupae overwinter for two years.

**HYLOICUS PINASTRI** Linnaeus *Pine Hawk-moth* **Pl. 1**

**Distribution.** Widespread throughout Europe. In the British Isles, confined to southern and eastern England.

**Description.** Length up to 80 mm; body green with blackish transverse lines; a broad band of reddish-brown runs along the back, sometimes extending down the sides to the level of the spiracles; three yellowish-white lines extend along the back, sometimes obscured by the reddish-brown band; a broken yellowish-white band extends along each side below the line of the spiracles; spiracles orange, rimmed with black; horn on segment 11 slightly roughened, black; head pale brown with black stripes. Young caterpillars are green with yellowish-white stripes.

**Habitat.** Pine forests.

**Foodplants.** Scots pine (*Pinus sylvestris*) and Norway spruce (*Picea abies*).

**Biology.** One generation a year. Eggs are laid in groups of two or three on the needles in July and hatch in about a fortnight. The caterpillars feed from August to September. They are active by day but are very sluggish, and are well camouflaged on the foodplant. Pupation takes place in the autumn beneath fallen pine needles or just below the surface of the soil. Moths emerge in the following June or July.

**MIMAS TILIAE** Linnaeus *Lime Hawk-moth* **Pl. 8**

**Distribution.** Widespread throughout Europe. In the British Isles mainly confined to central and southern England; occurs as a rarity in Wales.

**Description.** Length up to 60 mm; body green, finely spotted with yellowish-white, with seven diagonal yellow stripes along each side; spiracles white with red rims; horn on segment 11 blue above, yellow and purplish-red below; segment 13 has a distinctive, roughened plate which is yellow, marked with purplish-brown; head triangular, green with white stripes. Before pupation, body colour changes to purplish-brown.

**Habitat.** Woodland, parks and roadsides.

**Foodplants.** Lime (*Tilia*), elm (*Ulmus procera*), alder (*Alnus glutinosa*) and birch (*Betula*); in continental Europe, sometimes also oak (*Quercus*) and other deciduous trees.

**Biology.** One generation a year. Eggs are laid singly or in pairs on the undersides of leaves in June, hatching in 2–3 weeks. The caterpillars feed from July to September. They descend to the ground when fully grown and pupate in cocoons just below the surface of the soil. Moths emerge in May or June of the following year.

**SMERINTHUS OCELLATA** Linnaeus *Eyed Hawk-moth* **Pl. 2**

**Distribution.** Widespread throughout Europe. Widely distributed in England and Wales, becoming less common towards the north; absent from Scotland; local in Ireland.

**Description.** Length up to 80 mm; body bluish-green or yellowish-green, finely spotted with white, with seven diagonal, whitish or pale greenish-yellow stripes along each side; spiracles white with dark red rims; horn on segment 11 greyish-blue; head triangular, green with two yellow stripes. A form occurs with reddish spots along the sides.

**Habitat.** Woodland, hedgerows, riversides, parks and orchards.

**Foodplants.** Sallow and willow (*Salix*), aspen and poplar (*Populus*) and apple (*Malus*); also on birch (*Betula*) and hazel (*Corylus*) in continental Europe.

**Biology.** One generation a year. Eggs are laid singly or in pairs on the undersides of leaves in May or June, hatching in 2–3 weeks. The caterpillars feed from June to

September. When fully grown, they wander away from the foodplant and pupate in cocoons just below the surface of the soil. Moths emerge the next May or June.

**LAOTHOE POPULI** Linnaeus *Poplar Hawk-moth* **Pl. 3**

**Distribution.** Widespread throughout Europe. Widely distributed and often common throughout the British Isles.

**Description.** Length up to 65 mm; very plump; body yellowish-green or bluish-green, finely spotted with white, with seven diagonal, greenish-white stripes along each side; there is sometimes a row of reddish blotches above the line of the spiracles; spiracles white with dark red rims; horn on segment 11 yellowish-green, sometimes tipped with red; head triangular, green with two yellow stripes.

**Habitat.** Damp woodland and hedgerows, riversides, parks and other places where the foodplants grow.

**Foodplants.** Poplar and aspen (*Populus*), sallow and willow (*Salix*); in continental Europe, also recorded on birch (*Betula*), ash (*Fraxinus*) and apple (*Malus*).

**Biology.** One generation a year. Eggs are laid singly or in small groups on the undersides of leaves in June and hatch in 10–20 days. The caterpillars feed from July to September. When fully grown, they descend to the ground to pupate in cocoons just below the surface of the soil. Moths usually emerge in May of the following year, but sometimes a small second brood emerges in late summer or early autumn.

**HEMARIS TITYUS** Linnaeus *Narrow-bordered Bee Hawk-moth* **Pl. 28**

**Distribution.** Widespread throughout Europe. Widely distributed but local and uncommon in the British Isles.

**Description.** Length up to 35 mm; body whitish-green to bluish-green, variably marked with blotches of purplish- or brownish-red along the back and sides; underside purplish; horn on segment 11 rough, straight, reddish-brown; head green. Body becomes reddish just before pupation.

**Habitat.** Damp woodland, marshes, bogs and wet moorland.

**Foodplants.** Devilsbit scabious (*Succisa pratensis*) and field scabious (*Knautia arvensis*); in continental Europe, also on teasel (*Dipsacus*), bedstraw (*Galium*) and catchfly (*Lychnis*).

**Biology.** One generation a year. Eggs are laid singly on the undersides of leaves in June and hatch in 1–2 weeks. The caterpillars feed from July to August, readily dropping to the ground if disturbed. Pupation takes place in cocoons constructed just below the surface of the soil and moths emerge in May of the following year.

**HEMARIS FUCIFORMIS** Linnaeus **Pl. 28**
*Broad-bordered Bee Hawk-moth*

**Distribution.** Widespread in Europe. In the British Isles, restricted to central and southern England and Wales, where it is local and uncommon.

**Description.** Length up to 35 mm; body bright green, tinged with white on the back; underside reddish-brown; spiracles surrounded by patches of reddish-brown; horn on segment 11 violet at the base, becoming dark brown towards the tip; head dark bluish-green.

**Habitat.** Open woodland and woodland margins.

**Foodplants.** Honeysuckle (*Lonicera periclymenum*); in continental Europe, recorded on snowberry (*Symphoricarpos*) and other plants.

**Biology.** One generation a year. Eggs are laid singly on the undersides of leaves in May and June and hatch in about a fortnight. The caterpillars feed from June to

August on the undersides of leaves. When fully grown, they descend to the ground and pupate in cocoons just below the surface of the soil. Moths emerge in May of the following year.

**MACROGLOSSUM STELLATARUM** Linnaeus **Pl. 26**
*Humming-bird Hawk-moth*
**Distribution.** Common in southern Europe, migrating to other parts of Europe, including the British Isles, each year, where it produces a summer generation.
**Description.** Length up to 45 mm; body dark green or reddish-brown finely spotted with white, with two white lines on the back, becoming yellowish towards the head; a broad yellow line extends along each side below the line of the spiracles; horn on segment 11 is blue, tipped with yellow; head green or brown.
**Habitat.** Meadows and hedgerows.
**Foodplants.** Hedge bedstraw (*Galium mollugo*), lady's bedstraw (*G. verum*) and wild madder (*Rubia peregrina*).
**Biology.** Immigrants arrive in the British Isles in spring and summer. Eggs are laid singly on or near buds and flowers of the foodplant and hatch in about a week. Caterpillars have been found feeding in Britain in July and August. Pupation takes place in loosely-spun cocoons on the ground and moths emerge in about a month. These moths do not survive the winter in Britain.

**HYLES EUPHORBIAE** Linnaeus *Spurge Hawk-moth* **Pl. 22**
**Distribution.** Widespread in central and southern Europe. Occurs as a rare immigrant in southern England.
**Description.** Length up to 80 mm; body black, finely spotted with yellow; a rich red line extends along the middle of the back; back and sides variably marked with patches of red or yellow; a broad band of red or yellow extends along each side below the line of the spiracles; horn on segment 11 red with a black tip; red head.
**Habitat.** Field margins, waste ground and sea coasts.
**Foodplants.** Spurge (*Euphorbia*) and annual mercury (*Mercurialis annua*).
**Biology.** One or two generations a year in continental Europe. Eggs are laid singly or in small batches near the shoot-tips of the foodplant and hatch in about two weeks. Caterpillars have been found in Britain in August and September but these occurrences are very rare. Pupation takes place in fragile cocoons just below the surface of the soil. In continental Europe, first brood pupae may produce moths in about a fortnight but autumn pupae overwinter to produce moths in the following May.

**HYLES GALII** Rottemburg *Bedstraw Hawk-moth* **Pl. 26**
**Distribution.** Widespread throughout Europe. An infrequent migrant to the British Isles.
**Description.** Length up to 80 mm; body varying in colour from olive-green to brown or dark purplish-grey, sprinkled with fine yellowish dots; a line of large, round, yellow or pale yellowish-brown spots extends along each side above the level of the spiracles; legs black; horn on segment 11 reddish-brown, roughened and sharply pointed; pink head. Young caterpillars are green.
**Habitat.** Coastal sandhills, woodland margins and meadows, particularly in sandy regions.
**Foodplants.** Bedstraw (*Galium*), willowherb (*Epilobium*) and sometimes on *Fuchsia*.
**Biology.** One or two generations a year in continental Europe. Eggs are laid on leaves or flowers of the foodplant and hatch in about a fortnight. Caterpillars are

sometimes found in Britain in August and September. Pupation takes place in fragile cocoons constructed underground in sandy soil. In continental Europe, pupae of the summer brood produce moths within two or three months but autumn pupae overwinter, producing moths in the following May.

**HYLES VESPERTILIO** Esper **Pl. 23**

**Distribution.** Occurs locally in Mediterranean Europe, sometimes migrating as far north as central Europe. Not recorded from the British Isles.

**Description.** Length up to 80 mm; body greyish-brown freckled with ochreous-white, with a double line of large yellowish-white or red, black-edged spots along the back; one of the few European hawk-moths bearing no trace of a horn on segment 11; head greyish-brown. Young caterpillars are green.

**Habitat.** Hillsides and mountain slopes.

**Foodplants.** Willowherb (*Epilobium*), bedstraw (*Galium*) and loosestrife (*Lythrum*).

**Biology.** One or two generations a year. Eggs are usually laid in pairs on the undersides of leaves in June and again in August, and caterpillars may be found from June until October. Caterpillars feed mainly at night, hiding at the base of the foodplant by day. When full-grown, they pupate in flimsy silken cocoons among leaf litter on the ground. Moths are on the wing from May to June and from July to September although, at high altitudes, a single generation of moths emerges in July from overwintered pupae.

**DEILEPHILA ELPENOR** Linnaeus *Elephant Hawk-moth* **Pl. 23**

**Distribution.** Widespread throughout Europe, except for the extreme north. Widely distributed in the British Isles except for northern Scotland but more common in England and Wales.

**Description.** Length up to 80 mm; stout, strongly tapered towards the head; body pale ochre or occasionally green, heavily freckled and patterned with brownish-black but less strongly marked on the first five segments; segments 4 and 5 each have a pair of striking, kidney-shaped, white-rimmed, pale lilac 'eye-spots' on the back; horn on segment 11 small; head dark greyish-brown. Young caterpillars are green.

**Habitat.** Meadows, woodland clearings, waste ground, gardens, river valleys and other places where the foodplants grow.

**Foodplants.** Willowherb (*Epilobium*), bedstraw (*Galium*), vine (*Vitis vinifera*), bogbean (*Menyanthes trifoliata*) and evening primrose (*Oenothera*). In gardens, commonly found on *Fuchsia*.

**Biology.** One generation a year. Eggs are laid singly or in small groups on the undersides of leaves in June and hatch in about a fortnight. Caterpillars feed from July to September. When disturbed, the caterpillar retracts its head into the body causing the front segments to swell, making the eye-spots prominent. This alarming snake-like appearance is apparently successful in scaring off predators. Pupation takes place in late summer or early autumn in fragile cocoons among leaf litter on the ground, or just below the surface of the soil. Moths usually emerge in the following June but occasionally a partial second brood of moths appears in late summer.

**DEILEPHILA PORCELLUS** Linnaeus *Small Elephant Hawk-moth* **Pl. 23**

**Distribution.** Widespread throughout Europe. Widely distributed in the British Isles but very local in Scotland and Ireland.

**Description.** Length up to 60 mm; body pale grey or occasionally green, heavily freckled and patterned with black; segments 4 and 5 each have a pair of round,

white-rimmed, pale lilac 'eye-spots' on the back; segment 11 has a small hump instead of a horn; head greyish-black. Young caterpillars are green.
**Habitat.** Meadows, heathlands, chalk downland and coastal sandhills.
**Foodplants.** Bedstraw (*Galium*), willowherb (*Epilobium*) and purple loosestrife (*Lythrum salicaria*).
**Biology.** One generation a year. Eggs are laid singly on the foliage in June and hatch in 1–2 weeks. The caterpillars feed from July to September and are mainly active at night. When disturbed, they respond by dilating their eye spots in the same way as the Elephant Hawk-moth. Pupation takes place in September in fragile cocoons among leaf litter on the ground or just below the surface of the soil. Moths emerge in May of the following year.

# NOTODONTIDAE

This family of moths, known as the prominents, probably displays the greatest diversity of caterpillar forms. Some are very similar to those of the Noctuidae, with smooth skins and unmodified bodies but many have large humps and points on the back, while others have whip-like tails or long, spider-like legs. Some, such as the Buff-tip (*Phalera bucephala*) are covered with scattered fine hairs, while the chocolate-tips (*Clostera*) have both tufts of hairs and humps on the back. In Europe, most feed on the foliage of trees and shrubs.

**PHALERA BUCEPHALA** Linnaeus *Buff-tip* **Pl. 5**
**Distribution.** Widespread throughout Europe. Widely distributed in the British Isles, but rather local in Scotland and Ireland.
**Description.** Length up to 60 mm; covered with fine white hairs; body shining orange-yellow with broad, black bands along the back and sides, broken by transverse bands of orange and yellow; head black with a yellow, V-shaped marking.
**Habitat.** Woodland and commons.
**Foodplants.** Oak (*Quercus*), elm (*Ulmus*), sallow (*Salix*), lime (*Tilia*), hazel (*Corylus avellana*) and other deciduous trees and shrubs.
**Biology.** One generation a year. Eggs are laid in large groups on the undersides of leaves in July and caterpillars feed from July to September. They are gregarious for the greater part of their life, completely stripping an entire branch of its foliage before moving to another. When nearly fully fed, they become solitary. Pupation takes place in the soil in autumn but moths do not emerge until the following May or June.

**CERURA VINULA** Linnaeus *Puss Moth* **Pl. 2**
**Distribution.** Widespread in Europe. Widely distributed throughout the British Isles.
**Description.** Length up to 65 mm; very stout, tapering towards the rear end, which bears two long tails; body bright green with a white-edged, purplish-black,

saddle-shaped band along the back, narrowed at segment 3, which bears a small, pointed hump; head brown, marked with black. Young caterpillars are blackish-brown and have a conspicuous pair of ear-like projections behind the head.
**Habitat.** Woodland, hedgerows, commonland and other places where the food-plants grow.
**Foodplants.** Willow and sallow (*Salix*), poplar and aspen (*Populus*); probably on other deciduous trees in continental Europe.
**Biology.** One generation a year. Eggs are laid in small batches on leaves in May or June and hatch in about ten days. The caterpillars feed from July to early September. When disturbed, they adopt a threatening attitude, with the head reared up and the tails waving red filaments, which are retracted when not in use. They are also able to eject an acid spray from a gland situated just behind the head. Pupation takes place in September in tough cocoons of silk and chewed bark attached to the tree trunk. Moths emerge in the following May or June.

## FURCULA BICUSPIS Borkhausen *Alder Kitten* Pl. 5

**Distribution.** Occurs in central and northern Europe. In the British Isles, confined to England and Wales, where it is very locally distributed.
**Description.** Length up to 40 mm; stout, tapering towards the rear end which bears two long tails; body green with a white-edged, dark purplish-brown, saddle-shaped marking on the back of segments 4–11 and an elongate, triangular marking on the back of segments 1 and 2; segment 2 with a small, pointed hump on the back; head dark reddish-brown.
**Habitat.** Woodland.
**Foodplants.** Birch (*Betula*) and alder (*Alnus glutinosa*).
**Biology.** One generation a year. Eggs are laid in small groups on the upper surfaces of leaves in June and caterpillars feed from July to September. When disturbed, they react in a similar way to the Puss Moth. Pupation takes place in the autumn in tough cocoons spun on branches or tree trunks but moths do not emerge until the following May or June.

## FURCULA FURCULA Clerck *Sallow Kitten* Pl. 2

**Distribution.** Widespread in Europe. Widely distributed throughout the British Isles.
**Description.** Length up to 35 mm; body fairly stout, tapering towards the rear end which bears two long tails; body bright green with a yellow-edged, purplish-brown, saddle-shaped marking on the back, narrowed to a point on segment 3; segment 2 has a small hump on the back; head purplish-brown, marked with black at the rear.
**Habitat.** Woodland, wooded countryside and moorland.
**Foodplants.** Sallow (*Salix*) and sometimes aspen and poplar (*Populus*); also on birch (*Betula*) in continental Europe.
**Biology.** Two generations a year in the south, one generation in the north and west. Eggs are laid in small batches on the upper surfaces of leaves in June and August, hatching in about ten days. The caterpillars feed from June to July and August to September. When disturbed, they behave in a similar manner to the Puss Moth. Pupation takes place in tough cocoons of silk and chewed bark, attached to branches. First brood moths emerge in August but autumn pupae do not produce moths until the following May or June.

**FURCULA BIFIDA** Brahm *Poplar Kitten* **Pl. 3**

**Distribution.** Widely distributed throughout Europe. Widespread in southern and central England, local in Wales and apparently absent from Scotland and Ireland.

**Description.** Length up to 40 mm; body fairly stout, tapering towards the rear end, which bears two long tails; body bright green with a purplish-brown, saddle-shaped marking on the back of segments 4–11 and a shield-shaped marking on the back of segments 1 and 2; segment 2 with a very small hump on the back; head dark purplish-brown.

**Habitat.** Woodland and woodland margins.

**Foodplants.** Poplar, aspen (*Populus*) and sometimes sallow (*Salix*); in continental Europe also on birch (*Betula*).

**Biology.** One generation a year. Eggs are laid in small batches on the upper surfaces of leaves in June, and caterpillars feed from July to September. When disturbed, they behave in a similar manner to the Puss Moth. Pupation takes place in early autumn in tough cocoons of silk and chewed bark attached to branches or tree trunks. Moths usually emerge in the following May or June but may remain in the pupa state for a second winter.

**STAUROPUS FAGI** Linnaeus *Lobster* **Pl. 7**

**Distribution.** Widely distributed throughout Europe. In the British Isles, confined to southern England, parts of Wales and south-western Ireland.

**Description.** Length up to 60 mm; body fairly slender, narrowing towards the head; rear segments slightly flattened, bearing fin-like flanges on the sides, which, together with the strongly developed front legs, produce the characteristic, lobster-like appearance; segments 4–8 with double-pointed humps on the back; colour reddish-brown with a dark brown line above the spiracles; head large, reddish-brown marked with black.

**Habitat.** Woodland.

**Foodplants.** Beech (*Fagus sylvatica*), oak (*Quercus*), birch (*Betula*), hazel (*Corylus avellana*) and probably other deciduous trees and shrubs.

**Biology.** One generation a year. Eggs are laid singly on leaves in June or July, hatching in about ten days. The newly hatched caterpillars, which resemble ants, eat their eggshells before feeding on the foliage. Caterpillars become fully grown in September and pupate in slight silken cocoons amongst fallen leaves on the ground. Moths emerge in the following May or June.

**NOTODONTA DROMEDARIUS** Linnaeus *Iron Prominent* **Pl. 4**

**Distribution.** Widespread in central and northern Europe. Widely distributed throughout the British Isles and often common.

**Description.** Length up to 35 mm; body colour variable, ranging from yellowish-green to greyish-green or reddish-brown; segments 4–7 and 11 with pointed humps on the back; a broken, purplish-brown band extends along the back, becoming broader towards the head and fading towards the tail; a series of purplish-brown patches extends along the sides, below the spiracles; head pale green or brown with blackish-brown spotting.

**Habitat.** Woodland and wooded countryside.

**Foodplants.** Birch (*Betula*), alder (*Alnus glutinosa*), hazel (*Corylus avellana*), oak (*Quercus*) and, in continental Europe, also on sallow (*Salix*).

**Biology.** Two generations a year, except in the north. Eggs are laid singly or in pairs on the leaves in May and August. The caterpillars feed from June to July and August to September. Pupation takes place at the end of July and in the autumn in subterranean cocoons; moths emerge in August and May respectively.

**NOTODONTA TORVA** Hübner *Large Dark Prominent* **Pl. 3**

**Distribution.** Widely distributed in Europe but only recorded twice from the British Isles.

**Description.** Length up to 40 mm; body varying in colour from grey to yellowish-brown or dark purplish-brown; segments 5 and 6 have prominent humps on the back and segment 11 has a smaller hump; a dark purplish-brown band extends along the back, fading towards the tail; a whitish line extends along the spiracles on each side; head whitish with blackish-brown spotting.

**Habitat.** Woodland.

**Foodplants.** Poplar (*Populus*) and birch (*Betula*).

**Biology.** Two generations a year. Caterpillars may be found from June to October and moths from May to August. Autumn pupae overwinter.

**ELIGMODONTA ZICZAC** Linnaeus *Pebble Prominent* **Pl. 2**

**Distribution.** Widespread throughout Europe. Widely distributed and often common in the British Isles.

**Description.** Length up to 40 mm; body pale greyish-green, sometimes suffused with purplish-pink; rear segments sometimes yellowish or bright orange-brown; segments 5 and 6 with prominent humps on the back and segment 11 with a smaller hump; a broad, dark green band extends along the back of the first three segments; head whitish with blackish-green spotting.

**Habitat.** Damp woodland, fens and marshes.

**Foodplants.** Willow and sallow (*Salix*), poplar and aspen (*Populus*); in continental Europe, also on birch (*Betula*) and oak (*Quercus*).

**Biology.** Two generations a year in the south, one in the north. Eggs are laid in small groups on the leaves in May and June and again in August. The caterpillars feed from June to July and late August to September. They are extremely well camouflaged, resembling dead leaves. Pupation takes place in July and September and moths emerge in August and May respectively.

**HARPYIA MILHAUSERI** Fabricius *Tawny Prominent* **Pl. 33**

**Distribution.** Local in warm regions of central and southern Europe. A single specimen has been recorded from the British Isles.

**Description.** Length up to 45 mm; body green with two yellow lines along the back of the first three segments; segment 4 with a prominent hump, terminating in a forked spine; segments 5–9 and 11 with lesser humps and smaller spines; a brown, leaf-like marking extends along the sides of segments 7–9; head brown, slightly notched.

**Habitat.** Woodland.

**Foodplants.** Oak (*Quercus*), beech (*Fagus sylvatica*) and birch (*Betula*).

**Biology.** One generation a year. Caterpillars feed from June to August and pupate in cocoons spun on the bark. Pupae overwinter and produce moths in May or June of the following year.

**PERIDEA ANCEPS** Goeze *Great Prominent* **Pl. 33**

**Distribution.** Widespread in Europe, except for the extreme north. Widely distributed in Britain, except for northern Scotland; absent from Ireland.

**Description.** Length up to 40 mm; very plump, tapering slightly towards the extremities; body green, lightly spotted with pale yellow and with a pale yellow double line along the back; segments 1 and 2 with an oblique band of yellow and red on the sides; segments 5–11 each with a diagonal stripe of yellow and red; head large, green with four pale yellow lines and a broad yellow and red streak continuous with that on the body.
**Habitat.** Oak woodland.
**Foodplant.** Oak (*Quercus*).
**Biology.** One generation a year. Eggs are laid on the upper surfaces of leaves in May and June, hatching in about ten days. Caterpillars feed from June to August. They adopt a characteristic resting position, with the front segments of the body raised and the head thrown back. Pupation takes place in subterranean cocoons in late summer but moths do not emerge until the following May.

**PHEOSIA GNOMA** Fabricius *Lesser Swallow Prominent* **Pl. 4**
**Distribution.** Widespread throughout Europe. Widely distributed and often common in the British Isles.
**Description.** Length up to 40 mm; body very glossy, as though varnished; colour grey to purplish-brown with a broad blackish band down the back and a broad, bright yellow band along each side; segment 11 with a black, pointed hump; head whitish, with a network of blackish lines.
**Habitat.** Woodland.
**Foodplants.** Birch (*Betula*) and, in continental Europe, other deciduous trees.
**Biology.** Two generations a year. Eggs are laid in small batches on the upper surfaces of leaves in May and June and again in August. The caterpillars feed from June to July and late August to September. They rest on the undersides of the leaves. Pupation takes place in July and September in subterranean cocoons and moths emerge in August and May respectively.

**PHEOSIA TREMULA** Clerck *Swallow Prominent* **Pl. 3**
**Distribution.** Widespread throughout Europe. Widely distributed and common in many parts of the British Isles.
**Description.** Length up to 40 mm; body very glossy, as though varnished; colour either pale green or pale brown; green forms have a broad whitish band along the back and a yellow line along each side, below which the body is tinged with purple; brown forms are often pinkish between the segments and sometimes have a series of dark grey, transverse bands; segment 11 has a small hump, marked with a transverse black line; head whitish, with a network of greyish or greenish lines.
**Habitat.** Woodland.
**Foodplants.** Poplar and aspen (*Populus*), willow and sallow (*Salix*); in continental Europe, also on birch (*Betula*).
**Biology.** Two generations a year, only one generation in the north. Eggs are laid singly or in pairs on the upper surfaces of leaves in May and August. The caterpillars feed from June to July and September to October. Pupation of the first generation takes place in cocoons spun among leaves, but the autumn generation pupates beneath the soil. Moths emerge in May and August respectively.

**PTILODON CAPUCINA** Linnaeus *Coxcomb Prominent* **Pl. 4**
**Distribution.** Widespread throughout Europe. Widely distributed and often common in the British Isles.

**Description.** Length up to 35 mm; body pale bluish-green, sometimes suffused with pinkish-purple or pale ochre; a yellowish-white line extends along the sides, marked with red behind each spiracle; segment 11 has a pair of red-tipped, pointed warts on the back; head pale green or ochre.
**Habitat.** Woodland and wooded countryside.
**Foodplants.** Birch (*Betula*), hazel (*Corylus avellana*), poplar (*Populus*), sallow (*Salix*) and other deciduous trees.
**Biology.** Two generations a year. Eggs are laid in small batches on the upper surfaces of leaves in May and August. The caterpillars feed from June to July and August to September or October. Pupation takes place in subterranean cocoons at the foot of the tree in July and October and moths emerge in August and May respectively.

**PTILODONTELLA CUCULLINA** Denis & Schiffermüller **Pl. 8**
*Maple Prominent*
**Distribution.** Widely distributed but local in central and parts of northern Europe. In the British Isles, confined to parts of southern England.
**Description.** Length up to 30 mm; fairly stout in the middle, tapering towards the extremities; body greenish-white to pale green, with a dark purplish-green band along the back, narrowing towards the tail; segment 11 has a double-pointed, whitish or greyish hump, tipped with bright pink; underside tinged with purple; head brownish-white with a dark brown, V-shaped marking.
**Habitat.** Woods and downland.
**Foodplants.** Field maple (*Acer campestre*) and occasionally sycamore (*A. pseudoplatanus*).
**Biology.** One generation a year. Eggs are laid in small batches on the upper surfaces of leaves in June or July. The caterpillars feed from July to September, usually choosing shady situations and resting on the edges of leaves. Pupation takes place in the autumn in cocoons spun among leaf litter on the ground, but moths do not emerge until the following May.

**PTEROSTOMA PALPINA** Clerck *Pale Prominent* **Pl. 3**
**Distribution.** Widespread throughout Europe. Widely distributed in the British Isles, but more common in the southern half of England.
**Description.** Length up to 42 mm; body with numerous transverse wrinkles; colour greenish-blue, suffused with whitish above the line of the spiracles; four whitish lines extend along the back and a white line, edged above with black, extends along the spiracles; head bluish-green with a white stripe on each side.
**Habitat.** Woodland and wooded countryside.
**Foodplants.** Poplar and aspen (*Populus*) and sometimes sallow (*Salix*); in continental Europe, also on other deciduous trees.
**Biology.** Two generations a year in the south, one in the north. Eggs are laid in small batches on the upper surfaces of leaves in May and August. The caterpillars feed from June to July and August to September. Pupation takes place in July and again in autumn in silken cocoons in the earth at the foot of the tree. Moths emerge in August and May respectively.

**PTILOPHORA PLUMIGERA** Denis & Schiffermüller **Pl. 8**
*Plumed Prominent*
**Distribution.** Occurs in central and parts of northern Europe. In the British Isles, confined to a few localities in southern England and Wales.

**Description.** Length up to 30 mm; body pale bluish-green with pale yellowish-green lines between the segments; two broad, greenish-white lines extend along the back and a yellowish line along the spiracles on each side; head green.
**Habitat.** Woodland on chalk and limestone soils.
**Foodplants.** Field maple (*Acer campestre*) and sometimes sycamore (*A. pseudoplatanus*).
**Biology.** One generation a year. Eggs are laid on twigs in November but do not hatch until bud-burst in the following spring. The caterpillars feed from late April to early June. They rest in a characteristic, curled position on the undersides of leaves. Pupation takes place in June in cocoons under leaf litter or in the soil and moths emerge in November.

**CLOSTERA CURTULA** Linnaeus *Chocolate-tip* **Pl. 3**
**Distribution.** Widespread throughout Europe. In the British Isles, mainly confined to the southern half of England and south-eastern Wales, but recently recorded from a locality in Scotland.
**Description.** Length up to 35 mm; body covered in fine, greyish-white hairs, arising from small, yellowish warts; colour pale ochre with broken, black lines along the back and sides; segments 4 and 11 each with a small black hump in the middle of the back; head black with yellow markings.
**Habitat.** Wooded countryside, heaths and commons.
**Foodplants.** Poplar and aspen (*Populus*), willow and sallow (*Salix*); in continental Europe, also on other deciduous trees.
**Biology.** Two generations a year in the south, one in the north. Eggs are laid in small batches on the upper surfaces of leaves in May and August. The caterpillars feed from May to June and August to September. They are active at night, hiding by day between spun leaves. Pupation takes place in June and again in the autumn in cocoons spun between leaves. Autumn pupae fall to the ground with the leaves and remain there through the winter. Moths emerge in July and April respectively.

# DILOBIDAE

(now considered to be Dilobinae, a subfamily of the Noctuidae)

This family is represented by the Figure of Eight (*Diloba caeruleocephala*). The caterpillar is smooth-skinned and similar to those of the family Noctuidae but has the body hairs situated on conspicuous, raised black spots. It feeds on the foliage of trees and shrubs.

**DILOBA CAERULEOCEPHALA** Linnaeus *Figure of Eight* **Pl. 16**
**Distribution.** Widespread throughout Europe. Widely distributed and common in most parts of England and Wales; local and scarce in Scotland and Ireland.
**Description.** Length up to 40 mm; body ranging in colour from light bluish-grey to charcoal grey, with raised black spots; a broken line of deep yellow extends down the back, with similar lines along the spiracles on each side; head greyish-white with black markings.
*Cont. on p.* 201

## Structure of a Caterpillar

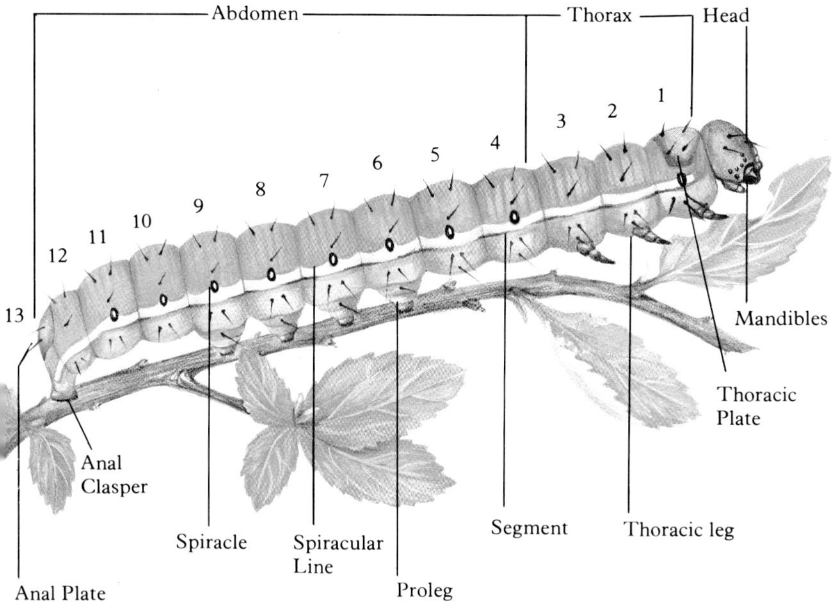

Abdomen
Thorax
Head
1
2
3
4
5
6
7
8
9
10
11
12
13
Mandibles
Thoracic Plate
Anal Clasper
Spiracle
Spiracular Line
Proleg
Segment
Thoracic leg
Anal Plate

## Front view of a Caterpillar Head

Mandible
Labrum
Ocellus
Antenna
Maxilla
Spinneret
Labium

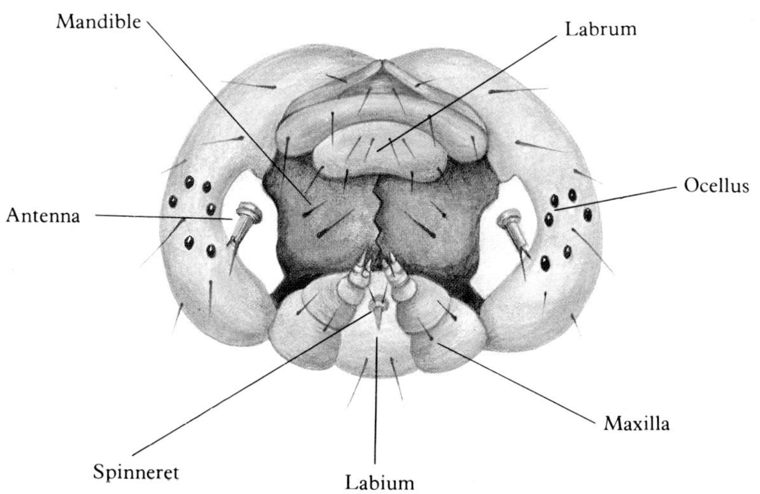

**Peacock Butterfly Life-cycle**

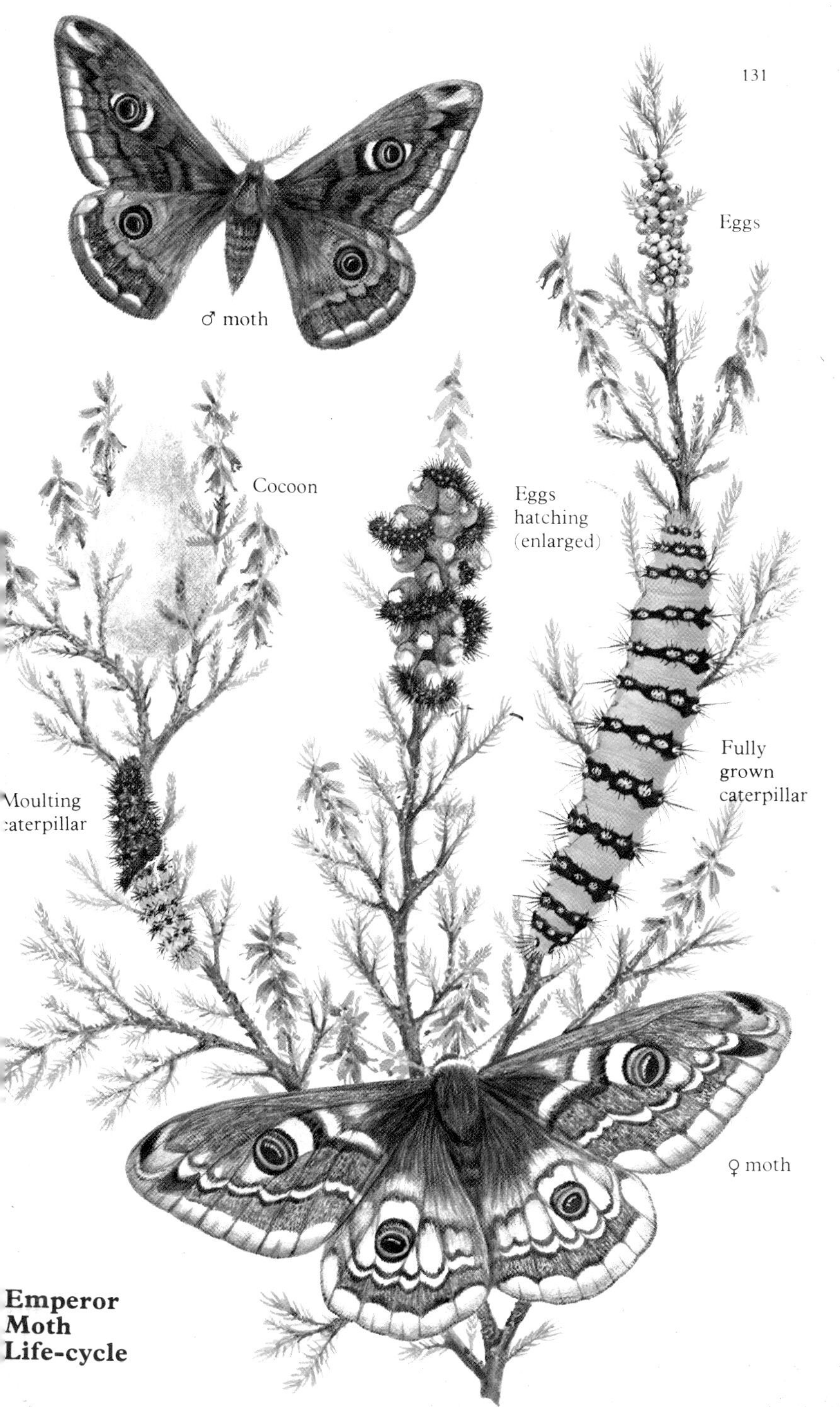


**Emperor Moth Life-cycle**

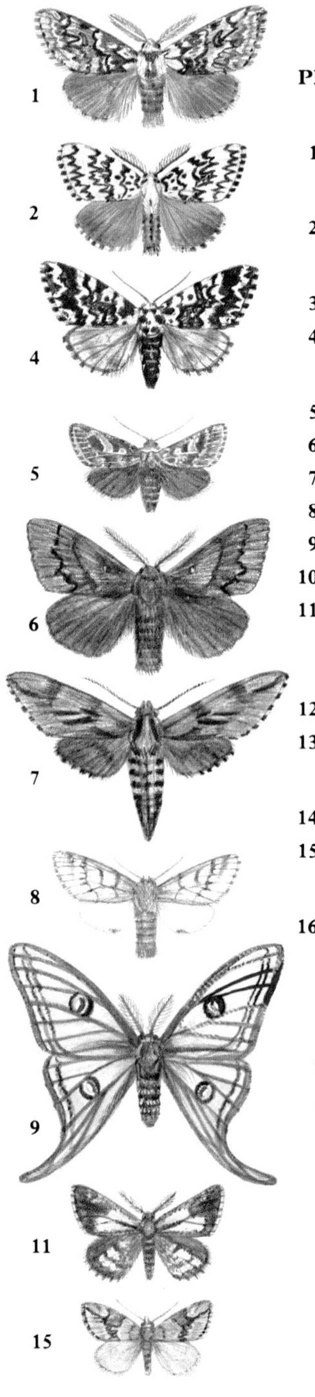


## PLATE 1

SILVER FIR *Abies alba* family: Pinaceae

1. **Dasychira abietis** 20

YEW *Taxus baccata* family: Taxaceae

2. **Lymantria monacha** *Black Arches* 20

NORWAY SPRUCE *Picea abies* family: Pinaceae

3. **Eupithecia abietaria** *Cloaked Pug* 9
4. **Panthea coenobita** 26

SCOTS PINE *Pinus sylvestris* family: Pinaceae

5. **Panolis flammea** *Pine Beauty* 23
6. **Dendrolimus pini** *Pine-tree Lappet* 6
7. **Hyloicus pinastri** *Pine Hawk-moth* 11
8. **Thaumetopoea pityocampa** *Pine Processionary* 20
9. **Graellsia isabellae** *Spanish Moon Moth* 6
10. **Thera firmata** *Pine Carpet* 8
11. **Bupalus piniaria** *Bordered White* 11

LAWSON'S CYPRESS *Chamaecyparis lawsoniana* family: Cupressaceae

12. **Lithophane leautieri** *Blair's Shoulder-knot* 24
13. **Eupithecia phoeniceata** *Cypress Pug* 9

JUNIPER *Juniperus communis* family: Cupressaceae

14. **Eupithecia pusillata** *Juniper Pug* 9
15. **Thera juniperata** *Juniper Carpet* 8

EUROPEAN LARCH *Larix decidua* family: Pinaceae

16. **Eupithecia lariciata** *Larch Pug* 9

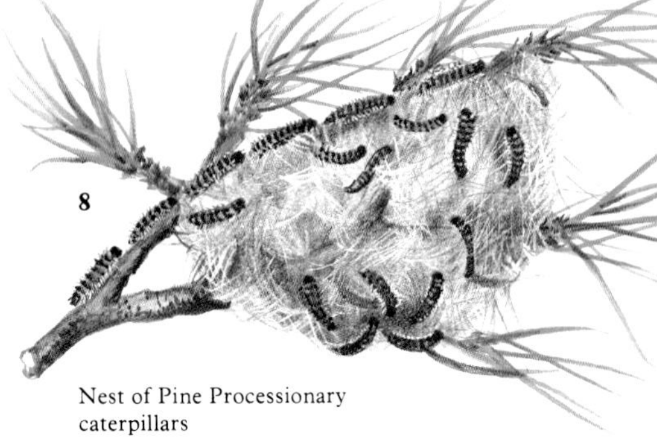


Nest of Pine Processionary caterpillars

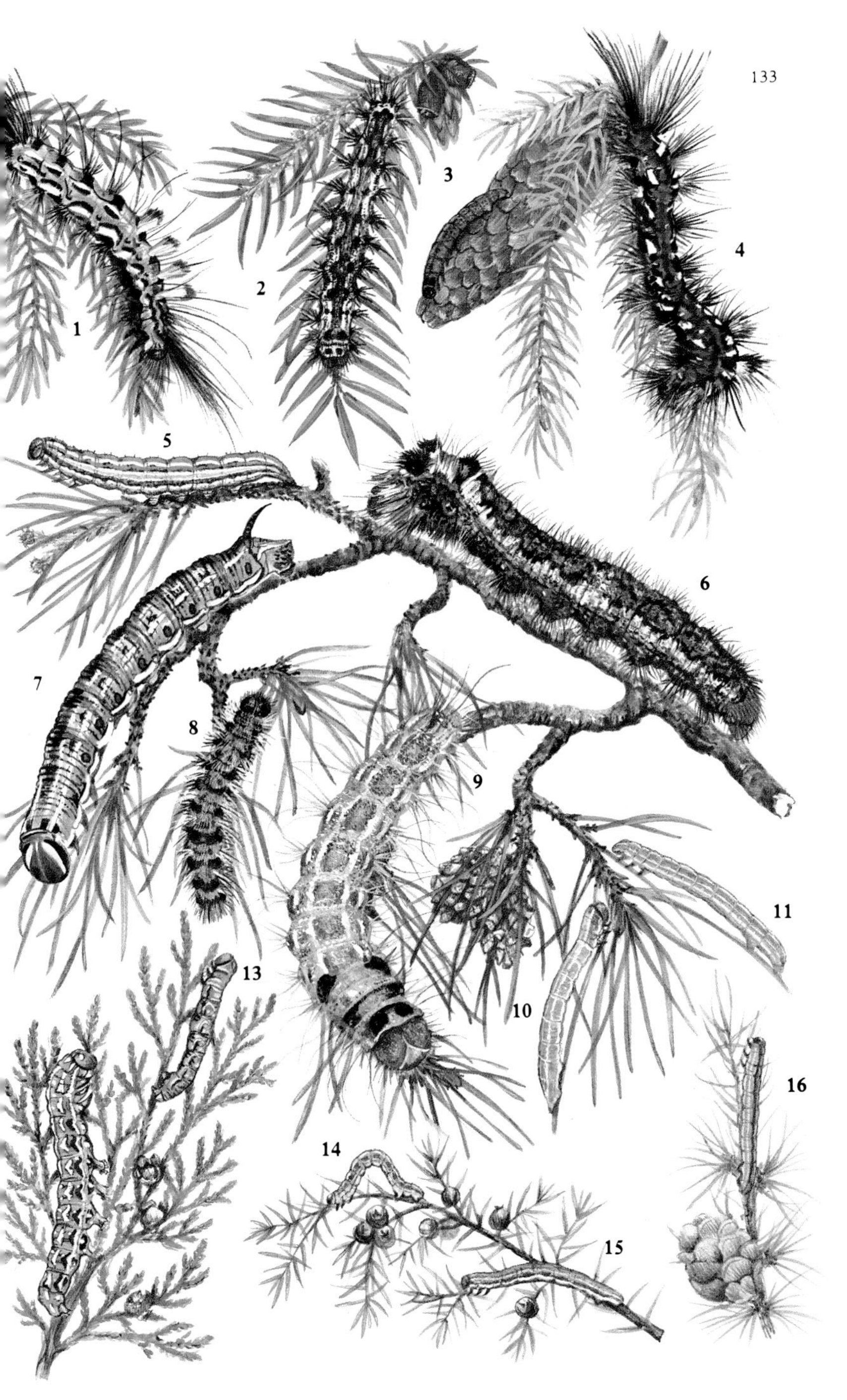
1
2
3
4
5
6
7
8
9
10
11
13
14
15
16

2 3 5 6 8 10 11 13 14 15

## PLATE 2

Grey Sallow *Salix cinerea* family: Salicaceae (*See also* Pl. 33)

1. **Lomaspilis marginata** *Clouded Border* 10
2. **Smerinthus ocellata** *Eyed Hawk-moth* 11
3. **Plagodis dolabraria** *Scorched Wing* 10
4. **Arctornis l-nigrum** *Black V Moth* 20
5. **Furcula furcula** *Sallow Kitten* 12
6. **Apatura iris** *Purple Emperor* 4

Osier *Salix viminalis* family: Salicaceae

7. **Earias clorana** *Cream-bordered Green Pea* 26
8. **Scoliopteryx libatrix** *Herald* 26

Goat Willow *Salix caprea* family: Salicaceae

9. **Eligmodonta ziczac** *Pebble Prominent* 12
10. **Colotois pennaria** *Feathered Thorn* 10
11. **Catocala nupta** *Red Underwing* 26
12. **Orgyia recens** *Scarce Vapourer* 20
13. **Cerura vinula** *Puss Moth* 12
14. **Xanthia icteritia** *Sallow* 24

White Sallow *Salix alba* family: Salicaceae

15. **Nymphalis antiopa** *Camberwell Beauty* 5
16. **Epione repandaria** *Bordered Beauty* 10

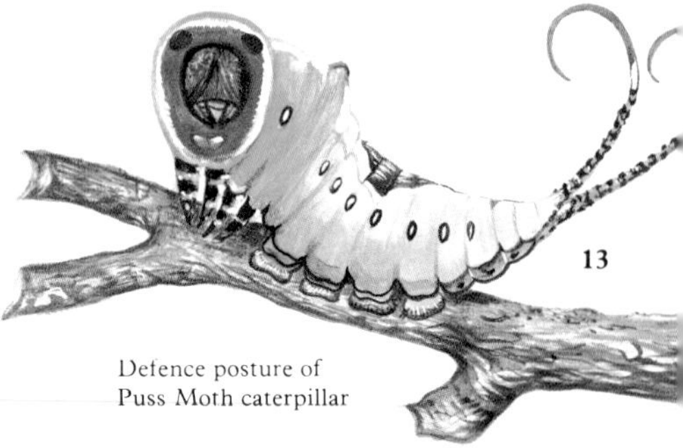

13

Defence posture of Puss Moth caterpillar

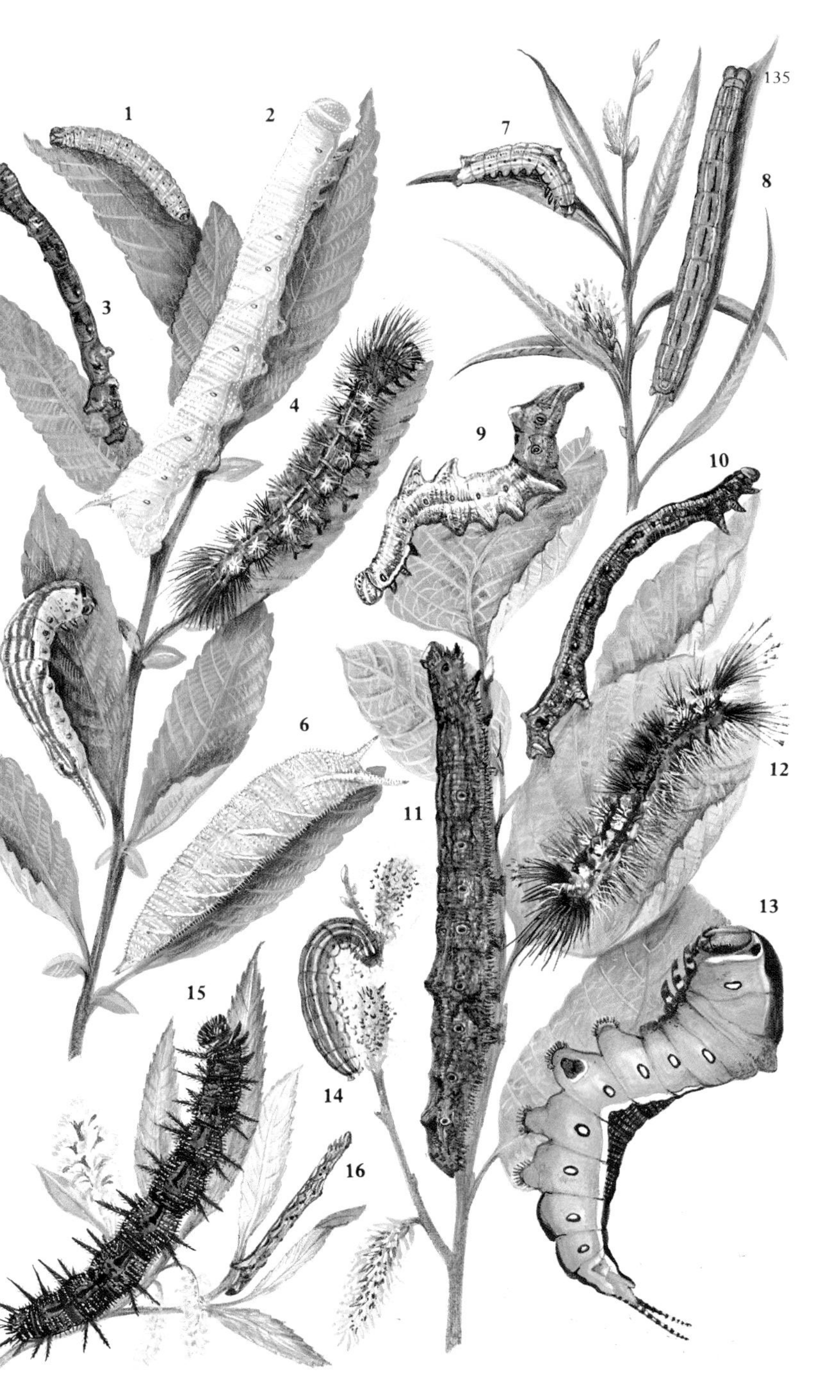
1
2
7
8
3
4
9
10
6
11
12
13
15
14
16

## PLATE 3

Aspen *Populus tremula* family: Salicaceae

1. **Apatura ilia** *Lesser Purple Emperor* 5
2. **Furcula bifida** *Poplar Kitten* 12
3. **Lobophora halterata** *Seraphim* 9
4. **Limenitis populi** *Poplar Admiral* 4
5. **Pterostoma palpina** *Pale Prominent* 12
6. **Tethea ocularis** *Figure of Eighty* 7
7. **Archiearis notha** *Light Orange Underwing* 7

Black Poplar *Populus nigra* family: Salicaceae

8. **Laothoe populi** *Poplar Hawk-moth* 11
9. **Clostera curtula** *Chocolate-tip* 12
10. **Tethea or** *Poplar Lutestring* 7
11. **Xanthia ocellaris** *Pale-lemon Sallow* 24
12. **Notodonta torva** *Large Dark Prominent* 12
13. **Pheosia tremula** *Swallow Prominent* 12
14. **Acronicta megacephala** *Poplar Grey* 24
15. **Poecilocampa populi** *December Moth* 6

Poplar Hawk-moth at rest on bark

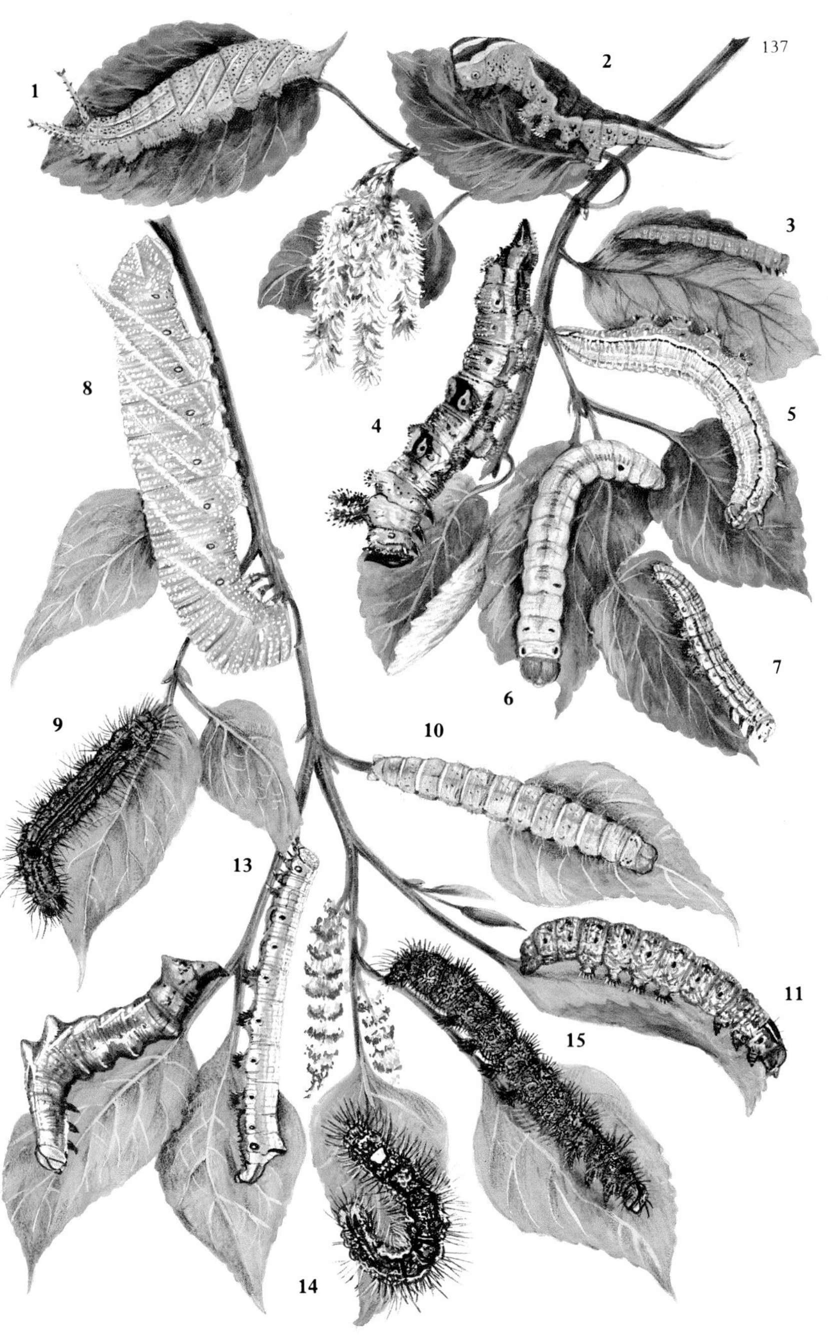
1
2
3
4
5
6
7
8
9
10
11
13
14
15

## PLATE 4

SILVER BIRCH *Betula pendula* family: Betulaceae

| | |
|---|---|
| 1. **Notodonta dromedarius** *Iron Prominent* | 124 |
| 2. **Acronicta leporina** *Miller* | 249 |
| 3. **Ennomos autumnaria** *Large Thorn* | 104 |
| 4. **Jodis lactearia** *Little Emerald* | 75 |
| 5. **Geometra papilionaria** *Large Emerald* | 74 |
| 6. **Pheosia gnoma** *Lesser Swallow Prominent* | 126 |
| 7. **Agriopis aurantiaria** *Scarce Umber* | 110 |
| 8. **Endromis versicolora** *Kentish Glory* | 67 |
| 9. **Semiothisa notata** *Peacock Moth* | 101 |
| 10. **Operophtera fagata** *Northern Winter Moth* | 89 |
| 11. **Falcaria lacertinaria** *Scalloped Hook-tip* | 68 |
| 12. **Cyclophora albipunctata** *Birch Mocha* | 76 |
| 13. **Ptilodon capucina** *Coxcomb prominent* | 126 |
| 14. **Achlya flavicornis** *Yellow Horned* | 72 |
| 15. **Selenia dentaria** *Early Thorn* | 105 |
| 16. **Drepana falcataria** *Pebble Hook-tip* | 69 |

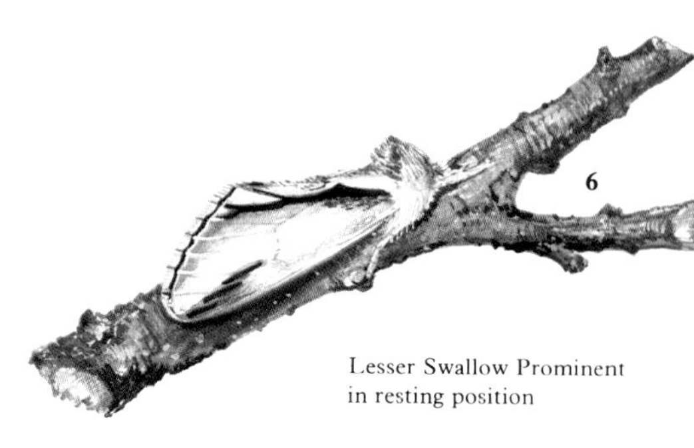


Lesser Swallow Prominent
in resting position

1
2
3
4
5
6
7
8
9
10
11
12
13
14
15
16

## PLATE 5

ALDER *Alnus* family: Betulaceae

1. **Ennomos alniaria** *Canary-shouldered Thorn* 104
2. **Ochropacha duplaris** *Common Lutestring* 71
3. **Selenia tetralunaria** *Purple Thorn* 106
4. **Furcula bicuspis** *Alder Kitten* 123
5. **Trichopteryx carpinata** *Early Tooth-striped* 99
6. **Acronicta alni** (early stage) *Alder Moth* 249
7. **Acronicta alni** (full-grown) *Alder Moth* 249

HORNBEAM *Carpinus betulus* family: Corylaceae

8. **Colocasia coryli** *Nut-tree Tussock* 264
9. **Agriopis marginaria** *Dotted Border* 110

BOG MYRTLE *Myrica gale* family: Salicaceae
(*See also* Pl. 33)

10. **Acronicta menyanthidis** *Light Knot Grass* 250
11. **Acronicta euphorbiae** *Sweet Gale Moth* 251
12. **Lacanobia contigua** *Beautiful Brocade* 229
13. Mniotype adusta *Dark Brocade* 243

HAZEL *Corylus avellana* family: Corylaceae

14. **Erannis defoliaria** *Mottled Umber* 110
15. **Hydriomena furcata** *July Highflyer* 86
16. **Phalera bucephala** *Buff-tip* 122

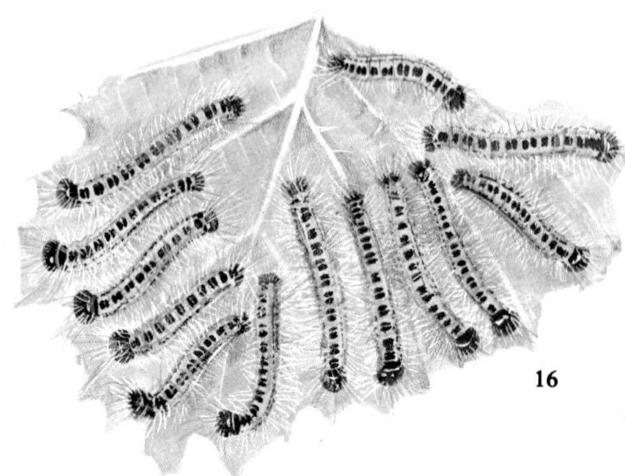


Young caterpillars
of the Buff-tip

1
2
3
4
5
6
7
8
9
11
12
13
14
15
16

## PLATE 6

OAK *Quercus* family: Fagaceae
(*See also* Pl. 33)

1. **Amphipyra pyramidea** *Copper Underwing* 252
2. **Conistra vaccinii** *Chestnut* 245
3. **Quercusia quercus** *Purple Hairstreak* 42
4. **Biston betularia** *Peppered Moth* 109
5. **Amphipyra berbera** *Svensson's Copper Underwing* 253
6. **Biston strataria** *Oak Beauty* 109
7. Orthosia cerasi fabricius *Common Quaker* 234
8. **Serraca punctinalis** *Pale Oak Beauty* 112
9. **Ennomos quercinaria** *August Thorn* 104
10. Hypomecis roboraria *Great Oak Beauty* 112
11. **Orthosia miniosa** *Blossom Underwing* 233
12. **Thaumetopoea processionea** *Oak Processionary* 201
13. **Apoda limacodes** *Festoon* 27
14. **Polyploca ridens** *Frosted Green* 72
15. **Dichonia aprilina** *Merveille du Jour* 243
16. **Pseudoips fagana** *Green Silver-lines* 263
17. **Drepana binaria** *Oak Hook-tip* 64
18. **Nycteola revayana** *Oak Nycteoline* 263

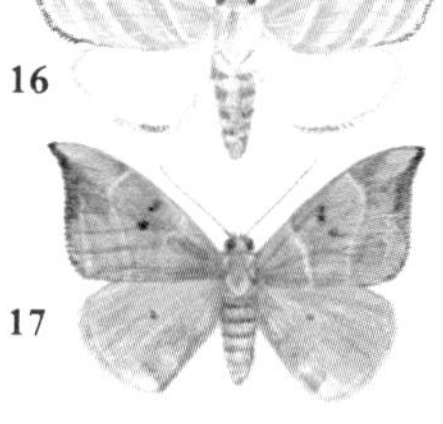

4

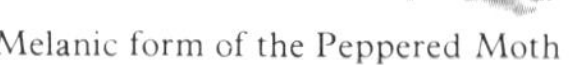

Melanic form of the Peppered Moth

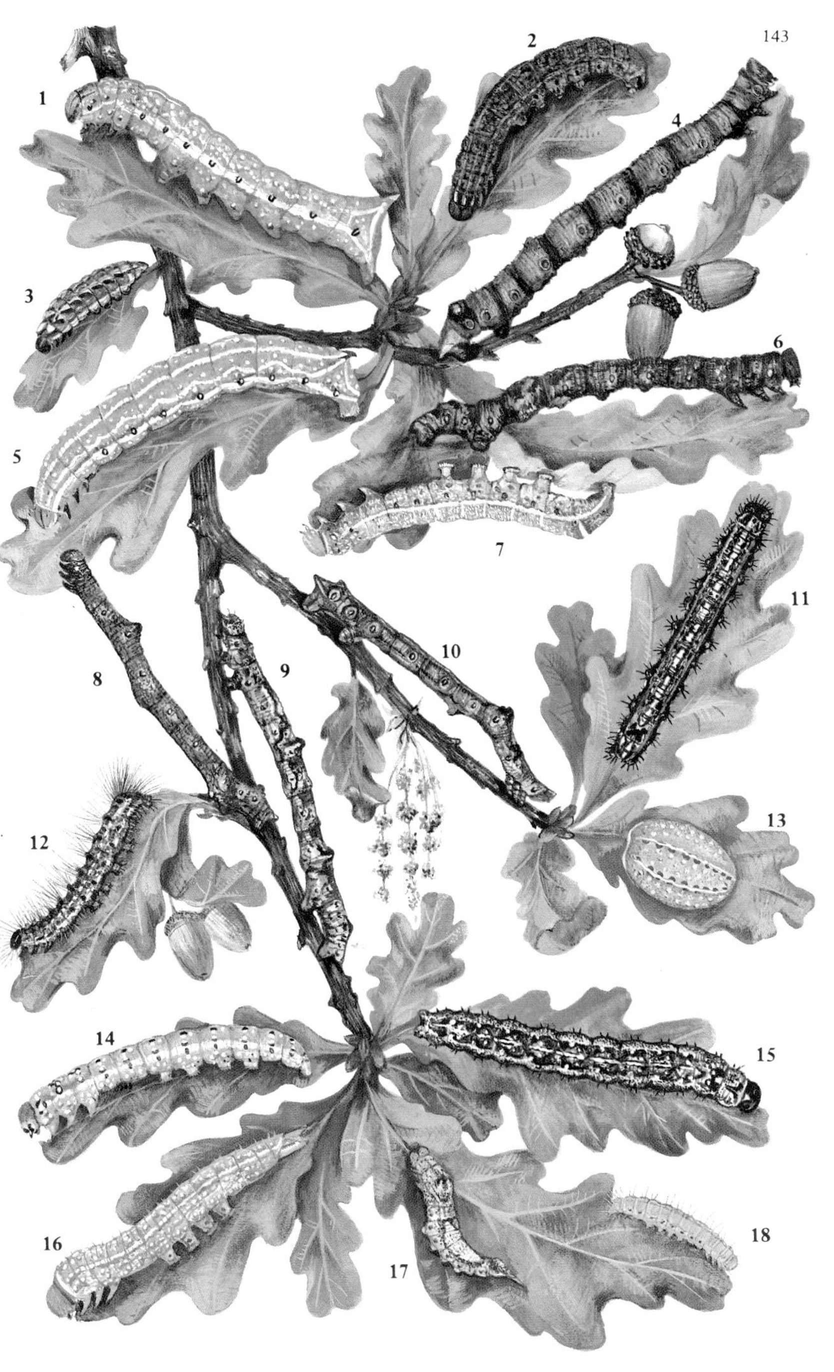
1
2
4
3
6
5
7
11
10
8
9
13
12
14
15
16
18
17

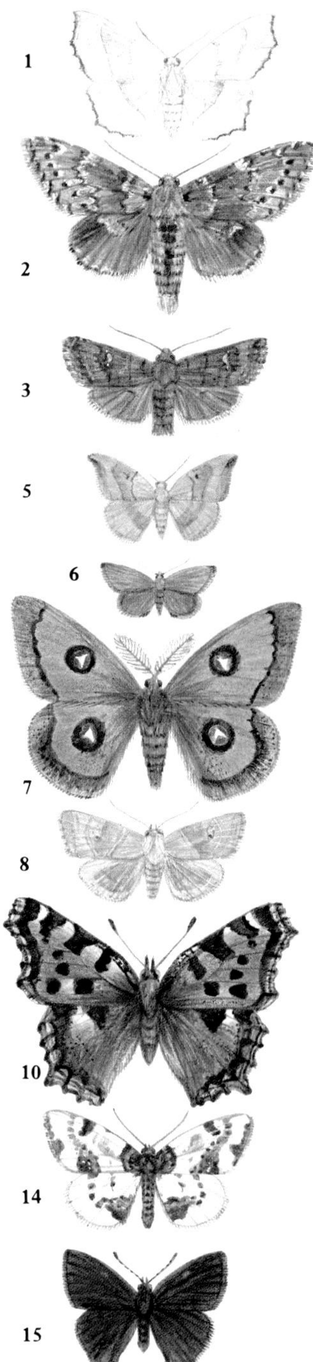


## PLATE 7

BEECH *Fagus sylvaticus* family: Fagaceae

1. **Campaea margaritata** *Light Emerald* 114
2. **Stauropus fagi** *Lobster* 124
3. **Eupsilia transversa** *Satellite* 244
4. **Brachionycha sphinx** *Sprawler* 240
5. **Drepana cultraria** *Barred Hook-tip* 69
6. **Heterogenea asella** *Triangle* 28
7. **Aglia tau** *Tau Emperor* 68

ELM *Ulmus campestris* family: Ulmaceae

8. **Cosmia trapezina** *Dun-bar* 255
9. **Lycia hirtaria** *Brindled Beauty* 109
10. **Nymphalis polychloros** *Large Tortoiseshell* 51
11. **Epirrita dilutata** *November Moth* 88
12. **Orthosia munda** *Twin-spotted Quaker* 235
13. **Alcis repandata** *Mottled Beauty* 111

WYCH ELM *Ulmus glabra* family: Ulmaceae

14. **Abraxas sylvata** *Clouded Magpie* 100
15. **Strymonidia w-album** *White Letter Hairstreak* 42
16. **Agrochola circellaris** *Brick* 245

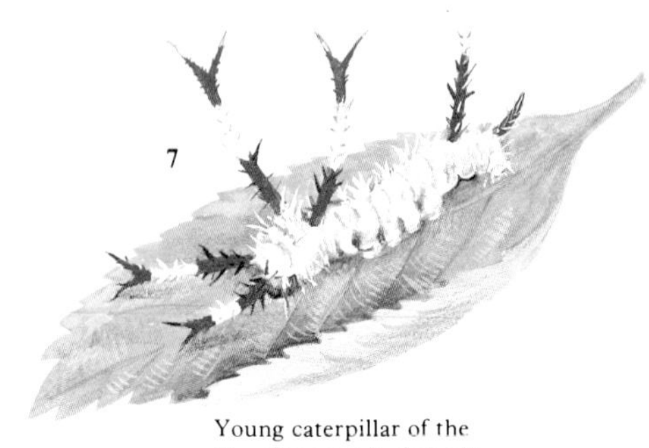


Young caterpillar of the Tau Emperor (enlarged)

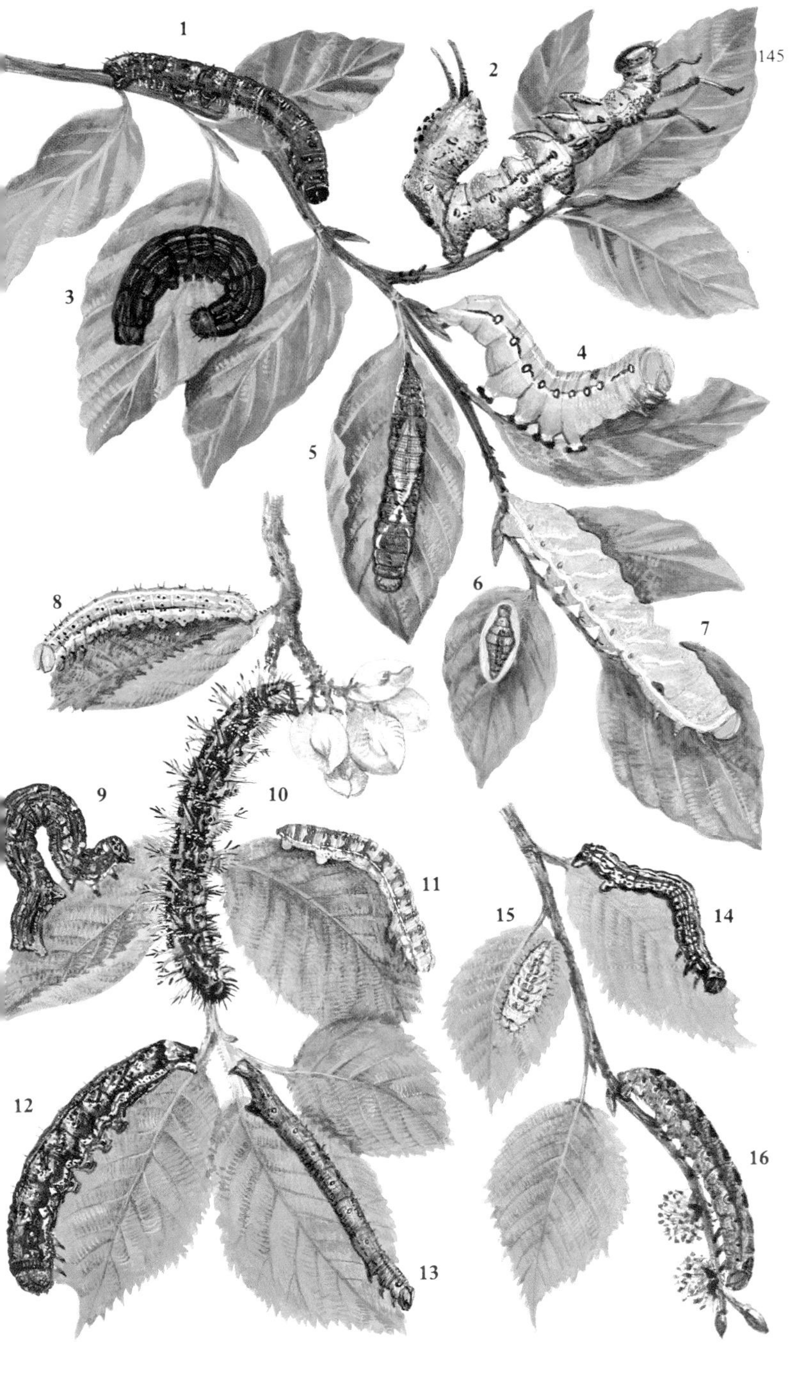
1
2
3
4
5
6
7
8
9
10
11
12
13
14
15
16

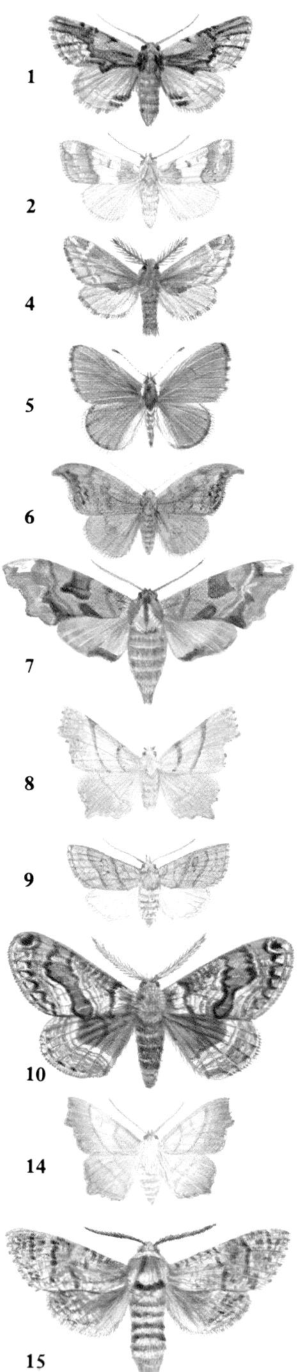


## PLATE 8

FIELD MAPLE *Acer campestris* family: Aceraceae

1. **Ptilodontella cucullina** *Maple Prominent* 12
2. **Xanthia aurago** *Barred Sallow* 24
3. **Cyclophora annulata** *Mocha* 7
4. **Ptilophora plumigera** *Plumed Prominent* 12
   (*For* Sycamore, *Acer pseudoplatanus*, *see* Pl. 33)

HOLLY *Ilex aquifolium* family: Aquifoliaceae

5. **Celastrina argiolus** *Holly Blue* 4

SMALL-LEAVED LIME *Tilia cordata* family: Tilia

6. **Sabra harpagula** *Scarce Hook-tip* 6

LIME *Tilia vulgaris* family: Tiliaceae

7. **Mimas tiliae** *Lime Hawk-moth* 11
8. **Ennomos erosaria** *September Thorn* 10
9. **Xanthia citrago** *Orange Sallow* 24

ASH *Fraxinus* family: Oleaceae

10. **Acanthobrahmaea europaea** *Hartig's Brahmaea* 6
11. **Atethmia centrago** *Centre-barred Sallow* 24
12. **Lithophane semibrunnea** *Tawny Pinion* 24
13. **Eupithecia fraxinata** *Ash Pug* 9
14. **Ennomos fuscantaria** *Dusky Thorn* 10
15. **Cossus cossus** *Goat Moth* 2

Pupae of the Holly Blue

1
2
3
4
5
6
7
8
9
11
12
14
15

## PLATE 9

NETTLE *Urtica dioica* family: Urticaceae

1. **Hypena proboscidalis** *Snout*
2. **Abrostola triplasia** *Spectacle*
3. **Araschnia levana** *European Map*
4. **Inachis io** *Peacock*
5. **Diachrysia chrysitis** *Burnished Brass*
6. **Aglais urticae** *Small Tortoiseshell*
7. **Vanessa atalanta** *Red Admiral*

HOP *Humulus* family: Cannabaceae

8. **Polygonia c-album** *Comma*
9. **Calliteara pudibunda** *Pale Tussock*
10. **Abrostola trigemina** *Dark Spectacle*

BIRTHWORT *Aristolochia* family: Aristolochiaceae

11. **Zerynthia polyxena** *Southern Festoon*

11a. **Zerynthia rumina** *Spanish Festoon*

12. **Archon apollinus** *False Apollo*

KNOTGRASS *Polygonum aviculare* family: Polygona

13. **Orthonama obstipata** *Gem*
14. **Dypterygia scabriuscula** *Bird's Wing*
15. **Rhodometra sacraria** *Vestal*
16. **Agrotis puta** *Shuttle-shaped Dart*
17. **Xylena vetusta** *Red Sword-grass*

Egg-strings of the European Map

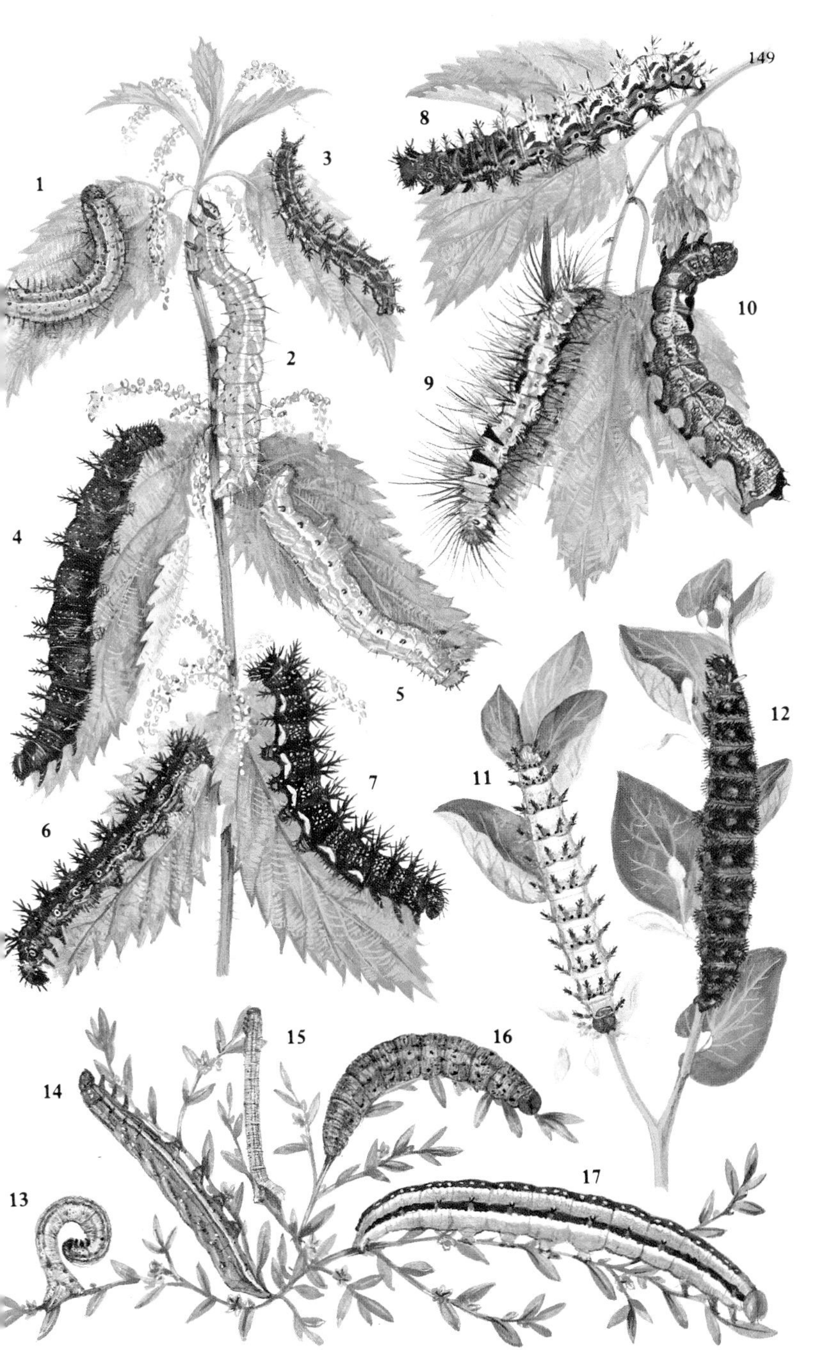
1
2
3
4
5
6
7
8
9
10
11
12
13
14
15
16
17

## PLATE 10

COMMON SORREL *Rumex acetosa*
family: Polygonaceae

1. **Timandra griseata** *Blood-vein* 7
2. **Lycaena phlaeas** *Small Copper* 4
3. **Aporophyla nigra** *Black Rustic* 24
4. **Eugnorisma depuncta** *Plain Clay* 21
5. **Adscita statices** *Forester* 2
6. **Bembecia chrysidiformis** *Fiery Clearwing* 3

FIDDLE DOCK *Rumex pulcher* family: Polygonaceae

7. **Diarsia dahlii** *Barred Chestnut* 22

SHEEP'S SORREL *Rumex acetosella*
family: Polygonaceae

8. **Xestia ashworthii** *Ashworth's Rustic* 22

WATER DOCK *Rumex hydrolapathum*
family: Polygonaceae

9. **Lycaena dispar** *Large Copper* 4

BROAD-LEAVED DOCK *Rumex obtusifolius*
family: Polygonaceae (*See also* Pl. 33)

10. **Camptogramma bilineata** *Yellow Shell* 8
11. **Spaelotis ravida** *Stout Dart* 22
12. **Diarsia mendica** *Ingrailed Clay* 22
13. **Arctia caja** *Garden Tiger* 20
14. **Diacrisia sannio** *Clouded Buff* 21
15. **Diaphora mendica** *Muslin Moth* 21
16. **Euxoa nigricans** *Garden Dart* 21
17. **Agrotis segetum** *Turnip Moth* 2

Garden Tiger in resting position

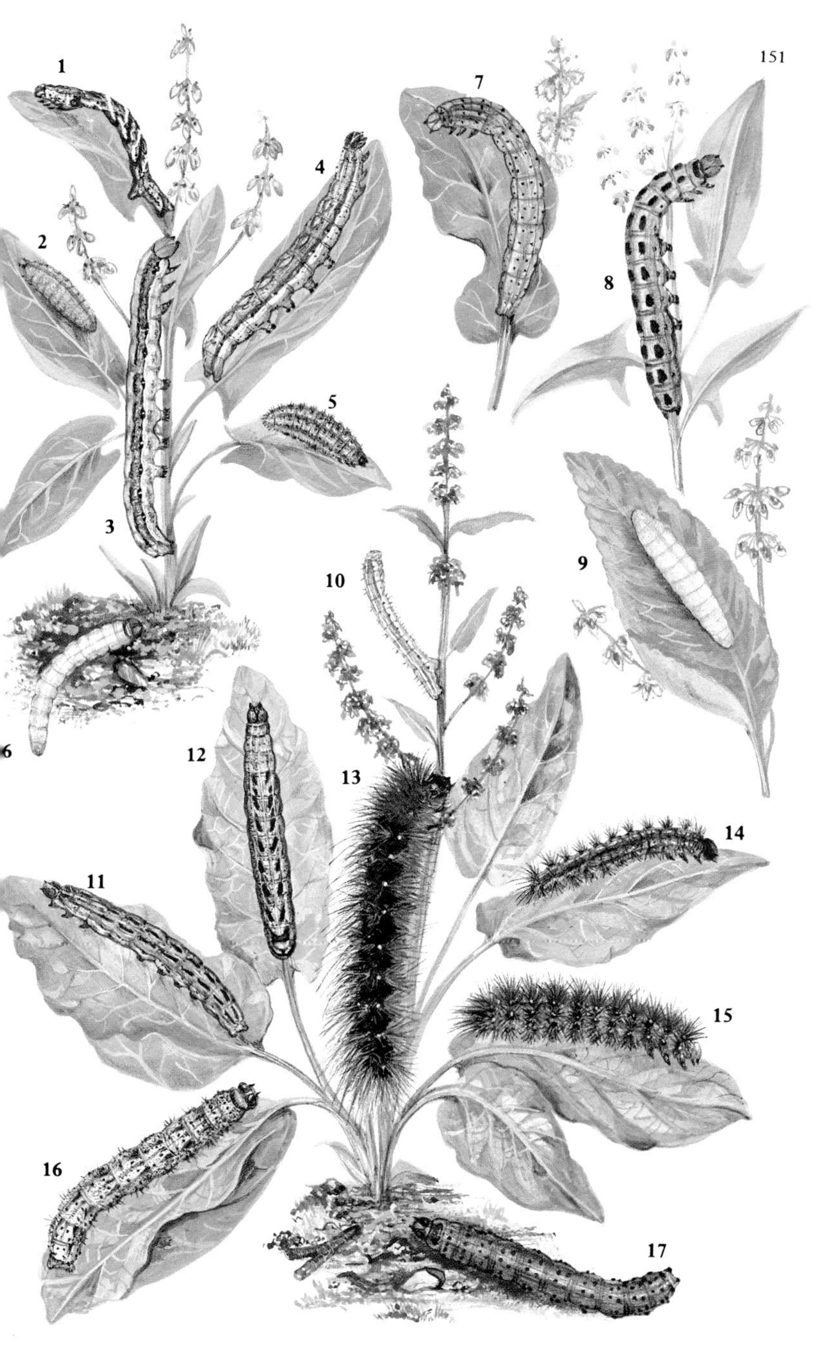
1
2
3
4
5
6
7
8
9
10
11
12
13
14
15
16
17

## PLATE 11

FAT HEN *Chenopodium album* family: Chenopodiaceae

**1. Eupithecia simpliciata** *Plain Pug* 9
**2 & 3. Lacanobia oleracea** *Bright-line Brown-eye* 23

COMMON ORACHE *Atriplex patulum* family: Chenopodiaceae

**4. Pelurga comitata** *Dark Spinach* 8
**5. Trachea atriplicis** *Orache Moth* 25

SEA BEET *Beta vulgaris* family: Chenopodiaceae

**6. Discestra trifolii** *Nutmeg* 22

PRICKLY SALTWORT *Salsola kali* family: Chenopodiaceae

**7. Agrotis ripae** *Sand Dart* 21

CHICKWEED *Stellaria media* family: Caryophyllaceae

**8. Hoplodrina blanda** *Rustic* 26
**9. Xestia xanthographa** *Square-spot Rustic* 22
**10. Xestia c-nigrum** *Setaceous Hebrew Character* 22
**11. Mythimna ferrago** *Clay* 23

GREATER STITCHWORT *Stellaria holostea* family: Caryophyllaceae

**12. Eupithecia pygmaeata** *Marsh Pug* 9

BLADDER CAMPION *Silene vulgaris* family: Caryophyllaceae

**13. Hadena confusa** *Marbled Coronet* 23

RAGGED ROBIN *Lychnis flos-cuculi* family: Caryophyllaceae

**14. Hadena rivularis** *Campion* 23
**15. Hadena bicruris** *Lychnis* 23

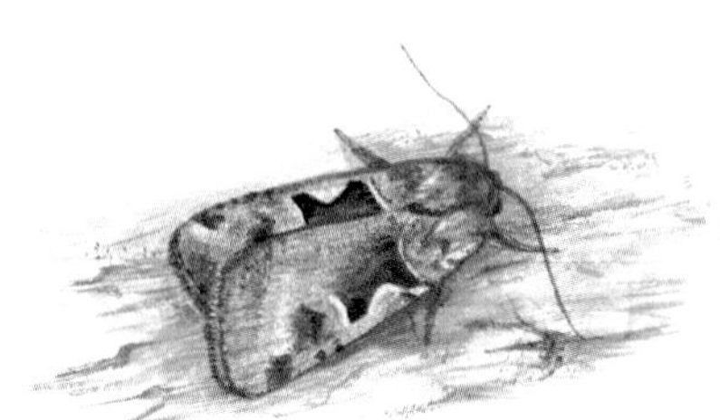


Setaceous Hebrew Character at rest

1
2
3
4
5
6
7
8
9
10
11
12
13
14
15

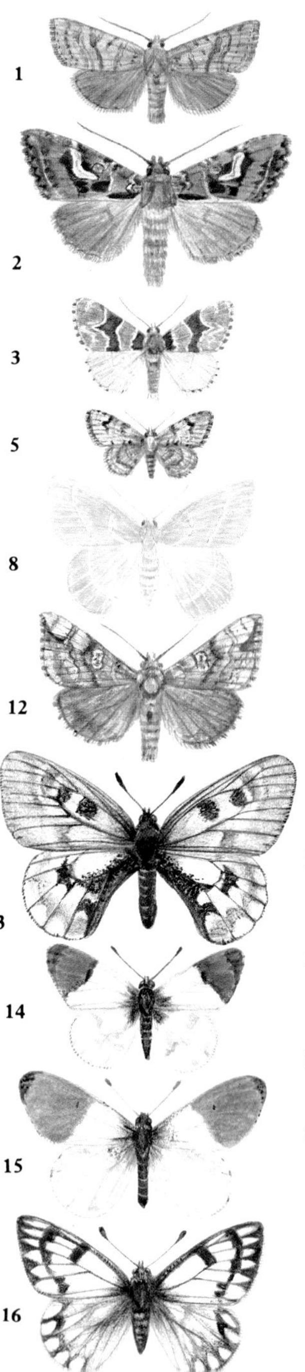


## PLATE 12

MEADOW BUTTERCUP *Ranunculus acris*
family: Ranunculaceae

1. **Agrochola lychnidis** *Beaded Chestnut* 246

LESSER CELANDINE *Ranunculus ficaria*
family: Ranunculaceae

2. **Trigonophora flammea** *Flame Brocade* 244

COMMON MEADOW-RUE *Thalictrum flavum*
family: Ranunculaceae

3. **Perizoma sagittata** *Marsh Carpet* 90

FLIXWEED *Descurainia sophia* family: Cruciferae

4. **Lithostege griseata** *Grey Carpet* 98

TRAVELLER'S JOY *Clematis vitalba*
family: Ranunculaceae

5. **Chloroclystis v-ata** *V-Pug* 96
6. **Eupithecia haworthiata** *Haworth's Pug* 90
7. **Scopula nigropunctata** *Sub-angled Wave* 77
8. **Hemistola chrysoprasaria** *Small Emerald* 75
9. **Melanthia procellata** *Pretty Chalk Carpet* 87
10. **Horisme vitalbata** *Small Waved Umber* 87
11. **Horisme tersata** *Fern* 87

*Delphinium* family: Ranunculaceae

12. **Polychrysia moneta** *Golden Plusia* 265

BULBOUS CORYDALIS *Corydalis solida*
family: Fumariaceae

13. **Parnassius mnemosyne** *Clouded Apollo* 34

BUCKLER MUSTARD *Biscutella laevigata*
family: Cruciferae

14. **Anthocharis belia** *Morocco Orange-tip* 40

HEDGE MUSTARD *Sisymbrium officinale*
family: Cruciferae

15. **Anthocharis cardamines** *Orange-tip* 40

*Erysimum pumilum* family: Cruciferae

16. **Pontia callidice** *Peak White* 40

12

Cocoon of Golden Plusia

1
2
3
4
5
6
7
8
9
10
11
12
13
14
15
16

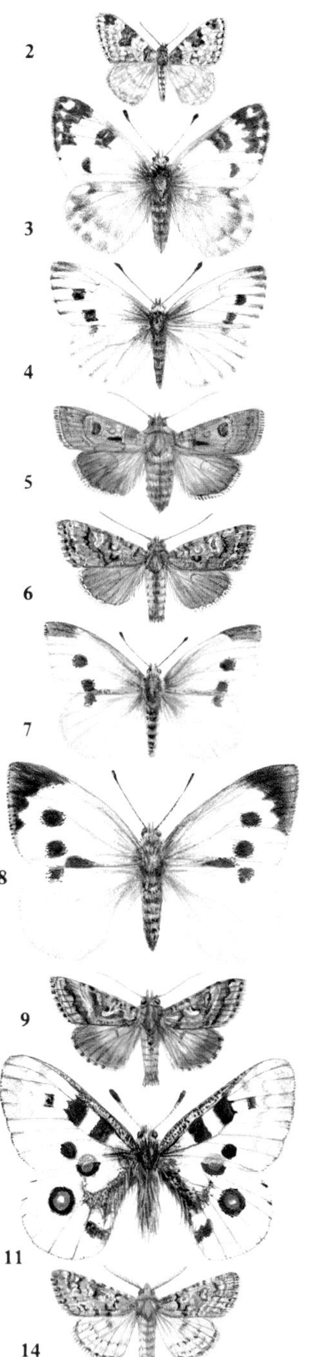


**PLATE 13**

HORSE-RADISH *Armoracia rusticana*
family: Cruciferae

| | | |
|---|---|---|
| 1. | **Euchloe simplonia** *Freyer's Dappled White* | 40 |
| 2. | **Xanthorhoe fluctuata** *Garden Carpet* | 80 |

WILD MIGNONETTE *Reseda lutea*
family: Resedaceae

| | | |
|---|---|---|
| 3. | **Pontia daplidice** *Bath White* | 39 |

GARLIC MUSTARD *Alliaria petiolata*
family: Cruciferae

| | | |
|---|---|---|
| 4. | **Pieris napi** *Green-veined White* | 39 |

TURNIP *Brassica rapa* family: Cruciferae

| | | |
|---|---|---|
| 5. | **Agrotis exclamationis** *Heart and Dart* | 216 |

CABBAGE *Brassica oleracea* family: Cruciferae

| | | |
|---|---|---|
| 6. | **Mamestra brassicae** *Cabbage Moth* | 228 |
| 7. | **Pieris rapae** *Small White* | 39 |
| 8. | **Pieris brassicae** *Large White* | 38 |
| 9. | **Autographa gamma** *Silver Y* | 265 |
| 10. | **Peridroma saucia** *Pearly Underwing* | 221 |

STONECROP *Sedum* family: Crassulaceae

| | | |
|---|---|---|
| 11. | **Parnassius apollo** *Apollo* | 33 |
| 12. | Gnophos glaucinaria | 115 |
| 13. | **Standfussiana lucernea** *Northern Rustic* | 218 |
| 14. | **Eumichtis lichenea** *Feathered Ranunculus* | 244 |

Egg batch of the Large White

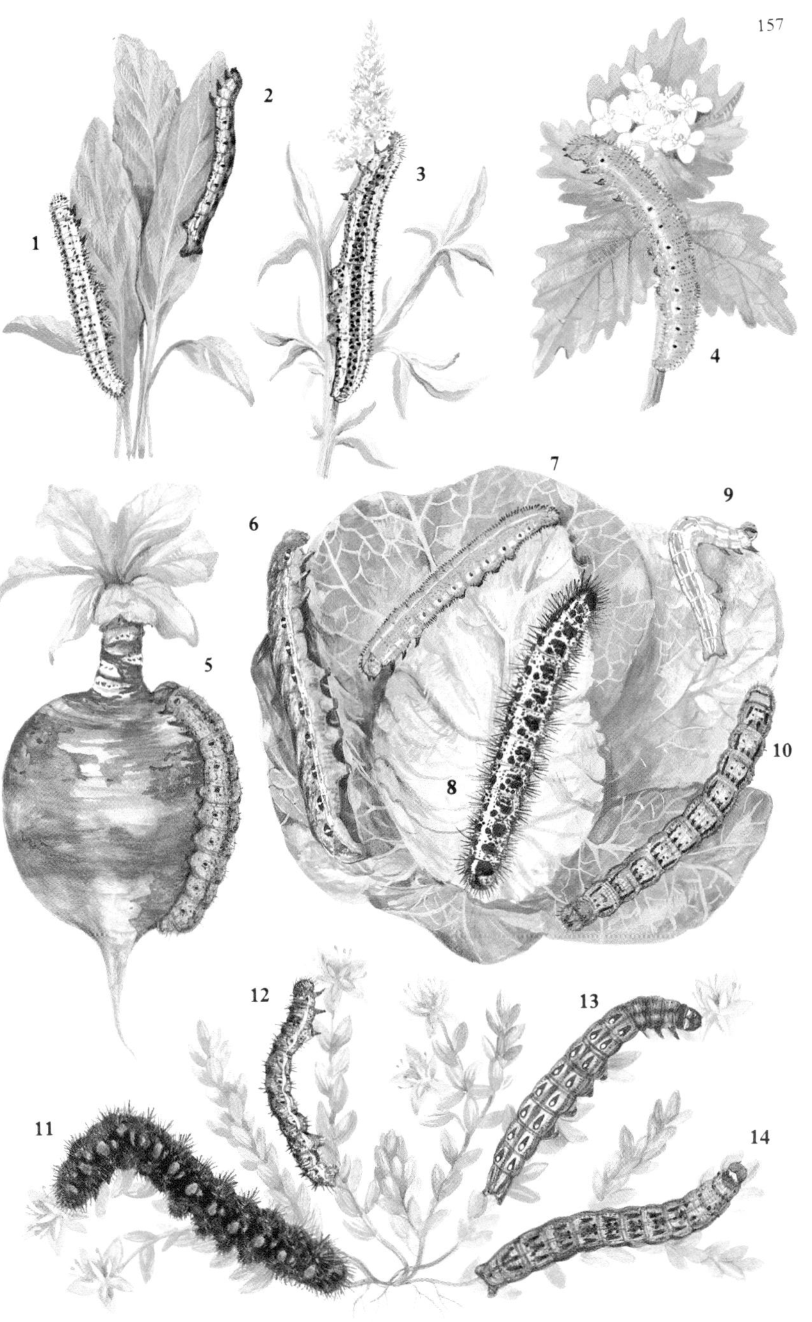
1
2
3
4
5
6
7
8
9
10
11
12
13
14

## PLATE 14

YELLOW SAXIFRAGE *Saxifraga aizoides*
family: Saxifragaceae

1. **Parnassius phoebus** *Small Apollo* 34

2. **Entephria flavicinctata** *Yellow-ringed Carpet* 82

SALAD BURNET *Sanguisorba minor* family: Rosaceae

3. Gnophos obscurata *Annulet* 115

LADY'S MANTLE *Alchemilla vulgaris*
family: Rosaceae

4. **Xanthorhoe munitata** *Red Carpet* 80

DOG ROSE *Rosa canina* family: Rosaceae

5. **Orthosia opima** *Northern Drab* 234

6 & 7. **Anticlea badiata** *Shoulder Stripe* 83

8. **Agrochola litura** *Brown-spot Pinion* 246

9. **Anticlea derivata** *Streamer* 83

10 & 11. **Orthosia cruda** *Small Quaker* 233

12. **Orgyia antiqua** *Vapourer* 203

13. **Cidaria fulvata** *Barred Yellow* 85

14. **Hemithea aestivaria** *Common Emerald* 75

Female Vapourer moth on cocoon

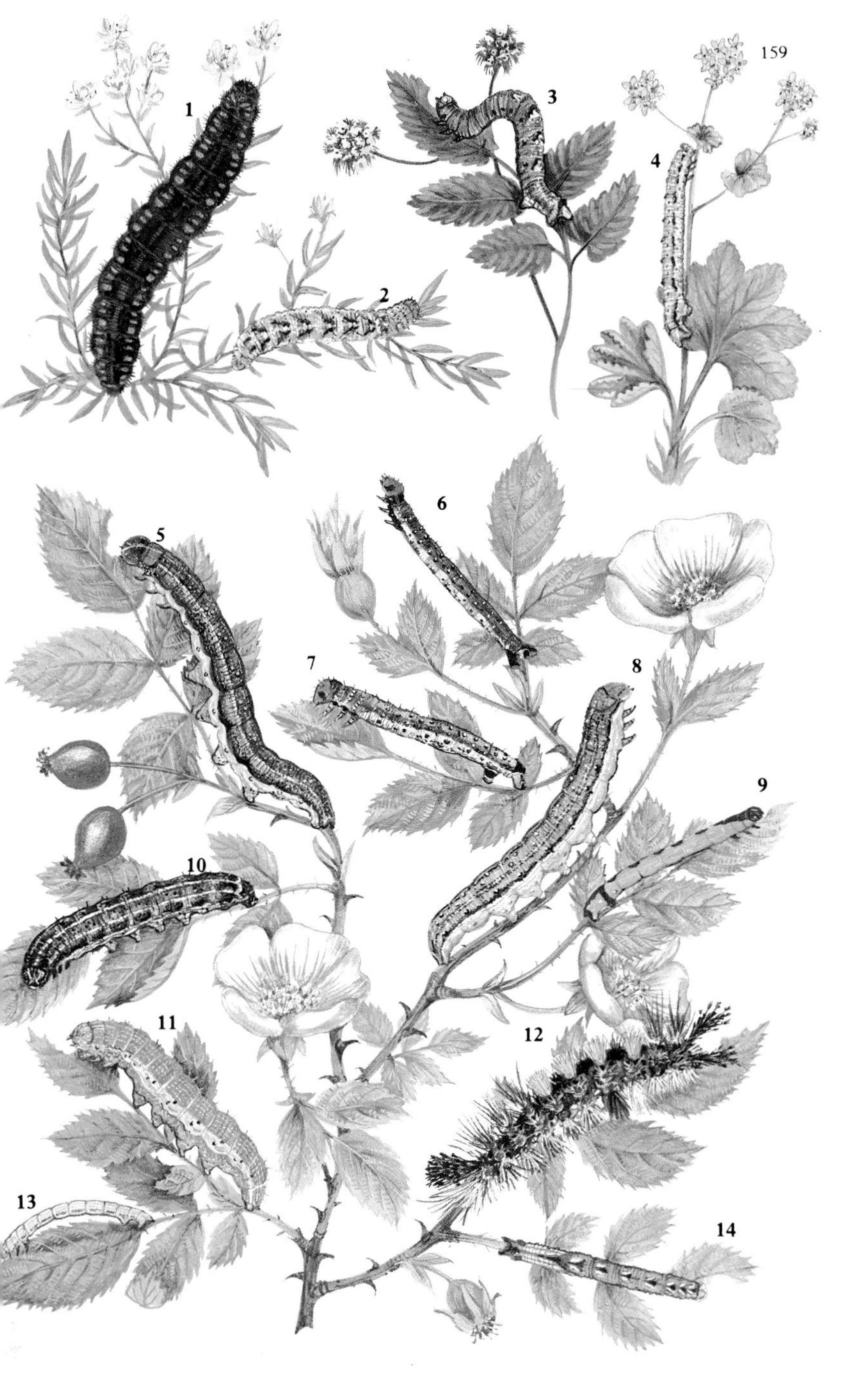
1
2
3
4
5
6
7
8
9
10
11
12
13
14

## PLATE 15

Raspberry *Rubus idaeus* family: Rosaceae

1. **Mesoleuca albicillata** *Beautiful Carpet* 83
2. **Acronicta auricoma** *Scarce Dagger* 250
3. **Spilosoma lutea** *Buff Ermine* 210

Wild Strawberry *Fragaria vesca* family: Rosaceae

4. **Pyrgus malvae** *Grizzled Skipper* 33

Bramble *Rubus fruticosus* family: Rosaceae

5. **Idaea biselata** *Small Fan-footed Wave* 77
6. **Habrosyne pyritoides** *Buff Arches* 71
7. **Lasiocampa quercus** *Oak Eggar* 63
8. **Idaea straminata** *Plain Wave* 79
9. **Xestia sexstrigata** *Six-striped Rustic* 224
10. **Eupithecia vulgata** *Common Pug* 93
11. **Diarsia brunnea** *Purple Clay* 222
12. **Polia nebulosa** *Grey Arches* 228
13. **Xestia ditrapezium** *Triple-spotted Clay* 223
14. **Anaplectoides prasina** *Green Arches* 226
15. **Hyppa rectilinea** *Saxon* 255
16. **Thyatira batis** *Peach Blossom* 70

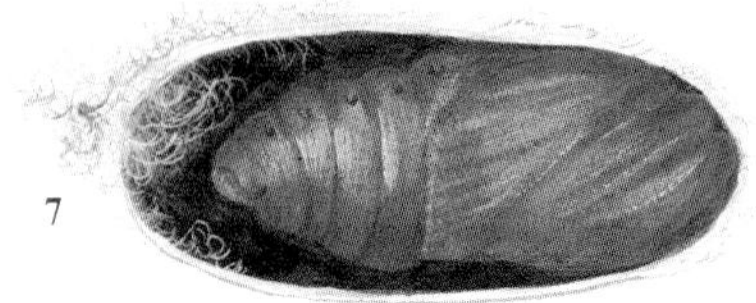


Cocoon of Oak Eggar opened to show pupa

1
2
4
3
8
5
7
9
6
10
11
12
13
14
16
15

## PLATE 16

CREEPING CINQUEFOIL *Potentilla reptans* family: Rosaceae

1. **Elaphria venustula** *Rosy Marbled*
2. **Aspitates gilvaria** *Straw Belle*

WATER AVENS *Geum rivale* family: Rosaceae

3. **Idaea aversata** *Riband Wave*

ROWAN *Sorbus aucuparia* family: Rosaceae

4. **Venusia cambrica** *Welsh Wave*

APPLE *Malus sylvestris* family: Rosaceae

5. **Malacosoma neustria** *Lackey*
6. **Chloroclystis rectangulata** *Green Pug*
7. **Operophtera brumata** *Winter Moth*
8. **Alsophila aescularia** *March Moth*
9. **Synanthedon myopaeformis** *Red-belted Clearwing*
10. **Diloba caeruleocephala** *Figure of Eight*
11. **Nola confusalis** *Least Black Arches*
12. **Naenia typica** *Gothic*
13. **Orthosia incerta** *Clouded Drab*

PEAR *Pyrus communis* family: Rosaceae

14. **Acronicta tridens** *Dark Dagger*
15. **Acronicta psi** *Grey Dagger*
16. **Zeuzera pyrina** *Leopard Moth*

3

5

8

9

10

12

13

15

16

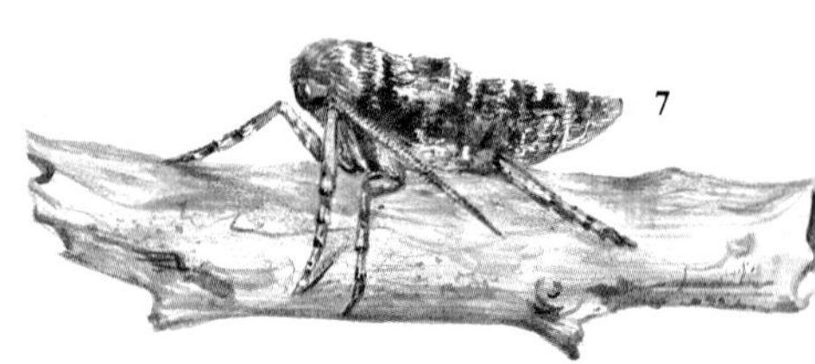


Female Winter Moth

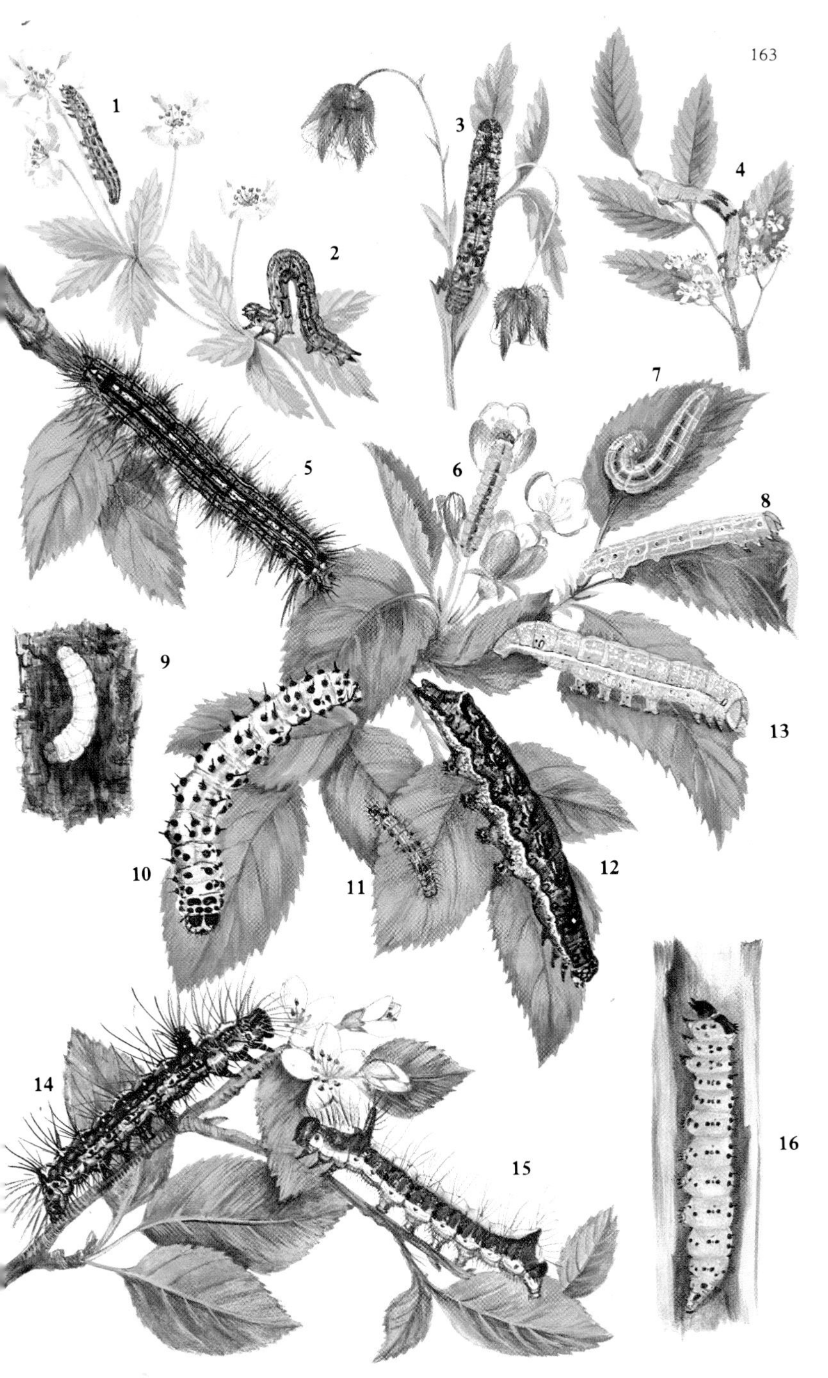

1
2
3
4
5
6
7
8
9
10
11
12
13
14
15
16

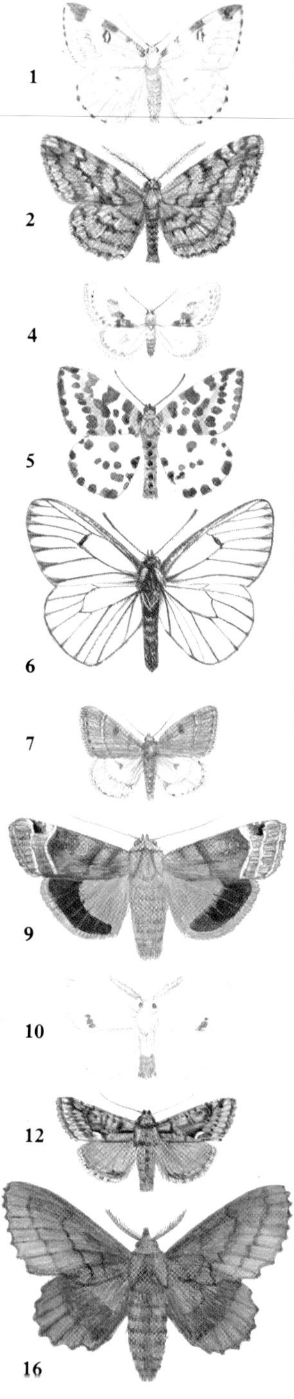

## PLATE 17

HAWTHORN *Crataegus monogyna* family: Rosaceae

1. **Opisthograptis luteolata** *Brimstone Moth*
2. **Peribatodes rhomboidaria** *Willow Beauty*
3. **Gymnoscelis rufifasciata** *Double-striped Pug* 9
4. **Cilix glaucata** *Chinese Character*
5. **Abraxas grossulariata** *Magpie Moth* 1
6. **Aporia crataegi** *Black-veined White* 3
7. **Theria primaria** *Early Moth* 11
8. **Eriogaster lanestris** *Small Eggar* 6
9. **Noctua fimbriata** *Broad-bordered Yellow Underwing* 21
10. **Euproctis similis** *Yellow-tail* 20
11. **Trichiura crataegi** *Pale Eggar* 6
12. **Allophyes oxyacanthae** *Green-brindled Crescent* 24
13. **Nola cucullatella** *Short-cloaked Moth* 21
14. **Noctua janthina** *Lesser Broad-bordered Yellow Underwing* 21
15. **Xestia triangulum** *Double Square-spot* 22
16. **Gastropacha quercifolia** *Lappet* 6

Lappet moth as leaf mimic

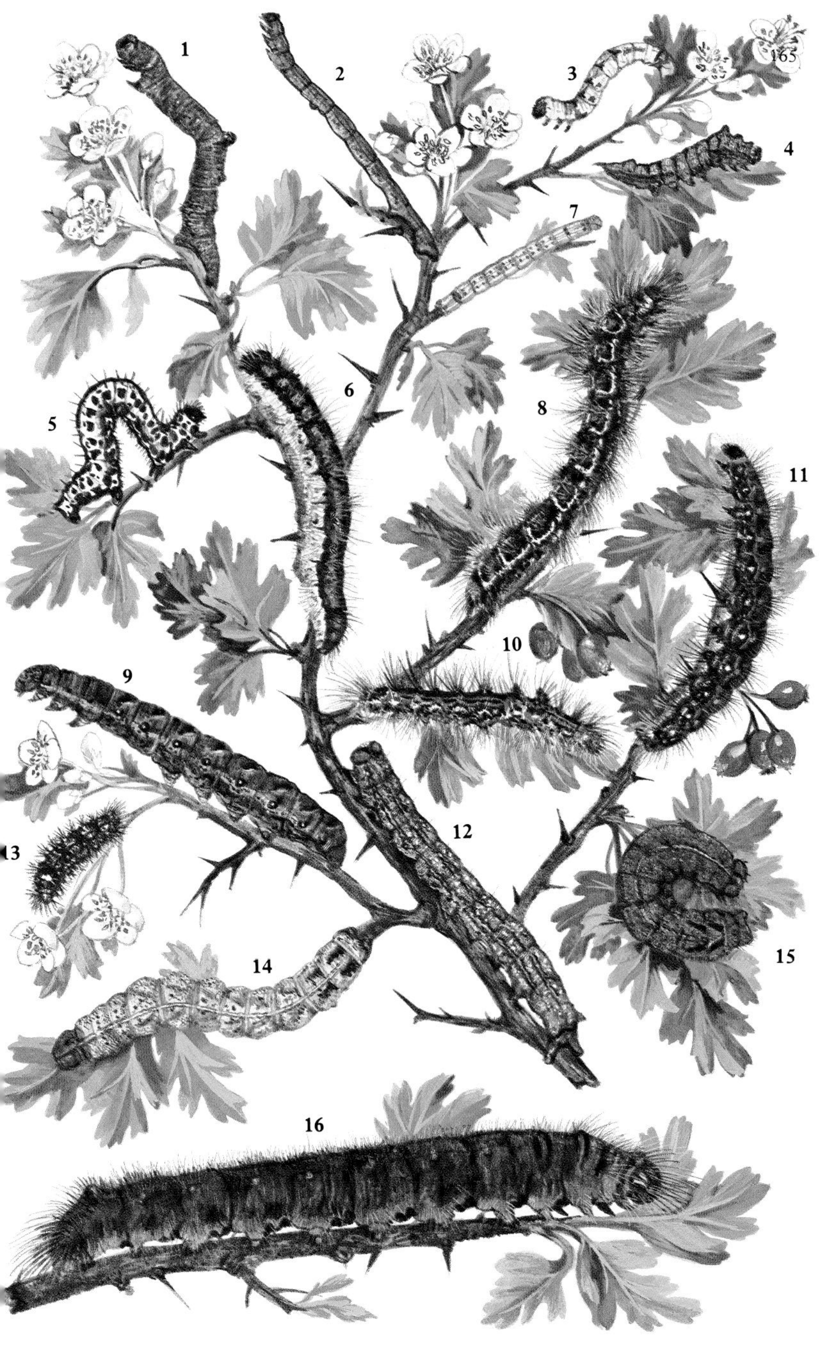
1
2
3
4
5
6
7
8
9
10
11
12
13
14
15
16

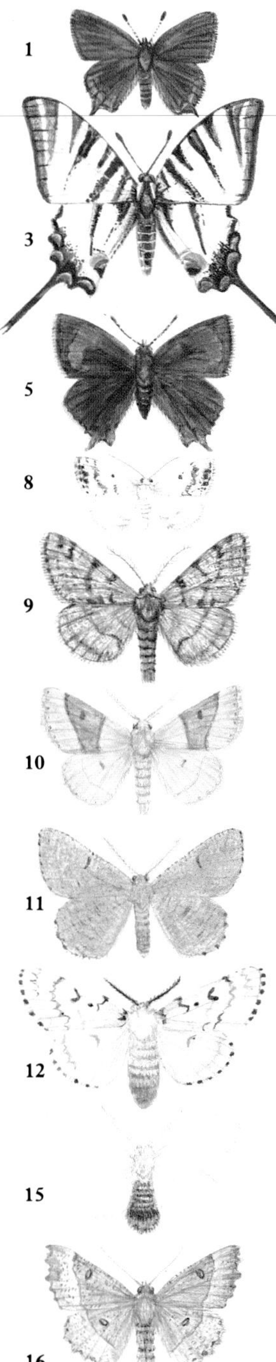


## PLATE 18

BLACKTHORN *Prunus spinosa* family: Rosaceae
(*See also* Pl. 33)

1. **Strymonidia pruni** *Black Hairstreak* 42
2. **Aleucis distinctata** *Sloe Carpet* 114
3. **Iphiclides podalirius** *Scarce Swallowtail* 36

4 & 6. **Semiothisa alternaria** *Sharp-angled Peacock* 101

5. **Thecla betulae** *Brown Hairstreak* 41

BIRD CHERRY *Prunus padus* family: Rosaceae

7. **Triphosia dubitata** *Tissue* 88
8. **Lomographa temerata** *Clouded Silver* 113

WILD PLUM *Prunus domestica* family: Rosaceae

9. **Apocheima pilosaria** *Pale Brindled Beauty* 108
10. **Crocallis elinguaria** *Scalloped Oak* 107
11. **Angerona prunaria** *Orange Moth* 108
12. **Lymantria dispar** *Gypsy Moth* 206
13. **Selenia lunularia** *Lunar Thorn* 106
14. **Conistra rubiginea** *Dotted Chestnut* 245
15. **Euproctis chrysorrhoea** *Brown-tail* 204
16. **Odontopera bidentata** *Scalloped Hazel* 106

Nest of Brown-tail caterpillars

1
2
3
4
5
6
7
8
9
10
11
12
13
14
15
16

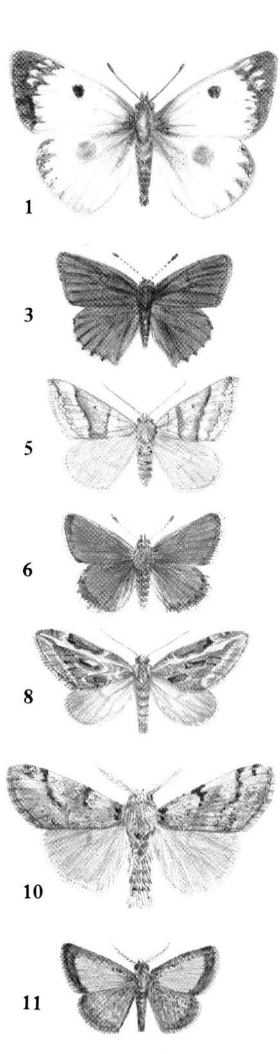

1

3

5

6

8

10

11

13

# PLATE 19

CROWN VETCH *Coronilla varia*
family: Leguminosae

1. **Colias australis** *Berger's Clouded Yellow* 37
2. **Zygaena transalpina** 27

GORSE *Ulex europaeus* family: Leguminosae

3. **Callophrys rubi** *Green Hairstreak* 41
4. **Perconia strigillaria** *Grass Wave* 116
5. **Scotopteryx mucronata** *Lead Belle* 81
6. **Plebejus argus** *Silver-studded Blue* 44

BROOM *Cytisus scoparius* family: Leguminosae
(*See also* Pl. 33)

7. **Chesias rufata** *Broom-tip* 98

8 & 9. **Chesias legatella** *Streak* 97

10. **Dicallomera fascelina** *Dark Tussock* 203
11. **Isturgia limbaria** *Frosted Yellow* 102
12. **Rhyparia purpurata** 210

DYER'S GREENWEED *Genista tinctoria*
family: Leguminosae

13. **Heterogynis penella** 28
14. **Lacanobia w-latinum** *Light Brocade* 230

PETTY WHIN *Genista anglica* family: Leguminosae

15. Gnophos obfuscata *Scotch Annulet* 115
16. **Pseudoterpna pruinata** *Grass Emerald* 74

14

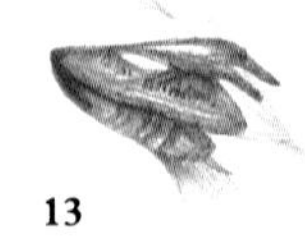

13

16

Cocoon and empty pupa shell of *Heterogynis penella* ♂

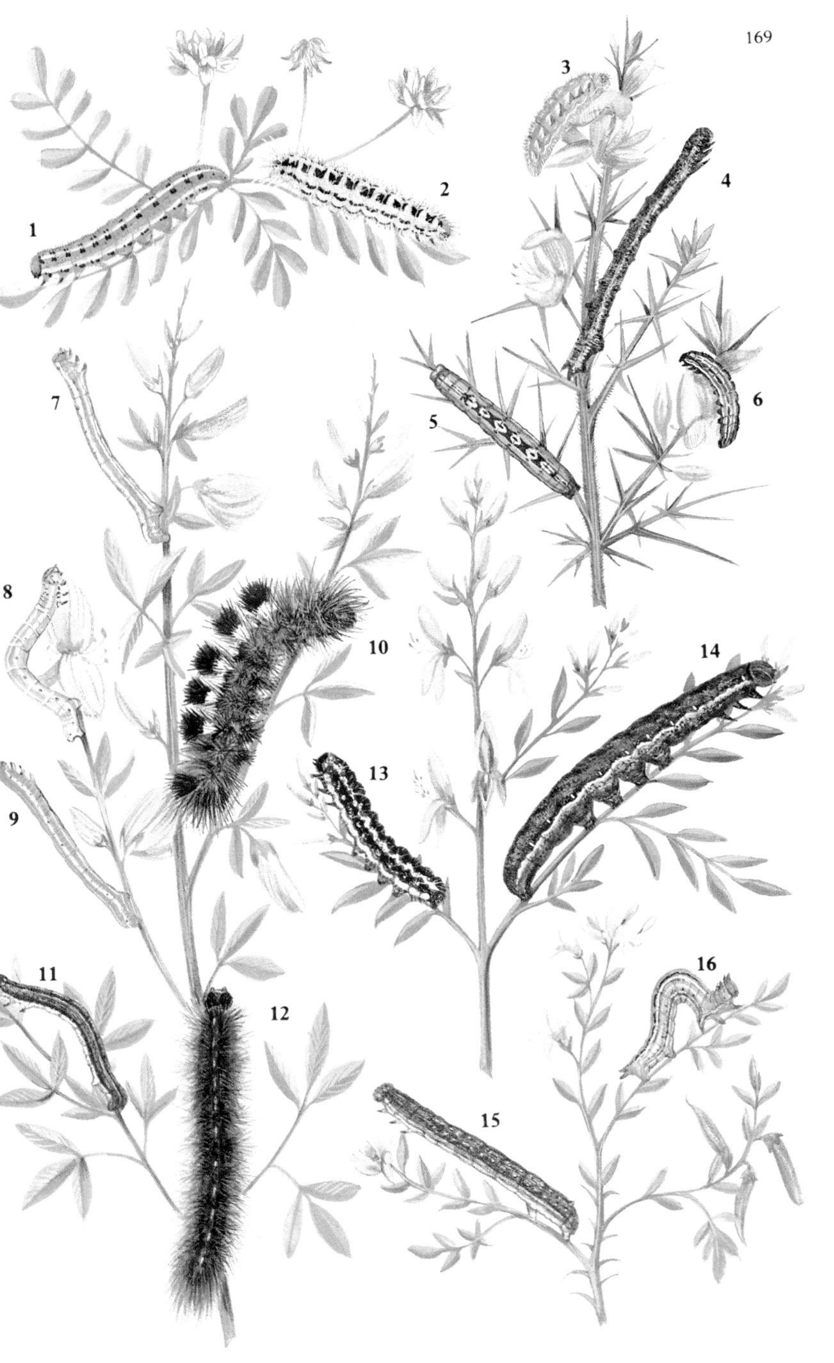
1
2
3
4
5
6
7
8
9
10
11
12
13
14
15
16

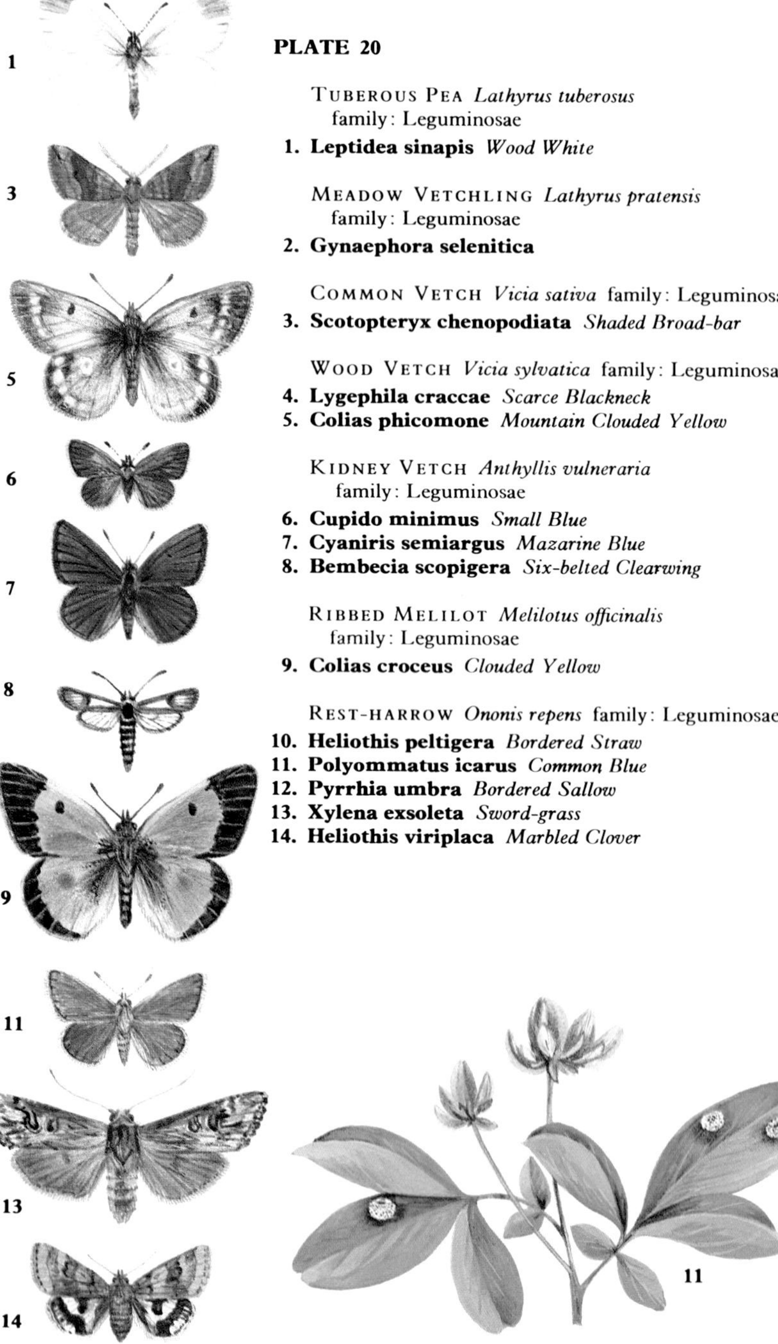


## PLATE 20

TUBEROUS PEA *Lathyrus tuberosus*
family: Leguminosae

1. **Leptidea sinapis** *Wood White* 3

MEADOW VETCHLING *Lathyrus pratensis*
family: Leguminosae

2. **Gynaephora selenitica** 20

COMMON VETCH *Vicia sativa* family: Leguminosae

3. **Scotopteryx chenopodiata** *Shaded Broad-bar* 8

WOOD VETCH *Vicia sylvatica* family: Leguminosae

4. **Lygephila craccae** *Scarce Blackneck* 26
5. **Colias phicomone** *Mountain Clouded Yellow* 3

KIDNEY VETCH *Anthyllis vulneraria*
family: Leguminosae

6. **Cupido minimus** *Small Blue* 4
7. **Cyaniris semiargus** *Mazarine Blue* 4
8. **Bembecia scopigera** *Six-belted Clearwing* 2

RIBBED MELILOT *Melilotus officinalis*
family: Leguminosae

9. **Colias croceus** *Clouded Yellow* 3

REST-HARROW *Ononis repens* family: Leguminosae

10. **Heliothis peltigera** *Bordered Straw* 26
11. **Polyommatus icarus** *Common Blue* 4
12. **Pyrrhia umbra** *Bordered Sallow* 26
13. **Xylena exsoleta** *Sword-grass* 24
14. **Heliothis viriplaca** *Marbled Clover* 26

Eggs of the Common Blue

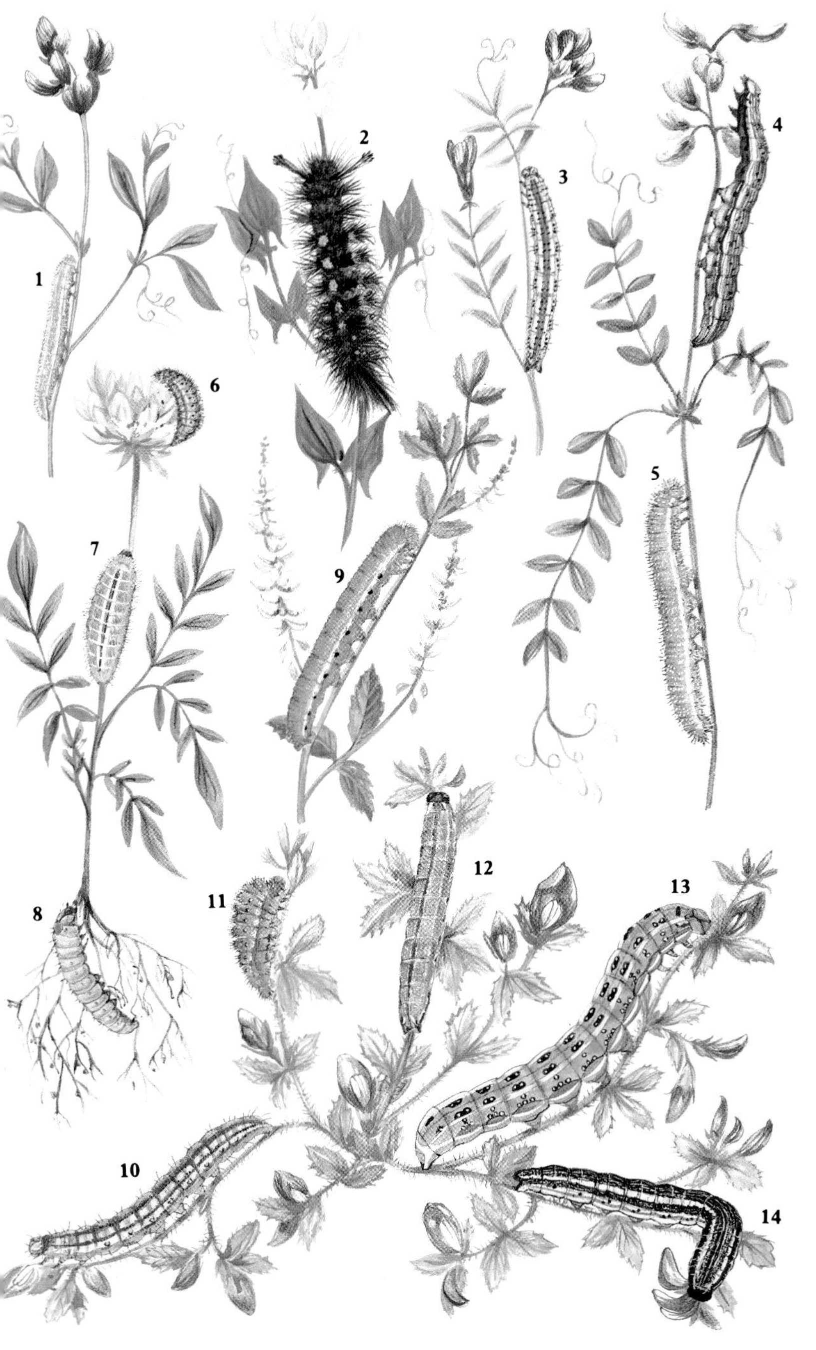
1
2
3
4
5
6
7
8
9
10
11
12
13
14

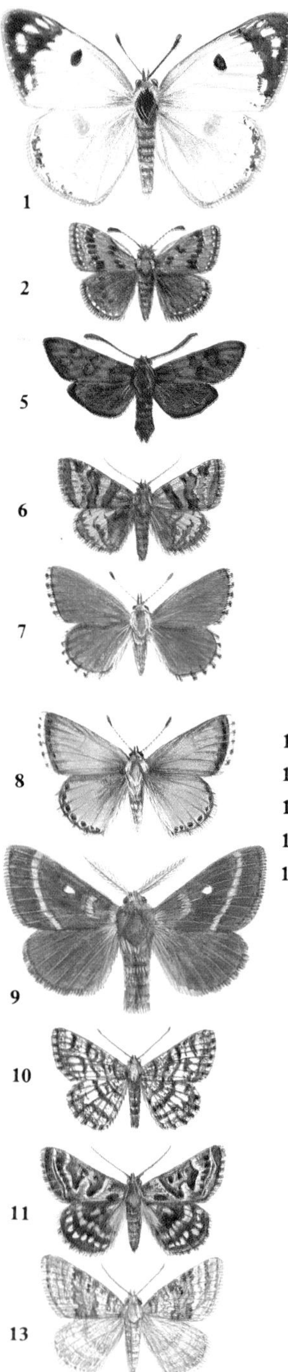


## PLATE 21

LUCERNE *Medicago sativa* family: Leguminosae

1. **Colias hyale** *Pale Clouded Yellow*

BIRDSFOOT TREFOIL *Lotus corniculatus* family: Leguminosae

2. **Erynnis tages** *Dingy Skipper*
3. **Everes argiades** *Short-tailed Blue*
4. **Zygaena trifolii** *Five-spot Burnet*
5. **Zygaena filipendulae** *Six-spot Burnet*

BLACK MEDICK *Medicago lupulina* family: Leguminosae

6. **Euclidia glyphica** *Burnet Companion*

HORSESHOE VETCH *Hippocrepis comosa* family: Leguminosae

7. **Lysandra bellargus** *Adonis Blue*
8. **Lysandra coridon** *Chalkhill Blue*

BIRDSFOOT *Ornithopus perpusillus* family: Leguminosae

9. **Lasiocampa trifolii** *Grass Eggar*

RED CLOVER *Trifolium pratense* family: Leguminosae

10. **Semiothisa clathrata** *Latticed Heath*
11. **Callistege mi** *Mother Shipton*
12. **Scopula rubiginata** *Tawny Wave*
13. **Scotopteryx bipunctaria** *Chalk Carpet*
14. **Zygaena lonicerae** *Narrow-bordered Five-spot Burnet*

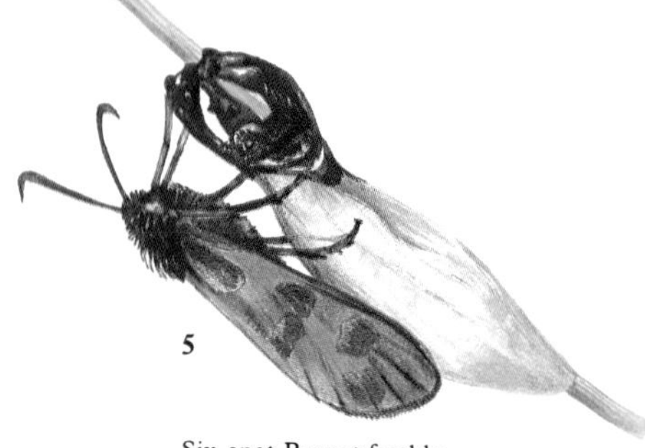


Six-spot Burnet freshly emerged from its cocoon

1
2
3
4
5
6
7
8
9
10
11
12
13
14

## PLATE 22

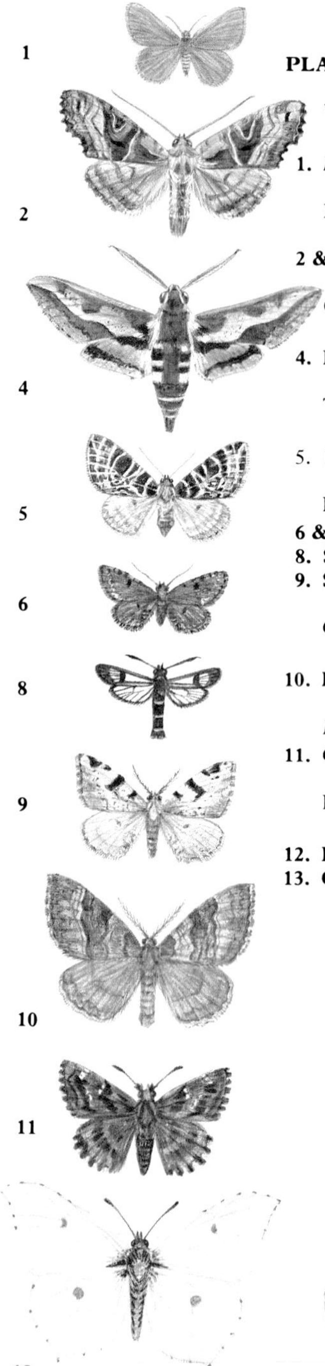

Wood Spurge *Euphorbia amagdyloides*
family Euphorbiaceae

1. **Minoa murinata** *Drab Looper*

Dog's Mercury *Mercurialis perennis*
family Euphoriaceae

2 & 3. **Phlogophora meticulosa** *Angle Shades*

Cypress Spurge *Euphorbia cyparissias*
family Euphorbiaceae

4. **Hyles euphorbiae** *Spurge Hawk-moth*

Touch-me-not Balsam *Impatiens noli-tangere*
family: Balsaminaceae

5. Eustroma reticulata *Netted Carpet*

Redcurrant *Ribes rubrum* family: Grossulariaceae

6 & 7. **Eupithecia assimilata** *Currant Pug*
8. **Symanthedon tipuliformis** *Currant Clearwing*
9. **Semiothisa wauaria** *V-Moth*

Common Mallow *Malva sylvestris*
family: Malvaceae

10. **Larentia clavaria** *Mallow*

Mallow *Malva* family: Malvaceae

11. **Carcharodus alceae** *Mallow Skipper*

Buckthorn *Rhamnus catharticus*
family: Rhamnaceae

12. **Philereme transversata** *Dark Umber*
13. **Gonepteryx rhamni** *Brimstone*

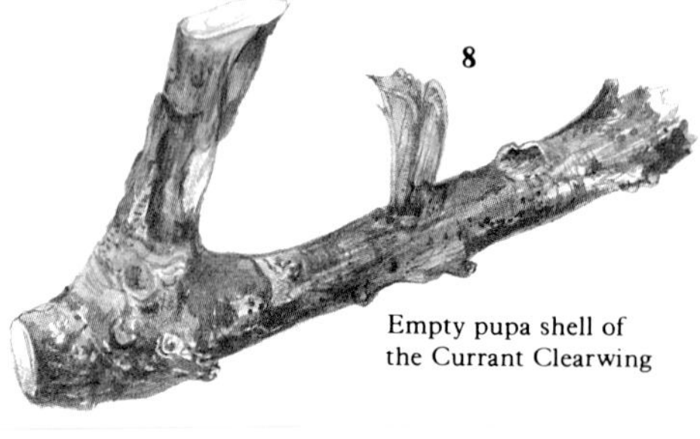

8

Empty pupa shell of the Currant Clearwing

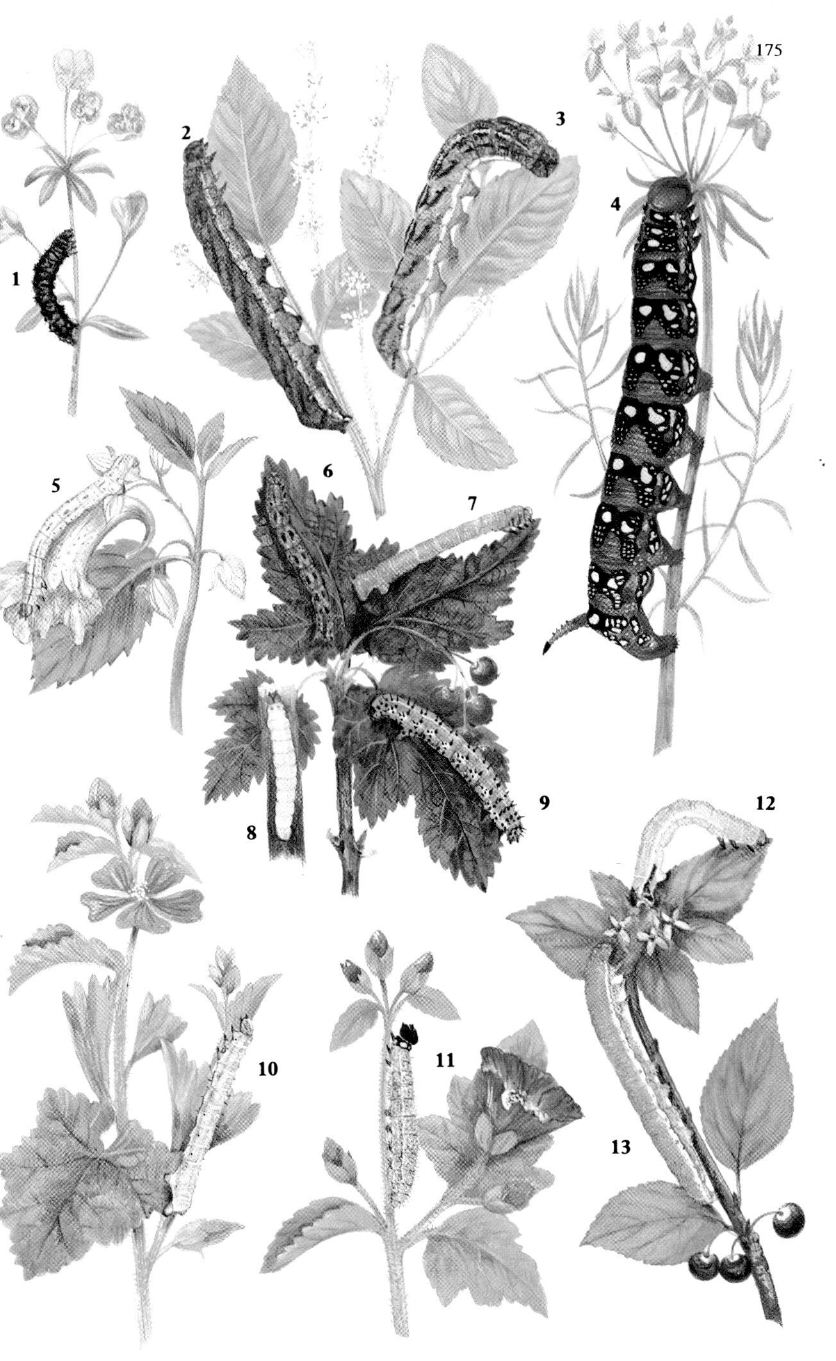
1
2
3
4
5
6
7
8
9
10
11
12
13

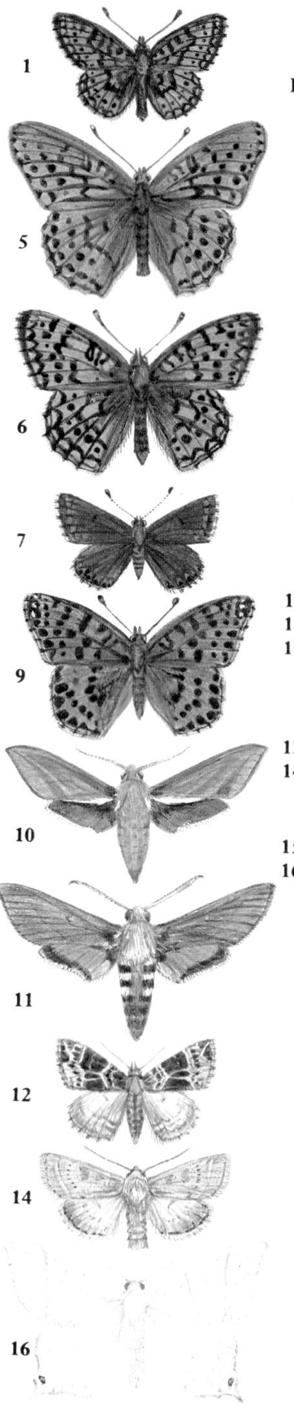


## PLATE 23

Dog Violet *Viola riviniana* family: Violaceae

1. **Boloria euphrosyne** *Pearl-bordered Fritillary* 5
2. **Boloria dia** *Violet Fritillary* 5
3. **Argynnis adippe** *High Brown Fritillary* 5
4. **Boloria selene** *Small Pearl-bordered Fritillary* 5
5. **Argynnis paphia** *Silver-washed Fritillary* 5
6. **Argynnis aglaja** *Dark Green Fritillary* 5

Common Rock Rose *Helianthemum nummularium* family: Cistaceae

7. **Aricia agestis** *Brown Argus* 4
8. **Aricia artaxerxes** *Northern Brown Argus* 4

Sweet Violet *Viola odorata* family: Violaceae

9. **Argynnis lathonia** *Queen of Spain Fritillary* 5

Rosebay Willowherb *Epilobium angustifolium* family: Onagraceae

10. **Deilephila elpenor** *Elephant Hawk-moth* 12
11. **Hyles vespertilio** 12
12. **Ecliptopera silaceata** *Small Phoenix* 8

Purple Loosestrife *Lythrum salicaria* family: Lythraceae

13. **Deilephila porcellus** *Small Elephant Hawk-moth* 12
14. **Orthosia gracilis** *Powdered Quaker* 23

Ivy *Hedera helix* family: Araliaceae

15. **Acasis viretata** *Yellow-barred Brindle* 9
16. **Ourapteryx sambucaria** *Swallow-tailed Moth* 10

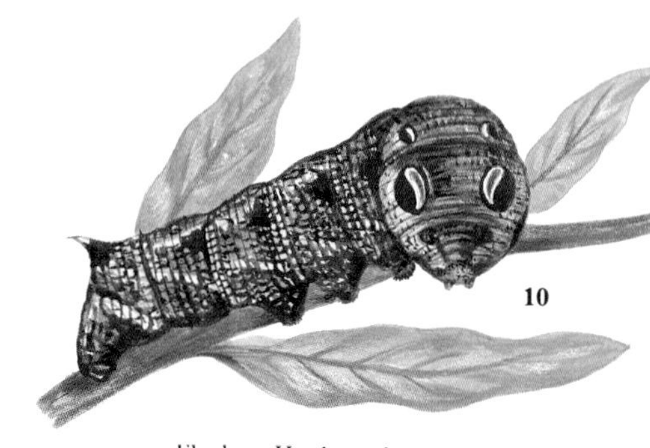


Elephant Hawk-moth caterpillar in defence posture

1
2
3
4
5
6
7
8
9
10
11
12
13
14
15
16

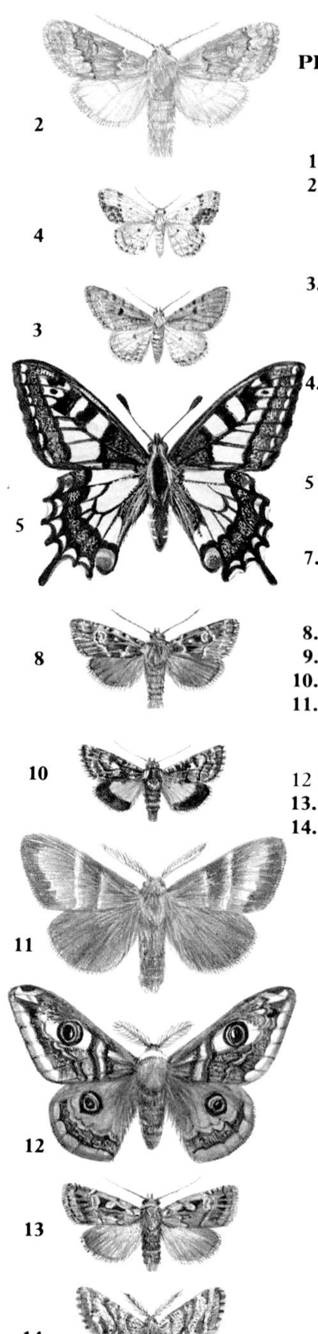


## PLATE 24

HOGWEED *Heracleum sphondylum*
family: Umbelliferae

1. **Eupithecia tripunctaria** *White-spotted Pug* 94
2. **Dasypolia templi** *Brindled Ochre* 240

BURNET SAXIFRAGE *Pimpinella saxifraga*
family: Umbelliferae

3. **Eupithecia pimpinellata** *Pimpinel Pug* 94

COW PARSLEY *Anthriscus sylvestris*
family: Umbelliferae

4. **Idaea dimidiata** *Single-dotted Wave* 78

MILK PARSLEY *Peucedanum palustre*
family: Umbelliferae

5 & 6 (young). **Papilio machaon** *Swallowtail* 35

HONEWORT *Trinia glauca* family: Umbelliferae

7. **Papilio alexanor** *Southern Swallowtail* 35

HEATHER *Calluna vulgaris* family: Ericaceae

8. **Lycophotia porphyrea** *True Lover's Knot* 221
9. **Eupithecia goosensiata** *Ling Pug* 93
10. **Anarta myrtilli** *Beautiful Yellow Underwing* 226
11. **Macrothylacia rubi** *Fox Moth* 63

BELL HEATHER *Erica cinerea* family: Ericaceae

12 (young) & 15. Pavonia pavonia *Emperor Moth* 65
13. **Xestia agathina** *Heath Rustic* 225
14. **Ematurga atomaria** *Common Heath* 113

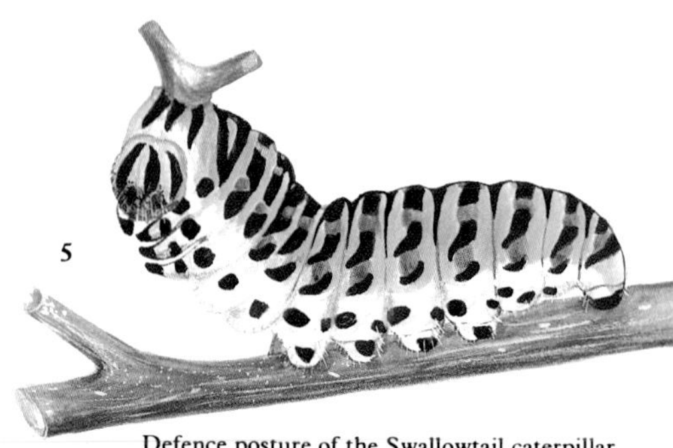


Defence posture of the Swallowtail caterpillar

1
2
3
4
5
6
7
8
9
10
11
12
13
14
15

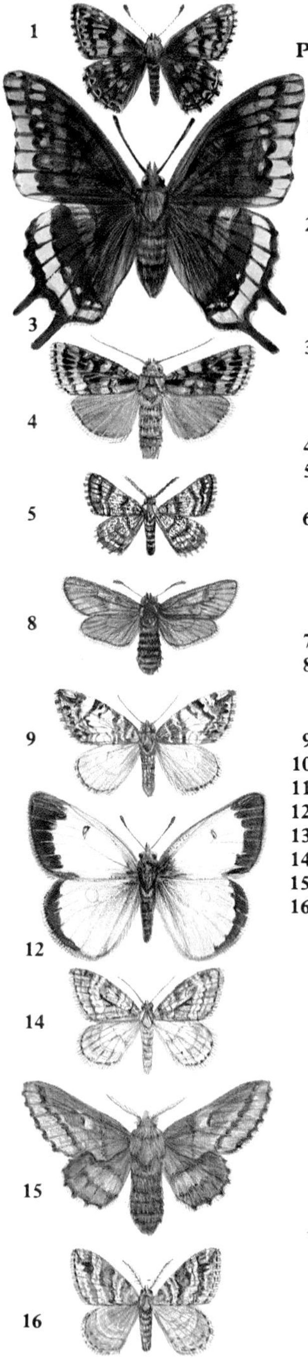

## PLATE 25

COWSLIP *Primula veris* family: Primulaceae

1. **Hamearis lucina** *Duke of Burgundy Fritillary* 48

COWBERRY *Vaccinium vitis-idaea* family: Ericaceae

2. **Anarta melanopa** *Broad-bordered White Underwing* 227

STRAWBERRY TREE *Arbutus unedo* family: Ericaceae

3. **Charaxes jasius** *Two-tailed Pasha* 48

ALPINE BEARBERRY *Arctostaphylos uva-ursi* family: Ericaceae

4. **Xestia alpicola** *Northern Dart* 222
5. **Semiothisa carbonaria** *Netted Mountain Carpet* 102
6. **Anarta cordigera** *Small Dark Yellow Underwing* 227

CROWBERRY *Empetrum nigrum* family: Empetraceae

7. **Idaea contiguaria** *Weaver's Wave* 78
8. **Zygaena exulans** *Scotch Burnet* 25

BILBERRY *Vaccinium myrtillus* family: Ericaceae

9. **Chloroclysta truncata** *Common Marbled Carpet* 85
10. **Chloroclystis debiliata** *Bilberry Pug* 97
11. **Eulithis populata** *Northern Spinach* 84
12. **Colias palaeno** *Moorland Clouded Yellow* 36
13. **Chloroclysta citrata** *Dark Marbled Carpet* 85
14. **Epirrita filigrammaria** *Small Autumnal Moth* 89
15. **Phyllodesma ilicifolia** *Small Lappet* 64
16. **Perizoma didymata** *Twin-spot Carpet* 90

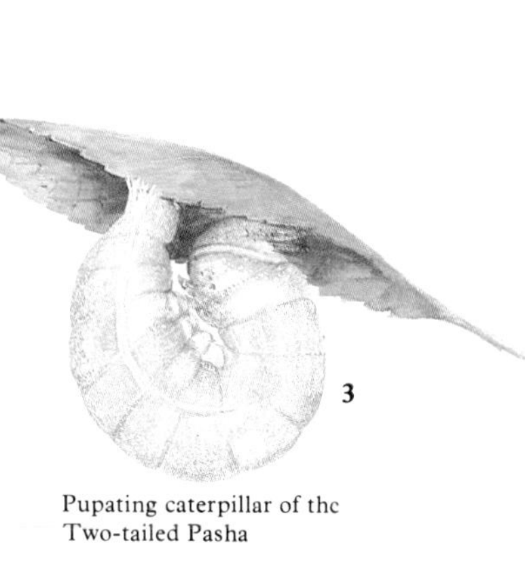

Pupating caterpillar of the Two-tailed Pasha

1
2
3
4
5
6
7
8
9
10
11
12
13
14
15
16

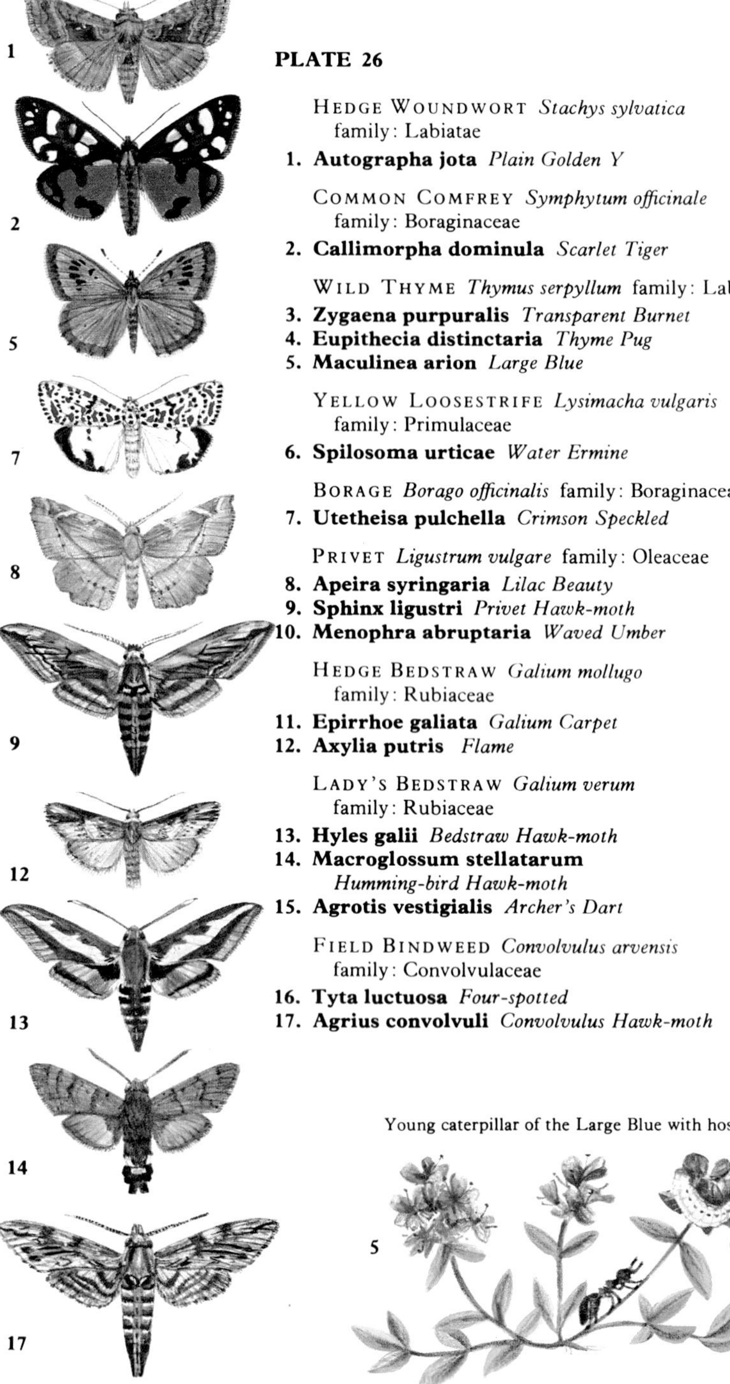


## PLATE 26

HEDGE WOUNDWORT *Stachys sylvatica*
family: Labiatae

1. **Autographa jota** *Plain Golden Y* 265

COMMON COMFREY *Symphytum officinale*
family: Boraginaceae

2. **Callimorpha dominula** *Scarlet Tiger* 212

WILD THYME *Thymus serpyllum* family: Labiatae

3. **Zygaena purpuralis** *Transparent Burnet* 27
4. **Eupithecia distinctaria** *Thyme Pug* 94
5. **Maculinea arion** *Large Blue* 47

YELLOW LOOSESTRIFE *Lysimacha vulgaris*
family: Primulaceae

6. **Spilosoma urticae** *Water Ermine* 211

BORAGE *Borago officinalis* family: Boraginaceae

7. **Utetheisa pulchella** *Crimson Speckled* 208

PRIVET *Ligustrum vulgare* family: Oleaceae

8. **Apeira syringaria** *Lilac Beauty* 103
9. **Sphinx ligustri** *Privet Hawk-moth* 117
10. **Menophra abruptaria** *Waved Umber* 111

HEDGE BEDSTRAW *Galium mollugo*
family: Rubiaceae

11. **Epirrhoe galiata** *Galium Carpet* 81
12. **Axylia putris** *Flame* 217

LADY'S BEDSTRAW *Galium verum*
family: Rubiaceae

13. **Hyles galii** *Bedstraw Hawk-moth* 120
14. **Macroglossum stellatarum** *Humming-bird Hawk-moth* 120
15. **Agrotis vestigialis** *Archer's Dart* 215

FIELD BINDWEED *Convolvulus arvensis*
family: Convolvulaceae

16. **Tyta luctuosa** *Four-spotted* 268
17. **Agrius convolvuli** *Convolvulus Hawk-moth* 116

Young caterpillar of the Large Blue with host ant

1
2
3
4
5
6
7
9
10
11
12
13
14
15
16
17

## PLATE 27

Great Mullein *Verbascum thapsus*
family: Scrophulariaceae

1. **Cucullia verbasci** *Mullein Moth* 239

Common Toadflax *Linaria vulgaris*
family: Scrophulariaceae

2. **Eupithecia linariata** *Toadflax Pug* 91

Dark Mullein *Verbascum nigrum*
family: Scrophulariaceae

3. **Cucullia lychnitis** *Striped Lychnis* 239

Common Figwort *Scrophularia nodosa*
family: Scrophulariaceae

4. **Cucullia scrophulariae** *Water Betony* 239

Sea Plantain *Plantago maritima*
family: Plantaginaceae

5. **Melitaea cinxia** *Glanville Fritillary* 56

Ribwort Plantain *Plantago lanceolata*
family: Plantaginaceae

6. **Parasemia plantaginis** *Wood Tiger* 208
7. **Hepialus lupulinus** *Common Swift* 23
8. **Melanchra persicariae** *Dot Moth* 229
9. **Melitaea didyma** *Spotted Fritillary* 55
10. **Euplexia lucipara** *Small Angle Shades* 254
11. **Hydraecia micacea** *Rosy Rustic* 257

Foxglove *Digitalis purpurea*
family: Scrophulariaceae

12. **Eupithecia pulchellata** *Foxglove Pug* 91
13. **Gortyna flavago** *Frosted Orange* 257

Common Cow-wheat *Melampyrum pratense*
family: Scrophulariaceae

14. **Mellicta athalia** *Heath Fritillary* 56
15. **Melitaea diamina** *False Heath Fritillary* 55

Potato *Solanum tuberosum* family: Solanaceae

16. **Acherontia atropos** *Death's Head Hawk-moth* 117

1 Cocoon of the Mullein Moth cut open to show pupa

1
2
3
4
5
6
7
8
9
10
11
12
13
14
15
16

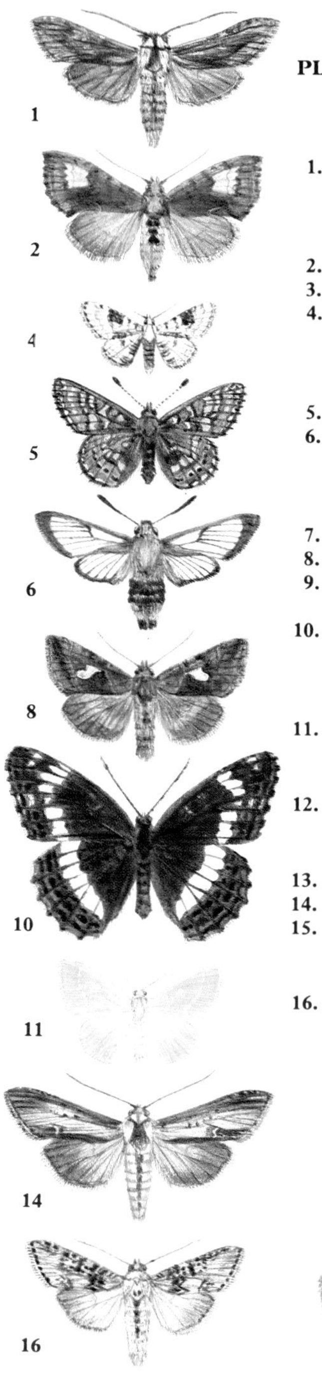


## PLATE 28

SCENTLESS MAYWEED *Matricaria perforata*
family: Compositae

1. **Cucullia chamomillae** *Chamomile Shark*

HEMP AGRIMONY *Eupatorium cannabinum*
family: Compositae

2. **Diachrysia chryson** *Scarce Burnished Brass*
3. **Eupithecia absinthiata** *Wormwood Pug*
4. **Eupithecia centaureata** *Lime-speck Pug*

DEVILSBIT SCABIOUS *Succisa pratensis*
family: Dipsacaceae

5. **Eurodryas aurinia** *Marsh Fritillary*
6. **Hemaris tityus** *Narrow-bordered Bee Hawk-moth*

HONEYSUCKLE *Lonicera periclymenum*
family: Caprifoliaceae

7. **Xylocampa areola** *Early Grey*
8. **Autographa bractea** *Gold Spangle*
9. **Hemaris fuciformis**
*Broad-bordered Bee Hawk-moth*
10. **Ladoga camilla** *White Admiral*

SEA WORMWOOD *Artemisia maritima*
family: Compositae

11. **Thetidea smaragdaria** *Essex Emerald*

DAISY *Bellis perennis* family: Compositae

12. **Apocheima alpina**

GOLDEN ROD *Solidago virgaurea* family: Compositae

13. **Eupithecia virgaureata** *Golden-rod Pug*
14. **Cucullia asteris** *Star-wort*
15. **Cucullia gnaphalii** *Cudweed*

WORMWOOD *Artemisia absinthium* family: Compositae

16. **Cucullia absinthii** *Wormwood*

16

The Wormwood in resting position

1
2
3
4
5
6
7
8
9
10
11
12
13
14
15
16

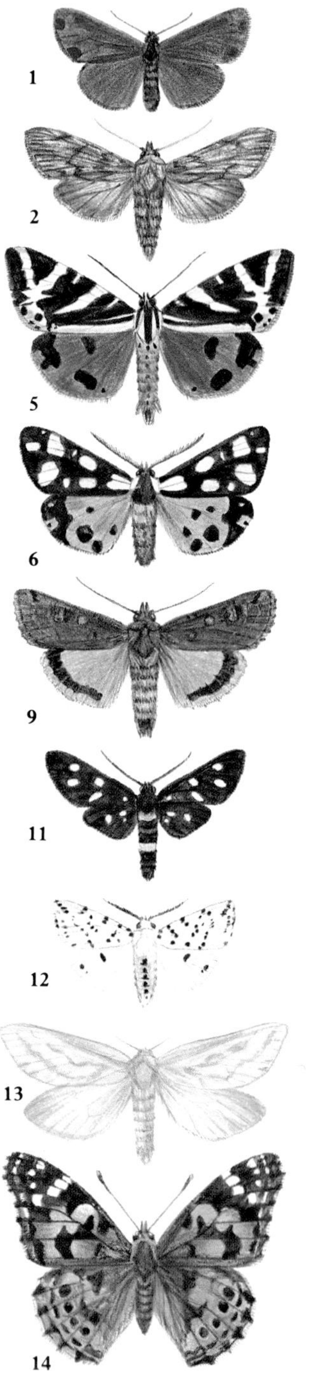


## PLATE 29

RAGWORT *Senecio jacobaea* family: Compositae

1. **Tyria jacobaeae** *Cinnabar* 2

LETTUCE *Lactuca sativa* family: Compositae

2. **Cucullia lactucae** *Lettuce Shark* 2
3. **Hecatera dysodea** *Ranunculus Moth* 2

DANDELION *Taraxacum vulgare* family: Composi

4. **Caradrina morpheus** *Mottled Rustic* 2
5. **Euplagia quadripunctaria** *Jersey Tiger* 2
6. **Arctia villica** *Cream-spot Tiger* 2
7. **Cerastis rubricosa** *Red Chestnut* 2
8. **Orthosia gothica** *Hebrew Character* 2
9. **Noctua pronuba** *Large Yellow Underwing* 2
10. **Phragmatobia fuliginosa** *Ruby Tiger* 2
11. **Syntomis phegea** *Nine-spotted* 2
12. **Spilosoma lubricipeda** *White Ermine* 2
13. **Hepialus humuli** *Ghost Moth*

CREEPING THISTLE *Cirsium arvense* family: Compositae

14. **Cynthia cardui** *Painted Lady*

BLACK KNAPWEED *Centaurea nigra* family: Compositae

15. **Melitaea phoebe** *Knapweed Fritillary*

Pupa of the Painted Lady

1
2
3
4
5
6
7
8
9
10
11
12
13
15

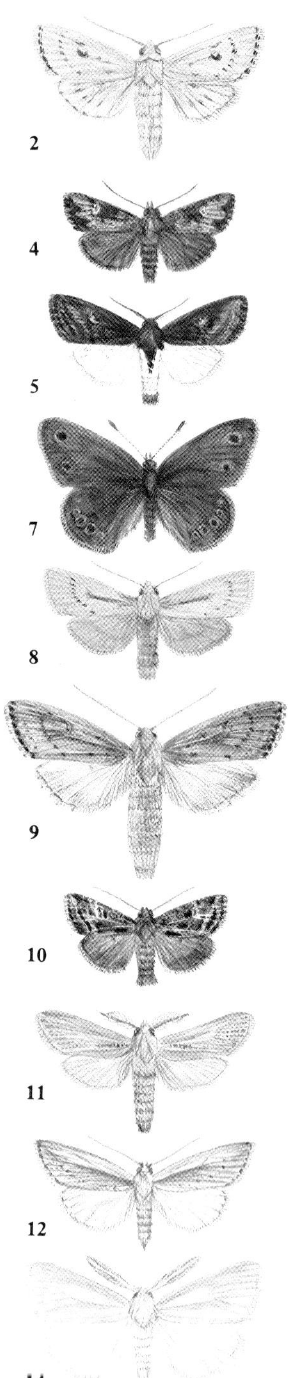


## PLATE 30

Yellow Iris *Iris pseudacorus* family: Iridaceae

1. **Celaena leucostigma** *Crescent*
2. **Archanara sparganii** *Webb's Wainscot*

Carnation Grass *Carex flacca* family: Cyperaceae

3. **Photedes captiuncula** *Least Minor*

Hairy Woodrush *Luzula pilosa* family: Juncaceae

4. **Mesapamea secalis** *Common Rustic*

Sea Daffodil *Pancratium maritimum* family: Amaryllidaceae

5. **Brithys crini** *Kew Arches*

Jointed Rush *Juncus articulatus* family: Juncaceae

6. **Coenobia rufa** *Small Rufous*

White Beak-sedge *Rhynchospora alba* family: Cyperaceae

7. **Coenonympha tullia** *Large Heath*

True Bulrush *Scirpus lacustris* family: Cyperaceae

8. **Archanara algae** *Rush Wainscot*

Great Reedmace *Typha latifolia* family: Typhacea

9. **Nonagria typhae** *Bulrush Wainscot*

Cotton Grass *Eriophorum vaginatum* family: Cyperaceae

10. **Celaena haworthii** *Haworth's Minor*

Reed *Phragmites communis* family: Gramineae

11. **Phragmataecia castaneae** *Reed Leopard*
12. **Senta flammea** *Flame Wainscot*
13. **Rhizedra lutosa** *Large Wainscot*
14. **Laelia coenosa** *Reed Tussock*

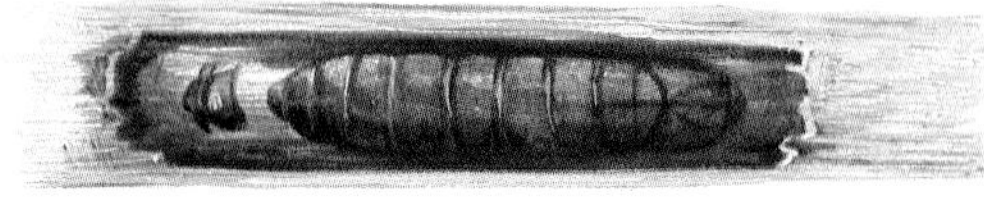

Pupa of the Bulrush Wainscot in stem of reedmace

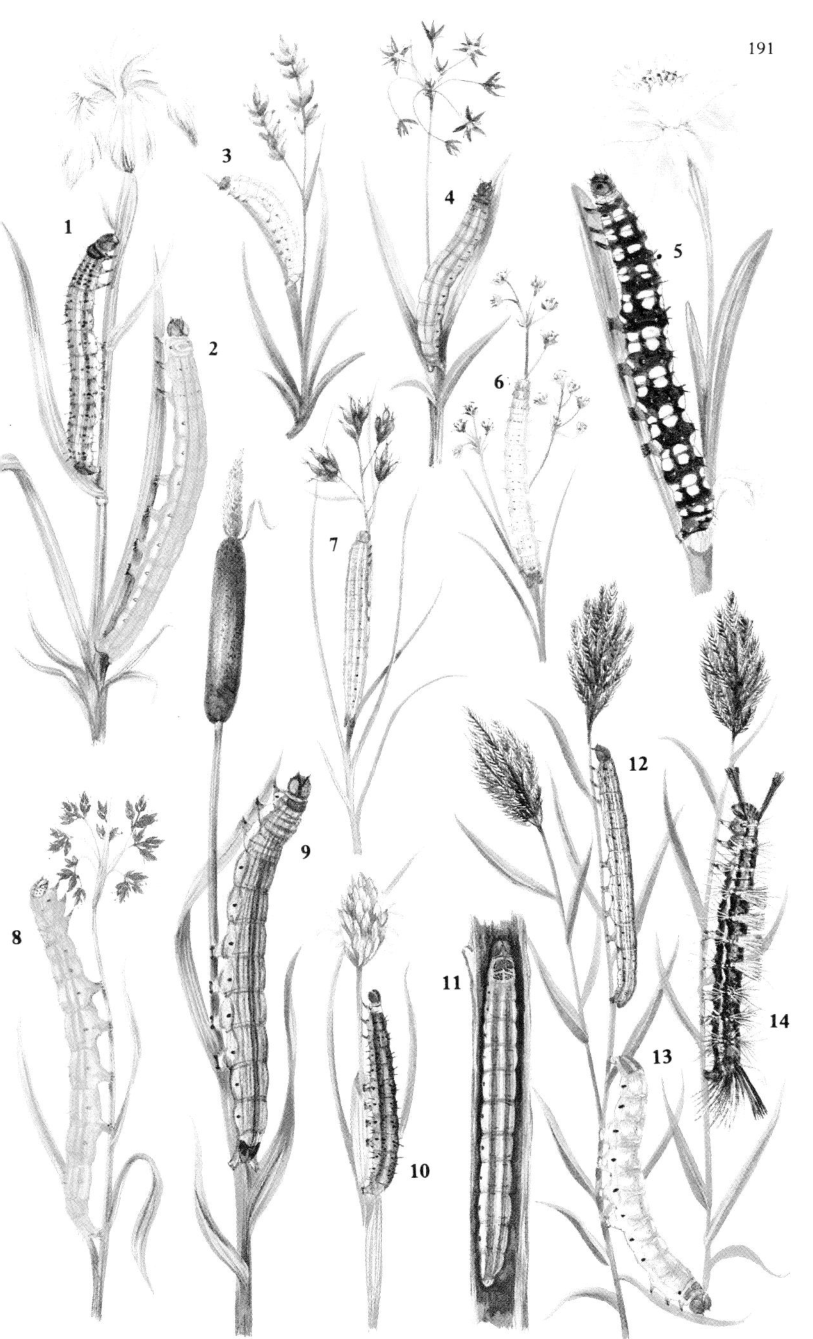
1
2
3
4
5
6
7
8
9
10
11
12
13
14

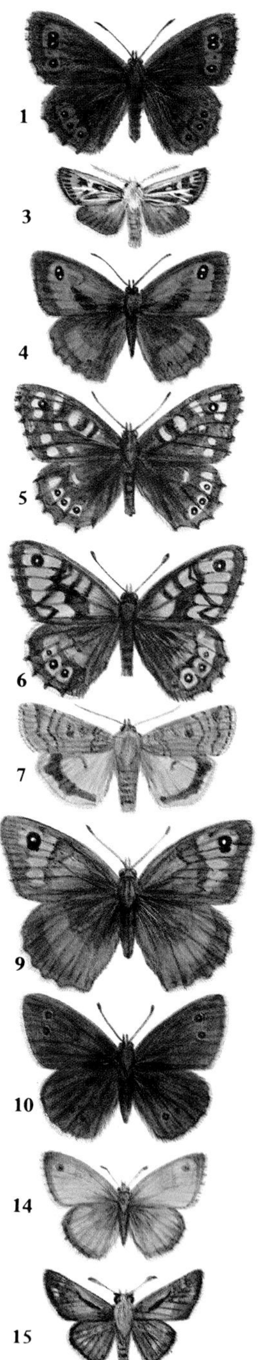


## PLATE 31

Purple Moor-grass *Molinia caerulea* family: Gramineae

1. **Erebia aethiops** *Scotch Argus* 5
2. Protodeltote pygarga *Marbled White Spot* 26
3. **Cerapteryx graminis** *Antler Moth* 23

Cock's-foot *Dactylis glomerata* family: Gramineae

4. **Pyronia tithonus** *Gatekeeper* 5
5. **Pararge aegeria** *Speckled Wood* 5
6. **Lasiommata megera** *Wall* 5
7. **Noctua comes** *Lesser Yellow Underwing* 21
8. **Mythimna comma** *Shoulder-striped Wainscot* 23

Annual Meadow-grass *Poa annua* family: Gramineae

9. **Maniola jurtina** *Meadow Brown* 6
10. **Aphantopus hyperantus** *Ringlet* 6
11. **Mythimna pallens** *Common Wainscot* 23
12. **Pachetra sagittigera** *Feathered Ear* 22

Meadow Fescue *Festuca pratensis* family: Gramineae

13. **Mesoligia furuncula** *Cloaked Minor* 25

Sheep's Fescue *Festuca ovina* family: Gramineae

14. **Coenonympha pamphilus** *Small Heath* 6
15. **Hesperia comma** *Silver-spotted Skipper* 3

Yorkshire Fog *Holcus lanatus* family: Gramineae

16. Thymelicus sylvestris *Small Skipper* 3

Wainscots at rest

1
2
3
4
5
6
7
8
9
10
11
12
13
14
15
16

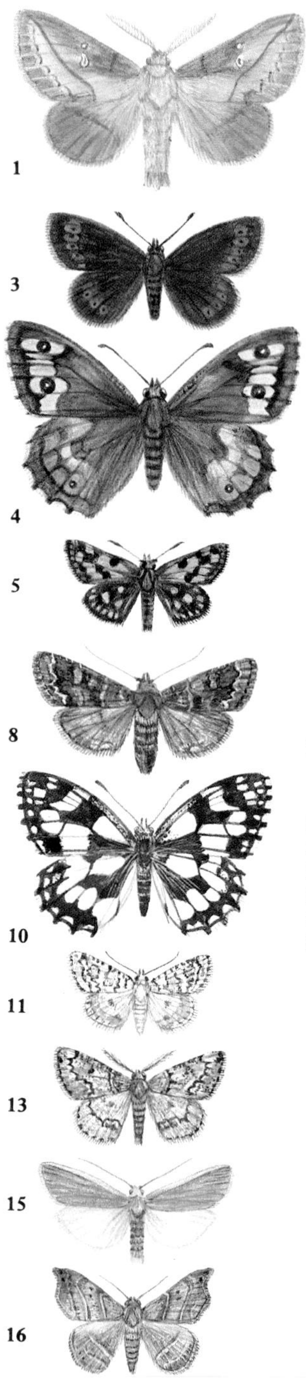


## PLATE 32

Couch-grass *Agropyron repens* family: Gramineae (*See also* Pl. 33)

1. **Philudoria potatoria** *Drinker* 64
2. **Apamea monoglypha** *Dark Arches* 255

Mat-grass *Nardus stricta* family: Gramineae

3. **Erebia epiphron** *Mountain Ringlet* 57

Early Hair-grass *Aira praecox* family: Gramine

4. **Hipparchia semele** *Grayling* 59

Slender False-brome *Brachypodium sylvaticum* family: Gramineae

5. **Carterocephalus palaemon** *Chequered Skipper* 30
6. **Ochlodes venata** *Large Skipper* 32
7. **Hipparchia fagi** *Woodland Grayling* 59

Bracken *Pteridium aquilinum* family: Polypodiaceae

8. **Ceramica pisi** *Broom Moth* 230

Heath False-brome *Brachypodium pinnatum* family: Gramineae

9. **Thymelicus acteon** *Lulworth Skipper* 31

Cat's Tail *Phleum pratense* family: Gramineae

10. **Melanargia galathea** *Marbled White* 58

Lichens

11. **Cryphia domestica** *Marbled Beauty* 252
12. **Nudaria mundana** *Muslin Footman* 207
13. **Cleorodes lichenaria** *Brussels Lace* 112
14. **Eilema griseola** *Dingy Footman* 207
15. **Eilema lurideola** *Common Footman* 207
16. **Laspeyria flexula** *Beautiful Hook-tip* 269

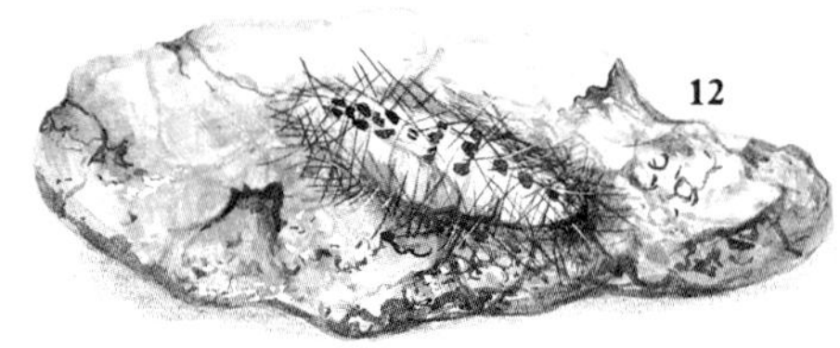


Pupa of the Muslin Footman in its network cocoon

1
2
3
4
5
6
7
8
9
10
11
12
13
14
15
16

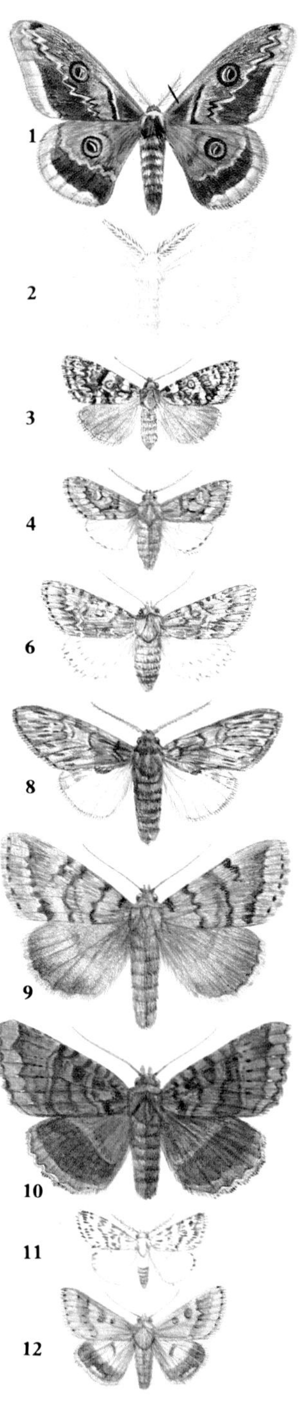


## PLATE 33

SALLOW *Salix* family: Salicaceae

1. **Saturnia pyri** *Great Peacock* 66
2. **Leucoma salicis** *White Satin* 205

DOCK *Rumex* family: Polygonaceae

3. **Acronicta rumicis** *Knot Grass* 252

COUCH-GRASS *Agropyron* family: Gramineae

4. **Luperina testacea** *Flounced Rustic* 257

BOG MYRTLE *Myrica gale* family: Salicaceae

5. **Eugraphe subrosea** *Rosy Marsh Moth* 220

SYCAMORE *Acer pseudoplatanus* family: Aceraceae

6. **Acronicta aceris** *Sycamore* 249

OAK *Quercus* family: Fagaceae

7. **Harpyia milhauseri** *Tawny Prominent* 125
8. **Peridea anceps** *Great Prominent* 125

BROOM *Cytisus scoparius* family: Leguminosae

9. **Apopestes spectrum** 268

BLACKTHORN *Prunus spinosa* family: Rosaceae

10. **Mormo maura** *Old Lady* 253
11. **Hyphantria cunea** *Fall Webworm* 210

*Chrysanthemum* family: Compositae

12. **Heliothis armigera** *Scarce Bordered Straw* 261

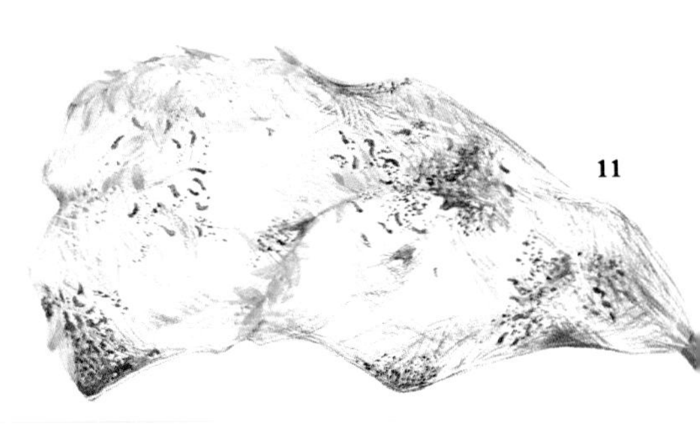


Caterpillar nest of the Fall Webworm

1
2
3
4
5
6
7
8
9
10
11
12

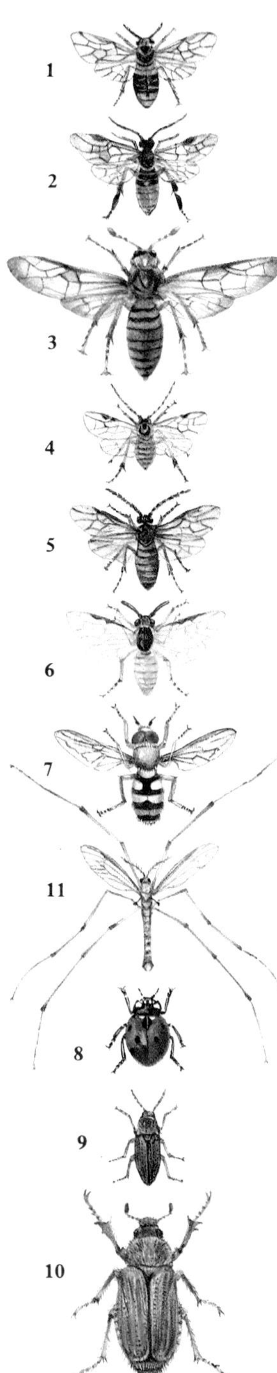


## PLATE 34

Larvae of insects often confused with caterpillars of butterflies and moths.

SAWFLIES (Hymenoptera: Symphyta)

1. **Diprion pini** *Pine Sawfly*

   This species occurs locally throughout the British Isles and is widespread in Europe. The larvae feed on pine (*Pinus*).

2. **Croesus septentrionalis** *Birch Sawfly*

   This is a common species in the British Isles and is widespread in Europe. The larvae feed on birch (*Betula*), alder (*Alnus*) and various other trees and shrubs.

3. **Cimbex femoratus** *Birch Sawfly*

   This large sawfly is widely distributed in the British Isles and Europe. The larvae feed on birch (*Betula*).

4. **Nematus ribesii** *Gooseberry Sawfly*

   A common and widespread species in Britain and Europe. The larvae are often pests on gooseberry and currant (*Ribes*).

5. **Phymatocera aterrima** *Solomon's Seal Sawfly*

   This insect has only recently become widespread in England and Wales, where it is sometimes a pest of solomon's seal (*Polygonatum*) in gardens. It is widespread in central and southern Europe.

6. **Arge ochropus** *Rose Sawfly*

   This species is locally common in southern England and widespread in Europe. The larvae feed on the foliage of roses (*Rosa*) and are sometimes a pest in gardens.

TWO-WINGED FLIES (Diptera)

7. **Syrphus sp.** *Hoverfly*

   The larvae of these common and widely distributed insects are often seen gliding over the surface of foliage. They feed on aphids (greenfly) and are beneficial in the garden.

11. **Tipula sp.** *Cranefly*

   The larvae of these flies are the well-known 'leather jackets' that feed on the roots of many plants but particularly on grasses. They are widespread and common, and are often pests.

BEETLES (Coleoptera)

8. **Coccinella 7-punctata** *Seven-spot Ladybird*

   This is a widespread species in Britain and Europe. Both the adults and larvae of this and other ladybirds feed on aphids and are beneficial in gardens.

9. **Agriotes sp.** *Click Beetle*

   The larvae of these common beetles feed on the roots of various plants and are the well-known 'wireworms' of agriculture and horticulture.

10. **Amphimallon solstitialis** *Summer Chafer*

   This is a common beetle in southern England and parts of Europe. The larvae of this and other species of chafers feed on the roots of various plants and are often found in gardens.

1
2
3
4
5
6
7
8
9
10
11

## PLATE 35: Caterpillar enemies

Coal tit with Winter Moth caterpillar.

Large White butterfly caterpillar killed by virus.

Predatory wasp with a noctuid caterpillar.

Dot Moth caterpillar killed by bacterial disease.

Vapourer caterpillar with larvae of parasitic *Apanteles* wasp.

Dot Moth caterpillar with pupae of a parasitic tachinid fly.

Shrivelled Ermine Moth caterpillar killed by granulosis virus.

Wood mouse eating a noctuid caterpillar.

Gypsy Moth caterpillar attacked by a predatory *Calosoma* beetle.

**Habitat.** Woodland, hedgerows and orchards.
**Foodplants.** Hawthorn (*Crataegus monogyna*), blackthorn (*Prunus spinosa*), apple (*Malus*) and other fruit trees.
**Biology.** One generation a year. Eggs are laid singly or in groups on twigs in October but do not hatch until the following spring. The caterpillars feed from April to June or July. They feed quite openly and their distinctive colours suggest that they are distasteful to birds. Pupation takes place in June or July in cocoons on or just below the soil and moths emerge in the late autumn.

# THAUMETOPOEIDAE

Caterpillars of this family are those of the well known processionary moths. They are easily recognised by their behaviour, living together in large communal nests, moving around in columns or processions. They are covered with poisonous hairs and should be handled with care. European species feed on conifers and oaks (*Quercus*).

**THAUMETOPOEA PITYOCAMPA** Denis & Schiffermüller **Pl. 1**
*Pine Processionary*
**Distribution.** Widely distributed in southern parts of Europe, particularly along the Mediterranean coast. Absent from the British Isles.
**Description.** Length up to 27 mm; body covered with fine white hairs along the sides, with tufts of reddish-yellow hairs on the back, arising from reddish-brown warts; colour bluish-black above the line of the spiracles, greyish-white below; head black. The hairs are highly irritant and may cause a painful rash.
**Habitat.** Coniferous forests.
**Foodplants.** Pine (*Pinus*) and sometimes cedar (*Cedrus*).
**Biology.** One generation a year. Eggs are laid in large numbers, forming 'sleeves' around pairs of needles, covered with scales from the body of the female. They are deposited in the summer and hatch in about a month. The caterpillars live in a communal nest in which they remain through the winter, coming out to feed when the weather is warm enough. They move in processions, head to tail, thus giving rise to their common name. When fully grown, from late winter to early summer, they leave the nest and pupate in subterranean cocoons. Moths emerge in the summer months but may remain in the pupa state for several years.

**THAUMETOPOEA PROCESSIONEA** Linnaeus **Pl. 6**
*Oak Processionary*
**Distribution.** Widely distributed in Europe but does not occur in the British Isles.
**Description.** Length up to 23 mm; body covered with long whitish hairs, arising from reddish warts; colour bluish-grey above the line of the spiracles, light greenish-grey below; segments 4–12 each have a velvety black patch on the back; head blackish-brown. The body hairs may cause an unpleasant rash.
**Habitat.** Forests.
**Foodplants.** Oak (*Quercus*) and sometimes walnut (*Juglans regia*).

**Biology.** One generation a year. Eggs are laid in July but do not hatch until the following spring. They are deposited on the branches in large groups, covered with scales from the body of the female. The caterpillars live in a communal nest, coming out at night to feed on the foliage. Their habit of moving in columns gives rise to the name 'processionary'. Pupation takes place within the nest in June and moths emerge in the following month.

# LYMANTRIIDAE

Moths of this family are known as tussocks. This refers to the characteristic, toothbrush-like tufts of hairs on the backs of the caterpillars. Also on the back of each caterpillar is a pair of small, raised glands. The hairs of some species are poisonous and should be treated with caution. Caterpillars of European species mainly feed on the foliage of trees and shrubs, although some feed on herbaceous plants and the Reed Tussock (*Laelia coenosa*) feeds on various reeds.

**LAELIA COENOSA** Hübner *Reed Tussock* **Pl. 30**

**Distribution.** Widespread in central Europe. Extinct in the British Isles.

**Description.** Length up to 35 mm; body dull ochreous-brown, covered with tufts of ochreous hairs, arising from small warts; segments 4–7 each with a central, brush-like tuft of hairs in the middle of the back; segment 1 has a pair of forward-pointing tufts of plumed black hairs and segment 11 a similar, backward-directed tuft on the back; head brown.

**Habitat.** Fens and marshes.

**Foodplants.** Branched bur-reed (*Sparganium erectum*), great fen-sedge (*Cladium mariscus*) and common reed (*Phragmites communis*).

**Biology.** One generation a year. Eggs are laid on stems in the summer and caterpillars feed until the autumn before going into hibernation. They resume feeding in the spring and, when fully grown, pupate in cocoons of silk, intermixed with body hairs, attached to stems of the foodplant. Moths emerge in the summer.

**ORGYIA RECENS** Hübner *Scarce Vapourer* **Pl. 2**

**Distribution.** Widely distributed in Europe. Formerly widespread in England and parts of Wales but now extremely local and apparently confined to parts of northern and eastern England.

**Description.** Length up to 35 mm; body black, covered with tufts of whitish hairs, arising from small warts; segments 4–7 each with a prominent, central, brush-like tuft of brown to reddish-brown hairs on the back; segment 1 with a pair of forward-pointing tufts of long, black, plumed hairs and segment 11 with a similar, backward-pointing tuft in the middle of the back; a double row of orange-red spots extends along the back and a broad red line along each side; head black.

**Habitat.** Woodland and hedgerows.

**Foodplants.** Willow and sallow (*Salix*), hawthorn (*Crataegus monogyna*), oak (*Quercus*) and other deciduous trees and shrubs.

**Biology.** Usually one generation a year. Eggs are laid in July in large batches on the outside of the cocoon from which the female has emerged. The caterpillars hibernate while quite small, completing their growth in the following spring. When fully grown, at the end of May, they pupate in tough cocoons incorporating hairs from the body, spun among leaves. Moths emerge in June. The females are virtually wingless.

**ORGYIA ANTIQUA** Linnaeus *Vapourer* **Pl. 14**

**Distribution.** Widespread throughout Europe. Widely distributed in the British Isles and often common in southern England.

**Description.** Length up to 35 mm; body dark grey, covered with tufts of greyish-white hairs, arising from small warts; segments 4–7 each have a prominent, central, brush-like tuft of brown, yellow or pale ochreous hairs; segment 1 with a pair of forward-pointing tufts of long, black plumed hairs, segment 11 with a similar, backward-pointing tuft in the middle of the back; four rows of dull red spots extend along the back and a broken white line extends along the spiracles on each side; head shining black. The body hairs may cause an irritating rash.

**Habitat.** Woodland, hedgerows, parks and gardens.

**Foodplants.** Almost any deciduous tree or shrub.

**Biology.** Usually one generation a year. Eggs are laid in July or August in a large batch on the outside of the cocoon from which the female has just emerged. Caterpillars do not hatch until the following spring. They feed until July or August and pupate in tough cocoons, incorporating hairs from the body, spun on twigs or in crevices of the bark. Moths emerge in July or August but may also occur as a partial second brood in October. It has been claimed that there is sometimes a third brood in southern England. The females are virtually wingless.

**GYNAEPHORA SELENITICA** Esper **Pl. 20**

**Distribution.** Local in central and southern Europe. Absent from the British Isles.

**Description.** Length up to 35 mm; body densely covered with long black hairs, with five pairs of whitish or yellowish-grey hair tufts along the back; segment 1 with a pair of forward-directed tufts of long, black, plumed hairs; segment 11 with a single tuft of similar, long black hairs; head black.

**Habitat.** Meadows and other open countryside where the foodplants grow.

**Foodplants.** Meadow vetchling (*Lathyrus pratensis*), sainfoin (*Onobrychis arenaria*) and broom (*Cytisus scoparius*).

**Biology.** One generation a year. Caterpillars feed from July to October, going into hibernation when fully grown and pupating in the following spring without further feeding. Pupation takes place in cocoons incorporating body hairs. Moths emerge in May.

**DICALLOMERA FASCELINA** Linnaeus *Dark Tussock* **Pl. 19**

**Distribution.** Widely distributed in central and northern Europe. Widespread and locally common in Britain and very local in Ireland.

**Description.** Length up to 40 mm; body black, covered with tufts of long grey and short ochreous hairs; segments 4–7 each with a prominent tuft of black and greyish-white hairs in the middle of the back; segment 1 with a pair of forward-pointing tufts of long black hairs and segment 11 with a similar backward-pointing tuft in the middle of the back; head black.

**Habitat.** Moorland and coastal sandhills.

**Foodplants.** Heather (*Calluna vulgaris*), broom (*Cytisus scoparius*), gorse (*Ulex* *europaeus*), sallow (*Salix*), hawthorn (*Crataegus monogyna*), bramble (*Rubus fruticosus*) and birch (*Betula*).

**Biology.** One generation a year. Eggs are laid on stems in July in large batches, covered with hairs from the body of the female. Caterpillars hatch in August and feed for a time before going into hibernation in small communal nests spun on the foliage or branches. They resume feeding in the spring and are fully grown by the end of May. Pupation takes place in cocoons incorporating body hairs, spun low down on the foodplant or on the ground, and moths emerge in July.

**CALLITEARA PUDIBUNDA** Linnaeus *Pale Tussock* **Pl. 9**

**Distribution.** Widespread in central and northern Europe. Widely distributed in England and Wales, local in Ireland and apparently absent from Scotland.

**Description.** Length up to 40 mm; body green, yellow or pale orange-brown, covered with tufts of fine grey hairs, arising from small warts; segments 4–7 each with a central tuft of dense yellowish or blackish-grey hairs, followed by a broad black band; segment 11 with a pointed tuft of long black or red hairs; head green or pale brown.

**Habitat.** Woodland.

**Foodplants.** Birch (*Betula*), oak (*Quercus*), elm (*Ulmus*) and other deciduous trees; also on hop (*Humulus lupulus*), on which it was at one time regarded as a pest and called the 'Hop Dog'.

**Biology.** One generation a year. Eggs are laid in batches in June and the caterpillars feed from July to September. When disturbed, they curl up, displaying the black bands on the back which are otherwise obscured by the body hairs. Pupation takes place in the autumn in cocoons incorporating body hairs. Moths emerge in the following May.

**DASYCHIRA ABIETIS** Denis & Schiffermüller **Pl. 1**

**Distribution.** Rather scarce in central and southern Europe.

**Description.** Length up to 38 mm; body yellowish-green with black markings along the back and sides and with two broad white lines along the back; segments 4–7 each with a dense tuft of brownish and pale yellow hairs; segment 1 with two forward-pointing tufts of long, black, plumed hairs and segment 11 with a tuft of long yellow hairs; head blackish.

**Habitat.** Coniferous woodland.

**Foodplants.** Norway spruce (*Picea abies*) and silver fir (*Abies alba*).

**Biology.** One generation a year. The caterpillars feed from the autumn to May of the following year, eating only the more tender needles. Moths are on the wing in June and July.

**EUPROCTIS CHRYSORRHOEA** Linnaeus *Brown-tail* **Pl. 18**

**Distribution.** Widespread throughout southern, central and parts of northern Europe. In the British Isles, mainly confined to coastal regions of southern and eastern England but sometimes moves further inland.

**Description.** Length up to 32 mm; body blackish-grey, covered with tufts of short, greyish-brown hairs arising from small warts; a broken, double, orange-red line extends down the back, on either side of which is a row of tufts of very short, white hairs; segments 9 and 10 each have a raised, red spot in the middle of the back; head shining black. The hairs of this caterpillar can cause a serious rash.

**Habitat.** Hedgerows, parks and gardens.

**Foodplants.** Hawthorn (*Crataegus monogyna*), blackthorn (*Prunus spinosa*), plum (*P. domestica*), sallow (*Salix*), sea buckthorn (*Hippophae rhamnoides*) and other deciduous trees and shrubs.
**Biology.** One generation a year. Eggs are laid on twigs in August in large batches, covered with scales from the body of the female. Caterpillars hatch in about three weeks and construct a communal silken nest in which they overwinter. In the following spring, they recommence feeding and spin a succession of nests as the food is exhausted. In June, when fully grown, they disperse and pupate in silken cocoons spun among the foliage. Moths emerge in July.

**EUPROCTIS SIMILIS** Fuessly *Yellow-tail* **Pl. 17**
**Distribution.** Widespread throughout Europe. Widely distributed in England and Wales; very local in southern Scotland and in Ireland.
**Description.** Length up to 40 mm; body black, covered with tufts of black and grey hairs arising from small warts; a bright, orange-red, double line extends along the middle of the back, on either side of which are tufts of short white hairs; a dull red line extends below the spiracles on each side; head black, marked with a whitish V-shape.
**Habitat.** Hedgerows, woodland and scrubland.
**Foodplants.** Hawthorn (*Crataegus monogyna*), blackthorn (*Prunus spinosa*), oak (*Quercus*), sallow (*Salix*) and other deciduous trees and shrubs.
**Biology.** One generation a year. Eggs are laid on undersides of leaves in July in large batches covered with hairs from the body of the female. The caterpillars feed from August to May, hibernating in small, cocoon-like shelters through the winter. Pupation takes place in brown cocoons, incorporating hairs from the body, spun among the foliage. Moths emerge in July.

**LEUCOMA SALICIS** Linnaeus *White Satin* **Pl. 33**
**Distribution.** Widespread in Europe. In the British Isles, mainly confined to England and eastern parts of Wales; occasionally recorded from Scotland, and occurs in Newcastle, Co. Wicklow in Ireland.
**Description.** Length up to 45 mm; body mottled grey with a broad band of black along the back, bordered on either side by a line of yellowish-white markings and bearing a line of large, creamy-white spots along the middle; tufts of whitish and reddish-brown hairs arise from raised orange-red warts; head black.
**Habitat.** Parks, roadsides, open wooded countryside and coastal regions.
**Foodplants.** Sallow (*Salix*) and poplar (*Populus*).
**Biology.** One generation a year. Eggs are laid in batches on twigs in August and hatch later in the month. Caterpillars hibernate in silken webs while still small, resuming their feeding in the following spring and becoming fully grown by the end of June. They sometimes feed gregariously but remain in individual webs. Pupation takes place in cocoons spun in crevices of the bark and moths emerge in July and August.

**ARCTORNIS L-NIGRUM** Müller *Black V Moth* **Pl. 2**
**Distribution.** Widespread in southern and central Europe and in Scandinavia. Occurs in the British Isles as a rare immigrant.
**Description.** Length up to 45 mm; body reddish-brown, blackish on the back, covered with tufts of reddish-brown and white hairs arising from small warts; head black.

**Habitat.** Woodland.
**Foodplants.** Sallow (*Salix*), poplar (*Populus*), elm (*Ulmus*), lime (*Tilia*) and other trees, including pine (*Pinus*).
**Biology.** One generation a year. Eggs are laid in small groups on the bark in July and caterpillars hatch in about two weeks. They feed for a time before going into hibernation and complete their growth in the following spring. Pupation takes place at the end of May in cocoons spun among the foliage, and moths emerge towards the end of June.

**LYMANTRIA MONACHA** Linnaeus *Black Arches* **Pl. 1**
**Distribution.** Widespread throughout Europe. In the British Isles, apparently confined to southern England and a few localities in Wales.
**Description.** Length up to 35 mm; body pale ochreous-white with a broad, blackish-grey band on the back, indented between the segments; tufts of shortish, grey hairs arise from small warts; segments 9 and 10 each have a small, red, raised spot in the middle of the back; head pale ochreous, strongly patterned with black.
**Habitat.** Woodland.
**Foodplants.** In the British Isles, mainly confined to oak (*Quercus*) but will eat the foliage of a wide range of trees, including yew (*Taxus baccata*). In continental Europe, primarily a pest of spruce (*Picea*), pine (*Pinus*) and other conifers.
**Biology.** One generation a year. Eggs are laid in August in large batches in crevices of the bark. Caterpillars hatch in the following spring and feed until the end of June. They are gregarious when at rest, gathering together in some sheltered place. Pupation takes place in July in cocoons spun in crevices of the bark and moths emerge in the following month.

**LYMANTRIA DISPAR** Linnaeus *Gypsy Moth* **Pl. 18**
**Distribution.** Widespread throughout Europe. Extinct in the British Isles but may occur as an occasional immigrant.
**Description.** Length up to 50 mm; body pale ochreous, suffused with blackish-grey and with three ochreous lines along the back; tufts of brownish or blackish hairs arise from small, reddish-brown, raised warts; segments 1–5 each have a pair of blue warts on the back, and segments 9 and 10 each have a raised red spot; head pale ochreous, patterned with black.
**Habitat.** Woodland.
**Foodplants.** Oak (*Quercus*), poplar (*Populus*) and many other trees, including conifers. The extinct British race fed primarily on bog myrtle (*Myrica gale*) and creeping willow (*Salix repens*).
**Biology.** One generation a year. Eggs are laid on tree trunks in August in large masses covered with scales from the body of the female. Caterpillars hatch in the following spring and feed until the end of June. Pupation takes place at the end of June or in July, in cocoons spun among the foliage; moths emerge in July or August.

# ARCTIIDAE

This family includes the tigers and footmen. The small to large caterpillars are usually covered with tufts of hairs, arising from raised warts. They have shiny heads with few hairs. The body hairs are often long and dense and some are known to be poisonous, although European species do not harm humans. They feed on a wide range of low-growing plants and sometimes on trees and shrubs. Many of the European footman caterpillars feed on lichens.

**NUDARIA MUNDANA** Linnaeus *Muslin Footman* **Pl. 32**
**Distribution.** Widespread in central and northern Europe. Widely distributed throughout the British Isles, probably more common in the west.
**Description.** Length up to 12 mm; body pale grey, variably marked with black, covered with tufts of black hairs arising from small, raised warts; a double line of yellow spots extends along the back; segment 7 has a large, velvety black spot in the middle of the back; head blackish.
**Habitat.** Stone walls, fences and hedges.
**Foodplants.** Various small lichens, particularly orange-coloured species.
**Biology.** One generation a year. Eggs are laid on lichens in July and caterpillars hatch towards the end of the month. They feed until the autumn and then go into hibernation until the following spring, when they resume feeding and become fully grown by the end of May. They are active by day and may be found feeding in bright sunshine. Pupation takes place in June in open network cocoons, sometimes several together, spun in crevices. Moths emerge in June and July.

**EILEMA GRISEOLA** Hübner *Dingy Footman* **Pl. 32**
**Distribution.** Widespread in central Europe. In the British Isles, confined to southern England and western Wales, where it is locally common.
**Description.** Length up to 25 mm; body velvety black above, blackish-brown below, covered with greyish hairs, arising from small, raised warts; two orange stripes extend along the back, sometimes broken into series of orange patches; head shining black.
**Habitat.** Damp woodland, fens and other marshy places.
**Foodplants.** Various lichens, such as *Peltigera canina*, growing on trees and bushes; possibly also on mosses and withered leaves.
**Biology.** One generation a year. Eggs are laid in groups on bark, close to patches of lichen, in July, and hatch by early August. The caterpillars feed until September when they go into hibernation. They become active again in the spring and are fully grown by the end of May. Pupation takes place in June in cocoons of silk mixed with fragments of lichen, spun in crevices of the bark. Moths emerge the following month.

**EILEMA LURIDEOLA** Zincken *Common Footman* **Pl. 32**
**Distribution.** Widespread in Europe. Widely distributed throughout the British Isles but most frequent in England and Wales.
**Description.** Length up to 22 mm; body velvety black above, brownish-grey below, covered with tufts of short, black and grey hairs, arising from small, raised

warts; an orange stripe extends along each side, except for the first three segments; head shining black.
**Habitat.** Woodland and hedgerows.
**Foodplants.** Various lichens growing on trees and bushes or on fences; in captivity, will eat the foliage of various deciduous trees.
**Biology.** One generation a year. Eggs are laid in groups on bark in July and hatch in August. The caterpillars feed for a time before going into hibernation and resume feeding in the spring, becoming fully grown by the end of May. Pupation takes place in June in silken cocoons spun in crevices of the bark and moths emerge within a month.

**UTETHEISA PULCHELLA** Linnaeus *Crimson Speckled* **Pl. 26**
**Distribution.** Widespread in the Mediterranean region, migrating to various parts of Europe, including the British Isles, where it is rare.
**Description.** Length up to 30 mm; body greyish with broad bands of yellowish-white along the back and sides; a series of black and orange-red transverse bands extends across the back of each segment; long grey and black hairs arise from small raised warts; head bright reddish-brown with a whitish, Y-shaped marking.
**Habitat.** Occurs in warm, sunny regions.
**Foodplants.** Borage (*Borago officinalis*), forgetmenot (*Myosotis*) and other herbaceous plants.
**Biology.** In warm regions and in captivity, this species is continuously brooded and may produce several generations in a year. Eggs are laid in large groups on the foliage. The caterpillars require plenty of warmth to complete their development and are unlikely to survive the winter in Britain. In southern Europe, caterpillars feed from May to June and August to September. Pupation takes place in white silken cocoons spun among foliage of the foodplant or on the ground. In the British Isles, moths mostly arrive as immigrants in the autumn.

**PARASEMIA PLANTAGINIS** Linnaeus *Wood Tiger* **Pl. 27**
**Distribution.** Widely distributed throughout Europe. Widespread in the British Isles but becoming less common, particularly in south-eastern England.
**Description.** Length up to 35 mm; body dark brownish-black, paler on the underside, covered with tufts of blackish hairs, arising from raised, shining black warts; segments 4–6 with tufts of reddish-brown hairs on the back, arising from reddish-brown warts; head shining black.
**Habitat.** Open woodland, downland and moors.
**Foodplants.** Plantain (*Plantago*), groundsel (*Senecio vulgaris*), dandelion (*Taraxacum*), common rock-rose (*Helianthemum nummularium*) and other low-growing herbaceous plants.
**Biology.** One generation a year. Eggs are laid in small groups on the foliage in June. Caterpillars hatch in July and feed until the autumn before hibernating. In the spring they resume feeding and are fully grown by the end of April. Pupation takes place in May in silken cocoons, incorporating hairs from the body, spun amongst the foliage of the foodplant.

**ARCTIA CAJA** Linnaeus *Garden Tiger* **Pl. 10**
**Distribution.** Widespread throughout Europe. Widely distributed and often common in the British Isles.

**Description.** Length up to 60 mm; body brownish-black, covered with dense tufts of hairs, arising from small, raised warts; the hairs on the back and sides above the level of the spiracles are long and black, tipped with greyish-white, but those below the spiracles are shorter and reddish-brown; all hairs on segments 1 and 2 are reddish-brown; spiracles shining white; head shining black.
**Habitat.** Open woodland, hedgerows, waste land, parks, gardens and other places where the foodplants grow.
**Foodplants.** Almost any low-growing plant, both wild and cultivated, and also the foliage of various deciduous trees and shrubs.
**Biology.** One generation a year. Eggs are laid in large batches on the undersides of leaves in July and caterpillars hatch in August. They feed for a time but go into hibernation while still quite small. Feeding is resumed in the spring and caterpillars are fully grown by the end of June. They are very active, particularly when in search for a pupation site, and are able to run very rapidly. Pupation takes place in silken cocoons spun among leaf litter on the ground and moths emerge in July and August.

**ARCTIA VILLICA** Linnaeus *Cream-spot Tiger* **Pl. 29**
**Distribution.** Widespread in central and southern Europe. In the British Isles, mainly confined to southern parts of England and Wales, although also recorded from north Wales.
**Description.** Length up to 50 mm; body black, covered with tufts of brownish hairs arising from raised warts; spiracles white; legs purplish-red; head reddish-brown.
**Habitat.** Woodland, downs and coastal sandhills.
**Foodplants.** A wide range of low-growing herbaceous plants and sometimes the young shoots of gorse (*Ulex europaeus*).
**Biology.** One generation a year. Eggs are laid in groups on the foliage in June and hatch in early July. The caterpillars feed for a time before going into hibernation and resume feeding in early spring. Pupation takes place in April or May in cocoons spun among the foliage or in leaf litter on the ground. Moths emerge in late May or in June.

**DIACRISIA SANNIO** Linnaeus *Clouded Buff* **Pl. 10**
**Distribution.** Widely distributed throughout Europe. Widespread and locally common in the British Isles.
**Description.** Length up to 40 mm; body reddish-brown, covered with tufts of short brown hairs, arising from small, raised warts; a broad, pale stripe extends along the back, bearing a series of yellow spots; a line of white spots extends along each side below the level of the spiracles; head dark greyish-brown. Young caterpillars have red dots on the back.
**Habitat.** Heaths, moors and downland.
**Foodplants.** Dandelion (*Taraxacum*), dock (*Rumex*), hawkweed (*Hieracium*), heather (*Calluna* and *Erica*), bog myrtle (*Myrica gale*) and various other low-growing plants.
**Biology.** One generation a year. Eggs are laid in small batches on the foliage in June and hatch in July. The caterpillars hibernate while still small and complete their growth in the following spring. When disturbed, they at first coil into a ring but soon become active and run off rapidly. Pupation takes place in May or June in fragile cocoons spun at the base of the foodplant. Moths emerge in June and July.

**RHYPARIA PURPURATA** Linnaeus **Pl. 19**

**Distribution.** Occurs in central and southern Europe. Absent from the British Isles.
**Description.** Length up to 45 mm; body blackish, extensively marked with white on the sides, with tufts of reddish-brown hairs on the back and greyish hairs along the sides, arising from small, raised warts; head shining black.
**Habitat.** Warm hillsides and other hot, dry places.
**Foodplants.** A wide range of low-growing herbaceous plants and shrubs.
**Biology.** One generation a year, with a second generation in the south. The caterpillars overwinter, completing their growth in the following spring. Pupation takes place in May in silken cocoons, incorporating body hairs, and moths emerge in June. Second brood moths are on the wing in September.

**HYPHANTRIA CUNEA** Drury *Fall Webworm* **Pl. 33**

**Distribution.** Occurs in warm regions of central and south-eastern Europe. Absent from the British Isles.
**Description.** Length up to 35 mm; body pale yellowish- or greenish-brown with a broad band of black mottling along the back; tufts of long hairs arise from raised warts which are black on the back and orange-brown on the sides; segment 1 has an orange-brown plate marked with brown; head black.
**Habitat.** Woodland, hedgerows and orchards.
**Foodplants.** Blackthorn (*Prunus spinosa*), cherry (*P. cerasus*), plum (*P. domestica*), apple (*Malus*), pear (*Pyrus*) and other deciduous trees and shrubs.
**Biology.** Two generations a year. Eggs are laid in large, hair-covered masses on the undersides of leaves in May and again in August, hatching in 1–3 weeks. Caterpillars feed from May to July and August to September, living together in a large communal silken web spun among the foliage. Pupation takes place in silken cocoons on the ground. Summer pupae produce moths in July but autumn pupae overwinter before producing moths in the following spring.

**SPILOSOMA LUBRICIPEDA** Linnaeus *White Ermine* **Pl. 29**

**Distribution.** Widespread throughout Europe. Widely distributed and common in the British Isles.
**Description.** Length up to 40 mm; body dark brownish-grey, covered with tufts of black hairs arising from raised, black warts; a red or orange stripe extends along the middle of the back; head shining black.
**Habitat.** Hedgerows, waste ground, gardens and other places where suitable foodplants grow.
**Foodplants.** A wide range of low-growing herbaceous plants, both wild and cultivated.
**Biology.** One generation a year. Eggs are laid in large batches on the foliage in July. Caterpillars feed from July or August until the autumn. They are extremely active, particularly when in search of a pupation site, and their rapid movement gives rise to the scientific name *lubricipeda*, meaning fleet-footed. Pupation takes place in the autumn in grey silken cocoons spun among leaf litter on the ground. Moths do not usually emerge until the following May or June but sometimes a partial second generation emerges in the autumn.

SPILOSOMA LUTEA Hufnagel *Buff Ermine* **Pl. 15**

**Distribution.** Widespread in Europe. Widely distributed and often common in the British Isles.

**Description.** Length up to 45 mm; body greyish-brown, darker on the back, covered with tufts of brown hairs, arising from raised, light brown warts; an indistinct, pale line runs along the middle of the back and a broad, whitish stripe extends along each side; head pale yellowish-brown.
**Habitat.** Hedgerows, waste ground, gardens, parks and other places where suitable foodplants grow.
**Foodplants.** A wide range of herbaceous plants and also the foliage of various trees and shrubs. One of the few species to feed on bracken (*Pteridium aquilinum*).
**Biology.** One generation a year. Eggs are laid in large batches on the foliage in June or July and caterpillars hatch in July or August. They feed until the autumn and pupate in grey cocoons of silk mixed with body hairs, spun among leaf litter on the ground. Moths emerge in May or June of the following year.

**SPILOSOMA URTICAE** Esper *Water Ermine* **Pl. 26**
**Distribution.** Widely distributed but local in Europe. In the British Isles, confined to a few localities in southern and eastern England.
**Description.** Length up to 45 mm; body dark greyish-brown, covered with tufts of dark brown hairs, arising from pale, raised warts; sometimes with a broken, yellowish line along the middle of the back; spiracles white, head shining black.
**Habitat.** Fenland, damp meadows and marshy places.
**Foodplants.** Yellow loosestrife (*Lysimacha vulgaris*), mint (*Mentha*), water dock (*Rumex hydrolapathum*), lousewort (*Pedicularis sylvatica*), yellow iris (*Iris pseudacorus*) and other marsh plants.
**Biology.** One generation a year. Eggs are laid in batches on the foodplant in June and caterpillars feed from July to August. When fully grown at the end of August, the caterpillars pupate in cocoons of silk mixed with body hairs, spun on the ground or between leaves of the foodplant. Moths emerge in the following June.

**DIAPHORA MENDICA** Clerck *Muslin Moth* **Pl. 10**
**Distribution.** Widespread in central and northern Europe. Widely distributed in England and Wales, becoming less common towards the north; local in Scotland; widespread and locally common in Ireland.
**Description.** Length up to 40 mm; body greyish-brown, covered with tufts of yellowish-brown hairs, arising from small, dark, raised warts; sometimes has traces of a pale line down the middle of the back; head yellowish-brown.
**Habitat.** Open woodland, downland, gardens and waste ground.
**Foodplants.** Dock (*Rumex*), chickweed (*Stellaria media*), plantain (*Plantago*), dandelion (*Taraxacum*) and other low-growing herbaceous plants.
**Biology.** One generation a year. Eggs are laid in groups, sometimes in double rows, on the foliage in May or June. The caterpillars feed from July to September. When disturbed, they roll into balls at first but soon uncoil and run away rapidly. Pupation takes place in the autumn in cocoons of silk mixed with body hairs, spun among the foliage or on the ground. Moths emerge in the following May.

**PHRAGMATOBIA FULIGINOSA** Linnaeus *Ruby Tiger* **Pl. 29**
**Distribution.** Widespread throughout Europe. Widely distributed and locally common in the British Isles.
**Description.** Length up to 35 mm; body velvety black, covered with dense tufts of blackish-brown or reddish-brown hairs, arising from small, raised warts; spiracles small, whitish; head shining black.

**Habitat.** Open woodland, downland, meadows, moorland and other places where the foodplants grow.
**Foodplants.** Dock (*Rumex*), dandelion (*Taraxacum*), golden-rod (*Solidago virgaurea*), yarrow (*Achillea millefolium*) and other herbaceous plants.
**Biology.** One generation a year. Eggs are laid in large batches on the foodplant in May. The caterpillars feed from May or June until the autumn, when they go into hibernation at the roots of the foodplant. Pupation takes place in the following spring without any further feeding. The brown silken cocoons are spun among the foodplant in April and moths emerge in May. A few caterpillars may feed up rapidly to produce a partial second brood of moths in the autumn.

**EUPLAGIA QUADRIPUNCTARIA** Poda *Jersey Tiger* **Pl. 29**
**Distribution.** Widely distributed in central and southern Europe. In the British Isles, confined to south-western England.
**Description.** Length up to 50 mm; body dark brown, covered with tufts of short, yellowish-brown or greyish hairs, arising from orange-brown warts; a broad, broken, orange-yellow band extends down the middle of the back and a broken stripe of yellowish-white along each side of the body; head shining black.
**Habitat.** Open countryside, waste land and gardens. In continental Europe, also on warm mountain slopes and in valleys.
**Foodplants.** A wide range of herbaceous plants.
**Biology.** One generation a year. Eggs are laid in groups on the foliage in August and hatch in 10–15 days. The caterpillars go into hibernation shortly after hatching and resume feeding the following spring. They are mainly active at night, hiding under leaves by day. Pupation takes place at the end of May in slight silken cocoons spun among leaf litter on the ground, and moths emerge in July or August.

**CALLIMORPHA DOMINULA** Linnaeus *Scarlet Tiger* **Pl. 26**
**Distribution.** Widespread throughout Europe. In the British Isles, confined to southern England and south-west Wales.
**Description.** Length up to 35 mm; body black with tufts of shortish, black and grey hairs, arising from small, raised warts; a broad, broken band of yellowish-white extends down the middle of the back and a similar band extends along each side of the body; head shining black.
**Habitat.** Damp meadows, river banks, damp woodland and other marshy places.
**Foodplants.** Comfrey (*Symphytum*), dock (*Rumex*), nettle (*Urtica*), bramble (*Rubus fruticosus*), blackthorn (*Prunus spinosa*) and various other plants.
**Biology.** One generation a year. Eggs are laid in batches on the foliage in July and hatch in about a fortnight. The caterpillars feed for a time before going into hibernation. They resume feeding in the spring and are fully grown by the end of May. They are active by day and often feed in full sunlight. Pupation takes place in silken cocoons spun among leaf litter on the ground and moths emerge in June.

**TYRIA JACOBAEAE** Linnaeus *Cinnabar* **Pl. 29**
**Distribution.** Widespread throughout Europe. Widely distributed in the British Isles; common in the southern half of England and in Wales, becoming less common and more coastal further north and in Ireland.
**Description.** Length up to 30 mm; body bright orange-yellow with conspicuous black, transverse bands; hairs short, black and inconspicuous; head shining black.

**Habitat.** Meadows, roadsides, downland, waste ground and other places where the foodplants grow.
**Foodplants.** Usually ragwort (*Senecio jacobaea*) but also on other species of *Senecio* such as groundsel (*S. vulgaris*).
**Biology.** One generation a year. Eggs are laid in large batches on the undersides of leaves in June. The caterpillars may be found from July to August. They feed gregariously by day and are very conspicuous. Their distinctive coloration warns potential predators that they are distasteful. Pupation takes place in cocoons spun on the ground in September and moths emerge in the following May or June.

# CTENUCHIDAE

Caterpillars of this family (more properly regarded as a subfamily of the Arctiidae) are small, with tufts of hairs arising from small warts. They are similar to those of the family Arctiidae but have long, slender thoracic legs and many fine hairs on the head. They feed on the foliage of various low-growing plants.

**SYNTOMIS PHEGEA** Linnaeus *Nine-spotted* **Pl. 29**
**Distribution.** Occurs in warm parts of central and southern Europe. Not recorded from the British Isles.
**Description.** Length up to 30 mm; body grey, covered with tufts of short grey hairs, arising from slightly raised, black warts; head reddish-brown.
**Habitat.** Woodland margins and sunny slopes.
**Foodplants.** Dandelion (*Taraxacum*), plantain (*Plantago*), scabious (*Scabiosa*), dead-nettle (*Lamium*) and other low-growing plants.
**Biology.** One generation a year. The caterpillars overwinter in communal webs spun under stones on the ground and resume feeding in the spring. When fully grown in May, they pupate on the ground in silken cocoons incorporating body hairs of the caterpillars. Moths emerge in June or July.

# NOLIDAE

Caterpillars of this family are small and have tufts of hair arising from small, slightly raised warts. They may be distinguished from those of the family Arctiidae by the absence of a pair of prolegs on body segement 6. They feed on the foliage of various trees, shrubs and low-growing plants.

**NOLA CUCULLATELLA** Linnaeus *Short-cloaked Moth* **Pl. 17**

**Distribution.** Occurs locally in central and northern Europe. Widely distributed in England and Wales but absent from Scotland and Ireland.

**Description.** Length up to 14 mm; short and stout, bearing many small warts, covered with short whitish or blackish hairs; body colour dark grey with a whitish line along the middle of the back, extending through a series of greyish-white patches; warts grey, yellowish or pinkish; head shining black.

**Habitat.** Woodland and hedgerows.

**Foodplants.** Hawthorn (*Crataegus monogyna*), blackthorn (*Prunus spinosa*), plum (*P. domestica*), apple (*Malus*) and pear (*Pyrus*).

**Biology.** One generation a year. Eggs are laid on the undersides of leaves in July and hatch in August. The young caterpillars feed for a short time before hiding themselves in depressions in the bark, covered with a few strands of silk, where they remain until the following April or May. They then resume feeding and become fully grown in early June. Pupation takes place in tough cocoons covered with fragments of bark on the branches and moths emerge in the same month.

**NOLA CONFUSALIS** Herrich-Schäffer *Least Black Arches* **Pl. 16**

**Distribution.** Widespread in Europe. Widely distributed in the British Isles but fairly local.

**Description.** Length up to 14 mm; back and sides covered with small warts, bearing long fine hairs; colour pale yellowish-brown to brownish-white with two broken bands of dark brown on the back between which are three dark, triangular markings; head yellowish-brown.

**Habitat.** Woodland and orchards.

**Foodplants.** Found on oak (*Quercus*), beech (*Fagus sylvatica*), apple (*Malus*) and blackthorn (*Prunus spinosa*) and other deciduous trees and shrubs, but probably feeds mostly on the lichens growing on them.

**Biology.** One generation a year. Eggs are laid in June and caterpillars feed from July to August or September. Pupation takes place in the autumn in rounded cocoons spun on the bark of the foodplant but moths do not emerge until the following May.

# NOCTUIDAE

Caterpillars of this large family include many of economic importance, such as the cutworms and armyworms. Most are smooth and lack warts or protuberances. Some, however, do have characteristic swellings on the back, and those of the copper underwings (*Amphipyra*) resemble the horns of hawk-moth caterpillars. Those of the Silver Y (*Autographa gamma*) and its relatives have reduced prolegs and are known as semi-loopers. Some caterpillars of this family, such as the Nut-tree Tussock (*Colocasia coryli*) and the various dagger moths (*Acronicta*) are covered with tufts of long hairs and are superficially similar to those of the family Arctiidae but may be distinguished by their characteristic markings. They feed mainly on the foliage of low-growing plants although some species live on trees and shrubs.

**EUXOA NIGRICANS** Linnaeus *Garden Dart* **Pl. 10**

**Distribution.** Widely distributed throughout Europe. Widespread in England and Wales but particularly common in eastern England. Widespread in Ireland and local in lowland Scotland.

**Description.** Length up to 40 mm; body ochreous or ochreous-brown, suffused with greenish-grey along the sides; a thin, black-edged, grey line runs along the back, sometimes passing through a series of dark brown, triangular and diamond-shaped markings; a double, pale brown stripe extends low down along each side; body hairs arise from blackish spots; head greyish-brown mottled and lined with black.

**Habitat.** Agricultural land, gardens, marshland and open downland.

**Foodplants.** Clover (*Trifolium*), plantain (*Plantago*), dock (*Rumex*), hogweed (*Heracleum sphondylium*) and many other low-growing herbaceous plants, both wild and cultivated.

**Biology.** One generation a year. Eggs are laid on the foodplant in August but apparently do not hatch until February of the following year. The caterpillars feed from early spring to June. They feed at night, eating stems at ground level and also feeding on foliage. They hide under the soil by day. Caterpillars are sometimes pests of sugar beet (*Beta vulgaris*). Pupation takes place in June in subterranean cocoons and moths emerge in August.

**AGROTIS VESTIGIALIS** Hufnagel *Archer's Dart* **Pl. 26**

**Distribution.** Widespread throughout Europe. Widely distributed in coastal areas of the British Isles, also occurring locally in sandy districts inland.

**Description.** Length up to 40 mm; body greyish-brown to greyish-green, tinged above with purple; three indistinct dark lines extend along the back; underside pale grey; body hairs arising from blackish dots; head light brown, banded with black.

**Habitat.** Coastal sandhills and sandy heaths.

**Foodplants.** Lady's bedstraw (*Galium verum*), hedge bedstraw (*G. mollugo*), stitchwort (*Stellaria*), chickweed (*S. media*), grasses and probably other low-growing herbaceous plants.

**Biology.** One generation a year. Eggs are laid in August. Some claim that caterpillars hatch in the summer and feed throughout the winter, while others suggest that they do not hatch until January. Feeding takes place at night, caterpillars hiding by day beneath the soil. They feed on roots and stem bases. When fully fed towards the end of May, they pupate beneath the soil. Moths emerge in June and July.

**AGROTIS SEGETUM** Denis & Schiffermüller *Turnip Moth* **Pl. 10**
**Distribution.** Widespread throughout Europe. Widely distributed in the British Isles, often abundant in England but less common in Scotland.
**Description.** Length up to 47 mm; glossy or greasy in appearance; body pale grey or greyish-brown, tinged with purplish or greenish above; underside yellowish-brown; sometimes with indistinct dark lines along the back; body hairs arise from blackish dots; head yellowish-brown, striped and spotted with blackish-brown.
**Habitat.** Agricultural land, gardens, meadows, waste land and other places where suitable foodplants grow.
**Foodplants.** Dock (*Rumex*), charlock (*Sinapis arvensis*), turnip (*Brassica rapa*), parsnip (*Pastinaca sativa*), carrot (*Daucus carota*) and a wide range of other herbaceous plants, both wild and cultivated.
**Biology.** One generation a year. Eggs are laid in June in small masses on stems or among leaf litter on the ground. Caterpillars hatch in the following month and feed at or below ground level, boring into roots and eating stem bases, causing plants to wither and die. They are sometimes serious agricultural pests, particularly of root crops. Caterpillars become fully grown by the end of October but remain in the soil throughout the winter without further feeding, and pupate in subterranean cocoons in the following May. Moths emerge in May and June.

**AGROTIS EXCLAMATIONIS** Linnaeus *Heart and Dart* **Pl. 13**
**Distribution.** Widespread throughout temperate Europe. Widely distributed and often common in the British Isles, although less common in northern Scotland.
**Description.** Length up to 38 mm; body reddish-brown, underside greyish-white; three dark reddish lines extend along the back and sometimes a series of dark, wedge-shaped markings are present; body hairs arise from dark brown spots; head yellowish-brown, marked with dark brown.
**Habitat.** Agricultural land, meadows, gardens, waste land and other places where suitable foodplants grow.
**Foodplants.** Dock (*Rumex*), plantain (*Plantago*), chickweed (*Stellaria media*), fat hen (*Chenopodium album*), turnip (*Brassica rapa*), sugar beet (*Beta vulgaris*) and many other herbaceous plants, both wild and cultivated.
**Biology.** One generation a year. Eggs are laid on leaves and stems in June and caterpillars hatch in July. They feed at night on roots, stems and foliage, hiding beneath the soil by day. They are sometimes agricultural pests, causing most damage to root crops. Caterpillars are fully grown by the autumn, when they burrow into the ground to construct cocoons in which they hibernate before pupating in the spring. Moths emerge in June.

**AGROTIS PUTA** Hübner *Shuttle-shaped Dart* **Pl. 9**
**Distribution.** Widespread in central and southern Europe. Widely distributed in central and southern England and parts of Wales, but most common in south-eastern England. Absent from Scotland and Ireland.
**Description.** Length up to 32 mm; body ochreous-brown or dirty greyish-brown, with three dark brown lines along the back which is sometimes mottled with dark brown; underside pale greenish-grey; head small, light brown, marked with dark brown.

**Habitat.** Agricultural land, waste land, gardens, marshes and woodland.
**Foodplants.** Dock (*Rumex*), knotgrass (*Polygonum aviculare*), dandelion (*Taraxacum*) and other low-growing herbaceous plants.
**Biology.** Two generations a year, possibly a third generation in some regions. Eggs are laid in large batches on leaves of the foodplant in May and again in August or September. Caterpillars of the first generation feed and pupate in the summer while those of the second generation overwinter and complete their growth the following spring, pupating in May. Pupation takes place in the earth. Moths are on the wing from May to June and again from July to August, and sometimes September to October.

**AGROTIS RIPAE** Hübner *Sand Dart* **Pl. 11**
**Distribution.** Occurs locally in sandy coastal regions of Europe. In the British Isles it is widely distributed along the coasts of England, Wales, eastern Scotland and eastern and southern Ireland.
**Description.** Length up to 40 mm; body pale ochreous-brown or dull green with greyish lines and spots and prominent black spiracles; head and plate on thorax light brown.
**Habitat.** Sand dunes and sea shores.
**Foodplants.** Prickly saltwort (*Salsola kali*), sea rocket (*Cakile maritima*), sea purslane (*Halimione portulacoides*), seablite (*Suaeda*) and other maritime plants.
**Biology.** One generation a year. Eggs are laid in July and caterpillars hatch in the following month. They feed at night, hiding in the sand by day, and are fully grown by late autumn. They then bury themselves deep in the sand where they overwinter before pupating in late spring of the following year. Moths emerge in June.

**AXYLIA PUTRIS** Linnaeus *Flame* **Pl. 26**
**Distribution.** Widespread in Europe. Widely distributed and common in lowland regions of the British Isles.
**Description.** Length up to 35 mm; body stout, tapering towards head; body greyish-brown, mottled with blackish and marked with black and greenish-grey, with a line of small yellowish spots along the back; body segments 4, 6 and 11 are distinctly swollen; raised dots blackish; head dark brown.
**Habitat.** Agricultural land, gardens, wasteland, hedgerows and woodland margins.
**Foodplants.** Hedge bedstraw (*Galium mollugo*), dock (*Rumex*), plantain (*Plantago*), fat hen (*Chenopodium album*), knotgrass (*Polygonum aviculare*), houndstongue (*Cynoglossum officinale*) and other herbaceous plants.
**Biology.** Usually one generation a year but sometimes a few second brood moths appear in the autumn. Eggs are laid in large batches on the undersides of leaves in July. Caterpillars hatch within a week and may be found until the end of September, feeding mainly at night. Pupation takes place in October in underground earthen cocoons. Moths usually emerge in June of the following year.

**EUGNORISMA DEPUNCTA** Linnaeus *Plain Clay* **Pl. 10**
**Distribution.** Widespread but local in Europe. In the British Isles locally common in parts of Scotland, northern England and north Wales; also in south-west England but scarce.
**Description.** Length up to 47 mm; body reddish-brown or greyish with a series of dark V-shaped markings along the back and a pale yellow or ochreous stripe below the spiracles on each side; spiracles sometimes surrounded with black, forming a

line of dark patches; head small, ochreous, with a dark brown streak on either side.
**Habitat.** Woodland.
**Foodplants.** Dock (*Rumex*), sorrel (*R. acetosa*), sheep's sorrel (*R. acetosella*), primrose (*Primula vulgaris*) and cowslip (*P. veris*).
**Biology.** One generation a year. Eggs are laid in August or September and caterpillars hatch after about three weeks, going into hibernation immediately in dry hollow stems of grasses. They become active in early spring and are fully grown by the end of May. Pupation takes place in the soil and moths emerge in July or August.

**STANDFUSSIANA LUCERNEA** Linnaeus *Northern Rustic* **Pl. 13**
**Distribution.** Widely distributed in upland and coastal regions of Europe. Widespread in coastal and highland regions of Scotland, Wales and Ireland and local in southern and western England.
**Description.** Length up to 45 mm; body varying in colour from greyish-green to purplish-brown, mottled with black; underside pale grey or greyish-green; a row of dark markings extends along the back, sometimes forming a series of V-shapes, on either side of which is a row of pale spots; head dark brown with two whitish spots.
**Habitat.** Rocky coasts, mountains, stony hillsides and quarries.
**Foodplants.** Biting stonecrop (*Sedum acre*), harebell (*Campanula rotundifolia*), cowslip (*Primula veris*), yellow saxifrage (*Saxifraga aizoides*), sheep's fescue (*Festuca ovina*) and other grasses.
**Biology.** One generation a year. Eggs are laid in August and caterpillars hatch in the following month. They feed for a time before hibernating and completing their growth the following spring. They are mainly active at night and may be found stretched out on rocks near their foodplants. Pupation takes place in the earth in May and moths emerge in July.

**NOCTUA PRONUBA** Linnaeus *Large Yellow Underwing* **Pl. 29**
**Distribution.** Widespread throughout Europe. Widely distributed in the British Isles but most common in lowland regions.
**Description.** Length up to 50 mm; body very variable in colour, ranging from ochreous to various shades of brown or even bright green; the most distinctive feature is a double row of dark brown or black longitudinal bars along the back, edged on the outside with whitish-brown or green; a further line of dark markings extends along the spiracles on either side; head light brown, banded and marked with dark brown.
**Habitat.** Agricultural land, gardens, waste ground, open countryside, moorland and other places where suitable foodplants grow.
**Foodplants.** Dandelion (*Taraxacum*), chickweed (*Stellaria media*), dock (*Rumex*), grasses and a wide range of herbaceous plants, both wild and cultivated.
**Biology.** One generation a year. Eggs are laid in compact, flat masses on the undersides of leaves in July and caterpillars hatch in August. They feed until mid-winter before going into hibernation, completing their growth in the spring. They eat foliage and stems, sometimes severing plants at ground level. The caterpillars are mostly active at night, hiding in the soil by day. Pupation takes place in May in subterranean cocoons and moths emerge in June or July.

**NOCTUA COMES** Hübner *Lesser Yellow Underwing* **Pl. 31**

**Distribution.** Widely distributed throughout Europe. Widespread and often common in all parts of the British Isles.

**Description.** Length up to 50 mm; body light brown or greyish-brown, sometimes tinged with green, mottled with ochre; hind segments of body with a double row of dark brown or black, wedge-shaped markings along the back, joined by a dark transverse bar on segment 11; a broad, pale yellowish-brown band extends below the spiracles on each side; head light brown, banded and mottled with dark brown.

**Habitat.** Meadows, gardens, waste ground, hedgerows, open woodland, heaths and other places where suitable foodplants grow.

**Foodplants.** Dock (*Rumex*), chickweed (*Stellaria media*), foxglove (*Digitalis purpurea*), primrose (*Primula vulgaris*), heather (*Calluna vulgaris*), cock's-foot (*Dactylis glomerata*), sallow (*Salix*), hawthorn (*Crataegus monogyna*), and many other low-growing plants and deciduous shrubs.

**Biology.** One generation a year. Eggs are laid in August and caterpillars hatch in the following month. They feed for a short time on low-growing plants before going into hibernation. Caterpillars become active again at bud-burst in the spring when they not only feed on low-growing plants but also ascend the trunks of deciduous trees and shrubs to eat the young foliage. They are mainly active at night. Pupation takes place in subterranean cocoons in May and moths emerge in July.

**NOCTUA FIMBRIATA** Schreber *Broad-bordered Yellow Underwing* **Pl. 17**

**Distribution.** Widespread in Europe. Widely distributed throughout the British Isles.

**Description.** Length up to 55 mm; body ochreous-brown or reddish-brown, underside paler; upperside with a pale central line down the back; body segments 11 and 12 have pale transverse bands behind dark, wedge-shaped markings on the back; spiracles surrounded by black spots; head pale brown, freckled with dark brown.

**Habitat.** Woodland.

**Foodplants.** Primrose (*Primula vulgaris*), dock (*Rumex*), sweet violet (*Viola odorata*), dead-nettle (*Lamium*), hawthorn (*Crataegus monogyna*), blackthorn (*Prunus spinosa*), silver birch (*Betula pendula*), sallow (*Salix*) and other low-growing plants and deciduous shrubs.

**Biology.** One generation a year. Eggs are laid in late summer and caterpillars feed in the autumn on low-growing plants before going into hibernation. In the following spring, they feed on the newly developed foliage of deciduous trees and shrubs. It has been claimed that eggs are laid on the foliage of trees and that caterpillars descend to the ground to hibernate. Caterpillars are usually full-grown by the middle of May and pupate on the ground. Moths emerge in July.

**NOCTUA JANTHINA** Denis & Schiffermüller **Pl. 17**
*Lesser Broad-bordered Yellow Underwing*

**Distribution.** Widespread in Europe. Widely distributed throughout the British Isles and often very common in southern England.

**Description.** Length up to 40 mm; body ochreous-brown, sometimes greyish above and tinged with greenish; a pale line extends along the back through a series of dark, V-shaped markings; body segments 10 and 11 each have a pair of black wedge-shaped markings on the back; head brown marked with dark brown.

**Habitat.** Woodland, hedgerows and gardens.

**Foodplants.** Dock (*Rumex*), primrose (*Primula vulgaris*), chickweed (*Stellaria media*), dead-nettle (*Lamium*) and other herbaceous plants, bramble (*Rubus fruticosus*), hawthorn (*Crataegus monogyna*), blackthorn (*Prunus spinosa*), elm (*Ulmus procera*), sallow (*Salix*) and hazel (*Corylus avellana*).
**Biology.** One generation a year. Eggs are laid in August and caterpillars feed on various low-growing plants and bramble before hibernation. In the following spring they climb the stems of various deciduous trees and shrubs to feed on the developing foliage. They are mainly active at night. Pupation takes place in May in fragile subterranean cocoons and moths emerge in July.

**SPAELOTIS RAVIDA** Denis & Schiffermüller *Stout Dart* **Pl. 10**
**Distribution.** Widely distributed in Europe but rather local in some areas. Widespread in England and Wales but most common in the Midlands and eastern England. Absent from Scotland and Ireland.
**Description.** Length up to 42 mm; body dull yellowish or greenish-brown, sometimes ochreous on the back, with a series of V-shaped markings through which runs a pale central line; sometimes with a series of dark-edged, oblique yellowish markings along the sides; head greyish-brown.
**Habitat.** Fens and margins of marshland.
**Foodplants.** Dock (*Rumex*), sow-thistle (*Sonchus*), dandelion (*Taraxacum*) and probably on other related plants.
**Biology.** One generation a year. Eggs are laid in September in large heaps covered by scales from the abdomen of the female. Caterpillars hatch in the autumn and feed slowly through the winter on young foliage and roots. Pupation takes place just below the surface of the soil among roots of the foodplant in May. Moths emerge in late June and early July.

**EUGRAPHE SUBROSEA** Stephens *Rosy Marsh Moth* **Pl. 33**
**Distribution.** Occurs in northern and central Europe. In the British Isles, confined to western Wales, although formerly occurred in the old county of Huntingdonshire, England.
**Description.** Length up to 35 mm; body pink with a broad band of black and purplish-grey along the back, through which runs a central yellowish-white line; further white lines extend along either side of the black band; a broad, creamy-white stripe extends along each side of the body, bordered above and below by bands of black or purplish-grey; head pale pinkish-brown with darker markings.
**Habitat.** Acid bogs.
**Foodplants.** Bog Myrtle (*Myrica gale*); in continental Europe, also recorded on northern bilberry (*Vaccinium uliginosum*), bog rosemary (*Andromeda polifolia*), Labrador tea (*Ledum palustre*) and heather (*Calluna vulgaris*). Feeds on narrow-leaved *Salix* species in captivity.
**Biology.** One generation a year. Eggs are laid singly or in small groups on the foodplant in July or August and hatch in about ten days. The caterpillars overwinter and complete their development in the following spring and early summer, becoming fully grown in June or July. They feed at night on buds and young shoots. Pupation takes place on the ground under moss and plant debris and moths emerge in July or August.

**LYCOPHOTIA PORPHYREA** Denis & Schiffermüller **Pl. 24**
*True Lover's Knot*
**Distribution.** Widely distributed and common throughout Europe. Widespread and common in the British Isles.
**Description.** Length up to 27 mm; body brown or reddish-brown, usually with three rows of ochreous-white rectangular markings along the back, bordered by dark brown or black lunules; a pale ochreous or pinkish-white stripe, edged above with dark brown, extends along each side; head ochreous, striped and mottled with dark brown.
**Habitat.** Heaths, moorland and other places where the foodplants grow.
**Foodplants.** Heather (*Calluna vulgaris*), bell heather (*Erica cinerea*) and cross-leaved heath (*E. tetralix*).
**Biology.** One generation a year. Eggs are laid in July and caterpillars hatch in the following month, feeding until the autumn and again in spring after hibernation. They are active at night, hiding by day among leaf litter at the base of the foodplant. When fully grown at the end of April, they pupate in flimsy cocoons on or just below the surface of the earth. Moths emerge in June or July.

**PERIDROMA SAUCIA** Hübner *Pearly Underwing* **Pl. 13**
**Distribution.** Resident in southern Europe but migrates to northern Europe. Occurs as a migrant throughout the British Isles but most frequent in south-western England.
**Description.** Length up to 42 mm; rather plump, with rear segments of abdomen appearing slightly swollen; body greyish-brown suffused with purplish-red above; two lines of black dashes extend along the back, joined by a transverse band on segment 11, behind which is a conspicuous whitish patch; head brown with blackish bands.
**Habitat.** May be found in almost any habitat in the British Isles but most often occurs in coastal regions. In southern Europe it is an agricultural pest.
**Foodplants.** Plantain (*Plantago*), dock (*Rumex*), clover (*Trifolium*), cabbage (*Brassica oleracea*), lettuce (*Lactuca sativa*) and other herbaceous plants, both wild and cultivated.
**Biology.** The life cycle of this species in the British Isles is little known. There are two or three generations a year in southern Europe but caterpillars do not survive the winter in Britain. Eggs are laid in large numbers on the foodplant and caterpillars hatch in about a fortnight. The caterpillars are active at night, burrowing beneath the soil by day. Pupation takes place within subterranean cocoons. Moths may occur in Britain in any month from May to November but are most frequent in the autumn.

**DIARSIA MENDICA** Fabricius *Ingrailed Clay* **Pl. 10**
**Distribution.** Widespread throughout Europe. Widely distributed and common in the British Isles.
**Description.** Length up to 33 mm; body reddish-brown to greyish-brown or greenish-grey with two rows of black, wedge-shaped dashes along the back; underside pale greyish-brown; a pale band extends below the line of the spiracles on either side; head small, pale brown with darker markings.
**Habitat.** Woodland, heaths and moorland.
**Foodplants.** Primrose (*Primula vulgaris*), knotgrass (*Polygonum aviculare*), dock (*Rumex*), bramble (*Rubus fruticosus*), bilberry (*Vaccinium myrtillus*), heather

(*Calluna vulgaris*), silver birch (*Betula pendula*) and probably other deciduous trees and herbaceous plants.

**Biology.** One generation a year. Eggs are laid in July and hatch in about a fortnight. Caterpillars feed in the summer and then hibernate before completing their growth in the following spring. They are fully grown by early May, when they burrow into the soil to pupate. Moths emerge in June.

**DIARSIA DAHLII** Hübner *Barred Chestnut* **Pl. 10**

**Distribution.** Widespread in northern Europe, becoming scarcer towards central Europe. Widely distributed in the British Isles but most commonly found from the Midlands of England northwards to Scotland.

**Description.** Length up to 35 mm; body pale ochreous to bluish-grey; underside pale grey; back rich reddish-brown to yellowish-brown with a series of diamond-shaped markings; head pale brown.

**Habitat.** Heaths, moors and woodland.

**Foodplants.** Dock (*Rumex*), plantain (*Plantago*) and sallow (*Salix*).

**Biology.** One generation a year. Eggs are laid in August and hatch in about a fortnight. The young caterpillars feed on leaves of dock and plantain in the autumn and then go into hibernation before completing their growth in the following spring, when they eat the newly developed foliage of sallow. Pupation takes place in the soil in June and moths emerge in August.

**DIARSIA BRUNNEA** Denis & Schiffermüller *Purple Clay* **Pl. 15**

**Distribution.** Widespread in Europe. Widely distributed and common throughout the British Isles.

**Description.** Length up to 33 mm; plump; body light or dark reddish-brown, paler below the line of the spiracles; a broken white line extends along the middle of the back, running through a series of pale chevron-shaped markings; a conspicuous yellowish-white transverse band extends across the back of segment 11; head shining brown with two dark bands.

**Habitat.** Woodland.

**Foodplants.** Dock (*Rumex*), great woodrush (*Luzula sylvatica*), bracken (*Pteridium aquilinum*), bramble (*Rubus fruticosus*), sallow (*Salix*), birch (*Betula*), bilberry (*Vaccinium myrtillus*) and various other deciduous trees and shrubs and low-growing herbaceous plants.

**Biology.** One generation a year. Eggs are laid in July and hatch in about a week. The caterpillars feed at night, hiding by day in the soil or under leaf litter. Before hibernation, they feed on dock and other low-growing plants but in the spring they eat the young foliage of various trees and shrubs. Pupation takes place in the ground in June and moths emerge in July.

**XESTIA ALPICOLA** Zetterstedt *Northern Dart* **Pl. 25**

**Distribution.** Occurs in various parts of the Alps and upland regions of northern Europe. In the British Isles it is confined to northern England, Scotland and Northern Ireland.

**Description.** Length up to 35 mm; skin rough and wrinkled; body dark reddish-brown to purplish-brown; underside reddish-brown; three indistinct pale lines and a double row of black dashes extend along the back; head brown.

**Habitat.** Mountains and upland moors.

**Foodplants.** Alpine Bearberry (*Arctostaphylos uva-ursi*), crowberry (*Empetrum*) and probably heather (*Calluna vulgaris*) and bilberry (*Vaccinium myrtillus*).
**Biology.** The caterpillars of this species take two years to complete their growth. Eggs are laid in July and caterpillars hatch in the same month. They burrow in moss and lichens surrounding the foodplants and feed on young shoots. When fully grown in May of the second year they pupate beneath lichens and moss. Moths emerge in June or July.

**XESTIA C-NIGRUM** Linnaeus *Setaceous Hebrew Character* **Pl. 11**
**Distribution.** Widespread throughout Europe. Widely distributed in the British Isles and often common in the south.
**Description.** Length up to 37 mm; body greyish-brown to greenish-grey; underside pale greyish-brown; a double row of black, wedge-shaped dashes extends along the back, becoming larger towards the tail, and a yellowish band extends along either side below the line of the spiracles; head pale brown with bands of darker brown.
**Habitat.** Woodland, meadows, gardens, waste ground, marshes and heathland.
**Foodplants.** Chickweed (*Stellaria media*), groundsel (*Senecio vulgaris*), dock (*Rumex*), plantain (*Plantago*), creeping willow (*Salix repens*), bilberry (*Vaccinium myrtillus*), white dead-nettle (*Lamium album*) and burdock (*Arctium*).
**Biology.** Apparently one generation a year in the British Isles, although development times of caterpillars can vary so greatly that overlapping broods may occur. Under laboratory conditions, up to six broods can be obtained in a year. Eggs are laid in summer or autumn, scattered on the foodplant or on the surrounding earth. Caterpillars hatch in about nine days and either become fully grown in the autumn or overwinter and complete their development in the following spring. Pupation takes place in the earth and moths are on the wing in autumn and also in late spring.

**XESTIA DITRAPEZIUM** Denis & Schiffermüller **Pl. 15**
*Triple-spotted Clay*
**Distribution.** Widespread in Europe. Widely distributed but local in the British Isles.
**Description.** Length up to 40 mm; body brown to greyish-brown; underside pale greyish-brown; a double row of blackish dashes extends along the back, terminating in a pair of conspicuous wedge-shaped markings on segment 11; head light brown with two blackish stripes.
**Habitat.** Damp woodland.
**Foodplants.** Dandelion (*Taraxacum*), chickweed (*Stellaria media*), primrose (*Primula vulgaris*), dock (*Rumex*), sallow (*Salix*), hazel (*Corylus avellana*), dogwood (*Cornus sanguinea*) and bramble (*Rubus fruticosus*).
**Biology.** One generation a year. Eggs are laid in July and the caterpillars are active in summer and autumn, feeding on low-growing plants. After hibernation, they resume feeding on the young foliage of deciduous trees and shrubs. They feed at night, hiding amongst leaf litter by day. Pupation takes place in the soil in June and moths emerge in the following month.

**XESTIA TRIANGULUM** Hufnagel *Double Square-spot* **Pl. 17**
**Distribution.** Widely distributed throughout Europe. Widespread in the British Isles but most common in south-eastern England.
**Description.** Length up to 42 mm; body yellowish-brown to reddish-brown, underside dull yellowish-grey; body segments 10 and 11 have conspicuous blackish,

wedge-shaped markings in pairs on the back; head light brown with two blackish stripes.

**Habitat.** Woodland and wooded countryside.

**Foodplants.** Dock (*Rumex*), chickweed (*Stellaria media*), primrose (*Primula vulgaris*), bramble (*Rubus fruticosus*), hawthorn (*Crataegus monogyna*), birch (*Betula*), blackthorn (*Prunus spinosa*), sallow (*Salix*) and hazel (*Corylus avellana*).

**Biology.** One generation a year. Eggs are laid in July and hatch in about a week. The caterpillars feed at first on low-growing plants but after hibernation eat the developing foliage of deciduous trees and shrubs. They are active at night, hiding on the ground by day. Pupation takes place in May in subterranean cocoons and moths emerge in the following month.

**XESTIA ASHWORTHII** Doubleday *Ashworth's Rustic* **Pl. 10**

**Distribution.** Occurs in mountainous regions of central Europe and coastal regions of Fennoscandia. In the British Isles it is restricted to the mountains of north Wales.

**Description.** Length up to 40 mm; body dark blackish-grey, sometimes tinged with green or purple, with a double row of black rectangular dashes along the back; head bright reddish-brown.

**Habitat.** Steep, rocky ground and scree on mountain sides.

**Foodplants.** Common rock-rose (*Helianthemum nummularium*), harebell (*Campanula rotundifolia*), wild thyme (*Thymus serpyllum*), sheep's sorrel (*Rumex acetosella*), salad burnet (*Sanguisorba minor*), creeping sallow (*Salix repens*) and probably various other plants.

**Biology.** One generation a year. Eggs are laid in July and the young caterpillars feed for a time before going into hibernation while still quite small. They resume feeding in the spring and are active both by day and night when the weather is warm enough. Pupation takes place in the soil or under moss in May and moths emerge in June or July.

**XESTIA SEXSTRIGATA** Haworth *Six-striped Rustic* **Pl. 15**

**Distribution.** Widely distributed in Europe. Widespread throughout the British Isles and often common.

**Description.** Length up to 33 mm; body pale greyish-brown, suffused with blackish-brown on the back; three pale lines and two rows of black dashes extend along the back; a broad blackish-brown band extends along the line of the spiracles on each side; underside grey; head yellowish-brown with two darker brown bands.

**Habitat.** Damp meadows and woodland, marshes and fens; sometimes also in hedgerows and gardens.

**Foodplants.** Dock (*Rumex*), ribwort plantain (*Plantago lanceolata*), hedge bedstraw (*Galium mollugo*), water figwort (*Scrophularia auriculata*) and bramble (*Rubus fruticosus*); probably feeds on many other herbaceous plants.

**Biology.** One generation a year. Eggs are laid in August and caterpillars may be found from September to May or June, feeding through the winter when the weather is mild. Pupation takes place in June or July in subterranean cocoons and moths usually emerge in July.

**XESTIA XANTHOGRAPHA** Denis & Schiffermüller **Pl. 11**
*Square-spot Rustic*

**Distribution.** Widespread throughout Europe. Widely distributed and common in the British Isles.

**Description.** Length up to 33 mm; very similar in appearance to *X. sexstrigata*; body pale ochreous-brown, banded with blackish-brown; three pale lines and two rows of black dashes on the back.
**Habitat.** Gardens, waste ground, meadows and many other places where suitable foodplants grow.
**Foodplants.** Dock (*Rumex*), plantain (*Plantago*), chickweed (*Stellaria media*), primrose (*Primula vulgaris*), annual meadowgrass (*Poa annua*) and other grasses, sallow (*Salix*), hawthorn (*Crataegus monogyna*) and other deciduous trees and shrubs.
**Biology.** One generation a year. Eggs are laid in August and hatch in about three weeks. Caterpillars feed on grasses and other low-growing plants through the winter, but in the spring they sometimes eat the foliage of deciduous trees and shrubs. They are active at night, hiding at the base of the plant or under stones by day. When fully grown in March or April the caterpillars burrow into the ground and make cocoons but do not pupate for a further six weeks. Moths emerge in August.

**XESTIA AGATHINA** Duponchel *Heath Rustic* **Pl. 24**
**Distribution.** Widely distributed in many parts of Europe. Widespread throughout the British Isles in suitable habitats.
**Description.** Length up to 30 mm; body varying in colour from bright green to greyish-green or brown with three broad white lines and two rows of black dashes extending along the back; a broad whitish band extends along either side below the line of the spiracles, broken by a series of orange, reddish-brown, pale purple or green patches; head yellowish-brown with two darker stripes.
**Habitat.** Heaths and moorland.
**Foodplants.** Heather (*Calluna vulgaris*), bell heather (*Erica cinerea*) and cross-leaved heath (*Erica tetralix*).
**Biology.** One generation a year. Eggs are laid in August or September and hatch in about three weeks. The caterpillars are active at night, feeding throughout the winter except in very cold weather. They cling closely to the stems of heather by day, when they are very well camouflaged. Pupation takes place in June in silken cocoons spun low down among stems of the foodplant. Moths emerge in August or September.

**NAENIA TYPICA** Linnaeus *Gothic* **Pl. 16**
**Distribution.** Widely distributed throughout Europe. Widespread in the British Isles.
**Description.** Length up to 48 mm; body greyish-brown with a broad wavy band of greyish-white extending along each side below the line of orange spiracles; a series of whitish V-shaped markings extends along the back; head greyish-white with dark brown markings.
**Habitat.** Hedgerows, gardens, orchards and waste ground.
**Foodplants.** Dock (*Rumex*), dandelion (*Taraxacum*), sow-thistle (*Sonchus*), primrose (*Primula vulgaris*), apple (*Malus*), sallow (*Salix*), hawthorn (*Crataegus monogyna*), blackthorn (*Prunus spinosa*) and many other herbaceous plants and deciduous trees and shrubs.
**Biology.** One generation a year. Eggs are laid in July on the foliage of trees and shrubs and hatch in about a fortnight. The caterpillars are gregarious at first, feeding on the surface of the leaves. After hibernation they become solitary and resume feeding on various low-growing plants. They are active at night, hiding by day at

the base of the foodplant. Pupation takes place in subterranean cocoons in May and moths emerge in the following month.

**ANAPLECTOIDES PRASINA** Denis & Schiffermüller **Pl. 15**
*Green Arches*

**Distribution.** Widespread in Europe. Widely distributed and locally common in the British Isles.

**Description.** Length up to 50 mm; body dark greyish-brown or chocolate-brown; pale greyish-white to brown below the line of the spiracles; each spiracle surrounded by a blackish blotch; head yellowish-brown with darker markings.

**Habitat.** Woodland.

**Foodplants.** Bramble (*Rubus fruticosus*), knotgrass (*Polygonum aviculare*), dock (*Rumex*), primrose (*Primula vulgaris*) and other low-growing plants, sallow (*Salix*) and bilberry (*Vaccinium myrtillus*).

**Biology.** One generation a year. Eggs are laid in July and hatch in about a week. The caterpillars feed at first on bramble and low-growing herbaceous plants, but after hibernation they also eat the young foliage of sallow and bilberry. They are active at night, remaining on the ground by day hidden under moss or leaf litter. Pupation takes place in May in subterranean cocoons and moths emerge in late June.

**CERASTIS RUBRICOSA** Denis & Schiffermüller *Red Chestnut* **Pl. 29**

**Distribution.** Widespread in Europe but scarce in the Mediterranean region. Widely distributed and often common in the British Isles.

**Description.** Length up to 41 mm; body reddish-brown, sometimes tinged with green, with a line of dark triangular-shaped markings along the back; two lines of yellowish streaks extend along the back, inside which are a series of black triangles, each with a central white dot; a broad, whitish band extends below the line of the spiracles on each side; head yellowish-brown with darker markings.

**Habitat.** Woods and woodland margins and boggy moorland.

**Foodplants.** Dandelion (*Taraxacum*), groundsel (*Senecio vulgaris*), chickweed (*Stellaria media*), dock (*Rumex*), bedstraw (*Galium*) and other low-growing herbaceous plants; also on sallow (*Salix*).

**Biology.** One generation a year. Eggs are laid in April, hatching in about a fortnight. The caterpillars are active at night but remain stretched out on stems or leaves of the foodplant by day. They feed up quite rapidly and are fully grown by the end of June. Pupation takes place in subterranean cocoons and moths emerge in March or April of the following year.

**ANARTA MYRTILLI** Linnaeus *Beautiful Yellow Underwing* **Pl. 24**

**Distribution.** Widespread in Europe. Widely distributed throughout the British Isles in suitable habitats.

**Description.** Length up to 30 mm; body dark green to bright yellowish-green spotted with white; a central line of yellow-centred, white markings extends along the back, on either side of which is a row of curved, yellow-centred, white dashes; a line of white, inverted V-shaped markings extends below the spiracles on either side; head green with pale brown mottling.

**Habitat.** Acid moorland and heaths.

**Foodplants.** Heather (*Calluna vulgaris*) and bell heather (*Erica cinerea*).

**Biology.** One generation a year in the north, two generations in the south. Eggs are laid singly or in pairs on the foliage in May and August and hatch in about a fortnight. Caterpillars may be found from April to October but are most common in the summer months. They are active by day and night and are often found on the upper twigs of the foodplant. Pupation takes place in July and again in the autumn in cocoons of silk and earth on the ground. Moths from July pupae emerge in August but autumn pupae overwinter and produce moths in the following spring. In the north, moths emerge in June.

**ANARTA CORDIGERA** Thunberg *Small Dark Yellow Underwing* **Pl. 25**

**Distribution.** Occurs in northern Europe and mountainous regions of central and southern Europe. In the British Isles it is confined to the highlands of Scotland.

**Description.** Length up to 30 mm; body slender, appearance velvety; colour varying from reddish-brown to purplish-brown or blackish; a fairly distinct central, whitish line extends down the back and a brown or yellowish stripe extends below the line of the spiracles on either side; head purplish-brown.

**Habitat.** Rocky mountain localities; also in lowland regions of Scandinavia.

**Foodplants.** Alpine bearberry (*Arctostaphylos uva-ursi*) and probably also related plants such as cowberry (*Vaccinium vitis-idaea*).

**Biology.** One generation a year. Eggs are laid singly on the foodplant in May and hatch in about a fortnight. Caterpillars feed at night, hiding low down on the foodplant by day. They are full-grown by the end of July and pupate in silken cocoons on the ground. Moths emerge in May of the following year.

**ANARTA MELANOPA** Thunberg *Broad-bordered White Underwing* **Pl. 25**

**Distribution.** Occurs in mountainous regions of central and southern Europe and also in Fennoscandia. In the British Isles it is confined to Northumberland in England and to mountainous parts of Scotland.

**Description.** Length up to 32 mm; body greyish-brown, suffused with reddish-brown or purplish-brown on the back and with whitish on the sides; underside grey; an indistinct dark line runs along the middle of the back, on either side of which is a line of yellowish-white dashes; head yellowish-brown with darker brown markings.

**Habitat.** Mountains and moorland.

**Foodplants.** Crowberry (*Empetrum nigrum*), bilberry (*Vaccinium myrtillus*), cowberry (*V. vitis-idaea*).

**Biology.** One generation a year. Eggs are laid singly or in pairs on leaves of the foodplant in May and hatch in about a fortnight. Caterpillars may be found from June to August. They feed at night, hiding under leaves of the foodplant by day. Pupation takes place in cocoons on the surface of the soil under moss in August but moths do not emerge until the following May.

**DISCESTRA TRIFOLII** Hufnagel *Nutmeg* **Pl. 11**

**Distribution.** Widespread throughout Europe. Widely distributed in Britain but rare in Ireland.

**Description.** Length up to 40 mm; body varying in colour from green to purplish-brown; two pale lines extend along the back, inside which are a series of black dashes; a conspicuous pinkish band, bordered with white extends below the line of the spiracles on either side; each spiracle, except the first and last, is surrounded by a black patch; head green or brown.

**Habitat.** Meadows, waste ground and agricultural land, particularly in coastal regions and other sandy areas.

**Foodplants.** Goosefoot (*Chenopodium*), orache (*Atriplex*), sea beet (*Beta vulgaris*), knotgrass (*Polygonum aviculare*) and occasionally onion (*Allium cepa*) and other plants.

**Biology.** One generation a year in the north but two generations in the south. Eggs are laid singly on stems and leaves of the foodplant in May and August and hatch in a week or less. The caterpillars feed at night, hiding on the ground at the base of the foodplant by day. They may be found from June to September. Pupation takes place in subterranean cocoons in summer and in the autumn. Moths emerge in May and August in the south, but a single generation emerges in late June further north.

**POLIA NEBULOSA** Hufnagel *Grey Arches* **Pl. 15**

**Distribution.** Widespread throughout Europe. Widely distributed in the British Isles.

**Description.** Length up to 50 mm; body yellowish-brown to greyish-brown, with a series of blackish, diamond-shaped markings down the back, on either side of which is a line of oblique dashes; spiracles orange; head yellowish-brown with darker markings.

**Habitat.** Woodland.

**Foodplants.** Dock (*Rumex*), bramble (*Rubus fruticosus*), sallow (*Salix*), hawthorn (*Crataegus monogyna*), birch (*Betula*) and other deciduous trees and shrubs.

**Biology.** One generation a year. Eggs are laid on low-growing plants in June or July, hatching in about a fortnight. The caterpillars feed at first on docks and probably on other low-growing plants, but after hibernation they eat the young foliage of various deciduous trees and shrubs. They are active at night, hiding at the base of the foodplant by day. Pupation takes place in subterranean cocoons in May and moths emerge in the following month.

**PACHETRA SAGITTIGERA** Hufnagel *Feathered Ear* **Pl. 31**

**Distribution.** Widely distributed in Europe. In the British Isles restricted to southern England where it is very local.

**Description.** Length up to 40 mm; body ochreous-brown; some forms are almost without markings but others have a pale central line bordered with black dashes on the back and a broad, dark brown band along the sides; head yellowish-brown. Young caterpillars are green.

**Habitat.** Downland and other localities with chalk or limestone soils.

**Foodplants.** Annual meadow-grass (*Poa annua*), wood meadow-grass (*P. nemoralis*), slender false-brome (*Brachypodium sylvaticum*), cock's-foot (*Dactylis glomerata*) and other grasses.

**Biology.** One generation a year. Eggs are laid on grasses in June and hatch in about twelve days. The caterpillars are active at night, hiding by day at the base of thick grass tufts. They probably feed throughout the winter in mild weather and are full-grown by March or April. Pupation takes place in fragile cocoons spun under moss on the ground in April and moths emerge in the following month.

**MAMESTRA BRASSICAE** Linnaeus *Cabbage Moth* **Pl. 13**

**Distribution.** Widespread throughout Europe. Widely distributed in the British Isles but most common in the south.

**Description.** Length up to 45 mm; body varying in colour from brown to greyish-green; two lines of black dashes extend along the back, joining to form a black

wedge-shape on segment 11; a broad band of orange, ochreous-yellow or pale green extends along the line of the spiracles on either side; head pale yellowish-brown or dark brown with paler markings. Young caterpillars are green with yellow rings between the segments.
**Habitat.** Agricultural land, gardens, waste ground and other places where suitable foodplants grow.
**Foodplants.** Almost any low-growing herbaceous plant but particularly cabbage (*Brassica oleracea*) and related plants; also on various deciduous trees and shrubs including oak (*Quercus*) and birch (*Betula*).
**Biology.** One generation a year. Eggs are laid in groups on the undersides of leaves in the summer months, hatching in about eight days. The caterpillars feed at night, hiding on the ground by day. They are sometimes serious pests of cabbages, boring into their hearts and remaining undetected until the crop is badly damaged. Pupation takes place in flimsy subterranean cocoons in the autumn but moths do not usually emerge until the following June.

## MELANCHRA PERSICARIAE Linnaeus *Dot Moth* **Pl. 27**

**Distribution.** Widespread in Europe. Widely distributed in England, particularly in the south, but more local in Wales and Ireland and only recorded from a few localities in southern Scotland.
**Description.** Length up to 40 mm; body varying in colour from purplish-brown to green; a pronounced hump present on segment 11; a white line extends along the back, passing through a series of dark, V-shaped markings which are particularly prominent on segments 4, 5 and 11; a series of oblique, dark stripes extend from the spiracles towards the underside; head pale brown.
**Habitat.** Hedgerows, waste ground, gardens and other places where suitable foodplants grow.
**Foodplants.** Nettle (*Urtica*), plantain (*Plantago*), *Anemone* and many other low-growing herbaceous plants; also on the foliage of elder (*Sambucus nigra*), sallow (*Salix*) and other deciduous trees and shrubs.
**Biology.** One generation a year. Eggs are laid singly or in masses on the foodplant in June or July, hatching in about a week. The caterpillars feed mostly at night, hiding by day under leaves of the foodplant. Pupation takes place in subterranean cocoons in the autumn but moths do not emerge until the following summer.

## LANCANOBIA CONTIGUA Denis & Schiffermüller **Pl. 5**

*Beautiful Brocade*
**Distribution.** Widespread but local in Europe. Widely distributed in the British Isles but most common in Scotland and southern England.
**Description.** Length up to 40 mm; body varying in colour from green to reddish-brown with green suffusion; three lines of purplish-brown or blackish dashes extend along the back; a purplish-brown line extends along the white spiracles on either side, below which is a whitish or pale green band of varying width; head greenish-brown.
**Habitat.** Lightly wooded acid heaths and moorland.
**Foodplants.** Bog myrtle (*Myrica gale*), sallow (*Salix*), birch (*Betula*), hazel (*Corylus avellana*), oak (*Quercus*), dock (*Rumex*), golden-rod (*Solidago virgaurea*), bracken (*Pteridium aquilinum*) and other plants.
**Biology.** One generation a year. Eggs are laid in large masses on the foodplant in

June and hatch in about a week. The caterpillars feed mainly at night, hiding on the ground by day. They are full-grown by the end of September and pupate in subterranean cocoons. Moths emerge in June of the following year.

**LACANOBIA W-LATINUM** Hufnagel *Light Brocade* **Pl. 19**
**Distribution.** Widely distributed in Europe. Widespread and common in southern England, becoming less common further north; scarce in Wales and Scotland and apparently absent from Ireland.
**Description.** Length up to 45 mm; fairly stout; body varying in colour from dull brown to grey or olive-green; a series of dark brown diamond and wedge-shaped markings extend along the back; below the whitish spiracles, the body colour is pale greyish-brown; head brown with two black streaks.
**Habitat.** Mainly chalk and limestone areas.
**Foodplants.** Broom (*Cytisus scoparius*), dyer's greenweed (*Genista tinctoria*), redshank (*Polygonum persicaria*), knotgrass (*P. aviculare*) and other plants.
**Biology.** One generation a year. Eggs are laid in large batches on the foodplant in June and hatch in about ten days. The caterpillars are active at night, hiding amongst the foodplant by day. They are full-grown by late summer and pupate in subterranean cocoons in the autumn. Moths emerge in May of the following year.

**LACANOBIA OLERACEA** Linnaeus *Bright-line Brown-eye* **Pl. 11**
**Distribution.** Widespread throughout Europe. Widely distributed in the British Isles and very common, except in the extreme north.
**Description.** Length up to 45 mm; body varying in colour from green to brown, grey or pink with fine white speckling; a broad line of pale yellow or white extends below the line of the spiracles on each side; head yellowish-brown or greenish-brown with pale markings.
**Habitat.** Cultivated ground, gardens, waste ground, margins of saltmarshes and other places where suitable foodplants grow.
**Foodplants.** Goosefoot (*Chenopodium*), orache (*Atriplex*), nettle (*Urtica dioica*), dock (*Rumex*) and other low-growing plants.
**Biology.** One generation a year. Eggs are laid in batches on the undersides of leaves in June and hatch in about a week. Caterpillars are mainly active at night, usually hiding at the base of the foodplant by day but sometimes basking stretched out on the foliage. This species is known as the Tomato Moth because of the damage that it sometimes causes to glasshouse crops. Pupation usually takes place in late August or in September in fragile subterranean cocoons. Moths do not emerge until the following June.

**CERAMICA PISI** Linnaeus *Broom Moth* **Pl. 32**
**Distribution.** Widespread throughout Europe. Widely distributed in the British Isles, except Shetland.
**Description.** Length up to 45 mm; body varying in colour from green to reddish-brown or dark purplish-brown with two broad yellow bands on the back and a broad yellow band along the line of the spiracles on either side; head brown or greenish-brown.
**Habitat.** Open country, heaths and moorland.
**Foodplants.** Bracken (*Pteridium aquilinum*), broom (*Cytisus scoparius*), bramble (*Rubus fruticosus*), sallow (*Salix*) and a wide range of other low-growing plants and deciduous trees and shrubs; sometimes also on young larch (*Larix decidua*).

**Biology.** One generation a year. Eggs are laid in batches on the foodplant in July and hatch in about ten days. Although the caterpillars are mainly active at night they may sometimes be seen by day, stretched out on fronds of bracken. They are usually full-grown in September and pupate in earthen cocoons beneath the ground. Moths do not emerge until the following June or July.

**HECATERA DYSODEA** Denis & Schiffermüller *Small Ranunculus* **Pl. 29**

**Distribution.** Widespread in central and southern Europe and parts of northern Europe. Although at one time this species was locally common in parts of south-eastern England, it no longer occurs in the British Isles.

**Description.** Length up to 30 mm; body ochreous or pale reddish-brown with black dots, pale greenish below line of spiracles; sometimes with three fine blackish lines on the back; head pale yellowish-brown.

**Habitat.** Fields and open countryside.

**Foodplants.** Lettuce (*Lactuca*), both wild and cultivated, smooth hawksbeard (*Crepis capillaris*) and sow-thistle (*Sonchus*).

**Biology.** One generation a year. Eggs are laid in June and caterpillars hatch in the following month, becoming full-grown by the end of August. They are mainly active at night, feeding on buds and flowers, but remain stretched out on the stems by day, when they are well camouflaged. Pupation takes place below the surface of the soil in autumn but moths do not emerge until the following June.

**HADENA RIVULARIS** Fabricius *Campion* **Pl. 11**

**Distribution.** Widespread throughout Europe except for the extreme north. Widely distributed in the British Isles.

**Description.** Length up to 35 mm; body brownish-yellow or pale greenish-brown, suffused with purplish-brown, especially towards the head and on the underside; a series of purplish-brown V-shaped markings extends along the back and similarly-coloured oblique stripes run through the spiracles on either side; head pale brown with darker markings.

**Habitat.** Damp meadows and other places where the foodplants grow.

**Foodplants.** Ragged robin (*Lychnis flos-cuculi*), sea campion (*Silene maritima*) and probably most other species of *Lychnis* and *Silene*.

**Biology.** One generation a year with a partial second brood in southern localities. Eggs are laid singly on or inside opening buds and flowers in June and hatch in about a week. The caterpillars feed on developing seeds but when these become ripe and hard, they will also eat the foliage. They are active at night, hiding by day among the lower leaves of the foodplant or in leaf litter on the ground. They are full-grown by the end of August and pupate in cocoons just below the surface of the soil. Moths emerge in the following May and June although second brood moths may be found in the autumn.

**HADENA CONFUSA** Hufnagel *Marbled Coronet* **Pl. 11**

**Distribution.** Widespread in Europe. Widely distributed and locally common in the British Isles.

**Description.** Length up to 30 mm; body dull yellowish-brown to reddish-brown; underside pale greyish, sometimes tinged with green; a line of greyish-brown V-shaped markings extends along the back; head reddish-brown with darker markings.

**Habitat.** Meadows, sea coasts and open countryside on chalk and limestone soils.

**Foodplants.** Sea campion (*Silene maritima*), bladder campion (*S. vulgaris*) and white campion (*S. alba*); possibly also on other species of *Silene* and *Lychnis*.
**Biology.** One generation a year. Eggs are laid singly on buds and flowers in June or July and hatch in about a week. When young the caterpillars live inside the seed capsules but as they grow larger they hide by day at the base of the foodplant, crawling up the stem at night to feed on the developing seeds. Caterpillars are usually full-grown by the end of August and pupate in fragile cocoons below the surface of the soil. Moths do not emerge until the following May or June and sometimes remain in the pupa for a second winter.

**HADENA BICRURIS** Hufnagel *Lychnis* **Pl. 11**
**Distribution.** Widespread in Europe. Widely distributed and common in the British Isles.
**Description.** Length up to 35 mm; body ochreous-brown with a series of blackish V-shaped markings down the back and a blackish band along the spiracles on either side; head pale brown with dark brown markings.
**Habitat.** Woodland, marshes, meadows, heaths and sand dunes.
**Foodplants.** Red campion (*Silene dioica*), ragged robin (*Lychnis flos-cuculi*) and other species of *Silene* and *Lychnis*; also sweet william (*Dianthus barbatus*).
**Biology.** Two generations a year in the south, one generation further north. Eggs are laid singly on flowers and buds and hatch in under a week. Caterpillars feed within the seed capsules at first but later remain on the outside with their heads thrust into the capsules. First brood caterpillars are fully grown by July and the second brood towards the end of August. Pupation takes place in fragile cocoons below the soil. Moths emerge in June and again in September.

**CERAPTERYX GRAMINIS** Linnaeus *Antler Moth* **Pl. 31**
**Distribution.** Widespread throughout Europe. Widely distributed in the British Isles.
**Description.** Length up to 35 mm; body dark bronze-brown above the line of the spiracles, pale orange-brown below; skin wrinkled and glossy; three broad, pale ochreous stripes extend along the back and a broad white band along the line of the spiracles; head yellowish-brown, marked with dark brown.
**Habitat.** Open countryside, particularly acid moorland.
**Foodplants.** Purple moor-grass (*Molinia caerulea*), mat-grass (*Nardus stricta*) and other coarse grasses, also rushes (*Juncus* and *Scirpus*).
**Biology.** One generation a year. Eggs are laid in August but do not hatch until March or April of the following year. They are laid at random by the female as she flies low over the ground. The caterpillars feed both by day and night and sometimes occur in such large numbers that they move in armies over grassland, completely destroying large areas of grazing. Pupation takes place in earthen cocoons amongst grass roots or under stones in June and moths emerge in July and August.

**PANOLIS FLAMMEA** Denis & Schiffermüller *Pine Beauty* **Pl. 1**
**Distribution.** Widely distributed throughout Europe. Widespread in Britain but local in Ireland.
**Description.** Length up to 40 mm; body greyish-green, occasionally brown, with three white stripes on the back and a broad, white band along the spiracles, bordered below with orange-yellow; spiracles orange; head reddish-brown with pale markings.
**Habitat.** Coniferous woodland.

**Foodplants.** Pine (*Pinus*) and sometimes other conifers such as spruce (*Picea*) and fir (*Abies*); occasionally on oak (*Quercus*) and birch (*Betula*).
**Biology.** One generation a year. Eggs are laid in single rows on the needles in May and hatch in about a week. Moths usually choose mature trees on which to lay eggs. The caterpillars feed on young shoots at first, later moving onto older needles where they are very well camouflaged. They are fully grown towards the end of July and pupate in flimsy cocoons spun in crevices of the bark or amongst leaf litter on the ground. Moths emerge in the following March or April.

**BRITHYS CRINI** Fabricius *Kew Arches* **Pl. 30**
**Distribution.** Occurs locally in southern Europe, particularly along the Mediterranean coast. Recorded once from the British Isles in Kew Gardens, Surrey.
**Description.** Length up to 49 mm; body purplish-black with broad, chequered bands of white; legs reddish-brown; head reddish-brown with black spots.
**Habitat.** Sea coasts.
**Foodplant.** Sea daffodil (*Pancratium maritimum*).
**Biology.** Caterpillars may be found in June, feeding on leaves, buds and stalks, boring down into the bulbs. Moths are on the wing in May.

**ORTHOSIA CRUDA** Denis & Schiffermüller *Small Quaker* **Pl. 14**
**Distribution.** Widespread in Europe, extending as far north as southern Scandinavia. Widely distributed in Britain and widespread but local in Ireland.
**Description.** Length up to 30 mm; body green or brown; green form freckled with white, and with yellowish rings between segments; a white central line extends down the back and a broad white band shaded with green and pink runs along the line of the spiracles. Brown form has distinct black dots; a broad white central line extends down the back with a narrower white line on either side of it and a white-bordered, ochreous stripe extends along the spiracles; both forms have a broad, white transverse line on the back of segment 11; head greenish or ochreous-white with darker spots.
**Habitat.** Woodland and woodland margins.
**Foodplants.** Oak (*Quercus*), sallow (*Salix*), hazel (*Corylus avellana*), hawthorn (*Crataegus monogyna*) and rose (*Rosa*).
**Biology.** One generation a year. Eggs are laid in April and hatch in about a week. Caterpillars are usually found in May and June. They feed mainly at night, hiding between two leaves spun together with silk. In captivity these caterpillars may be cannibalistic. Pupation takes place in July in subterranean cocoons but moths do not emerge until the following March.

**ORTHOSIA MINIOSA** Denis & Schiffermüller *Blossom Underwing* **Pl. 6**
**Distribution.** Widely distributed in Europe. Widespread in England but most common in the south; local in Wales and scarce in Ireland.
**Description.** Length up to 35 mm; body bluish-grey to brown, spotted and finely marked with black; three yellow lines extend along the back, the central line being much broader than the others; a broad yellow band, spotted with black and margined with white extends along the spiracles; head pale grey or brown with dark spots.
**Habitat.** Woodland and hedgerows.
**Foodplants.** Oak (*Quercus*) and occasionally hawthorn (*Crataegus monogyna*),

blackthorn (*Prunus spinosa*), bramble (*Rubus fruticosus*) and various low-growing plants.

**Biology.** One generation a year. Eggs are laid in small batches on oak twigs in April, hatching in about a fortnight. At first, the young caterpillars are gregarious, living under a communal web, but later become solitary. Some leave the oak at this stage to feed on surrounding undergrowth. Caterpillars are full-grown by the middle of June and pupation takes place in subterranean cocoons. Moths emerge in the following March or April.

**ORTHOSIA OPIMA** Hübner *Northern Drab* **Pl. 14**

**Distribution.** Widely distributed in western and central Europe. Widespread but local in the British Isles; scarce in Scotland and Ireland.

**Description.** Length up to 40 mm; body above spiracles dark purplish-brown or greyish-green, below spiracles pale green; three fine, whitish lines extend along the back; head pale ochre.

**Habitat.** Sandhills, heaths, downland and marshes.

**Foodplants.** Sallow (*Salix*), birch (*Betula*), rose (*Rosa*), dyer's greenweed (*Genista tinctoria*), ragwort (*Senecio jacobaea*), houndstongue (*Cynoglossum officinale*) and other plants.

**Biology.** One generation a year. Eggs are laid in large groups in April and hatch in about a week. The caterpillars are active at night, hiding by day under leaves. They are reported to eat the flowers of dyer's greenweed but usually feed on foliage. They become fully fed towards the end of June and pupate in July in subterranean cocoons. Moths emerge in April of the following year.

**ORTHOSIA GRACILIS** Denis & Schiffermüller *Powdered Quaker* **Pl. 23**

**Distribution.** Widely distributed in Europe. Widespread in England, Wales and Ireland; widely distributed but local in Ireland.

**Description.** Length up to 45 mm; body above spiracles reddish-brown or greyish-green, below spiracles green, yellowish-green or greenish-brown; a pale green or brown band extends along the line of the spiracles, bordered above with black; head brown.

**Habitat.** Open countryside, particularly in marshy areas.

**Foodplants.** Sallow (*Salix*), bog myrtle (*Myrica gale*), purple loosestrife (*Lythrum salicaria*), yellow loosestrife (*Lysimacha vulgaris*), meadowsweet (*Filipendula ulmaria*) and other plants.

**Biology.** One generation a year. Eggs are laid in large batches in April, hatching in about ten days. The caterpillars spin the leaves of growing shoots together and feed within, moving to a fresh plant when the first is exhausted. As they grow larger the caterpillars feed externally, hiding on the ground by day. Pupation takes place in the soil in July but moths do not emerge until the following spring.

ORTHOSIA CERASI FABRICIUS Denis & Schiffermuller *Common Quaker* **Pl. 6**

**Distribution.** Widely distributed throughout Europe, except for the extreme north. Widespread in the British Isles but less common in northern Scotland.

**Description.** Length up to 40 mm; plump; body green, speckled with yellowish-white, with yellowish rings between the segments; a yellowish-white line runs along the middle of the back and a similar line extends along the spiracles on either side;

conspicuous yellowish transverse bands are present behind the head and on the back of segment 11; head pale brownish-green.
**Habitat.** Woods, woodland margins and hedgerows.
**Foodplants.** Oak (*Quercus*), sallow (*Salix*) and elm (*Ulmus*).
**Biology.** One generation a year. Eggs are laid in irregular batches on twigs in April and hatch in about ten days. The caterpillars feed at first in spun shoots and later exposed on the foliage. They feed by day and night and are full-grown by the end of June. Pupation takes place in subterranean cocoons. Moths do not usually emerge until the following spring, although some may emerge during mild days in winter.

**ORTHOSIA INCERTA** Hufnagel *Clouded Drab* **Pl. 16**
**Distribution.** Widespread in Europe. Widely distributed throughout the British Isles and often common.
**Description.** Length up to 40 mm; body varying in colour from bluish-green to yellowish-green or dark greyish-green, heavily speckled with white; a broad white line extends down the middle of the back with a narrower white line on either side; a white or yellowish band bordered above with black extends along the line of the spiracles; head pale green or greenish-brown.
**Habitat.** Woodland and orchards.
**Foodplants.** Oak (*Quercus*), sallow (*Salix*) and other deciduous trees and shrubs, including apple (*Malus*) and also hop (*Humulus lupulus*).
**Biology.** One generation a year. Eggs are laid in masses on the foodplant in March, hatching in about ten days. The caterpillars feed at night, hiding between spun leaves by day. They become fully grown in June or July and pupate in fragile subterranean cocoons. Moths do not usually emerge until the following March but some may emerge in the winter months.

**ORTHOSIA MUNDA** Denis & Schiffermüller *Twin-spotted Quaker* **Pl. 7**
**Distribution.** Widespread in Europe, except in the south. Widely distributed in the British Isles; common in southern and central England and in Wales but more local elsewhere.
**Description.** Length up to 40 mm; body above line of spiracles dark greyish-brown; below spiracles pale grey or greenish-grey; a broad ochreous band extends along the middle of the back, bearing a series of darker, arrow-shaped markings; an ochreous band, margined above with black, extends along the line of the spiracles, with conspicuous white spots on segments 4 and 5; a transverse ochreous band is present on the back of segment 11; head reddish-brown with darker markings.
**Habitat.** Woodland.
**Foodplants.** Sallow (*Salix*), elm (*Ulmus*), oak (*Quercus*), aspen (*Populus tremula*), blackthorn (*Prunus spinosa*), hop (*Humulus lupulus*) and honeysuckle (*Lonicera periclymenum*).
**Biology.** One generation a year. Eggs are laid in masses on the foodplant in April and hatch in about ten days. The caterpillars feed at night and are fully grown by the end of June. Pupation takes place in subterranean cocoons in July and moths usually emerge in the following spring although some may emerge earlier.

**ORTHOSIA GOTHICA** Linnaeus *Hebrew Character* **Pl. 29**
**Distribution.** Widespread throughout Europe. Widely distributed and often common in the British Isles.

**Description.** Length up to 40 mm; body green, finely marked with yellowish-white, with narrow, yellow rings between the segments; three yellowish-white lines extend along the back; a pale green or white band, edged above with black, extends along the line of the spiracles; head green.
**Habitat.** Woodland, hedgerows, meadows and any other place where suitable foodplants grow.
**Foodplants.** Oak (*Quercus*), sallow (*Salix*), hawthorn (*Crataegus monogyna*) and many other trees and shrubs; also on dock (*Rumex*), dandelion (*Taraxacum*), meadowsweet (*Filipendula ulmaria*), clover (*Trifolium*) and other low-growing plants.
**Biology.** One generation a year. Eggs are laid in irregular masses on the foliage in April and hatch in about ten days. The caterpillars are active at night but remain hidden on the foodplant by day. They become fully grown in June or July and pupate in fragile subterranean cocoons. Moths usually emerge in the following spring although some may emerge during mild spells in the winter.

**MYTHIMNA FERRAGO** Fabricius *Clay* **Pl. 11**
**Distribution.** Widely distributed in Europe. Widespread throughout the British Isles.
**Description.** Length up to 45 mm; body bright ochre, underside paler; three white lines, bordered with black or dark brown, extend along the back and a broad, brownish band extends along the spiracles on either side; head pale ochre with a network of dark brown markings.
**Habitat.** Woodland, woodland margins and other places where suitable foodplants grow.
**Foodplants.** Wood meadow-grass (*Poa nemoralis*) and other grasses, chickweed (*Stellaria media*), plantain (*Plantago*) and dandelion (*Taraxacum*).
**Biology.** One generation a year. Eggs are laid in rows in folded grass blades in July and hatch in about a week. Caterpillars hide at the base of the foodplant by day, climbing up to feed on the tips of the blades at night. They feed slowly at first, but after hibernation resume feeding at a greater rate, and are fully grown by the end of May. Pupation takes place in subterranean cocoons and moths emerge in June or July.

**MYTHIMNA PALLENS** Linnaeus *Common Wainscot* **Pl. 31**
**Distribution.** Widespread in Europe. Widely distributed throughout the British Isles and common except in the extreme north.
**Description.** Length up to 40 mm; body ochreous, pale greyish below; three white lines, bordered with brown, extend along the back; a broad band of dark brown extends above the line of the spiracles; head pale brown with a network of darker markings.
**Habitat.** Marshes, meadows and other grassland.
**Foodplants.** Annual meadow-grass (*Poa annua*), cock's-foot (*Dactylis glomerata*), couch-grass (*Agropyron repens*) and other grasses.
**Biology.** Two generations a year in the south but only one generation a year further north. Eggs are laid in rows on grass blades in July and September, hatching in about a week. The caterpillars are active at night, hiding amongst the roots by day. The first generation feeds up rapidly and is full-grown in August, but the second generation hibernates while still small, completing growth in the following spring and pupating in May. Pupation takes place in subterranean cocoons. Moths of the

first generation emerge in September, while those of the second generation emerge in the following July.

**MYTHIMNA COMMA** Linnaeus *Shoulder-striped Wainscot* **Pl. 31**
**Distribution.** Widespread throughout Europe. Widely distributed in the British Isles but less common in Ireland and northern Scotland.
**Description.** Length up to 40 mm; fairly stout, body pale reddish-brown to greyish-brown; three pale lines, edged with darker brown, extend along the back and a pale brown or whitish band extends below the line of the spiracles on either side; head pale brown with dark brown stripes.
**Habitat.** Fens, marshes and other places where suitable foodplants grow.
**Foodplants.** Cock's-foot (*Dactylis glomerata*) and other grasses, also dock (*Rumex*).
**Biology.** One generation a year. Eggs are laid in irregular rows on grass blades in June and hatch in about a week. Caterpillars feed at the tips of the grass blades at night, hiding at the roots by day. They are full-grown by the autumn and burrow into the ground, where they remain through the winter in their cocoons before pupating the following April. Moths emerge in May or June.

**SENTA FLAMMEA** Curtis *Flame Wainscot* **Pl. 30**
**Distribution.** Occurs locally in parts of western, central and northern Europe. In the British Isles, it is restricted to parts of eastern and southern England, where it is very local.
**Description.** Length up to 30 mm; body ochreous to reddish-brown, sometimes with reddish rings between the segments; a pale ochreous line, bordered with dark brown, runs down the middle of the back, with two less distinct pale lines on either side; a pale ochreous band extends below the line of the spiracles, bordered above by a darker brown band; underside pale grey; head pale brown with a network of larger brown markings.
**Habitat.** Marshland and fens.
**Foodplant.** Common reed (*Phragmites communis*).
**Biology.** One generation a year. Eggs are laid in double rows on the leaves in June or July and hatch in about a fortnight. The caterpillars feed on the foliage at night, hiding by day in old hollow stems. They become fully grown in the autumn and pupate in hollow reed stems. Moths emerge in the following May or June.

**CUCULLIA ABSINTHII** Linnaeus *Wormwood* **Pl. 28**
**Distribution.** Widely distributed but local in Europe. In the British Isles it is restricted to scattered localities in England, Wales and southern Ireland.
**Description.** Length up to 40 mm; body greyish-white, variably patterned with transverse bands of greyish-green, between which are patches of brown; head whitish with pale brown markings.
**Habitat.** Sea coasts, waste land and other places where the foodplants grow.
**Foodplants.** Wormwood (*Artemisia absinthium*) and sometimes mugwort (*A. vulgaris*).
**Biology.** One generation a year. Eggs are laid on buds of the foodplant in July. Caterpillars feed from August to September or October. They are active by day, eating flowers and developing seeds. When at rest on the foodplant they are extremely well camouflaged. Pupation takes place in cocoons on or below the surface of the soil. Moths emerge in July of the following year.

**CUCULLIA CHAMOMILLAE** Denis & Schiffermüller **Pl. 28**
*Chamomile Shark*

**Distribution.** Widespread in warmer parts of Europe. Widely distributed in the British Isles but absent from northern Scotland and confined to coastal localities in Ireland.

**Description.** Length up to 45 mm; body yellowish-green to greenish-white, underside darker green; two lines of diagonal green markings extend along the back, forming a series of V-shapes, between which are a series of purplish-pink markings; a broken line of green extends along the spiracles, below which is a line of purplish-pink dashes; head greenish-white with darker markings.

**Habitat.** Open countryside with sandy or chalky soil, particularly in coastal localities.

**Foodplants.** Chamomile (*Chamaemelum nobile*), corn chamomile (*Anthemis arvensis*), stinking chamomile (*A. cotula*), scented mayweed (*Chamomilla recutita*), scentless mayweed (*Matricaria perforata*), and related plants; also on feverfew (*Tanacetum parthenium*).

**Biology.** One generation a year. Eggs are laid singly on stems of the foodplant in April or May. The caterpillars may be active by day or night, feeding on flowers and developing seeds from May to July. Pupation takes place in large cocoons constructed well below the surface of the soil. Moths do not emerge until April of the following year and sometimes remain in the pupa for a second winter.

**CUCULLIA LACTUCAE** Denis & Schiffermüller *Lettuce Shark* **Pl. 29**

**Distribution.** Widespread but local in central and southern Europe.

**Description.** Length up to 50 mm; body yellowish-white with bright yellow stripes down the middle of the back and along each side, between which are series of large, black, rectangular patches; legs black; head black.

**Habitat.** Open countryside.

**Foodplants.** Lettuce (*Lactuca*), purple lettuce (*Prenanthes purpurea*), sow-thistle (*Sonchus*), mouse-ear hawkweed (*Hieracium pilosella*) and related plants.

**Biology.** One generation a year. Caterpillars feed on the flowers and foliage from June to September. The pupae overwinter, producing moths in the following May or June.

**CUCULLIA ASTERIS** Denis & Schiffermüller *Star-wort* **Pl. 28**

**Distribution.** Widely distributed in Europe. In the British Isles, confined to England and Wales where it occurs locally, mainly in coastal regions.

**Description.** Length up to 45 mm; body green, pink or purplish-red with a broad yellow stripe, edged with black, down the middle of the back, on either side of which is a series of narrow black lines; a black-edged, yellow band extends below the line of the spiracles; head green to pink with black spots.

**Habitat.** Salt-marshes and woodland.

**Foodplants.** Sea aster (*Aster tripolium*) and golden-rod (*Solidago virgaurea*).

**Biology.** One generation a year. Eggs are laid singly on the foodplant in July and caterpillars hatch in the same month. They are active during the day and will only feed in sunshine. Those living in woodland localities are full-grown by the end of August, but salt-marsh caterpillars feed for a further month. Pupation takes place in cocoons on or below the surface of the soil. Moths emerge the following June.

**CUCULLIA GNAPHALII** Hübner *Cudweed* **Pl. 28**

**Distribution.** Local in Europe but more common towards Fennoscandia. In the British Isles it is confined to parts of south-eastern England, where it is very local, and to one locality in Oxfordshire.

**Description.** Length up to 42 mm; body dull green to yellowish-green with a broad purplish-brown band bearing a series of darker, diamond-shaped markings extending along the back; a series of reddish- or purplish-brown oblique dashes extend along the spiracles on either side; head green with purplish-brown markings.

**Habitat.** Woodland clearings.

**Foodplant.** Golden-rod (*Solidago virgaurea*).

**Biology.** One generation a year. Eggs are laid singly on leaves of the foodplant in June and hatch in about a week. The caterpillars usually feed on the leaves, particularly those growing just below the flowerheads. They are fully grown by the end of August and pupate in cocoons on the surface of the ground. Moths emerge in May or June of the following year.

**CUCULLIA LYCHNITIS** Rambur *Striped Lychnis* **Pl. 27**

**Distribution.** Widely distributed but local and seldom common in Europe. In the British Isles it is confined to a few localities in southern England.

**Description.** Length up to 50 mm; body pale green with a series of transverse yellow bands, each bearing a characteristic pattern of black stripes and spots; head yellowish-brown with black spotting. The extent of the yellow bands and black markings on caterpillars of this species is very variable.

**Habitat.** Open countryside, downland and roadsides.

**Foodplants.** Dark mullein (*Verbascum nigrum*), white mullein (*V. lychnitis*) and sometimes figworts (*Scrophularia*).

**Biology.** One generation a year. Eggs are laid singly on the undersides of leaves in July and caterpillars feed from August to September. They eat the flowers of mullein and figwort, often feeding on plants already attacked by the more common Mullein Moth (*Cucullia verbasci*). Pupation takes place in the autumn in cocoons on or below the surface of the soil but moths do not emerge until the following June and sometimes remain in the pupa for several years.

**CUCULLIA SCROPHULARIAE** Denis & Schiffermüller **Pl. 27**
*Water Betony*

**Distribution.** Widely distributed in Europe. There is only one definite record in the British Isles, from Dorset in southern England.

**Description.** Length up to 50 mm; intermediate in appearance between *C. lychnitis* and *C. verbasci* but can be distinguished from the former by the presence of black rings between the segments and from the latter by its stronger and simpler pattern, lacking the black vertical streaks present on the sides of *C. verbasci*.

**Habitat.** Open countryside and roadsides.

**Foodplants.** Figwort (*Scrophularia*) and sometimes mullein (*Verbascum*).

**Biology.** One generation a year. Caterpillars feed from June to August or September according to locality. The pupae overwinter, sometimes twice, before producing moths in the following April.

**CUCULLIA VERBASCI** Linnaeus *Mullein Moth* **Pl. 27**

**Distribution.** Widely distributed throughout Europe, except for the extreme north. In the British Isles it is widely distributed in England and Wales but absent from Scotland and Ireland; it is most common in southern England.

**Description.** Length up to 50 mm; body greenish-white to pale bluish-green with a series of transverse bands of yellow across the back, each bearing a characteristic pattern of black spots; there are further black spots below the line of the spiracles; head yellow with black dots.
**Habitat.** Open countryside, where the foodplants grow; sometimes in gardens.
**Foodplants.** Mullein (*Verbascum*), figwort (*Scrophularia*) and sometimes cultivated *Buddleia*.
**Biology.** One generation a year. Eggs are laid singly on the undersides of leaves in May. The caterpillars may be found in June and July, feeding fully exposed on the foliage, sometimes in large numbers on one plant. Pupation takes place in August in large cocoons, constructed well below the surface of the soil. Moths usually emerge the next April or May but may remain in the pupa for up to five years.

**BRACHIONYCHA SPHINX** Hufnagel *Sprawler* **Pl. 7**
**Distribution.** Widespread and common in Europe, except for the extreme north. In the British Isles it is mainly confined to England and Wales, where it is locally common; it is local and scarce in Ireland.
**Description.** Length up to 50 mm; plump, with a hump on the back of segment 11; body bright green with three yellowish-white lines along the back and a whitish, transverse band just behind the head; a yellowish-white line runs along the black-rimmed spiracles on either side.
**Habitat.** Woodland.
**Foodplants.** Oak (*Quercus*), sallow (*Salix*), beech (*Fagus sylvatica*), hawthorn (*Crataegus monogyna*) and a wide range of other deciduous trees and shrubs.
**Biology.** One generation a year. Eggs are laid in crevices of tree trunks in autumn but do not hatch until the following April. The caterpillars feed until the end of June. They are strongly cannibalistic, especially when young. The characteristic defensive posture adopted by these caterpillars, stretched out with the head and thorax thrown backward, gives rise to the name 'sprawler'. Pupation takes place in the summer in cocoons deep below the ground and moths emerge in late autumn.

**DASYPOLIA TEMPLI** Thunberg *Brindled Ochre* **Pl. 24**
**Distribution.** Occurs in northern Europe and mountainous regions of central Europe. It is widely distributed in the British Isles but is more common in the north, particularly northern Scotland; very local in Ireland.
**Description.** Length up to 50 mm; plump; body pale ochreous-grey, suffused with brownish-pink on the back, with conspicuous black spots; head reddish-brown.
**Habitat.** Coasts, mountains and other rocky places.
**Foodplants.** Hogweed (*Heracleum sphondylium*) and angelica (*Angelica sylvestris*); possibly on other related plants.
**Biology.** One generation a year. Eggs are laid singly or in small groups on stems or foliage of the foodplant in March or April. Caterpillars hatch in about a month and feed until July or early August. They burrow into stems and bore down into the roots. When fully grown, they leave the foodplant and pupate amongst grass roots or in the soil. Moths emerge in September or October but overwinter before laying their eggs.

**APOROPHYLA NIGRA** Haworth *Black Rustic* **Pl. 10**
**Distribution.** Widely distributed in Europe, except in the south. Widespread in the British Isles but particularly common in southern England and in Scotland.

**Description.** Length up to 50 mm; slender; body very variable in colour, ranging from green to reddish-brown, pink or grey; a band of dark, arrow-shaped markings extends down the middle of the back with a dark line on either side; a white line extends along the black-rimmed spiracles, below which is a band of yellowish-green; green specimens are often suffused and marked with brown; head brown or brownish-green.

**Habitat.** Heaths, moorland and coastal regions.

**Foodplants.** Dock and sorrel (*Rumex*), plantain (*Plantago*), heather (*Calluna vulgaris*), chickweed (*Stellaria media*), square-stemmed willowherb (*Epilobium tetragonum*) and tufted hair-grass (*Deschampsia cespitosa*); also on hawthorn (*Crataegus monogyna*) and other deciduous trees and shrubs.

**Biology.** One generation a year. Eggs are laid singly or in small groups on the foodplant in September or October and hatch in about a month. Caterpillars feed at first on low-growing plants but often complete their growth on buds and young foliage of deciduous trees and shrubs in the spring. They become fully grown in May or June and pupate in large subterranean cocoons. Moths emerge in September or October.

**LITHOPHANE SEMIBRUNNEA** Haworth *Tawny Pinion* **Pl. 8**

**Distribution.** Widespread but local in Europe. In the British Isles it is confined to Wales and the southern half of England.

**Description.** Length up to 40 mm; slightly tapered towards the extremities; body yellowish-green with a whitish-yellow stripe down the middle of the back and finer, ill-defined, whitish lines on either side; a band of pale yellow extends below the line of the spiracles; head pale bluish-green with darker markings. Before pupation, the caterpillar becomes brownish in colour.

**Habitat.** Marshland and other damp open country.

**Foodplant.** Ash (*Fraxinus excelsior*). In captivity, will also eat leaves of privet (*Ligustrum vulgare*) and plum (*Prunus domestica*).

**Biology.** One generation a year. Eggs are laid singly on twigs of the foodplant in spring, hatching in about three weeks. Caterpillars feed in May and June, burrowing into the ground to pupate when fully grown. Moths emerge in October but overwinter before mating and laying eggs in the spring.

**LITHOPHANE LEAUTIERI** Boisduval *Blair's Shoulder-knot* **Pl. 1**

**Distribution.** Occurs in southern, western and parts of central Europe. In the British Isles it is at present confined to southern England and Wales but is gradually spreading northwards.

**Description.** Length up to 38 mm; body green with a broad white stripe down the middle of the back and a line of slightly curved, white markings on either side; a sinuous white line extends below the line of the spiracles, each of which is set in a deep maroon patch; head green with lighter markings.

**Habitat.** Parks, gardens and other places where suitable foodplants grow.

**Foodplants.** Monterey cypress (*Cupressus macrocarpa*), Lawson's cypress (*Chamaecyparis lawsoniana*) and, in continental Europe, also on funeral cypress (*Cupressus sempervirens*) and juniper (*Juniperus communis*).

**Biology.** One generation a year. Eggs are laid on the undersides of young sprays of the foodplant and hatch in February or March. The caterpillars feed at first on male buds and flowers but later on the young foliage. When fully grown in June or July they construct large cocoons of silk and earth in which they remain for some weeks before pupating. Moths emerge in October.

**XYLENA VETUSTA** Hübner *Red Sword-grass* **Pl. 9**

**Distribution.** Widespread throughout Europe, becoming more common towards the north. Widely distributed in the British Isles.

**Description.** Length up to 60 mm; body usually green but sometimes brown; a pale yellow line extends along the back, running through the middle of a broad, blackish-green band, dotted with white and bordered with yellow; a black line extends along the red spiracles, bordered below with greenish-white; head brown. Some caterpillars are apparently much less strongly marked.

**Habitat.** Moorland and marshes.

**Foodplants.** Almost any low-growing herbaceous plants; also yellow iris (*Iris pseudacorus*), sedges (*Carex*), grasses and deciduous trees and shrubs.

**Biology.** One generation a year. Eggs are laid in batches on the foodplants in April, hatching in about ten days. The caterpillars feed both by day and night on low-growing plants and the young foliage of trees and shrubs, and are fully grown by the end of July. Pupation takes place in subterranean cocoons and moths emerge in the autumn, overwintering before laying eggs in the following spring.

**XYLENA EXSOLETA** Linnaeus *Sword-grass* **Pl. 20**

**Distribution.** Widely distributed but somewhat local in Europe. Widespread in the British Isles but less common than formerly, especially in southern England.

**Description.** Length up to 65 mm; large and plump; body bright green with two yellow lines on the back, between which is a series of white-centred, black spots, sometimes absent; a white line extends below the spiracles on each side, bordered above by a broken line of bright red; head brownish-green to yellowish-green.

**Habitat.** Moorland and open woodland.

**Foodplants.** A wide range of low-growing herbaceous plants and young foliage of deciduous trees and shrubs.

**Biology.** One generation a year. Eggs are laid in batches in April and hatch in about ten days. The caterpillars feed from May to July and are active both by day and night. Pupation takes place on or under the ground in August and moths emerge in the autumn but do not lay eggs until the following spring.

**XYLOCAMPA AREOLA** Esper *Early Grey* **Pl. 28**

**Distribution.** Widely distributed in Europe, except in the extreme north. Widespread in the British Isles but most common in southern England.

**Description.** Length up to 40 mm; slender, tapered towards the extremities; body ochreous to pale grey with a pale brown to whitish central band along the back, interrupted by a square, blackish marking on segment 7; dots white, ringed with black; a pale band extends along either side, below the level of the spiracles; head pale grey or brown.

**Habitat.** Open woodland and lightly wooded countryside.

**Foodplant.** Honeysuckle (*Lonicera periclymenum*).

**Biology.** One generation a year. Eggs are laid singly on stems of the foodplant in April and hatch in about ten days. The caterpillars feed at night, remaining on the foodplant by day, stretched out on stems, where they are well camouflaged. They are fully grown by the end of June and pupate in cocoons beneath the ground or under leaf litter. Moths do not emerge until the following spring.

**ALLOPHYES OXYACANTHAE** Linnaeus **Pl. 17**
*Green-brindled Crescent*

**Distribution.** Widespread throughout Europe. Widely distributed in the British Isles and often common.

**Description.** Length up to 45 mm; fairly slender but with a backward-directed hump on segment 11 bearing four small points; body colour very variable, ranging from brown to purplish-grey or greyish-green; a complex pattern of diamond-shapes extends along the back, broken by two pale, oblique streaks on segment 4; a series of broken, wavy lines, outlined with black, extend along the sides; underside whitish; head whitish with a blackish transverse bar and other dark markings.

**Habitat.** Woodland margins, hedgerows and lightly wooded country.

**Foodplants.** Hawthorn (*Crataegus monogyna*), blackthorn (*Prunus spinosa*) and other related plants.

**Biology.** One generation a year. Eggs are laid singly or in small groups on tree trunks in the autumn. Eggs overwinter before hatching in the spring and caterpillars may be found from April to May or June. They are active at night, concealing themselves on the bark of branches by day. They are well camouflaged, with green forms occurring where there is strong growth of lichens. Pupation takes place in subterranean cocoons and moths emerge from September onwards.

**DICHONIA APRILINA** Linnaeus *Merveille du Jour* **Pl. 6**

**Distribution.** Widespread but local throughout Europe. Widely distributed in Britain but more common in the south. Widespread but local in Ireland.

**Description.** Length up to 45 mm; fairly stout; body variable in colour, ranging from reddish-brown to greenish-brown or greyish-green; a broken, whitish central line runs along the back, through a blackish band, often broken into a series of diamond-shapes; a dark band extends above the line of the spiracles on either side; head brown with pale markings.

**Habitat.** Woodland.

**Foodplant.** Oak (*Quercus*).

**Biology.** One generation a year. Eggs are laid singly or in small groups on branches or in crevices of the bark in autumn, but do not hatch until the following spring. Caterpillars may be found from March to June, boring into buds at first but later feeding openly on the foliage. They are active at night, hiding in crevices of the bark by day. Pupation takes place in large cocoons in the ground among the tree roots and moths emerge in September or October.

MNIOTYPE ADUSTA Esper *Dark Brocade* **Pl. 5**

**Distribution.** Widespread throughout Europe. Widely distributed in the British Isles but more common in the north.

**Description.** Length up to 45 mm; body very variable in colour, usually green, with or without brown shading on the back, but sometimes yellow or pinkish; three dark lines extend along the back, the central line being thicker and sometimes broken into a series of diamond-shaped markings; head pale yellowish-brown or greenish-brown.

**Habitat.** Downland, fens, heaths, moorland and mountains.

**Foodplants.** Bog myrtle (*Myrica gale*), goat willow (*Salix caprea*), alder (*Alnus glutinosa*), hawthorn (*Crataegus monogyna*), knotgrass (*Polygonum aviculare*), bladder campion (*Silene vulgaris*) and various other low-growing herbaceous plants and grasses.

**Biology.** One generation a year. Eggs are laid in small batches on the leaves in June and hatch in about a fortnight. The caterpillars feed at night, hiding among the roots by day. When fully grown, in August, they darken in colour and construct cocoons in the soil or under moss, in which they overwinter before pupating in the following spring. Moths emerge in May or June.

**TRIGONOPHORA FLAMMEA** Esper *Flame Brocade* **Pl. 12**

**Distribution.** Occurs in southern and western Europe. Although at one time a resident species in Britain, it now occurs only as an occasional immigrant along the south coast.

**Description.** Length up to 55 mm; body green or brown with a pale central line down the back, bordered with dark brown or green; a dark line extends along the spiracles on either side; head brownish-white with darker markings.

**Habitat.** Chalk downland and marshy ground.

**Foodplants.** Lesser celandine (*Ranunculus ficaria*) and related plants; also on broom (*Cytisus scoparius*), blackthorn (*Prunus spinosa*), ash (*Fraxinus excelsior*) and privet (*Ligustrum*).

**Biology.** One generation a year. Little is known of the life cycle of this species in the wild. Caterpillars overwinter while small and feed up in late winter and spring, becoming fully grown in April. Moths are on the wing from September to November.

**EUMICHTIS LICHENEA** Hübner *Feathered Ranunculus* **Pl. 13**

**Distribution.** Occurs in many parts of Europe, particularly along coasts. Widely distributed in coastal localities in Britain, except northern Scotland; occurs locally in Ireland.

**Description.** Length up to 45 mm; body varying in colour from green to grey or pinkish-brown; underside pale grey; a pale central line margined with darker green or grey extends along the back through a series of diamond-shaped markings outlined in dark grey or brown; a pale band extends along the line of the spiracles; head pale brown.

**Habitat.** Cliffs, sandhills, limestone hills and hedgerows.

**Foodplants.** Biting stonecrop (*Sedum acre*), thrift (*Armeria maritima*), sea plantain (*Plantago maritima*), wild cabbage (*Brassica oleracea*), ragwort (*Senecio jacobaea*) and a wide range of other herbaceous plants.

**Biology.** One generation a year. Eggs are laid singly or in small groups on the foodplant in September and hatch in about three weeks. The caterpillars overwinter while small, completing their growth in the spring. They are active at night, hiding by day at the roots of the foodplants. Pupation takes place in subterranean cocoons in May and moths emerge in August or September.

**EUPSILIA TRANSVERSA** Hufnagel *Satellite* **Pl. 7**

**Distribution.** Widespread and common in Europe. Widely distributed in the British Isles but more common in the south.

**Description.** Length up to 45 mm; body velvety brownish-black; underside paler greyish-brown; three fine, greyish, indistinct lines extend along the back; plate on segment 1 black with two orange lines; a broken white line extends along the spiracles, expanded on the first four segments and on segment 12 to form large white patches; head reddish-brown, heavily marked with black.

**Habitat.** Woodland, parks and other places where the foodplants grow.

**Foodplants.** Oak (*Quercus*), beech (*Fagus sylvatica*), silver birch (*Betula pendula*),

elm (*Ulmus*), sallow (*Salix*), poplar (*Populus*), maple (*Acer campestre*) and other deciduous trees and shrubs.
**Biology.** One generation a year. Eggs are laid singly or in masses on the foodplant in March and hatch in about a fortnight. The caterpillars feed at night, hiding by day in spun shoots. Besides eating the foliage, they readily feed on other caterpillars, both of their own and of other species. When fully grown at the end of June they construct subterranean cocoons in which they remain for about a fortnight before pupating. Moths emerge in September or October but do not lay eggs until the following spring.

**CONISTRA VACCINII** Linnaeus *Chestnut* **Pl. 6**
**Distribution.** Widespread in Europe, except for the extreme north. Widely distributed in the British Isles.
**Description.** Length up to 34 mm; body purplish-brown to greenish-grey, finely mottled with greyish-white; three indistinct, pale lines extend along the back; plate on segment 1 brownish-black with three conspicuous white lines; an indistinct, pale stripe extends along the line of the spiracles on either side; head brown with pale brown mottling.
**Habitat.** Woodland and other places where the foodplants grow.
**Foodplants.** Oak (*Quercus*), silver birch (*Betula pendula*), elm (*Ulmus*) and other deciduous trees and shrubs; also low-growing herbaceous plants.
**Biology.** One generation a year. Eggs are laid singly or in heaps on the foodplant in March or April and hatch in about a fortnight. Young caterpillars feed on flowers and foliage of trees and shrubs but may later descend to feed on the undergrowth. They are fully grown by the end of June, when they construct large subterranean cocoons in which they remain for some weeks before pupating. Moths emerge in September or October but do not lay eggs until the following spring.

**CONISTRA RUBIGINEA** Denis & Schiffermüller *Dotted Chestnut* **Pl. 18**
**Distribution.** Widely distributed but local in Europe. In the British Isles it is confined to scattered localities in England and south Wales.
**Description.** Length up to 40 mm; head and body covered with fine, reddish-brown hairs; body soft, brown or grey, becoming darker on the back; a line of square, black spots extends along the back; plate on segment 1 is black; head shining black.
**Habitat.** Woodland and wooded heaths.
**Foodplants.** Apple (*Malus sylvestris*), wild plum (*Prunus domestica*), blackthorn (*P. spinosa*), and probably oak (*Quercus*) and other deciduous trees and shrubs, and low-growing herbaceous plants.
**Biology.** One generation a year. Eggs are laid singly or in small batches in April, hatching in about three weeks. Little appears tc be known of the biology of the caterpillars in the wild. It seems that they will feed on the foliage of a wide range of trees and shrubs and later on low-growing plants and also on other caterpillars. When fully grown in June or July, they pupate in cocoons spun on the surface of the soil. Moths emerge in October but do not lay eggs until the following spring.

**AGROCHOLA CIRCELLARIS** Hufnagel *Brick* **Pl. 7**
**Distribution.** Widespread in Europe. Widely distributed in the British Isles but most common in southern England.
**Description.** Length up to 35 mm; body reddish-brown to greyish-brown, often

with a row of shield-shaped, chocolate-brown markings along the back, divided by a pale greyish central line; body below line of spiracles pale greyish-brown; head brown with darker markings.

**Habitat.** Woodland.

**Foodplants.** Wych elm (*Ulmus glabra*), poplar (*Populus*) and ash (*Fraxinus excelsior*).

**Biology.** One generation a year. Eggs are laid singly or in small batches near the buds in autumn but do not hatch until the following spring. The caterpillars show a preference for flowers and seeds but will also eat the foliage. They are full-grown in June and descend to the ground to make subterranean cocoons in which they remain for some weeks before pupating. Moths emerge in August or September.

**AGROCHOLA LITURA** Linnaeus *Brown-spot Pinion* **Pl. 14**

**Distribution.** Widely distributed in Europe but often local and scarce. Widely distributed in Britain but absent from Ireland.

**Description.** Length up to 40 mm; body greyish-green or brown with white dots; a pale line bordered with dark green or brown extends along the middle of the back, sometimes with a less distinct line on either side; a white line, bordered above with black or dark brown, extends along the spiracles, below which the body is yellowish-green; head brown with faint markings.

**Habitat.** Woodlands, commons and heaths.

**Foodplants.** Meadowsweet (*Filipendula ulmaria*), dock (*Rumex*), chickweed (*Stellaria media*), dead-nettles (*Lamium*), rose (*Rosa*), bramble (*Rubus fruticosus*), oak (*Quercus*), sallow (*Salix*) and other herbaceous plants and deciduous trees and shrubs.

**Biology.** One generation a year. Eggs are laid in October but do not hatch until the following spring. The caterpillars feed at first on low-growing plants and may remain on these until fully grown but often complete their feeding on the foliage of trees and shrubs. The full-grown caterpillars construct subterranean cocoons in June, in which they remain for some weeks before pupating. Moths emerge in September or October.

**AGROCHOLA LYCHNIDIS** Denis & Schiffermüller **Pl. 12**
*Beaded Chestnut*

**Distribution.** Widely distributed in Europe. Widespread in Wales and England, becoming less common towards the north; scarce in Scotland and Ireland.

**Description.** Length up to 45 mm; body pale purplish-brown or bright green; green form has narrow yellow rings between the segments; three indistinct, dark lines extend along the back; a broad, pale yellow band extends along each side below the level of the spiracles; head green or brown.

**Habitat.** Woodland margins, hedgerows and many other places where suitable foodplants grow.

**Foodplants.** Buttercup (*Ranunculus*), chickweed (*Stellaria media*), dock (*Rumex*), dandelion (*Taraxacum*), groundsel (*Senecio jacobaea*) and other low-growing herbaceous plants and grasses; also sallow (*Salix*), hawthorn (*Crataegus monogyna*) and other deciduous shrubs and trees.

**Biology.** One generation a year. Eggs are laid in the autumn but do not hatch until the following spring. Caterpillars feed at first on low-growing plants but may later move onto the foliage of trees and shrubs. They are active at night and in the early morning, hiding near the ground for the rest of the day. In June, the fully grown caterpillars make subterranean cocoons in which they remain for some weeks before pupating. Moths emerge in September.

**ATETHMIA CENTRAGO** Haworth *Centre-barred Sallow* **Pl. 8**
**Distribution.** Widely distributed in western and central Europe. Widespread and locally common throughout the British Isles.
**Description.** Length up to 30 mm; body grey, mottled with blackish-grey on the back; a row of whitish blotches extends along the middle of the back, with less distinct lines of pale spots on either side; a wavy black line extends above the spiracles on each side; head black with greyish-brown markings.
**Habitat.** Woodland and hedgerows.
**Foodplant.** Ash (*Fraxinus excelsior*).
**Biology.** One generation a year. Eggs are laid in small batches near leaf buds or in crevices of the bark in September, but do not hatch until the following spring. The caterpillars feed inside buds while small but later eat shoots and flowers. They are active at night, hiding by day in crevices of the bark or on the ground. In June, the fully grown caterpillars make subterranean cocoons in which they remain for some weeks before pupating. Moths emerge in August.

**XANTHIA CITRAGO** Linnaeus *Orange Sallow* **Pl. 8**
**Distribution.** Widespread in Europe. Widely distributed in Britain but not known from Ireland.
**Description.** Length up to 35 mm; body greenish-brown to purplish or dark greyish-brown with whitish dots; a pale line extends along the middle of the back, with a row of more or less distinct, blackish dashes on either side; a broad, pale brown or white band extends below the line of the spiracles; underside pale grey or brown; head brown.
**Habitat.** Woodland, hedgerows and wooded countryside.
**Foodplant.** Lime (*Tilia*).
**Biology.** One generation a year. Eggs are laid singly or in small groups near the buds in September but do not hatch until the following spring. The caterpillars are active at night but hide by day. Young caterpillars conceal themselves in spun leaves but when larger, they hide at the base of the tree, climbing the trunk at dusk to resume feeding. In June, the fully grown caterpillars construct subterranean cocoons in which they remain for several weeks before pupating. Moths emerge in August and September.

**XANTHIA AURAGO** Denis & Schiffermüller *Barred Sallow* **Pl. 8**
**Distribution.** Widespread in Europe. Widespread and locally common in southern Britain, becoming scarcer further north; absent from Ireland.
**Description.** Length up to 25 mm; body pale ochre or purplish-brown, paler between segments; dots white; a whitish line extends along the middle of the back, with a less distinct, fine white line on either side; a pale brown or whitish line extends along the spiracles, below which the body is pale ochre or greyish-white; head small, brown.
**Habitat.** Woodland, downland and hedgerows.
**Foodplants.** Field maple (*Acer campestre*) and beech (*Fagus sylvatica*).
**Biology.** One generation a year. Eggs are laid singly on twigs in the autumn but do not hatch until the following spring. Young caterpillars bore into buds to feed but later eat the flowers and foliage, hiding at first between spun leaves but later feeding

more openly. In June the fully grown caterpillars construct subterranean cocoons in which they remain for some weeks before pupating. Moths emerge in September and October.

**XANTHIA ICTERITIA** Hufnagel *Sallow* **Pl. 2**

**Distribution.** Widespread throughout Europe. Widely distributed and often common in the British Isles.

**Description.** Length up to 30 mm; body reddish-brown to purplish-brown; a pale brown or whitish line bordered with black extends along the middle of the back, but is sometimes broken into a series of pale dashes; sides darker than back above the level of the spiracles but paler below; underside pale grey; head small, reddish-brown.

**Habitat.** Damp woodland and commonland, heaths, moorland and other places where the foodplants grow.

**Foodplants.** Goat willow (*Salix caprea*), grey sallow (*S. cinerea*) and black poplar (*Populus nigra*); also on low-growing herbaceous plants.

**Biology.** One generation a year. Eggs are laid singly or in short rows near buds, covered with hairs from the abdomen of the female. They are laid in the autumn but do not hatch until the following spring. Caterpillars feed at first in catkins but later eat the leaves or descend to the undergrowth and feed on low-growing plants. In June, when fully grown, they construct subterranean cocoons in which they remain for some weeks before pupating. Moths emerge in August or September.

**XANTHIA OCELLARIS** Borkhausen *Pale-lemon Sallow* **Pl. 3**

**Distribution.** Widely distributed in Europe but sometimes rather local. In the British Isles, confined to the south and east of England.

**Description.** Length up to 30 mm; stout, tapering towards head; body dark brown to purplish-brown, finely marked with brownish-white; divisions between segments distinct, tinged with orange-brown; an indistinct, whitish line extends along the middle of the back, sometimes running through a series of blackish-brown, chevron-shaped markings, plate on segment 1 blackish-brown with two broad white lines; head reddish-brown.

**Habitat.** Hedgerows, roadsides, parkland and other places where the foodplant grows.

**Foodplants.** Black poplar (*Populus nigra*) and various low-growing herbaceous plants.

**Biology.** One generation a year. Eggs are laid singly or in small groups near buds of poplar in the autumn but do not hatch until the following spring. The young caterpillars feed at first in the catkins but later eat the foliage and then descend to feed on the undergrowth, at which stage they are active at night, hiding by day under leaf litter. When fully grown in June, they construct subterranean cocoons in which they remain for several weeks before pupating. Moths emerge in September and October.

**ACRONICTA MEGACEPHALA** Denis & Schiffermüller **Pl. 3**
*Poplar Grey*

**Distribution.** Widespread throughout Europe. Widely distributed in the British Isles but local in Scotland.

**Description.** Length up to 35 mm; body sparsely covered with long, fine, pale grey hairs; colour dull greyish-white, patterned with darker grey; a band of black markings, each bearing reddish or orange spots, extends along the back, except for

segment 10, which has a large patch of ochreous-white; legs pale ochre; head large, whitish with dark grey markings or dark grey with pale markings.
**Habitat.** Woodland, commons and other places where the foodplants grow.
**Foodplants.** Black poplar (*Populus nigra*) and other species of *Populus*, also on goat willow (*Salix caprea*).
**Biology.** One generation a year. Eggs are laid singly on the foliage in July, hatching in about a week. The caterpillars feed by day and may be found resting with the head curled to the side in a characteristic 'question-mark' shape. Pupation takes place in September in cocoons spun in crevices of the bark or sometimes beneath the soil at the foot of the tree. Moths do not emerge until the following May or June.

**ACRONICTA ACERIS** Linnaeus *Sycamore* **Pl. 33**
**Distribution.** Widespread in Europe, except for the extreme north. Widely distributed in southern and central England and parts of Wales but apparently absent from northern England, Scotland and Ireland.
**Description.** Length up to 40 mm; body greyish-brown, covered with dense tufts of long pale yellow or orange hairs, with four pairs of reddish hair tufts on the back; a line of black-edged, diamond-shaped, white spots extends along the middle of the back; head dark brown.
**Habitat.** Wooded countryside, parks, gardens and roadsides.
**Foodplants.** Horse chestnut (*Aesculus hippocastanum*), sycamore (*Acer pseudoplatanus*), field maple (*A. campestre*) and sometimes oak (*Quercus*) and other trees.
**Biology.** One generation a year. Eggs are laid singly on leaves in July and hatch in about a week. Caterpillars curl into a 'U' shape when at rest. They become fully grown in late August or September and pupate in double cocoons of silk and body hairs, spun in crevices of the bark. Moths usually emerge in the following June or July but may remain in the pupa stage for a second winter.

**ACRONICTA LEPORINA** Linnaeus *Miller* **Pl. 4**
**Distribution.** Widespread throughout Europe. Widely distributed in Britain but local in Ireland where it is mainly a coastal species.
**Description.** Length up to 37 mm; body covered with dense, fine, recurved hairs which tend to be white in specimens from the south and yellow in those from the north; body pale green; head pale green. Prior to pupation, the body darkens and the hairs become black.
**Habitat.** Woodland, heathland, moors and roadsides.
**Foodplants.** Silver birch (*Betula pendula*), alder (*Alnus glutinosa*), oak (*Quercus*), poplar (*Populus*) and sallow (*Salix*).
**Biology.** One generation a year. Eggs are laid singly on the foliage in July, hatching in about seven days. The caterpillars feed openly on the foliage from July to early October, resting curled on the undersides of leaves, where they are difficult to detect. Pupation takes place in the autumn in tunnels bored in rotten wood, closed with hairs from the caterpillar's body. Moths do not emerge until the following summer and sometimes remain in the pupa for two or three years.

**ACRONICTA ALNI** Linnaeus *Alder Moth* **Pl. 5**
**Distribution.** Widely distributed in Europe but apparently local and rather scarce. Widespread but local in England, Wales and Ireland.
**Description.** Length up to 35 mm; body black with pairs of large, paddle-shaped hairs on the back arising from conspicuous, transverse bands of yellow; head and

legs shining black. Young caterpillars do not have the yellow bands, and the hairs on the back are not so strongly developed, but a large patch of greyish-white on the back makes them look like bird droppings when curled on leaves.
**Habitat.** Woodland and commons.
**Foodplants.** Birch (*Betula*), alder (*Alnus glutinosa*), oak (*Quercus*), sallow (*Salix*), hawthorn (*Crataegus monogyna*) and other deciduous trees and shrubs.
**Biology.** One generation a year. Eggs are laid singly on leaves in June and hatch in about a week. The caterpillars feed in July and August and, when fully grown, bore into rotten wood to pupate. Moths emerge in the following May or June.

**ACRONICTA TRIDENS** Denis & Schiffermüller *Dark Dagger* **Pl. 16**
**Distribution.** Widespread in Europe. Widely distributed in Britain but more common in the south; not recorded from Ireland.
**Description.** Length up to 38 mm; a prominent, squarish hump on segment 4 and a less prominent hump on segment 11; body greyish-black with a broad orange-yellow stripe down the middle of the back, on either side of which is a line of orange-red spots; a wide band of white, marked with red and pink, extends along the sides; head shining black.
**Habitat.** Woodland, orchards and hedgerows.
**Foodplants.** Hawthorn (*Crataegus monogyna*), blackthorn (*Prunus spinosa*), wild plum (*P. domestica*), pear (*Pyrus communis*), apple (*Malus domestica*), sallow (*Salix*), rose (*Rosa*) and probably on other deciduous trees and shrubs.
**Biology.** One generation a year. Eggs are laid singly on the foliage in June and hatch in about a week. The caterpillars are fully grown by the autumn and pupate in crevices in the bark. Moths do not emerge until the following June and sometimes remain in the pupa for two years.

**ACRONICTA PSI** Linnaeus *Grey Dagger* **Pl. 16**
**Distribution.** Widely distributed and common in Europe. Widespread throughout the British Isles.
**Description.** Length up to 38 mm; a blunt spike is present on the back of segment 4 and a hump on segment 11; body bluish-grey with a broad, pale yellow band down the middle of the back; a broad white band extends below the line of the spiracles, above which is a line of red spots; head shining black.
**Habitat.** Woodland, hedgerows, commons, gardens and other places where the foodplants grow.
**Foodplants.** Birch (*Betula*), alder (*Alnus glutinosa*), hawthorn (*Crataegus monogyna*), blackthorn (*Prunus spinosa*), plum (*P. domestica*), pear (*Pyrus*), apple (*Malus*) and many other deciduous trees and shrubs.
**Biology.** One generation a year. Eggs are laid singly on leaves in July or August and hatch in about a week. Caterpillars feed from August to early October and may often be found wandering on tree trunks in the autumn. Pupation takes place in October in cocoons spun in cracks in the bark, in rotten wood or in the soil. Moths emerge in June of the following year. It has been claimed that there are two generations in southern England with moths on the wing from late May to September.

**ACRONICTA MENYANTHIDIS** Esper *Light Knot Grass* **Pl. 5**
**Distribution.** Widespread in Fennoscandia and also occurs in mountainous areas of central Europe. In Britain it is confined to Wales, northern England and Scotland; local in Ireland, occurring mainly in the west.

**Description.** Length up to 40 mm; body blackish-brown or black with tufts of black hairs on the back and sides; a row of red spots extends below the line of white spiracles on each side; head and legs shining black.
**Habitat.** Heathland, moors, mountains and marshy places.
**Foodplants.** Heather (*Calluna vulgaris*), bog myrtle (*Myrica gale*), bilberry (*Vaccinium myrtillus*), sallow (*Salix*), birch (*Betula*) and other low-growing plants and trees.
**Biology.** One generation a year. Eggs are laid in overlapping batches of twenty or more on the foodplant in June and hatch in about a week. The caterpillars are active by day, usually feeding at the tops of low-growing moorland plants. Pupation takes place at the base of the foodplant in the autumn but moths do not emerge until the following May or June.

**ACRONICTA AURICOMA** Denis & Schiffermüller *Scarce Dagger* **Pl. 15**
**Distribution.** Widespread throughout Europe. Apparently now extinct in the British Isles, occurring only as an occasional immigrant.
**Description.** Length up to 40 mm; body dark grey, banded with velvety black on the back; each band with four orange-red spots, each bearing a tuft of reddish hairs; spiracles white, ringed with black; head shining black.
**Habitat.** Woodland.
**Foodplants.** Bramble (*Rubus fruticosus*), birch (*Betula*), oak (*Quercus*), bilberry (*Vaccinium myrtillus*) and raspberry (*Rubus idaeus*).
**Biology.** Two generations a year. Eggs are laid in small batches in May and August and caterpillars may be found from June to July and again in September. Pupation takes place in cocoons spun on the undersides of leaves. Moths of the first generation emerge in July or August but second generation pupae overwinter before producing moths in the following May.

**ACRONICTA EUPHORBIAE** Denis & Schiffermüller **Pl. 5**
*Sweet Gale Moth*
**Distribution.** Widely distributed throughout Europe. In the British Isles it is confined to Scotland and western Ireland.
**Description.** Length up to 36 mm; body with tufts of hair, pale brown on the back, whitish on the sides; body colour dark grey with a conspicuous red transverse marking on the back of segment 2; a double row of large pale yellow spots extends along the back; below the line of the white spiracles is a band of pale red; head shining black.
**Habitat.** Moorland and heaths.
**Foodplants.** Bog myrtle (*Myrica gale*), heather (*Calluna vulgaris*), sallow (*Salix*), birch (*Betula*), bramble (*Rubus fruticosus*), plantain (*Plantago*) and many other plants.
**Biology.** One generation a year in Scotland, two generations in Ireland. Eggs are laid singly or in small batches on the foodplant or sometimes on the ground. Caterpillars may be found from July to September, feeding by day in bright sunshine. Pupation takes place in the autumn in tough cocoons under rocks but moths do not emerge until the following April or May. In Ireland, a second brood of moths appears in August.

**ACRONICTA RUMICIS** Linnaeus *Knot Grass* **Pl. 33**

**Distribution.** Widespread in Europe. Widely distributed throughout the British Isles, although less common in Scotland.

**Description.** Length up to 38 mm; body black with tufts of reddish-brown hairs; a line of red spots extends along the middle of the back, flanked on either side by a line of larger white patches; a band of orange and red markings extends along each side below the level of the white spiracles; head black, marked with brown.

**Habitat.** Hedgerows, waste ground, rough meadows and other places where the foodplants grow.

**Foodplants.** Plantain (*Plantago*), dock (*Rumex*), bramble (*Rubus fruticosus*), thistles (*Cirsium* and *Carduus*), hop (*Humulus lupulus*), sallow (*Salix*), hawthorn (*Crataegus monogyna*) and other plants.

**Biology.** One or two generations a year. Eggs are laid in batches on the foodplant in May and again in August, hatching in about a week. Caterpillars may be found from June to September, according to locality. Pupation takes place in cocoons of silk and body hairs spun near the ground. Summer brood moths emerge in August but autumn pupae overwinter, producing moths in the following May.

**CRYPHIA DOMESTICA** Hufnagel *Marbled Beauty* **Pl. 32**

**Distribution.** Widespread throughout Europe. Widely distributed in Britain, except for northern Scotland; very local in Ireland.

**Description.** Length up to 20 mm; bluish-grey, sometimes heavily suffused with blackish-grey; a band of orange, arrowhead-shaped markings extends along the back; underside pale bluish-grey; head shining black.

**Habitat.** Gardens, parks, cliffs and other places where the foodplant grows.

**Foodplant.** Lichen (*Lecidea confluens*).

**Biology.** One generation a year. Eggs are laid singly or in small groups near to the foodplant in August, hatching in about three weeks. Caterpillars feed for a short time before going into hibernation, completing their growth in the following spring. They construct silken tunnels among the food in which they hide during the day, coming out to feed at night. Pupation takes place within the tunnels in June and moths emerge in July.

**AMPHIPYRA PYRAMIDEA** Linnaeus *Copper Underwing* **Pl. 6**

**Distribution.** Widely distributed in Europe. Widespread in southern and midland England and in Wales, becoming less common further north; widely distributed in Ireland.

**Description.** Length up to 42 mm; body plump, pale greenish-blue or bright green; greenish-blue forms have the first two segments yellowish-green; segment 11 with a prominent, triangular hump, tipped with yellow; a white line runs down the middle of the back, on either side of which is a pattern of white lines and dots; a white line extends along the spiracles; all white markings become yellowish on the first two segments; head pale green with a white stripe on the sides.

**Habitat.** Woodland and hedgerows.

**Foodplants.** Oak (*Quercus*), hornbeam (*Carpinus betulus*), ash (*Fraxinus excelsior*) and probably on other deciduous trees.

**Biology.** One generation a year. Eggs are laid singly or in small groups in September or October but do not hatch until the following spring. The caterpillars feed in April and May, pupating in subterranean cocoons in June. Moths emerge in August or September.

**AMPHIPYRA BERBERA** Rungs *Svensson's Copper Underwing* **Pl. 6**
**Distribution.** Probably widespread in Europe but distribution is uncertain due to confusion with *A. pyramidea*. In the British Isles, it has a similar distribution to *pyramidea* but has not yet been recorded from Ireland.
**Description.** Length up to 42 mm; similar to *A. pyramidea* but hump on segment 11 less acutely triangular and tipped with a sharply pointed red spike; white markings on the back join to form a wavy line; thoracic legs sometimes black.
**Habitat.** Woodland.
**Foodplants.** Oak (*Quercus*), lime (*Tilia*) and sallow (*Salix*); probably also on other deciduous trees.
**Biology.** One generation a year. Eggs are laid in late summer but do not hatch until the following spring. The caterpillars feed in April and May, pupating in subterranean cocoons in June. Moths emerge in July and August.

**MORMO MAURA** Linnaeus *Old Lady* **Pl. 33**
**Distribution.** Widespread in central and southern Europe. Widely distributed throughout the British Isles, except for the northern half of Scotland.
**Description.** Length up to 70 mm; fairly stout, tapering gradually towards the head; body pale brownish-grey or ochreous, with a white dotted line extending along the back through a band of dark grey, triangular markings, on either side of which is a series of oblique black streaks; an undulating, ochreous-white line extends along each side below the level of the black-rimmed, orange spiracles; head pale brown with darker markings.
**Habitat.** Hedgerows, waste ground, gardens and damp, marshy places.
**Foodplants.** Blackthorn (*Prunus spinosa*), hawthorn (*Crataegus monogyna*), birch (*Betula*), sallow (*Salix*), ivy (*Hedera helix*) and various other shrubs and low-growing herbaceous plants.
**Biology.** One generation a year. Eggs are laid in July and August and hatch in September. The caterpillars feed at first on low-growing plants, but after hibernation they feed on the young foliage of various trees and shrubs. They are active at night, hiding in the soil during the day. Pupation takes place in the soil towards the end of June and moths emerge in July or August.

**DYPTERYGIA SCABRIUSCULA** Linnaeus *Bird's Wing* **Pl. 9**
**Distribution.** Widely distributed in Europe. In the British Isles it is mainly confined to the midlands and south-east of England with scattered records from other parts of England and Wales.
**Description.** Length up to 35 mm; body stout, reddish-brown speckled with yellow and black; a white line runs down the middle of the back, with three dark brown lines on either side; a broad yellow band extends below the line of the spiracles; head small, brown with black lines.
**Habitat.** Woodland.
**Foodplants.** Knotgrass (*Polygonum aviculare*), sorrel and dock (*Rumex*) and probably other low-growing plants.
**Biology.** One generation a year. Eggs are laid on the foodplant in June, hatching in about a week. The caterpillars feed in July and August. They are active at night, hiding under leaf litter on the ground by day. Pupation takes place in subterranean cocoons in the autumn but moths do not emerge until the following May or June.

**TRACHEA ATRIPLICIS** Linnaeus *Orache Moth* **Pl. 11**

**Distribution.** Widespread in Europe. Extinct in the British Isles but occurred at one time in eastern England.

**Description.** Length up to 48 mm; body variable in colour, ranging from purplish-grey to greyish-green or reddish-brown with white dots; a black line runs along the middle of the back and an orange-yellow or reddish band extends below the line of the spiracles on either side, sometimes bordered above with black; a conspicuous yellow or red spot is present above the spiracle on segment 11; head reddish-brown.

**Habitat.** Fens, riversides, damp meadows and marshy places.

**Foodplants.** Orache (*Atriplex*), goosefoot (*Chenopodium*) and other low-growing herbaceous plants.

**Biology.** One generation a year. Eggs are laid in June and caterpillars may be found from July to September. Caterpillars are said to feed at night. Pupation takes place in the autumn in tough, subterranean cocoons of silk, earth and small stones. Moths emerge in June of the following year.

**EUPLEXIA LUCIPARA** Linnaeus *Small Angle Shades* **Pl. 27**

**Distribution.** Widely distributed throughout Europe. Widespread in the British Isles and often common.

**Description.** Length up to 35 mm; body deep green or purplish-brown with a series of dark, V-shaped markings along the back; a pair of conspicuous white spots on the back of segment 11; a white line extends below the spiracles on either side, below which the body is yellowish-green or greenish-brown; head pale brown or greenish-brown with blackish markings.

**Habitat.** Woodland, commons and gardens.

**Foodplant.** Bracken (*Pteridium aquilinum*), willowherb (*Epilobium*), plantain (*Plantago*), birch (*Betula*), sallow (*Salix*) and other deciduous trees and low-growing plants.

**Biology.** One generation a year. Eggs are laid in July and hatch in about a week. Caterpillars may be found in August and September. They are active at night, concealing themselves by day under leaves or stones on the ground. Pupation takes place in subterranean cocoons in the autumn but moths do not emerge until June. Occasionally, moths of a second generation appear in the autumn.

**PHLOGOPHORA METICULOSA** Linnaeus *Angle Shades* **Pl. 22**

**Distribution.** Widespread throughout Europe. Widely distributed in the British Isles but most common in southern England.

**Description.** Length up to 40 mm; plump and rather soft; colour varies from bright green to brownish-green, brown or pinkish-brown; a broken white line extends along the middle of the back, on either side of which is a series of dark, oblique lines; a pale band extends below the line of the spiracles; head pale green or brown with darker brown markings.

**Habitat.** Parks, gardens, woodland, hedgerows and other places where the foodplants grow.

**Foodplants.** Chickweed (*Stellaria media*), dock (*Rumex*), nettle (*Urtica*), dog's mercury (*Mercurialis perennis*), bramble (*Rubus fruticosus*), oak (*Quercus*), birch (*Betula*) and other trees, shrubs and low-growing plants, including those cultivated in gardens.

**Biology.** Probably two generations a year but broods overlap so that caterpillars and moths may be found in almost any month of the year. Eggs are laid singly or in small groups on foliage and hatch in about ten days. The caterpillars feed at night, usually hiding under plants by day but sometimes wandering about, particularly when fully grown. Pupation takes place in cocoons just below the surface of the soil.

**COSMIA TRAPEZINA** Linnaeus *Dun-bar* **Pl. 7**

**Distribution.** Widespread in Europe. Widely distributed throughout the British Isles and often common.

**Description.** Length up to 28 mm; body bright green with black-centred, white spots and with narrow, yellowish bands between the segments; a broad, yellowish-white line runs down the middle of the back with a finer, broken line on either side; a broad, yellowish-white band, tinged with green, extends along the spiracles, sometimes edged above with blackish-green; head pale green.

**Habitat.** Woodland and hedgerows.

**Foodplants.** Elm (*Ulmus*), oak (*Quercus*), birch (*Betula*), sallow (*Salix*), hawthorn (*Crataegus monogyna*) and many other deciduous trees and shrubs.

**Biology.** One generation a year. Eggs are laid in batches, covered with scales from the body of the female in August or September but do not hatch until the following spring. The caterpillars feed from April to early June on a wide range of trees and shrubs but also attack and eat other caterpillars, particularly those of the Winter Moth (*Operophtera brumata*). Pupation takes place in cocoons under leaf litter on the ground or just below the soil in June and moths emerge in the following month.

**HYPPA RECTILINEA** Esper *Saxon* **Pl. 15**

**Distribution.** Widespread and sometimes common in northern Europe, also occurs further south at high altitudes. In the British Isles it is confined to Scotland, north-western England and parts of western Ireland.

**Description.** Length up to 45 mm; body reddish-brown to greyish-brown with three black-edged, grey lines along the back, sometimes with wedge-shaped markings forming a diamond-like pattern; segment 11 with a distinct hump on the back; a dark brown band extends along the line of the small, white spiracles on either side; head shining blackish-brown.

**Habitat.** Light woodland and moors.

**Foodplants.** Bramble (*Rubus fruticosus*), raspberry (*R. idaeus*), sallow (*Salix*) and alpine bearberry (*Arctostaphylos uva-ursi*).

**Biology.** One generation a year. Eggs are laid on the foliage in June and caterpillars feed through the summer. They are fully grown by October when they construct hibernacula of silk and debris on the ground, in which they remain curled up through the winter. In the spring they come out of hibernation and pupate in subterranean cocoons without further feeding. Moths emerge in May or June.

**APAMEA MONOGLYPHA** Hufnagel *Dark Arches* **Pl. 32**

**Distribution.** Widespread throughout Europe. Widely distributed and common in the British Isles.

**Description.** Length up to 45 mm; stout; body glossy, pale brownish-grey with shining black dots, plates and legs; head shining black.

**Habitat.** Meadows, moorland and other grassy places.

**Foodplants.** Cock's-foot (*Dactylis glomerata*), couch-grass (*Agropyron repens*) and other grasses.

**Biology.** One generation a year. Eggs are laid in July and hatch in about ten days.

The caterpillars may be found from August to June. They feed at night at the bases of the grass stems, hiding in small chambers constructed among the roots by day. Pupation takes place in May under the soil or beneath stones and moths emerge in June or July. Occasionally a partial second brood of moths appears in the autumn.

**MESOLIGIA FURUNCULA** Denis & Schiffermüller **Pl. 31**
*Cloaked Minor*

**Distribution.** Widely distributed in Europe. Widespread throughout the British Isles except the outer Hebrides and Shetland.

**Description.** Length up to 20 mm; body plump in the middle, tapering at either end; colour bright yellow to dull yellowish-white, sometimes with a reddish line down the middle of the back; a small reddish-brown plate is present on the back of segment 1; spiracles very small, black; head small, reddish-brown.

**Habitat.** Coastal cliffs and sand dunes, chalk downland, road verges and railway embankments.

**Foodplants.** Meadow fescue (*Festuca pratensis*), tall fescue (*F. arundinacea*), tufted hair-grass (*Deschampsia cespitosa*) and other grasses.

**Biology.** One generation a year. The biology of this species is not fully known but it appears that eggs are laid in late summer and that the young caterpillars overwinter, completing their growth in the following spring and becoming fully fed by the end of May or June. They feed within the grass stems and pupate in chambers hollowed out in the base of the foodplant. Moths emerge in July and August.

**MESAPAMEA SECALIS** Linnaeus *Common Rustic* **Pl. 30**

**Distribution.** Widespread and often common in Europe. Widely distributed and common throughout the British Isles, except at high altitude.

**Description.** Length up to 25 mm; body tapered at both ends; colour bright green to greyish-green, sometimes with a pinkish band down the middle of the back; spiracles black; head small, pale brown.

**Habitat.** Meadows and other grassy places.

**Foodplants.** Cock's-foot (*Dactylis glomerata*), tufted hair-grass (*Deschampsia cespitosa*) and other grasses; also hairy woodrush (*Luzula pilosa*) and cultivated cereals.

**Biology.** One generation a year. Eggs are laid in rows on the leaves in August and hatch in about a week. Caterpillars bore into the shoots and feed through the winter, moving from one plant to another. In spring, they eat the developing flowers within the leaf sheaths. Pupation takes place in subterranean cocoons at the end of May and moths emerge in June or July.

**PHOTEDES CAPTIUNCULA** Treitschke *Least Minor* **Pl. 30**

**Distribution.** Occurs in Scandinavia and the mountains of France. In the British Isles it is confined to a few localities in northern England and western Ireland.

**Description.** Length up to 15 mm; body slightly wrinkled; colour ochreous, tinged with purplish-red on the back; spiracles black; head shining reddish-brown.

**Habitat.** Limestone countryside and coasts.

**Foodplant.** Glaucous sedge (*Carex flacca*).

**Biology.** One generation a year. Eggs are laid in July or August, hatching in about a fortnight. The caterpillars feed until the autumn and again in the spring after hibernation. They bore down into the hearts of the stems, moving to fresh plants as the contents are consumed. Pupation takes place in flimsy cocoons just below the surface of the soil in June and moths emerge in June or July.

**LUPERINA TESTACEA** Denis & Schiffermüller *Flounced Rustic* **Pl. 33**

**Distribution.** Widespread in Europe, except for the extreme north. Widely distributed throughout Britain but less common in Scotland. In Ireland, mostly restricted to coastal localities.

**Description.** Length up to 35 mm; plump, skin glossy and wrinkled; body dirty yellowish-white, darker on the back; plates on segments 1 and 13 yellowish-brown; spiracles pinkish, rimmed with black; head shining yellowish-brown.

**Habitat.** Grassland on sand and chalk, sand dunes and coastal cliffs.

**Foodplants.** Various grasses.

**Biology.** One generation a year. Eggs are laid in irregular rows on grass stems near the ground in late summer, hatching in 2–3 weeks. The caterpillars live underground from September to June, feeding on roots and sometimes at the bases of stems. Pupation takes place in the soil in July and moths emerge in August.

**HYDRAECIA MICACEA** Esper *Rosy Rustic* **Pl. 27**

**Distribution.** Widespread throughout Europe. Widely distributed and often common in the British Isles.

**Description.** Length up to 37 mm; body dull greyish-pink with brown spots; a dark line extends along the middle of the back; plate on first segment pale shining ochreous with the front margin dark brown; head yellowish-brown.

**Habitat.** Cultivated and waste ground, marshes and sea cliffs.

**Foodplants.** Dock (*Rumex*), plantain (*Plantago*), burdock (*Arctium*), horsetail (*Equisetum*), woundwort (*Stachys*) and other plants, both wild and cultivated including cereals, rhubarb (*Rheum rhaponticum*) and potato (*Solanum tuberosum*).

**Biology.** One generation a year. Eggs are laid on lower leaves of the foodplant in September but do not hatch until the following spring. The caterpillars feed from May to August, boring into the plant at ground level and either boring down into the root or up into the stem. Pupation takes place in the soil at the roots of the foodplant in August and moths emerge in the following month.

**GORTYNA FLAVAGO** Denis & Schiffermüller *Frosted Orange* **Pl. 27**

**Distribution.** Widespread and common in most parts of Europe. Widely distributed throughout the British Isles, except for the north-west of Scotland; scarce in Ireland.

**Description.** Length up to 35 mm; body yellowish-white, sometimes suffused with purplish-red, with dark brown spots and plate on segment 1; head ochreous-brown.

**Habitat.** Meadows, waste ground, marshes, open woodland and other places where the foodplants grow.

**Foodplants.** Foxglove (*Digitalis purpurea*), burdock (*Arctium*), thistle (*Cirsium* and *Carduus*) and many other plants, both wild and cultivated, including potato (*Solanum tuberosum*) and rhubarb (*Rheum rhaponticum*).

**Biology.** One generation a year. Eggs are laid in heaps near the base of the stem in August or September but do not hatch until the following spring. The caterpillars feed from March to July, boring in stems and moving to fresh plants when the first are exhausted. Pupation takes place in July or August within tunnels in the stems near the ground and moths emerge in August or September.

**CELAENA HAWORTHII** Curtis *Haworth's Minor* **Pl. 30**

**Distribution.** Widely distributed in Europe. Widespread in the British Isles but most common in northern Britain.

**Description.** Length up to 18 mm; body purplish-brown, paler below the line of the spiracles; dots shining blackish-brown; plates on segments 1 and 13 pale ochreous; head pale reddish-brown.

**Habitat.** Marshy places, particularly boggy moorland and heaths.

**Foodplants.** Cotton-grass (*Eriophorum vaginatum*) and other grasses; also recorded on various rushes (*Juncus* and *Scirpus*) in continental Europe.

**Biology.** One generation a year. Eggs are laid in late summer but do not hatch until the following spring. The caterpillars feed from April to July within the stems, leaving when fully grown to pupate in flimsy cocoons at the base of the foodplant or under stones. Moths emerge in August.

**CELAENA LEUCOSTIGMA** Hübner *Crescent* **Pl. 30**

**Distribution.** Occurs in central Europe and parts of northern Europe. Widely distributed in the British Isles but rather local.

**Description.** Length up to 32 mm; skin soft and smooth, slightly glistening; body dark greyish-brown, sometimes with a greenish tint, with three slightly paler lines on the back; dots dark brown, conspicuous; plate on segment 1 shining black; head shining brown.

**Habitat.** Fens, marshes, wet moorland and damp woodland.

**Foodplants.** Yellow iris (*Iris pseudacorus*), cut-sedge (*Cladium mariscus*) and probably on other related plants.

**Biology.** One generation a year. Eggs are laid in long rows on dead reed stems in late summer but do not hatch until the following spring. The caterpillars feed within leaves or stems from March to July. When fully grown they descend to the ground and pupate in slight cocoons spun among leaf litter. Moths emerge in late July or in August.

**NONAGRIA TYPHAE** Thunberg *Bulrush Wainscot* **Pl. 30**

**Distribution.** Widespread throughout Europe, except for the extreme north. Widely distributed and locally common in the British Isles but absent from highland and northern Scotland.

**Description.** Length up to 60 mm; long and slender; pale yellowish-brown tinged with reddish, slightly darker on the back; a pale stripe extends along the line of the black spiracles on either side; plate on segment one reddish-brown; head reddish-brown.

**Habitat.** Reed-beds.

**Foodplants.** Great reedmace (*Typha latifolia*) and sometimes lesser reedmace (*T. angustifolia*).

**Biology.** One generation a year. Eggs are laid in late summer but do not hatch until the following spring. The caterpillars mine at first into the upper parts of the stems but later make large tunnels lower down. Pupation takes place in August within the stems and moths emerge in the same month.

**ARCHANARA SPARGANII** Esper *Webb's Wainscot* **Pl. 30**

**Distribution.** Widely distributed throughout Europe. In the British Isles, confined to the south and east of England and to a few localities in south Wales and Ireland.

**Description.** Length up to 50 mm; long and slender; body translucent yellowish-

green with four dark green lines on the back and a line through the spiracles on either side; spiracles pale reddish, rimmed with black; head shining, pale brown.
**Habitat.** Fenland and marshes, particularly in coastal regions.
**Foodplants.** Yellow iris (*Iris pseudacorus*), great reedmace (*Typha latifolia*), lesser reedmace (*T. angustifolia*) and bur-reed (*Sparganium erectum*).
**Biology.** One generation a year. Eggs are laid in late summer but do not hatch until the following spring. The caterpillars feed within leaves and stems and are fully grown by the middle of August. Pupation takes place within the stems and moths emerge in a few weeks.

**ARCHANARA ALGAE** Esper *Rush Wainscot* **Pl. 30**
**Distribution.** Widely distributed in Europe but often more local than *A. sparganii*. In the British Isles, confined to the east and south-east of England.
**Description.** Length up to 50 mm; long and slender; body pale, translucent green; very similar to *A. sparganii* but head with darker freckling.
**Habitat.** Fenland, lakes and ponds.
**Foodplants.** Bulrush (*Scirpus lacustris*), reedmace (*Typha*) and yellow iris (*Iris pseudacorus*).
**Biology.** One generation a year. Eggs are laid in late summer but do not hatch until the following spring. The caterpillars feed at first in shoot-tips but later bore into stems. When fully grown in August, they pupate within the stems. Moths emerge in the same month.

**RHIZEDRA LUTOSA** Hübner *Large Wainscot* **Pl. 30**
**Distribution.** Widespread throughout Europe. Widely distributed in the British Isles.
**Description.** Length up to 38 mm; plump, soft and wrinkled; body pale pinkish-brown, with a diffuse, greyish line along the middle of the back; spiracles black; plates on segments 1 and 13 reddish-brown; head shining, bright reddish-brown.
**Habitat.** Reed-beds, ditches and riversides.
**Foodplant.** Common reed (*Phragmites communis*).
**Biology.** One generation a year. Eggs are laid in the autumn but do not hatch until the following spring. The caterpillars feed in the stem bases and rhizomes, causing leaves of affected plants to turn white. They are fully grown in July and leave the plants to pupate in the ground among the rhizomes. Moths emerge in August or September.

**COENOBIA RUFA** Haworth *Small Rufous* **Pl. 30**
**Distribution.** Widespread in central and western Europe. Widely distributed in the British Isles and locally common, but absent from northern Scotland and local and scarce in Ireland.
**Description.** Length up to 22 mm; long and slender, with smooth, shining skin; body pinkish-white, shaded with darker pink on the back; a dark-centred, pale line extends along the middle of the back; a pale, wavy line extends along the spiracles on either side; head small and rounded, shining yellowish-brown.
**Habitat.** Fens, bogs and other marshy places.
**Foodplants.** Jointed rush (*Juncus articulatus*) and soft rush (*J. effusus*); probably on other *Juncus* species.
**Biology.** One generation a year. Eggs are laid in old stems of rush in August and hatch in about three weeks. The young caterpillars bore into the pith of the stem,

remaining there throughout the winter before attacking fresh growing stems in the spring. When fully grown at the end of May, they pupate in old stems of the foodplant and moths emerge in July.

**HOPLODRINA BLANDA** Denis & Schiffermüller *Rustic* **Pl. 11**

**Distribution.** Widespread throughout Europe. Widely distributed in the British Isles and common in England, Wales and Ireland.

**Description.** Length up to 28 mm; rather stout; body brownish-grey with a broad band of pinkish-ochre along the back; a pale line extends along the middle of the back, passing through a series of diffuse, blackish, V-shaped markings; a whitish-grey band extends along either side below the level of the spiracles; head small, yellowish-brown.

**Habitat.** Commonland, heaths, gardens and other places where the foodplants grow.

**Foodplants.** Chickweed (*Stellaria media*), dock (*Rumex*), plantain (*Plantago*) and other low-growing plants.

**Biology.** One generation a year. Eggs are laid in July and hatch in about a week. The caterpillars feed through the winter until April or May. They are mainly active at night, hiding by day at the roots of the foodplant. Pupation takes place in earthen cocoons in May and moths emerge in the following month.

**CARADRINA MORPHEUS** Hufnagel *Mottled Rustic* **Pl. 29**

**Distribution.** Widely distributed in Europe. Widespread throughout Britain, except for the extreme north of Scotland; scarce and local in Ireland.

**Description.** Length up to 29 mm; body brownish-grey with a broad, pale band along the back, sometimes tinged with ochre; a conspicuous, broken white line extends along the back of segments 1–3; a series of blackish, V-shaped markings extends along the pale band, edged on either side by a line of blackish dashes, which become wedge-shaped towards the rear; a diffuse, whitish band extends along the spiracles on each side; head shining, dark brown.

**Habitat.** Commonland, hedgerows, woodland, salt marshes and other places where the foodplants grow.

**Foodplants.** Nettle (*Urtica*), dandelion (*Taraxacum*), chickweed (*Stellaria media*), knotgrass (*Polygonum aviculare*), and other low-growing plants.

**Biology.** One generation a year. Eggs are laid in July or August and hatch in about a week. The caterpillars are active at night, hiding under leaf litter by day. They feed slowly until late autumn, when they construct large cocoons of earth and silk among roots or in tufts of grass, in which they remain through the winter before pupating in spring. Moths emerge in June or July.

**ELAPHRIA VENUSTULA** Hübner *Rosy Marbled* **Pl. 16**

**Distribution.** Local but widespread in Europe. In the British Isles, confined to south-east England.

**Description.** Length up to 15 mm; tapered towards the head and with a slight hump towards the rear; body deep purplish-brown with a series of dark reddish, diamond-shaped markings along the back; segment 3 with a pair of conspicuous, large, white or reddish spots; underside grey; head brown with pale markings.

**Habitat.** Open woodland.

**Foodplants.** Tormentil (*Potentilla erecta*) and other species of *Potentilla*; bramble

(*Rubus fruticosus*), lady's mantle (*Alchemilla*), greenweed (*Genista*) and broom (*Cytisus scoparius*).
**Biology.** One generation a year. Eggs are laid singly on the undersides of leaves in June. The caterpillars feed on the flowers from June to August before pupating in subterranean cocoons. Moths do not emerge until May or June of the following year.

**PYRRHIA UMBRA** Hufnagel *Bordered Sallow* **Pl. 20**
**Distribution.** Widespread throughout Europe. Widely distributed but local in the British Isles, with the exception of northern Scotland.
**Description.** Length up to 37 mm; body very variable in colour, ranging from green to brown, pink, grey or blackish; usually with a dark central line along the middle of the back and a paler line on either side; a white or yellow stripe extends along each side below the line of the spiracles; head pale green or brown.
**Habitat.** Downland, coastal sand dunes and beaches.
**Foodplants.** Rest-harrow (*Ononis*), henbane (*Hyoscyamus niger*) and sea sandwort (*Honkenya peploides*).
**Biology.** One generation a year. Eggs are laid on shoots of the foodplant in June or early July. The caterpillars feed on flowers and developing seeds and are fully grown by the end of August. Pupation takes place in the earth in September but moths do not emerge until late May or June of the following year.

**HELIOTHIS ARMIGERA** Hübner *Scarce Bordered Straw* **Pl. 33**
**Distribution.** Widespread in southern and parts of central Europe. Occurs as an occasional immigrant in the British Isles; the caterpillars are regularly imported on tomatoes and other fruit.
**Description.** Length up to 40 mm; skin rough, covered with minute spines, visible under a hand lens; body ranging in colour from green to brown, variably marked with irregular, longitudinal lines of yellowish-white; usually with a dark band along each side above the line of the spiracles; below spiracular line, body is usually pale or finely spotted with white; segment 11 with a slight hump on the back; head pale ochre, marked with dark green or brown.
**Habitat.** Cultivated fields, market gardens and open countryside.
**Foodplants.** A wide range of wild and cultivated plants, including tomato (*Lycopersicon*), maize (*Zea*), carnation (*Dianthus*) and *Chrysanthemum*.
**Biology.** Two or three generations a year in southern Europe. Eggs are laid singly on the foodplant and hatch in about a week. Caterpillars feed on leaves, buds, flowers and fruits of a wide range of plants and are important pests in southern Europe and other warm regions of the world. They sometimes become established in glasshouses in the British Isles, arriving on imported chrysanthemums. Pupation takes place in the soil. Migrant moths usually arrive in southern England in the autumn.

**HELIOTHIS VIRIPLACA** Hufnagel *Marbled Clover* **Pl. 20**
**Distribution.** Widely distributed in Europe. In the British Isles, confined to southern and eastern England.
**Description.** Length up to 42 mm; body very variable in colour, ranging from various shades of green to reddish-brown, pinkish or purplish; usually finely patterned with small dots and lines of yellow; two yellow bands extend along the back and a further yellow band along the line of the spiracles, bordered below with white; head pale green or brown with black spots.

**Habitat.** Sandy and chalky places, waste land, downland and beaches.
**Foodplants.** Campion (*Silene*), rest-harrow (*Ononis*), clover (*Trifolium*), toadflax (*Linaria*), hawksbeard (*Crepis*) and other low-growing plants.
**Biology.** One generation a year, possibly with a partial second brood in southern England. Eggs are laid in July and caterpillars may be found in August and September feeding on flowers and developing seeds. Pupation takes place just below the surface of the soil in the autumn but moths do not emerge until the following June.

**HELIOTHIS PELTIGERA** Denis & Schiffermüller *Bordered Straw* **Pl. 20**
**Distribution.** Widespread in southern and western Europe, migrating northwards each year. A sporadic immigrant in the British Isles, occurring most commonly along the southern coast of England.
**Description.** Length up to 38 mm; body very variable in colour, ranging from green to brown or purplish, usually with a dark line along the middle of the back, with paler lines on either side; a yellow or white stripe extends along each side below the line of small, black-rimmed spiracles; head green or brown.
**Habitat.** Coastal regions and other places where suitable foodplants grow.
**Foodplants.** Sticky groundsel (*Senecio viscosus*), rest-harrow (*Ononis repens*) and garden marigold (*Calendula*).
**Biology.** Usually one generation a year but unlikely to survive the winter in the British Isles. Immigrant moths lay eggs in June and caterpillars are found feeding on flowers from late June until the autumn. It seems that few caterpillars complete their development in the British Isles but those that become fully grown pupate beneath the soil and may produce moths late in the year. In southern Europe there are several generations a year.

PROTODELTOTE PYGARGA Hufnagel *Marbled White Spot* **Pl. 31**
**Distribution.** Widely distributed in Europe. In the British Isles, it is confined to southern and eastern England, parts of Wales and the south-west of Ireland.
**Description.** Length up to 20 mm; slender, tapering slightly towards the rear; body yellow or reddish-brown with a dark line down the middle of the back and a pale line on either side; a reddish line extends along the black spiracles on either side; head rounded, brown.
**Habitat.** Woodland, heaths, moorland and bogs, mainly on acid soils.
**Foodplants.** Purple moor-grass (*Molinia caerulea*), slender false-brome (*Brachypodium sylvaticum*) and probably on other grasses.
**Biology.** One generation a year. Eggs are laid in June or July and caterpillars feed from July to September. Pupation takes place in earthen cocoons in the autumn but moths do not emerge until the following May or June.

**EARIAS CLORANA** Linnaeus *Cream-bordered Green Pea* **Pl. 2**
**Distribution.** Widely distributed but local in Europe. In the British Isles, mainly confined to southern and eastern England, with a few records from northern England and southern Scotland.
**Description.** Length up to 19 mm; short and plump, tapering towards the rear; body whitish, sometimes tinged with pink, with brown lines along the back and sides; underside pale bluish-green; segments 5 and 11 each have a pair of dark brown, raised warts on the back; spiracles black; head pale green, sometimes drawn back into the body.

**Habitat.** Damp woodland, fens and marshes.
**Foodplants.** Osier (*Salix viminalis*) and other *Salix* species.
**Biology.** One generation a year. Eggs are laid in June or July and caterpillars feed from July to August. They live in the spun terminal shoots of various willows and, when fully grown, construct boat-shaped silken cocoons attached to stems or twigs of the foodplant. The pupae normally overwinter, producing moths in the following May or June, but a small second generation of moths sometimes appears in August.

**PSEUDOIPS FAGANA** Fabricius *Green Silver-lines* **Pl. 6**
**Distribution.** Widespread throughout Europe. Widely distributed in Britain, except for the extreme north of Scotland; widely distributed but scarce in Ireland.
**Description.** Length up to 35 mm; body plump, tapered strongly towards the rear; colour green, spotted and patterned with yellowish-white; two yellowish-white, broad lines extend along the back; the rear claspers are elongated and striped with red; head pale green.
**Habitat.** Woodland.
**Foodplants.** Oak (*Quercus*), beech (*Fagus sylvatica*), birch (*Betula*), hazel (*Corylus avellana*) and sometimes other deciduous trees.
**Biology.** One generation a year. Eggs are laid singly on leaves in June and hatch in about a week. The caterpillars are rather sluggish and may often be found resting on the undersides of leaves. They become fully grown in September or October, when they construct tough, papery brown cocoons on the undersides of leaves, in cracks in the bark or beneath leaf litter on the ground. Moths do not emerge until June of the following year.

**NYCTEOLA REVAYANA** Scopoli *Oak Nycteoline* **Pl. 6**
**Distribution.** Widespread throughout Europe, except for the extreme north. Widely distributed in the British Isles but most common in southern England.
**Description.** Length up to 20 mm; body bright green with narrow, greenish-yellow lines between the segments, with sparse, fine white hairs; spiracles yellowish with black rims; head pale yellowish-green.
**Habitat.** Woodland.
**Foodplant.** Oak (*Quercus*).
**Biology.** One generation a year. Eggs are laid in the spring and caterpillars feed from May to July. When fully grown, they construct whitish, boat-shaped cocoons on the undersides of leaves or on twigs. Moths emerge in late summer but overwinter before laying eggs.

**PANTHEA COENOBITA** Esper **Pl. 1**
**Distribution.** Occurs in central and south-eastern Europe. Absent from the British Isles.
**Description.** Length up to 60 mm; covered with tufts of black and white hairs arising from small, yellowish-brown warts; body reddish-brown with lines of black markings along the back and sides; a line of white patches extends down the middle of the back and a further line along each side below the level of the spiracles; head black.
**Habitat.** Coniferous woodland.
**Foodplants.** Spruce (*Picea*), pine (*Pinus*), silver fir (*Abies alba*) and European larch (*Larix decidua*).
**Biology.** One generation a year. Caterpillars feed from August to the beginning of

October and pupate in papery cocoons on or below the surface of the soil at the foot of the tree. Moths emerge in May or June of the following year.

**COLOCASIA CORYLI** Linnaeus *Nut-tree Tussock* **Pl. 5**

**Distribution.** Widespread throughout Europe but rather local. Widely distributed in the British Isles.

**Description.** Length up to 35 mm; plump; body usually pinkish-orange but sometimes brown, ochreous or grey, covered with tufts of fine, whitish hairs; segment 2 with a pair of forward-directed tufts of brown or blackish hairs; segments 4, 5 and 11 each have a single tuft of reddish-brown or blackish hairs on the back; a series of dark, rectangular markings extends along the middle of the back, sometimes joined to form a continuous band; a whitish band extends along each side; head reddish-brown or greyish.

**Habitat.** Woodland.

**Foodplants.** Beech (*Fagus sylvatica*), hazel (*Corylus avellana*), birch (*Betula*), hornbeam (*Carpinus betulus*), and field maple (*Acer campestre*).

**Biology.** Two generations a year in southern England, one in the north. Eggs are laid singly on the leaves in May and August and caterpillars feed from June to July and September to early October. When at rest, they conceal themselves between spun leaves. Pupation takes place in cocoons at the base of the tree in July and October and moths emerge in August and April respectively.

**DIACHRYSIA CHRYSITIS** Linnaeus *Burnished Brass* **Pl. 9**

**Distribution.** Widespread throughout Europe and often common. Widely distributed in the British Isles.

**Description.** Length up to 35 mm; a semi-looper with only three pairs of prolegs; body pale bluish-green with a series of whitish, arrow-shaped markings along the back and a whitish line along the black-rimmed spiracles; head yellowish-green.

**Habitat.** Cultivated land, waste ground, gardens and other places where suitable foodplants grow.

**Foodplants.** Nettle (*Urtica dioica*), dead-nettle (*Lamium*), hemp-nettle (*Galeopsis*) and probably other similar plants.

**Biology.** Two generations a year in southern England, one generation in the north. Eggs are laid singly on leaves in June and August and hatch in about a week. Caterpillars of the second generation hibernate under leaf litter on the ground while still quite small and continue feeding in the following spring. They are mainly active at night, hiding in folded leaves by day. Pupation takes place in pale brown, silken cocoons spun on the undersides of leaves in May and July, and moths emerge in June and August respectively.

DIACHRYSIA CHRYSON Esper *Scarce Burnished Brass* **Pl. 28**

**Distribution.** Widely distributed but rather local and scarce in many parts of Europe. In the British Isles it is confined to southern England and parts of south Wales.

**Description.** Length up to 30 mm; a semi-looper with only three pairs of prolegs; body bright yellowish-green, bearing a broken, dark-centred, white line along the middle of the back with a series of oblique white lines on either side; a black-edged, white line extends along the spiracles; head shining green.

**Habitat.** River valleys, marshes and fenland.

**Foodplant.** Hemp agrimony (*Eupatorium cannabinum*).

**Biology.** One generation a year. Eggs are laid in August and the caterpillars go into hibernation while still small, completing their growth the following spring. They are mainly active at night, hiding on the undersides of leaves by day. Pupation takes place in July in whitish silken cocoons spun on the undersides of leaves. Moths emerge in late July and August.

**POLYCHRYSIA MONETA** Fabricius *Golden Plusia* **Pl. 12**

**Distribution.** Widespread in Europe. Widely distributed in England but scarce in Scotland, and in Ireland confined to the Dublin area.

**Description.** Length up to 35 mm; a semi-looper with only three pairs of prolegs; body bright green, whitish between segments; a dark line extends along the middle of the back and a white line above the level of the spiracles on each side, becoming less distinct towards the head; head shining green. Young caterpillars are dark greyish-green with black spots.

**Habitat.** Gardens.

**Foodplants.** Delphinium (*Delphinium*), monkshood (*Aconitum*) and globe flower (*Trollius europaeus*).

**Biology.** Usually one generation a year but sometimes there is a partial second brood in southern England. Eggs are normally laid in July, and the caterpillars either feed up rapidly in late summer or overwinter at the base of the foodplant, completing their growth in the following spring. They feed on leaves, buds and developing seeds. Pupation takes place in June and sometimes in August in golden yellow silken cocoons spun on the undersides of leaves. Moths emerge within a month.

**AUTOGRAPHA GAMMA** Linnaeus *Silver Y* **Pl. 13**

**Distribution.** Resident in southern Europe, migrating to the rest of Europe as far north as the Arctic Circle. Occurs as a migrant throughout the British Isles but most common in southern and eastern England.

**Description.** Length up to 25 mm; a semi-looper with only three pairs of prolegs; body varying in colour from yellowish-green to bluish-green or dark greenish-grey; the back is patterned with fine white lines and rings, and a white or yellowish band extends along the spiracles on each side; head usually green with a characteristic black stripe on either side but sometimes lacks the stripe or is completely black.

**Habitat.** Agricultural land, waste land and gardens.

**Foodplants.** Clover (*Trifolium*), pea (*Pisum sativum*), cabbage (*Brassica oleracea*), lettuce (*Lactuca sativa*) and many other wild and cultivated plants.

**Biology.** Two generations a year in Britain from migrants arriving in the spring. Eggs are laid singly or in small batches in May and August and hatch in about a fortnight. Caterpillars may be found throughout the summer and autumn, although those occurring late in the year do not survive the winter. They are sometimes serious pests of field crops. Pupation takes place within translucent, whitish cocoons spun amongst the foliage. Moths emerge in late summer.

**AUTOGRAPHA JOTA** Linnaeus *Plain Golden Y* **Pl. 26**

**Distribution.** Widespread in Europe. Widely distributed in the British Isles but less common in Ireland and Scotland.

**Description.** Length up to 38 mm; a semi-looper with only three pairs of prolegs; body bright green with traces of four indistinct, pale lines on the back; a fine yellow line extends above the spiracles on each side; head green with a strong black stripe on either side.

**Habitat.** Hedgerows, woodland and waste ground.

**Foodplants.** Dead-nettle (*Lamium*), hedge woundwort (*Stachys sylvatica*), nettle

(*Urtica dioica*) and other low-growing plants; probably also deciduous trees and shrubs.
**Biology.** One generation a year. Eggs are laid singly on leaves in July and caterpillars hatch in about a week. They feed for a time before going into hibernation while still quite small. In the following spring they resume feeding, mostly at night, and become fully grown by the end of May. Pupation takes place in yellowish-white silken cocoons spun on the undersides of leaves. Moths emerge in June or July.

**AUTOGRAPHA BRACTEA** Denis & Schiffermüller *Gold Spangle* **Pl. 28**
**Distribution.** Widely distributed in central and northern Europe. Widespread in Britain except for southern England; local in Ireland.
**Description.** Length up to 35 mm; a semi-looper with only three pairs of prolegs; body pale green with six irregular, white lines on the back and a white line above the spiracles on each side; head green with a black stripe on each side.
**Habitat.** Hedgerows, waste ground and moorland.
**Foodplants.** Nettle (*Urtica*), dead-nettle (*Lamium*), dandelion (*Taraxacum*), groundsel (*Senecio vulgaris*), honeysuckle (*Lonicera periclymenum*) and other plants.
**Biology.** One generation a year. Eggs are laid in July and caterpillars hibernate when still small, completing their growth in the following spring. Pupation takes place in May in cocoons spun on leaves of the foodplant; moths emerge in July.

**ABROSTOLA TRIGEMINA** Werneburg *Dark Spectacle* **Pl. 9**
**Distribution.** Widespread throughout Europe. Widely distributed in the British Isles but local in Scotland.
**Description.** Length up to 35 mm; body with a hump on segment 11; colour green, greenish-brown or purplish-brown with blackish triangular markings on the back of segments 4, 5 and 11; a whitish line extends along the spiracles on each side; head pale green or brown with a dark band on each side.
**Habitat.** Hedgerows, waste ground and other places where the foodplants grow.
**Foodplants.** Nettle (*Urtica dioica*) and hop (*Humulus lupulus*).
**Biology.** One generation a year except in south-west England, where there is a second brood. Eggs are laid in July and the caterpillars usually feed in August and September. Pupation takes place in the autumn in silken cocoons spun inside folded leaves but moths do not emerge until June of the following year.

**ABROSTOLA TRIPLASIA** Linnaeus *Spectacle* **Pl. 9**
**Distribution.** Widespread in Europe. Widely distributed and often common in the British Isles, although more local in Ireland.
**Description.** Length up to 35 mm; body varying in colour from green to purplish-brown; whitish on the back, with a series of dark green or brown V-shaped markings; segment 11 with a distinct hump; a whitish line extends along the spiracles on each side; head pale green or brown with a dark stripe on each side.
**Habitat.** Hedgerows, waste ground, open woodland and other places where the foodplant grows.
**Foodplant.** Nettle (*Urtica dioica*).
**Biology.** One generation a year, with a partial second brood in parts of southern England. Eggs are laid singly on leaves of the foodplant in July and hatch in about a week. The caterpillars are active by day, and may be found resting on the upper leaves of the foodplant. They are fully grown in late summer and pupate in cocoons spun among leaf litter on the ground. Moths do not emerge until the following May or June but a second brood may appear in late summer.

**CATOCALA NUPTA** Linnaeus *Red Underwing* **Pl. 2**

**Distribution.** Widely distributed in Europe. In the British Isles, confined to southern and central England and parts of Wales.

**Description.** Length up to 70 mm; long and slender, tapering towards the rear; body colour brown or brownish-grey with two blackish bands on the back, sometimes indistinct; a pair of ochreous spots present on the back of each segment; segment 8 has a prominent projection on the back, and segment 11 a slight hump; rear claspers elongate; head pale grey with a black band.

**Habitat.** Woodland and other places where the foodplants grow.

**Foodplants.** Willow (*Salix*), poplar (*Populus*) and plum (*Prunus domestica*).

**Biology.** One generation a year. Eggs are laid singly or in small groups in crevices of the bark in September, but do not hatch until the following spring. The caterpillars feed at night, hiding in cracks in the bark by day. They are fully grown in late June or July and pupate in open silken cocoons spun between leaves or in crevices of the bark. Moths emerge in August or September.

**CALLISTEGE MI** Clerck *Mother Shipton* **Pl. 21**

**Distribution.** Widespread throughout Europe. Widely distributed in the British Isles, becoming less common towards the north.

**Description.** Length up to 40 mm; long and slender; a semi-looper with only three pairs of prolegs; body pale ochreous-white or pale yellow, with two dark bands extending along the back on either side of a central ochreous line, these markings sometimes appearing as a number of fine brown lines; a yellowish-white band extends along each side below the line of the spiracles; head whitish with fine brown lines continuous with those on the body.

**Habitat.** Downland, meadows and open woodland.

**Foodplants.** Clover (*Trifolium*), melilot (*Melilotus*) and probably other related plants.

**Biology.** One generation a year. Eggs are laid in June and hatch in about three weeks. The caterpillars feed by day and night and are often found at rest on grasses. If disturbed, they readily fall to the ground in a characteristic, curled posture. When fully grown in September, they pupate in cocoons attached to leaves or grass blades close to the ground. Moths emerge in the following May or June.

**EUCLIDIA GLYPHICA** Linnaeus *Burnet Companion* **Pl. 21**

**Distribution.** Widespread throughout Europe. Widely distributed in the British Isles but less common towards the north and absent from many parts of Scotland.

**Description.** Length up to 40 mm; long and slender, a semi-looper with only three pairs of functional prolegs; body brownish-white lined with yellowish-brown; a whitish or pinkish stripe extends along the sides below the line of the spiracles, sometimes bordered below with dark brown; head whitish with markings continuous with those on the body.

**Habitat.** Downland, meadows and open woodland, mainly on chalk or limestone.

**Foodplants.** Black medick (*Medicago lupulina*), lucerne (*M. sativa*), clover (*Trifolium*) and other related plants.

**Biology.** One generation a year. Eggs are laid in small groups on the leaves in June and hatch in about a fortnight. The caterpillars are active at night, remaining stretched out along stems of the foodplant by day. When fully grown at the end of September, they pupate in the soil at the base of the foodplant. Moths emerge in the following May or June.

**TYTA LUCTUOSA** Denis & Schiffermüller *Four-spotted* **Pl. 26**

**Distribution.** Widely distributed but local in Europe. In the British Isles, confined to a few localities in southern England; apparently much less common in recent years.

**Description.** Length up to 35 mm; pale reddish-ochre with two broken, dark brown bands on the back, bearing white spots; a broad, brownish-white band extends below the line of black spiracles on each side; head brownish-white with dark brown lines.

**Habitat.** Downland, embankments and waste ground on chalky soils.

**Foodplant.** Field bindweed (*Convolvulus arvensis*).

**Biology.** One generation a year. Eggs are laid singly on stems or buds of the foodplant in June. The caterpillars feed in July and August. Pupation takes place in September in strong subterranean cocoons but moths do not emerge until the following June.

**LYGEPHILA CRACCAE** Denis & Schiffermüller *Scarce Blackneck* **Pl. 20**

**Distribution.** Occurs locally in central and southern Europe. In the British Isles, confined to a few coastal localities in south-west England.

**Description.** Length up to 36 mm; fairly slender, tapering towards the head; body pale brown with a broad stripe of mottled dark brown along the back, through which runs a pale-bordered, blackish-brown line; a double line of dark brown extends along the sides; head brown.

**Habitat.** Cliffs and rocky places.

**Foodplants.** Wood vetch (*Vicia sylvatica*) and probably on other related plants.

**Biology.** One generation a year. Eggs are laid singly on leaves of the foodplant in the summer but do not hatch until the following spring. Caterpillars feed until June and pupate in cocoons on the surface of the soil. Moths emerge in July and August.

APOPESTIS SPECTRUM Esper **Pl. 33**

**Distribution.** Occurs in southern Europe.

**Description.** Length up to 80 mm; body yellow with four black stripes along the back and a complex pattern of white-ringed black markings along the sides; head yellowish-white with black spots.

**Habitat.** Hillsides and open countryside where the foodplants grow.

**Foodplants.** Hairy greenweed (*Genista pilosa*), broom (*Cytisus scoparius*) and probably other related plants.

**Biology.** One generation a year. Eggs are laid on stems of the foodplant in March. The caterpillars may be found from April to June or July, feeding mainly on flowers. They sit openly on stems of the foodplant and their bright colouring suggests that they are distasteful to predators. Pupation takes place in greyish-white cocoons on the foodplant and moths emerge in about a month. Moths overwinter before laying eggs in the following spring.

**SCOLIOPTERYX LIBATRIX** Linnaeus *Herald* **Pl. 2**

**Distribution.** Widespread throughout Europe, although less common in the south. Widely distributed in the British Isles.

**Description.** Length up to 50 mm; long and slender, with a velvety appearance; body green with an indistinct dark line extending along the middle of the back and a black-edged, greenish-yellow line on either side; an indistinct whitish line extends along the spiracles on each side; head strongly rounded, yellowish-green with a central black line.

**Habitat.** Woodland, common land and gardens.

**Foodplants.** Sallow (*Salix*) and poplar (*Populus*).

**Biology.** Two generations a year in southern England but only one generation from the Midlands northwards. Eggs are laid singly or in small batches on twigs and leaves and hatch in about a week. The caterpillars may be found from June to September and when fully grown pupate in whitish silken cocoons, usually spun between leaves. Moths emerging in the autumn overwinter before mating and laying eggs, but broods may overlap and moths can be found in most months of the year.

## LASPEYRIA FLEXULA Denis & Schiffermüller **Pl. 32**

*Beautiful Hook-tip*

**Distribution.** Widespread in Europe. In the British Isles, mostly confined to southern England and south Wales.

**Description.** Length up to 24 mm; body slightly swollen behind the head and towards the rear; first two pairs of prolegs very small; body bluish-green, intricately patterned with black and greenish-white; segment 11 with a pair of raised warts on the back; head greenish-white with black markings.

**Habitat.** Woodland and neglected orchards.

**Foodplants.** Lichens (*Physcia stellaris* and *Xanthoria parietana*).

**Biology.** One generation a year. Eggs are laid singly or in small heaps on twigs or lichens in August. The caterpillars overwinter while still small, resuming their feeding in the following spring. They are active at night, feeding on lichens growing on various trees and shrubs, but remain on the food by day, when they are extremely well camouflaged. When fully grown in May, they pupate in yellowish-grey cocoons spun among the food. Moths emerge in June or July.

## HYPENA PROBOSCIDALIS Linnaeus *Snout* **Pl. 9**

**Distribution.** Widespread throughout Europe. Widely distributed in the British Isles and often common.

**Description.** Length up to 25 mm; long and slender, with long legs; body varying from yellowish-green to dark green with yellowish bands between the segments; two greenish-white lines extend along the back and a broad, white line extends along the spiracles on each side; dots pale green, slightly raised; head green with black spotting.

**Habitat.** Open woodland, hedgerows, gardens and waste ground.

**Foodplant.** Nettle (*Urtica dioica*).

**Biology.** One generation a year, with a partial second brood in the south. Eggs are laid in July or August and the caterpillars overwinter before completing their growth in the following spring. Pupation takes place in May and moths emerge in the following month or later. Second brood moths emerge in the autumn.

# Bibliography


Allan, P. B. M., 1949. *Larval foodplants*. Watkins & Doncaster. London.

Ancilotto, A., Grollo, A. & Zangheri, S., 1970. *i bruchi*. Mondadori. Milan.

Bodi, E., 1985. *The caterpillars of European butterflies*. Sciences Nat. Compiegne.

Brooks, M. & Knight, C., 1982. *A complete guide to British butterflies*. Jonathan Cape. London.

Buckler, W., (editors Stainton, H. T. & Porritt, G. T.), 1886–1901. *The larvae of the British butterflies and moths*. Vols 1–9. Ray Society. London.

Carter, D. J., 1979. *The Observer's Book of Caterpillars*. Warne. London.

Carter, D., 1982. *Butterflies and Moths in Britain and Europe*. Heinemann, Pan & British Museum (Nat. Hist.). London.

Cribb, P. W., 1983. *Breeding the British Butterflies*. Amateur Entomologists' Society. Hanworth.

Dickson, R., 1976. *A Lepidopterist's Handbook*. Amateur Entomologists' Society. Hanworth.

Forster, W. & Wohlfahrt, T., 1954–74. *Die Schmetterlinge Mitteleuropas*. (5 vols) Keller. Stuttgart.

Friedrich, E., 1983. *Breeding Butterflies and Moths*. Harley Books. Colchester.

Gardiner, B. O. C., 1982. *A silkmoth rearer's handbook*. (3rd edition) Amateur Entomologists' Society. Hanworth.

Gómez-Bustillo, M. R. & Fernández-Rubio, F., 1974–9. *Mariposas de la Peninsula Ibérica*. (4 vols) Ministerio de Agricultura Madrid.

Guilbot, R., 1982. *Élevage des papillons*. Boubée. Paris.

Haggett, G. M., 1981. *Larvae of British Lepidoptera not figured by Buckler*. British Entomological & Natural History Society. London.

Heath, J., et al. 1976-1991. *The Moths and Butterflies of Great Britain and Ireland*. (6 vols) Harley Books. Colchester.

Higgins, L. & Hargreaves, B., 1983. *The Butterflies of Britain and Europe*. Collins. London.

Higgins, L. G. & Riley, N. D., 1983. *A field guide to the Butterflies of Britain and Europe*. (5th edition) Collins. London.

Howarth, T. G., 1973. *South's British Butterflies*. Warne. London.

Howarth, T. G., 1984. *Colour identification guide to butterflies of the British Isles*. (2nd edition) Viking. London.

Hyde, G., 1977. *British caterpillars: Butterflies*. Jarrold. Norwich.

Hyde, G., 1977. *British caterpillars: Moths*. (2 vols) Jarrold. Norwich.

Kloet, G. S. & Hincks, W. D., 1972. *A check list of British Insects. Part 2: Lepidoptera*. (2nd edition) Royal Entomological Society of London.

Le Cerf, F. & Herbulot, C., 1963–71. *Atlas des Lépidoptères de France*. (3 vols) Boubée. Paris.

Leraut, P., 1980. *Liste systématique et synonymique des lépidoptères de France, Belgique et Corse*.

Merz, E. & Pfletschinger, H., 1982. *Die Raupen unserer Schmetterlinge*. Kosmos. Stuttgart.

Newman, L. H., 1965. *Hawk-moths of Great Britain and Europe*. Cassell. London.

Novak, I., 1980. *A field guide in colour to butterflies and moths*. Octopus. London.

Reichholf-Riehm, H., 1983. *Schmetterlinge*. Mosaik. Munich.

Rougeot, P-C. & Viette, P., 1978. *Guide des papillons nocturnes d'Europe et d'Afrique du Nord*. Delachaux & Niestlé. Paris.

Sauer, F., 1982. *Raupe und Schmetterlinge*. Fauna-Verlag. Karlsfeld.

Skinner, B., 1984. *Colour identification guide to moths of the British Isles*. Viking. London.

Sokoloff, P., 1984. *Breeding the British and European hawk-moths*. Amateur Entomologists' Society. Hanworth.

South, R., 1961. *The moths of the British Isles*. (2 vols, 4th edition) Warne. London.

Spuler, A. in Hofmann, E., 1910. *Die Schmetterlinge Europas*. Vol. 4. *Die Raupen der Schmetterlinge Europas*. Stuttgart.

Stokoe, W. J. & Stovin, G. H. T., 1944. *The caterpillars of the British butterflies*. Warne. London.

Stokoe, W. J. & Stovin, G. H. T., 1948. *The caterpillars of British moths*. (2 vols) Warne. London.

Wilson, S. & Wilson, E., 1880. *The larvae of the British lepidoptera*. Reeve. London.

# Foodplant lists

In the following section, major foodplants are arranged in the same order as in the colour plates. The caterpillars of butterflies and moths that feed on them are listed by family in the same order as the descriptive text. Those that do not feed on that particular plant in the British Isles are marked by a †, while those that do not occur in the British Isles at all are indicated by an *.

Species of caterpillars feeding on other plants may be traced through the foodplant index.

## PINE *Pinus* **Pl. 1**

**Lasiocampidae**
*Pine-tree Lappet *Dendrolimus pini*

**Saturniidae**
*Spanish Moon Moth *Graellsia isabellae*

**Geometridae**
Pine Carpet *Thera firmata*
†Cloaked Pug *Eupithecia abietaria*
Willow Beauty *Peribatodes rhomboidaria*
Bordered White *Bupalus piniaria*

**Sphingidae**
Pine Hawk-moth *Hyloicus pinastri*

**Thaumetopoeidae**
*Pine Processionary *Thaumetopoea pityocampa*

**Lymantriidae**
†Black V Moth *Arctornis l-nigrum*
†Black Arches *Lymantria monacha*

**Noctuidae**
Pine Beauty *Panolis flammea*
**Panthea coenobita*

## WILLOW and SALLOW *Salix* **Pl. 2**

**Cossidae**
Leopard Moth *Zeuzera pyrina*
Goat Moth *Cossus cossus*

**Nymphalidae**
Purple Emperor *Apatura iris*
*Lesser Purple Emperor *Apatura ilia*
Large Tortoiseshell *Nymphalis polychloros*
Camberwell Beauty *Nymphalis antiopa*
Comma *Polygonia c-album*

**Lasiocampidae**
Pale Eggar *Trichiura crataegi*
Small Eggar *Eriogaster lanestris*
Lackey *Malacosoma neustria*
Grass Eggar *Lasiocampa trifolii*
Oak Eggar *Lasiocampa quercus*
Fox Moth *Macrothylacia rubi*
†Small Lappet *Phyllodesma ilicifolia*
Lappet *Gastropacha quercifolia*

**Saturniidae**
Emperor Moth *Saturnia pavonia*
*Great Peacock *Saturnia pyri*

**Thyatiridae**
†Poplar Lutestring *Tethea or*

**Geometridae**
Northern Spinach *Eulithis populata*
Dark Marbled Carpet *Chloroclysta citrata*
Common Marbled Carpet *Chloroclysta truncata*
July Highflyer *Hydriomena furcata*
Seraphim *Lobophora halterata*
Early Tooth-striped *Trichopteryx carpinata*
Clouded Border *Lomaspilis marginata*
Sharp-angled Peacock *Semiothisa alternaria*
Netted Mountain Carpet *Semiothisa carbonaria*
Scorched Wing *Plagodis dolabraria*
Bordered Beauty *Epione repandaria*
Canary-shouldered Thorn *Ennomos alniaria*
Early Thorn *Selenia dentaria*
Purple Thorn *Selenia tetralunaria*
Feathered Thorn *Colotois pennaria*
Pale Brindled Beauty *Apocheima pilosaria*
Brindled Beauty *Lycia hirtaria*
Peppered Moth *Biston betularia*
Dotted Border *Agriopis marginaria*
Pale Oak Beauty *Serraca punctinalis*

**Sphingidae**
Eyed Hawk-moth *Smerinthus ocellata*
Poplar Hawk-moth *Laothoe populi*

**Notodontidae**
Buff-tip *Phalera bucephala*
Puss Moth *Cerura vinula*
Sallow Kitten *Furcula furcula*
Poplar Kitten *Furcula bifida*
Iron Prominent *Notodonta dromedarius*
Pebble Prominent *Eligmodonta ziczac*
Swallow Prominent *Pheosia tremula*
Coxcomb Prominent *Ptilodon capucina*
Pale Prominent *Pterostoma palpina*
Chocolate-tip *Clostera curtula*

**Lymantriidae**
Scarce Vapourer *Orgyia recens*
Dark Tussock *Dicallomera fascelina*
Brown-tail *Euproctis chrysorrhoea*
Yellow-tail *Euproctis similis*
White Satin *Leucoma salicis*
†Black V Moth *Arctornis l-nigrum*

**Noctuidae**
Lesser Yellow Underwing *Noctua comes*
Broad-bordered Yellow Underwing *Noctua fimbriata*
Lesser Broad-bordered Yellow Underwing *Noctua janthina*
Barred Chestnut *Diarsia dahlii*
Purple Clay *Diarsia brunnea*
Setaceous Hebrew Character *Xestia c-nigrum*
Triple-spotted Clay *Xestia ditrapezium*
Double Square-spot *Xestia triangulum*
Ashworth's Rustic *Xestia ashworthii*
Square-spot Rustic *Xestia xanthographa*
Gothic *Naenia typica*
Green Arches *Anaplectoides prasina*
Red Chestnut *Cerastis rubricosa*
Grey Arches *Polia nebulosa*
Dot Moth *Melanchra persicariae*
Beautiful Brocade *Lacanobia contigua*
Broom Moth *Ceramica pisi*
Small Quaker *Orthosia cruda*
Northern Drab *Orthosia opima*
Powdered Quaker *Orthosia gracilis*
Common Quaker *Orthosia stabilis*
Clouded Drab *Orthosia incerta*
Twin-spotted Quaker *Orthosia munda*
Hebrew Character *Orthosia gothica*
Sprawler *Brachionycha sphinx*
Dark Brocade *Blepharita adusta*
Satellite *Eupsilia transversa*
Brown-spot Pinion *Agrochola litura*
Beaded Chestnut *Agrochola lychnidis*
Sallow *Xanthia icteritia*
Poplar Grey *Acronicta megacephala*
Miller *Acronicta leporina*
Alder Moth *Acronicta alni*
Dark Dagger *Acronicta tridens*
Light Knot Grass *Acronicta menyanthidis*
Sweet Gale Moth *Acronicta euphorbiae*
Knot Grass *Acronicta rumicis*
Svensson's Copper Underwing *Amphipyra berbera*
Old Lady *Mormo maura*
Small Angle Shades *Euplexia lucipara*
Dun-bar *Cosmia trapezina*
Saxon *Hyppa rectilinea*
Cream-bordered Green Pea *Earias clorana*
Red Underwing *Catocala nupta*
Herald *Scoliopteryx libatrix*

## POPLAR and ASPEN *Populus* Pl. 3

**Limacodidae**
Triangle *Heterogenea asella*

**Nymphalidae**
*Poplar Admiral *Limenitis populi*
*Lesser Purple Emperor *Apatura ilia*
Large Tortoiseshell *Nymphalis polychloros*

**Lasiocampidae**
December Moth *Poecilocampa populi*

**Saturniidae**
*Great Peacock *Saturnia pyri*

**Thyatiridae**
Figure of Eighty *Tethea ocularis*
Poplar Lutestring *Tethea or*
†Common Lutestring *Ochropacha duplaris*

**Geometridae**
Light Orange Underwing *Archiearis notha*
July Highflyer *Hydriomena furcata*
Seraphim *Lobophora halterata*
Clouded Border *Lomaspilis marginata*
Bordered Beauty *Epione repandaria*
Feathered Thorn *Colotois pennaria*
Pale Brindled Beauty *Apocheima pilosaria*

**Sphingidae**
Eyed Hawk-moth *Smerinthus ocellata*
Poplar Hawk-moth *Laothoe populi*

**Notodontidae**
Puss Moth *Cerura vinula*
Sallow Kitten *Furcula furcula*
Poplar Kitten *Furcula bifida*
†Large Dark Prominent *Notodonta torva*

Pebble Prominent *Eligmodonta ziczac*
Swallow Prominent *Pheosia tremula*
Coxcomb Prominent *Ptilodon capucina*
Pale Prominent *Pterostoma palpina*
Chocolate-tip *Clostera curtula*

**Lymantriidae**
White Satin *Leucoma salicis*
†Black V Moth *Arctornis l-nigrum*
*Gypsy Moth *Lymantria dispar*

**Noctuidae**
Twin-spotted Quaker *Orthosia munda*
Satellite *Eupsilia transversa*
Brick *Agrochola circellaris*
Sallow *Xanthia icteritia*
Pale-lemon Sallow *Xanthia ocellaris*
Poplar Grey *Acronicta megacephala*
Miller *Acronicta leporina*
Red Underwing *Catocala nupta*
Herald *Scoliopteryx libatrix*

**BIRCH** *Betula* **Pl. 4**

**Cossidae**
Goat Moth *Cossus cossus*

**Lycaenidae**
†Brown Hairstreak *Thecla betulae*

**Nymphalidae**
Large Tortoiseshell *Nymphalis polychloros*
Camberwell Beauty *Nymphalis antiopa*

**Lasiocampidae**
December Moth *Poecilocampa populi*
Pale Eggar *Trichiura crataegi*
Small Eggar *Eriogaster lanestris*

**Saturniidae**
*Tau Emperor *Aglia tau*
Emperor Moth *Pavonia Pavonia*

**Endromidae**
Kentish Glory *Endromis versicolora*

**Drepanidae**
Scalloped Hook-tip *Falcaria lacertinaria*
Pebble Hook-tip *Drepana falcataria*

**Thyatiridae**
Common Lutestring *Ochropacha duplaris*
Yellow Horned *Achlya flavicornis*

**Geometridae**
Large Emerald *Geometra papilionaria*
Common Emerald *Hemithea aestivaria*
Little Emerald *Jodis lactearia*
†Mocha *Cyclophora annulata*
Birch Mocha *Cyclophora albipunctata*
Dark Marbled Carpet *Chloroclysta citrata*
Common Marbled Carpet *Chloroclysta truncata*
November Moth *Epirrita dilutata*
Winter Moth *Operophtera brumata*
Northern Winter Moth *Operophtera fagata*
Early Tooth-striped *Trichopteryx carpinata*
Peacock Moth *Semiothisa notata*
Netted Mountain Carpet *Semiothisa carbonaria*
Scorched Wing *Plagodis dolabraria*
Large Thorn *Ennomos autumnaria*
August Thorn *Ennomos quercinaria*
Canary-shouldered Thorn *Ennomos alniaria*
September Thorn *Ennomos erosaria*
Early Thorn *Selenia dentaria*
Lunar Thorn *Selenia lunularia*
Scalloped Hazel *Odontopera bidentata*
Feathered Thorn *Colotois pennaria*
Orange Moth *Angerona prunaria*
Pale Brindled Beauty *Apocheima pilosaria*
Oak Beauty *Biston strataria*
Peppered Moth *Biston betularia*
Scarce Umber *Agriopis aurantiaria*
Dotted Border *Agriopis marginaria*
Mottled Umber *Erannis defoliaria*
Willow Beauty *Peribatodes rhomboidaria*
Mottled Beauty *Alcis repandata*
Great Oak Beauty *Hypomecis roboraria*
Pale Oak Beauty *Serraca punctinalis*
Light Emerald *Campaea margaritata*

**Sphingidae**
Lime Hawk-moth *Mimas tiliae*
†Eyed Hawk-moth *Smerinthus ocellata*
†Poplar Hawk-moth *Laothoe populi*

**Notodontidae**
Alder Kitten *Furcula bicuspis*
†Sallow Kitten *Furcula furcula*
†Poplar Kitten *Furcula bifida*
Lobster *Stauropus fagi*
Iron Prominent *Notodonta dromedarius*
†Large Dark Prominent *Notodonta torva*
†Pebble Prominent *Eligmodonta ziczac*
*Tawny Prominent *Harpyia milhauseri*
Lesser Swallow Prominent *Pheosia gnoma*
†Swallow Prominent *Pheosia tremula*
Coxcomb Prominent *Ptilodon capucina*

**Lymantriidae**
Dark Tussock *Dicallomera fascelina*
Pale Tussock *Calliteara pudibunda*

**Noctuidae**
Broad-bordered Yellow Underwing *Noctua fimbriata*
Ingrailed Clay *Diarsia mendica*
Purple Clay *Diarsia brunnea*
Double Square-spot *Xestia triangulum*
Grey Arches *Polia nebulosa*
Cabbage Moth *Mamestra brassicae*
Beautiful Brocade *Lacanobia contigua*
Pine Beauty *Panolis flammea*
Northern Drab *Orthosia opima*
Satellite *Eupsilia transversa*
Chestnut *Conistra vaccinii*
Miller *Acronicta leporina*
Alder Moth *Acronicta alni*
Grey Dagger *Acronicta psi*
Light Knot Grass *Acronicta menyanthidis*
Scarce Dagger *Acronicta auricoma*
Sweet Gale Moth *Acronicta euphorbiae*
Old Lady *Mormo maura*
Small Angle Shades *Euplexia lucipara*
Angle Shades *Phlogophora meticulosa*
Dun-bar *Cosmia trapezina*
Green Silver-lines *Pseudoips fagana*
Nut-tree Tussock *Colocasia coryli*

## ALDER *Alnus* Pl. 5

**Endromidae**
Kentish Glory *Endromis versicolora*

**Drepanidae**
†Oak Hook-tip *Drepana binaria*
Pebble Hook-tip *Drepana falcataria*

**Thyatiridae**
Common Lutestring *Ochropacha duplaris*

**Geometridae**
Large Emerald *Geometra papilionaria*
Little Emerald *Jodis lactearia*
Early Tooth-striped *Trichopteryx carpinata*
Sharp-angled Peacock *Semiothisa alternaria*
Bordered Beauty *Epione repandaria*
Large Thorn *Ennomos autumnaria*
Canary-shouldered Thorn *Ennomos alniaria*
Early Thorn *Selenia dentaria*
Purple Thorn *Selenia tetralunaria*

**Sphingidae**
Lime Hawk-moth *Mimas tiliae*

**Notodontidae**
Alder Kitten *Furcula bicuspis*
Iron Prominent *Notodonta dromedarius*

**Noctuidae**
Dark Brocade *Mniotype adusta*
Miller *Acronicta leporina*
Alder Moth *Acronicta alni*
Grey Dagger *Acronicta psi*

## HAZEL *Corylus* Pl. 5

**Lasiocampidae**
Pale Eggar *Trichiura crataegi*

**Thyatiridae**
†Common Lutestring *Ochropacha duplaris*

**Geometridae**
Large Emerald *Geometra papilionaria*
July Highflyer *Hydriomena furcata*
Winter Moth *Operophtera brumata*
Clouded Border *Lomaspilis marginata*
Mottled Umber *Erannis defoliaria*
Mottled Beauty *Alcis repandata*

**Sphingidae**
†Eyed Hawk-moth *Smerinthus ocellata*

**Notodontidae**
Buff-tip *Phalera bucephala*
Lobster *Stauropus fagi*
Iron Prominent *Notodonta dromedarius*
Coxcomb Prominent *Ptilodon capucina*

**Noctuidae**
Lesser Broad-bordered Yellow Underwing *Noctua janthina*
Triple-spotted Clay *Xestia ditrapezium*
Double Square-spot *Xestia triangulum*
Beautiful Brocade *Lacanobia contigua*
Small Quaker *Orthosia cruda*
Green Silver-lines *Pseudoips fagana*
Nut-tree Tussock *Colocasia coryli*

## OAK *Quercus* Pl. 6

**Cossidae**
Leopard Moth *Zeuzera pyrina*

**Limacodidae**
Festoon *Apoda limacodes*
Triangle *Heterogenea asella*

**Lycaenidae**
Purple Hairstreak *Quercusia quercus*

**Lasiocampidae**
December Moth *Poecilocampa populi*
Pale Eggar *Trichiura crataegi*
Oak Eggar *Lasiocampa quercus*

**Saturniidae**
*Tau Emperor *Aglia tau*

**Drepanidae**
Oak Hook-tip *Drepana binaria*

**Thyatiridae**
Common Lutestring *Ochropacha duplaris*
Frosted Green *Polyploca ridens*

**Geometridae**
Common Emerald *Hemithea aestivaria*
Little Emerald *Jodis lactearia*
November Moth *Epirrita dilutata*
Winter Moth *Operophtera brumata*
Scorched Wing *Plagodis dolabraria*
August Thorn *Ennomos quercinaria*
September Thorn *Ennomos erosaria*
Lunar Thorn *Selenia lunularia*
Purple Thorn *Selenia tetralunaria*
Scalloped Hazel *Odontopera bidentata*
Scalloped Oak *Crocallis elinguaria*
Feathered Thorn *Colotois pennaria*
Pale Brindled Beauty *Apocheima pilosaria*
Oak Beauty *Biston strataria*
Peppered Moth *Biston betularia*
Scarce Umber *Agriopis aurantiaria*
Dotted Border *Agriopis marginaria*
Mottled Umber *Erannis defoliaria*
Great Oak Beauty *Hypomecis roboraria*
Pale Oak Beauty *Serraca punctinalis*
Light Emerald *Campaea margaritata*

**Sphingidae**
†Lime Hawk-moth *Mimas tiliae*

**Notodontidae**
Buff-tip *Phalera bucephala*
Lobster *Stauropus fagi*
Iron Prominent *Notodonta dromedarius*
†Pebble Prominent *Eligmodonta ziczac*
*Tawny Prominent *Harpyia milhauseri*
Great Prominent *Peridea anceps*

**Thaumetopoeidae**
*Oak Processionary *Thaumetopoea processionea*

**Lymantriidae**
Scarce Vapourer *Orgyia recens*
Pale Tussock *Calliteara pudibunda*
Yellow-tail *Euproctis similis*
Black Arches *Lymantria monacha*
*Gypsy Moth *Lymantria dispar*

**Nolidae**
Least Black Arches *Nola confusalis*

**Noctuidae**
Cabbage Moth *Mamestra brassicae*
Beautiful Brocade *Lacanobia contigua*
Pine Beauty *Panolis flammea*
Small Quaker *Orthosia cruda*
Blossom Underwing *Orthosia*
Common Quaker *Orthosia cerasi fabricius*
Clouded Drab *Orthosia incerta*
Twin-spotted Quaker *Orthosia munda*
Hebrew Character *Orthosia gothica*
Sprawler *Brachionycha sphinx*
Merveille du Jour *Dichonia aprilina*
Satellite *Eupsilia transversa*
Chestnut *Conistra vaccinii*
Dotted Chestnut *Conistra rubiginea*
Brown-spot Pinion *Agrochola litura*
Sycamore *Acronicta aceris*
Miller *Acronicta leporina*
Alder Moth *Acronicta alni*
Scarce Dagger *Acronicta auricoma*
Copper Underwing *Amphipyra pyramidea*
Svensson's Copper Underwing *Amphipyra berbera*
Angle Shades *Phlogophora meticulosa*
Dun-bar *Cosmia trapezina*
Green Silver-lines *Pseudoips fagana*
Oak Nycteoline *Nycteola revayana*

## BEECH *Fagus* Pl. 7

**Limacodidae**
Festoon *Apoda limacodes*
Triangle *Heterogenea asella*

**Lycaenidae**
†Brown Hairstreak *Thecla betulae*

**Saturniidae**
*Tau Emperor *Aglia tau*

**Drepanidae**
†Oak Hook-tip *Drepana binaria*
Barred Hook-tip *Drepana cultraria*

**Geometridae**
Large Emerald *Geometra papilionaria*
Northern Winter Moth *Operophtera fagata*
Clouded Magpie *Abraxas sylvata*
September Thorn *Ennomos erosaria*
Peppered Moth *Biston betularia*
Light Emerald *Campaea margaritata*

**Notodontidae**
Lobster *Stauropus fagi*
*Tawny Prominent *Harpyia milhauseri*

**Nolidae**
Least Black Arches *Nola confusalis*

**Noctuidae**
Sprawler *Brachionycha sphinx*
Satellite *Eupsilia transversa*
Barred Sallow *Xanthia aurago*
Green Silver-lines *Pseudoips fagana*
Nut-tree Tussock *Colocasia coryli*

## ELM *Ulmus* **Pl. 7**

**Cossidae**
Leopard Moth *Zeuzera pyrina*
Goat Moth *Cossus cossus*

**Lycaenidae**
White Letter Hairstreak *Strymonidia w-album*

**Nymphalidae**
Large Tortoiseshell *Nymphalis polychloros*
Camberwell Beauty *Nymphalis antiopa*
Comma *Polygonia c-album*

**Geometridae**
November Moth *Epirrita dilutata*
Clouded Magpie *Abraxas sylvata*
Canary-shouldered Thorn *Ennomos alniaria*
Pale Brindled Beauty *Apocheima pilosaria*
Brindled Beauty *Lycia hirtaria*
Oak Beauty *Biston strataria*
Peppered Moth *Biston betularia*
Mottled Beauty *Alcis repandata*
Light Emerald *Campaea margaritata*

**Sphingidae**
Lime Hawk-moth *Mimas tiliae*

**Notodontidae**
Buff-tip *Phalera bucephala*

**Lymantriidae**
Pale Tussock *Calliteara pudibunda*
†Black V Moth *Arctornis l-nigrum*

**Noctuidae**
Lesser Broad-bordered Yellow Underwing *Noctua janthina*
Common Quaker *Orthosia cerasi fabricius*
Twin-spotted Quaker *Orthosia munda*
Satellite *Eupsilia transversa*
Chestnut *Conistra vaccinii*
Brick *Agrochola circellaris*
Dun-bar *Cosmia trapezina*

## LIME *Tilia* **Pl. 8**

**Lycaenidae**
†White Letter Hairstreak *Strymonidia w-album*

**Saturniidae**
*Tau Emperor *Aglia tau*

**Drepanidae**
Scarce Hook-tip *Sabra harpagula*

**Geometridae**
August Thorn *Ennomos quercinaria*
Canary-shouldered Thorn *Ennomos alniaria*
September Thorn *Ennomos erosaria*
Pale Brindled Beauty *Apocheima pilosaria*
Brindled Beauty *Lycia hirtaria*
Peppered Moth *Biston betularia*

**Sphingidae**
Lime Hawk-moth *Mimas tiliae*

**Notodontidae**
Buff-tip *Phalera bucephala*

**Lymantriidae**
†Black V Moth *Arctornis l-nigrum*

**Noctuidae**
Sprawler *Brachionycha sphinx*
Orange Sallow *Xanthia citrago*
Grey Dagger *Acronicta psi*
Svensson's Copper Underwing *Amphipyra berbera*

## ASH *Fraxinus* **Pl. 8**

**Cossidae**
Leopard Moth *Zeuzera pyrina*
Goat Moth *Cossus cossus*

**Brahmaeidae**
*Hartig's Brahmaea *Acanthobrahmaea europaea*

**Geometridae**
Ash Pug *Eupithecia fraxinata*
Dusky Thorn *Ennomos fuscantaria*
Lunar Thorn *Selenia lunularia*
Feathered Thorn *Colotois pennaria*
Brindled Beauty *Lycia hirtaria*

**Sphingidae**
Privet Hawk-moth *Sphinx ligustri*
†Poplar Hawk-moth *Laothoe populi*

**Noctuidae**
Sprawler *Brachionycha sphinx*
Tawny Pinion *Lithophane semibrunnea*
Flame Brocade *Trigonophora flammea*
Brick *Agrochola circellaris*
Centre-barred Sallow *Atethmia centrago*
Copper Underwing *Amphipyra pyramidea*

## NETTLE *Urtica* Pl. 9

**Nymphalidae**
Red Admiral *Vanessa atalanta*
Painted Lady *Cynthia cardui*
Small Tortoiseshell *Aglais urticae*
Peacock *Inachis io*
Comma *Polygonia c-album*
*European Map *Araschnia levana*

**Arctiidae**
Cream-spot Tiger *Arctia villica*
Scarlet Tiger *Callimorpha dominula*

**Noctuidae**
Dot Moth *Melanchra persicariae*
Bright-line Brown-eye *Lacanobia oleracea*
Angle Shades *Phlogophora meticulosa*
Mottled Rustic *Caradrina morpheus*
Burnished Brass *Diachrysia chrysitis*
Silver Y *Autographa gamma*
Plain Golden Y *Autographa jota*
Gold Spangle *Autographa bractea*
Dark Spectacle *Abrostola trigemina*
Spectacle *Abrostola triplasia*
Snout *Hypena proboscidalis*

## KNOTGRASS *Polygonum* Pl. 9

**Geometridae**
Blood-vein *Timandra griseata*
Tawny Wave *Scopula rubiginata*
Small Fan-footed Wave *Idaea biselata*
Riband Wave *Idaea aversata*
Vestal *Rhodometra sacraria*
Gem *Orthonama obstipata*
Straw Belle *Aspitates gilvaria*

**Noctuidae**
Heart and Dart *Agrotis exclamationis*
Shuttle-shaped Dart *Agrotis puta*
Flame *Axylia putris*
Ingrailed Clay *Diarsia mendica*
Green Arches *Anaplectoides prasina*
Nutmeg *Discestra trifolii*
Beautiful Brocade *Lacanobia contigua*
Light Brocade *Lacanobia w-latinum*
Red Sword-grass *Xylena vetusta*
Dark Brocade *Mniotype adusta*
Bird's Wing *Dypterygia scabriuscula*
Orache Moth *Trachea atriplicis*
Mottled Rustic *Caradrina morpheus*

## DOCK and SORREL *Rumex* Pl. 10

**Zygaenidae**
Forester *Adscita statices*

**Sesiidae**
Fiery Clearwing *Bembecia chrysidiformis*

**Lycaenidae**
Small Copper *Lycaena phlaeas*
*Large Copper *Lycaena dispar*

**Geometridae**
Common Emerald *Hemithea aestivaria*
Blood-vein *Timandra griseata*
Riband Wave *Idaea aversata*
Plain Wave *Idaea straminata*
Gem *Orthonama obstipata*
Yellow Shell *Camptogramma bilineata*

**Arctiidae**
Garden Tiger *Arctia caja*
Clouded Buff *Diacrisia sannio*
Muslin Moth *Diaphora mendica*
Ruby Tiger *Phragmatobia fuliginosa*
Scarlet Tiger *Callimorpha dominula*

**Noctuidae**
Garden Dart *Euxoa nigricans*
Turnip Moth *Agrotis segetum*
Heart and Dart *Agrotis exclamationis*
Shuttle-shaped Dart *Agrotis puta*
Flame *Axylia putris*
Plain Clay *Eugnorisma depuncta*
Large Yellow Underwing *Noctua pronuba*
Lesser Yellow Underwing *Noctua comes*
Broad-bordered Yellow Underwing *Noctua fimbriata*
Lesser Broad-bordered Yellow Underwing *Noctua janthina*
Stout Dart *Spaelotis ravida*
Pearly Underwing *Peridroma saucia*
Ingrailed Clay *Diarsia mendica*
Barred Chestnut *Diarsia dahlii*
Purple Clay *Diarsia brunnea*
Setaceous Hebrew Character *Xestia c-nigrum*
Triple-spotted Clay *Xestia ditrapezium*
Double Square-spot *Xestia triangulum*
Ashworth's Rustic *Xestia ashworthii*
Six-striped Rustic *Xestia sexstrigata*
Square-spot Rustic *Xestia xanthographa*

Gothic *Naenia typica*
Green Arches *Anaplectoides prasina*
Red Chestnut *Cerastis rubricosa*
Grey Arches *Polia nebulosa*
Beautiful Brocade *Lacanobia contigua*
Bright-line Brown-eye *Lacanobia oleracea*
Hebrew Character *Orthosia gothica*
Shoulder-striped Wainscot *Mythimna comma*
Black Rustic *Aporophyla nigra*
Brown-spot Pinion *Agrochola litura*
Beaded Chestnut *Agrochola lychnidis*
Knot Grass *Acronicta rumicis*
Bird's Wing *Dypterygia scabriuscula*
Angle Shades *Phlogophora meticulosa*
Rosy Rustic *Hydraecia micacea*
Rustic *Hoplodrina blanda*

## CHICKWEED *Stellaria* Pl. 11

**Geometridae**
Blood-vein *Timandra griseata*
Riband Wave *Idaea aversata*
Plain Wave *Idaea straminata*
Red Carpet *Xanthorhoe munitata*
Yellow Shell *Camptogramma bilineata*
Twin-spot Carpet *Perizoma didymata*

**Arctiidae**
Muslin Moth *Diaphora mendica*

**Noctuidae**
Archer's Dart *Agrotis vestigialis*
Heart and Dart *Agrotis exclamationis*
Large Yellow Underwing *Noctua pronuba*
Lesser Yellow Underwing *Noctua comes*
Lesser Broad-bordered Yellow Underwing *Noctua janthina*
Setaceous Hebrew Character *Xestia c-nigrum*
Triple-spotted Clay *Xestia ditrapezium*
Double Square-spot *Xestia triangulum*
Square-spot Rustic *Xestia xanthographa*
Red Chestnut *Cerastis rubricosa*
Clay *Mythimna ferrago*
Black Rustic *Aporophyla nigra*
Brown-spot Pinion *Agrochola litura*
Beaded Chestnut *Agrochola lychnidis*
Angle Shades *Phlogophora meticulosa*
Rustic *Hoplodrina blanda*
Mottled Rustic *Caradrina morpheus*

## ROSE *Rosa* Pl. 14

**Geometridae**
March Moth *Alsophila aescularia*
Common Emerald *Hemithea aestivaria*
Streamer *Anticlea derivata*
Shoulder Stripe *Anticlea badiata*
Barred Yellow *Cidaria fulvata*
Lunar Thorn *Selenia lunularia*
Pale Brindled Beauty *Apocheima pilosaria*
Brindled Beauty *Lycia hirtaria*
Oak Beauty *Biston strataria*
Peppered Moth *Biston betularia*
Mottled Umber *Erannis defoliaria*
Willow Beauty *Peribatodes rhomboidaria*

**Lymantriidae**
Vapourer *Orgyia antiqua*
Brown-tail *Euproctis chrysorrhoea*

**Arctiidae**
Buff Ermine *Spilosoma luteum*
Jersey Tiger *Euplagia quadripunctaria*

**Noctuidae**
Small Quaker *Orthosia cruda*
Northern Drab *Orthosia opima*
Brown-spot Pinion *Agrochola litura*
Dark Dagger *Acronicta tridens*
Grey Dagger *Acronicta psi*
Copper Underwing *Amphipyra pyramidea*
Angle Shades *Phlogophora meticulosa*

## BRAMBLE *Rubus* Pl. 15

**Hesperiidae**
Grizzled Skipper *Pyrgus malvae*

**Lycaenidae**
Green Hairstreak *Callophrys rubi*

**Nymphalidae**
*Violet Fritillary *Clossiana dia*

**Lasiocampidae**
Pale Eggar *Trichiura crataegi*
Grass Eggar *Lasiocampa trifolii*
Oak Eggar *Lasiocampa quercus*
Fox Moth *Macrothylacia rubi*

**Saturniidae**
Emperor Moth *Pavonia pavonia*

**Drepanidae**
Chinese Character *Cilix glaucata*

**Thyatiridae**
Peach Blossom *Thyatira batis*
Buff Arches *Habrosyne pyritoides*

**Geometridae**
Small Fan-footed Wave *Idaea biselata*

Plain Wave *Idaea straminata*
Beautiful Carpet *Mesoleuca albicillata*
Common Pug *Eupithecia vulgata*

**Lymantriidae**
Dark Tussock *Dicallomera fascelina*

**Arctiidae**
Scarlet Tiger *Callimorpha dominula*

**Noctuidae**
Lesser Broad-bordered Yellow Underwing *Noctua janthina*
Ingrailed Clay *Diarsia mendica*
Purple Clay *Diarsia brunnea*
Triple-spotted Clay *Xestia ditrapezium*
Double Square-spot *Xestia triangulum*
Six-striped Rustic *Xestia sexstrigata*
Green Arches *Anaplectoides prasina*
Grey Arches *Polia nebulosa*
Broom Moth *Ceramica pisi*
Blossom Underwing *Orthosia miniosa*
Brown-spot Pinion *Agrochola litura*
Scarce Dagger *Acronicta auricoma*
Sweet Gale Moth *Acronicta euphorbiae*
Knot Grass *Acronicta rumicis*
Angle Shades *Phlogophora meticulosa*
Saxon *Hyppa rectilinea*
Rosy Marbled *Elaphria venustula*

## APPLE *Malus* Pl. 16

**Cossidae**
Leopard Moth *Zeuzera pyrina*

**Sesiidae**
Red-belted Clearwing *Synanthedon myopaeformis*

**Pieridae**
*Black-veined White *Aporia crataegi*

**Lasiocampidae**
Lackey *Malacosoma neustria*
Lappet *Gastropacha quercifolia*

**Saturniidae**
*Great Peacock *Saturnia pyri*

**Drepanidae**
Chinese Character *Cilix glaucata*

**Geometridae**
March Moth *Alsophila aescularia*
Winter Moth *Operophtera brumata*
Northern Winter Moth *Operophtera fagata*
Green Pug *Chloroclystis rectangulata*
Brimstone Moth *Opisthograptis luteolata*
Scalloped Oak *Crocallis elinguaria*
Brindled Beauty *Lycia hirtaria*
Peppered Moth *Biston betularia*

**Sphingidae**
Eyed Hawk-moth *Smerinthus ocellata*
†Poplar Hawk-moth *Laothoe populi*

**Dilobidae**
Figure of Eight *Diloba caeruleocephala*

**Arctiidae**
*Fall Webworm *Hyphantria cunea*

**Nolidae**
Short-cloaked Moth *Nola cucullatella*
Least Black Arches *Nola confusalis*

**Noctuidae**
Gothic *Naenia typica*
Clouded Drab *Orthosia incerta*
Dotted Chestnut *Conistra rubiginea*
Dark Dagger *Acronicta tridens*
Grey Dagger *Acronicta psi*

## HAWTHORN *Crataegus* Pl. 17

**Cossidae**
Leopard Moth *Zeuzera pyrina*

**Sesiidae**
Red-belted Clearwing *Synanthedon myopaeformis*

**Papilionidae**
*Scarce Swallowtail *Iphiclides podalirius*

**Pieridae**
*Black-veined White *Aporia crataegi*

**Lasiocampidae**
December Moth *Poecilocampa populi*
Pale Eggar *Trichiura crataegi*
Small Eggar *Eriogaster lanestris*
Lackey *Malacosoma neustria*
Oak Eggar *Lasiocampa quercus*
Lappet *Gastropacha quercifolia*

**Saturniidae**
Emperor Moth *Pavonia pavonia*

**Drepanidae**
Chinese Character *Cilix glaucata*

**Geometridae**
March Moth *Alsophila aescularia*

Common Emerald *Hemithea aestivaria*
Little Emerald *Jodis lactearia*
Common Marbled Carpet *Chloroclysta truncata*
November Moth *Epirrita dilutata*
Winter Moth *Operophtera brumata*
Northern Winter Moth *Operophtera fagata*
Common Pug *Eupithecia vulgata*
Double-striped Pug *Gymnoscelis rufifasciata*
Magpie Moth *Abraxas grossulariata*
Brimstone Moth *Opisthograptis luteolata*
Large Thorn *Ennomos autumnaria*
August Thorn *Ennomos quercinaria*
Early Thorn *Selenia dentaria*
Scalloped Hazel *Odontopera bidentata*
Swallow-tailed Moth *Ourapteryx sambucaria*
Feathered Thorn *Colotois pennaria*
Orange Moth *Angerona prunaria*
Pale Brindled Beauty *Apocheima pilosaria*
Scarce Umber *Agriopis aurantiaria*
Dotted Border *Agriopis marginaria*
Mottled Umber *Erannis defoliaria*
Willow Beauty *Peribatodes rhomboidaria*
Mottled Beauty *Alcis repandata*
Early Moth *Theria primaria*
Light Emerald *Campaea margaritata*

**Dilobidae**
Figure of Eight *Diloba caeruleocephala*

**Lymantriidae**
Scarce Vapourer *Orgyia recens*
Dark Tussock *Dicallomera fascelina*
Brown-tail *Euproctis chrysorrhoea*
Yellow-tail *Euproctis similis*

**Nolidae**
Short-cloaked Moth *Nola cucullatella*

**Noctuidae**
Lesser Yellow Underwing *Noctua comes*
Broad-bordered Yellow Underwing *Noctua fimbriata*
Lesser Broad-bordered Yellow Underwing *Noctua janthina*
Double Square-spot *Xestia triangulum*
Square-spot Rustic *Xestia xanthographa*
Gothic *Naenia typica*
Grey Arches *Polia nebulosa*
Small Quaker *Orthosia cruda*
Blossom Underwing *Orthosia miniosa*
Hebrew Character *Orthosia gothica*
Sprawler *Brachionycha sphinx*
Black Rustic *Aporophyla nigra*
Green-brindled Crescent *Allophyes oxyacanthae*
Dark Brocade *Mniotype adusta*
Beaded Chestnut *Agrochola lychnidis*
Alder Moth *Acronicta alni*
Dark Dagger *Acronicta tridens*
Grey Dagger *Acronicta psi*
Knotgrass *Acronicta rumicis*
Old Lady *Mormo maura*
Dun-bar *Cosmia trapezina*

## BLACKTHORN *Prunus spinosa* Pl. 18

**Papilionidae**
*Scarce Swallowtail *Iphiclides podalirius*

**Pieridae**
*Black-veined White *Aporia crataegi*

**Lycaenidae**
Brown Hairstreak *Thecla betulae*
Black Hairstreak *Strymonidia pruni*

**Lasiocampidae**
Pale Eggar *Trichiura crataegi*
Small Eggar *Eriogaster lanestris*
Lackey *Malacosoma neustria*
Lappet *Gastropacha quercifolia*

**Saturniidae**
Emperor Moth *Pavonia pavonia*

**Drepanidae**
Chinese Character *Cilix glaucata*

**Geometridae**
Common Emerald *Hemithea aestivaria*
Little Emerald *Jodis lactearia*
November Moth *Epirrita dilutata*
Winter Moth *Operophtera brumata*
Green Pug *Chloroclystis rectangulata*
Magpie Moth *Abraxas grossulariata*
Sharp-angled Peacock *Semiothisa alternaria*
Brimstone Moth *Opisthograptis luteolata*
Large Thorn *Ennomos autumnaria*
Early Thorn *Selenia dentaria*
Lunar Thorn *Selenia lunularia*
Scalloped Hazel *Odontopera bidentata*
Scalloped Oak *Crocallis elinguaria*
Swallow-tailed Moth *Ourapteryx sambucaria*
Feathered Thorn *Colotois pennaria*
Orange Moth *Angerona prunaria*
Pale Brindled Beauty *Apocheima pilosaria*
Oak Beauty *Biston strataria*
Scarce Umber *Agriopis aurantiaria*
Dotted Border *Agriopis marginaria*
Mottled Umber *Erannis defoliaria*
Clouded Silver *Lomographa temerata*

Sloe Carpet *Aleucis distinctata*
Early Moth *Theria primaria*
Light Emerald *Campaea margaritata*

**Dilobidae**
Figure of Eight *Diloba caeruleocephala*

**Lymantriidae**
Brown-tail *Euproctis chrysorrhoea*
Yellow-tail *Euproctis similis*

**Arctiidae**
*Fall Webworm *Hyphantria cunea*
Scarlet Tiger *Callimorpha dominula*

**Nolidae**
Short-cloaked Moth *Nola cucullatella*
Least Black Arches *Nola confusalis*

**Noctuidae**
Broad-bordered Yellow Underwing *Noctua fimbriata*
Lesser Broad-bordered Yellow Underwing *Noctua janthina*
Double Square-spot *Xestia triangulum*
Gothic *Naenia typica*
Blossom Underwing *Orthosia miniosa*
Twin-spotted Quaker *Orthosia munda*
Green-brindled Crescent *Allophyes oxyacanthae*
Flame Brocade *Trigonophora flammea*
Dotted Chestnut *Conistra rubiginea*
Dark Dagger *Acronicta tridens*
Grey Dagger *Acronicta psi*
Old Lady *Mormo maura*

## BROOM *Cytisus* Pl. 19

**Heterogynidae**
**Heterogynis penella*

**Lycaenidae**
Green Hairstreak *Callophrys rubi*
Silver-studded Blue *Plebejus argus*

**Lasiocampidae**
Grass Eggar *Lasiocampa trifolii*

**Geometridae**
Grass Emerald *Pseudoterpna pruinata*
Large Emerald *Geometra papilionaria*
Lead Belle *Scotopteryx mucronata*
Double-striped Pug *Gymnoscelis rufifasciata*
Streak *Chesias legatella*
Broom-tip *Chesias rufata*
Frosted Yellow *Isturgia limbaria*
Orange Moth *Angerona prunaria*
Scotch Annulet *Gnophos obfuscata*

**Lymantriidae**
**Gynaephora selenitica*
Dark Tussock *Dicallomera fascelina*

**Arctiidae**
**Rhyparia purpurata*

**Noctuidae**
Lesser Yellow Underwing *Noctua comes*
Light Brocade *Lacanobia w-latinum*
Broom Moth *Ceramica pisi*
Flame Brocade *Trigonophora flammea*
Rosy Marbled *Elaphria venustula*
**Apopestes spectrum*

## CLOVER *Trifolium* Pl. 21

**Zygaenidae**
Narrow-bordered Five-spot Burnet *Zygaena lonicerae*

**Pieridae**
Clouded Yellow *Colias croceus*

**Lycaenidae**
Common Blue *Polyommatus icarus*
*Mazarine Blue *Cyaniris semiargus*

**Geometridae**
Tawny Wave *Scopula rubiginata*
Chalk Carpet *Scotopteryx bipunctaria*
Shaded Broad-bar *Scotopteryx chenopodiata*
Latticed Heath *Semiothisa clathrata*
**Apocheima alpina*

**Noctuidae**
Garden Dart *Euxoa nigricans*
Pearly Underwing *Peridroma saucia*
Hebrew Character *Orthosia gothica*
Marbled Clover *Heliothis viriplaca*
Silver Y *Autographa gamma*
Mother Shipton *Callistege mi*
Burnet Companion *Euclidia glyphica*

## HEATHER *Calluna* and *Erica* Pl. 24

**Lycaenidae**
Silver-studded Blue *Plebejus argus*

**Lasiocampidae**
Pale Eggar *Trichiura crataegi*
Oak Eggar *Lasiocampa quercus*
Fox Moth *Macrothylacia rubi*

**Saturniidae**
Emperor Moth *Saturnia pavonia*

**Geometridae**
Weaver's Wave *Idaea contiguaria*
Dark Marbled Carpet *Chloroclysta citrata*
Common Marbled Carpet *Chloroclysta truncata*
July Highflyer *Hydriomena furcata*
Small Autumnal Moth *Epirrita filigrammaria*
Winter Moth *Operophtera brumata*
Ling Pug *Eupithecia goossensiata*
Double-striped Pug *Gymnoscelis rufifasciata*
Magpie Moth *Abraxas grossulariata*
Mottled Beauty *Alcis repandata*
Common Heath *Ematurga atomaria*
Scotch Annulet *Gnophos obfuscatus*
Annulet *Gnophos obscuratus*

**Lymantriidae**
Dark Tussock *Dicallomera fascelina*

**Arctiidae**
Clouded Buff *Diacrisia sannio*

**Noctuidae**
Lesser Yellow Underwing *Noctua comes*
†Rosy Marsh Moth *Eugraphe subrosea*
True Lover's Knot *Lycophotia porphyrea*
Ingrailed Clay *Diarsia mendica*
Northern Dart *Xestia alpicola*
Heath Rustic *Xestia agathina*
Beautiful Yellow Underwing *Anarta myrtilli*
Black Rustic *Aporophyla nigra*
Light Knot Grass *Acronicta menyanthidis*
Sweet Gale Moth *Acronicta euphorbiae*

## BILBERRY *Vaccinium* Pl. 25

**Zygaenidae**
Scotch Burnet *Zygaena exulans*

**Pieridae**
*Moorland Clouded Yellow *Colias palaeno*

**Lycaenidae**
Green Hairstreak *Callophrys rubi*

**Nymphalidae**
†Small Pearl-bordered Fritillary *Clossiana selene*

**Lasiocampidae**
Pale Eggar *Trichiura crataegi*
Oak Eggar *Lasiocampa quercus*
Fox Moth *Macrothylacia rubi*
Small Lappet *Phyllodesma ilicifolia*

**Saturniidae**
Emperor Moth *Pavonia pavonia*

**Geometridae**
Little Emerald *Jodis lactearia*
Plain Wave *Idaea straminata*
Northern Spinach *Eulithis populata*
Dark Marbled Carpet *Chloroclysta citrata*
Common Marbled Carpet *Chloroclysta truncata*
July Highflyer *Hydriomena furcata*
Small Autumnal Moth *Epirrita filigrammaria*
Twin-spot Carpet *Perizoma didymata*
Common Pug *Eupithecia vulgata*
Bilberry Pug *Chloroclystis debiliata*
Mottled Beauty *Alcis repandata*
Early Moth *Theria primaria*

**Noctuidae**
†Rosy Marsh Moth *Eugraphe subrosea*
Ingrailed Clay *Diarsia mendica*
Purple Clay *Diarsia brunnea*
Northern Dart *Xestia alpicola*
Setaceous Hebrew Character *Xestia c-nigrum*
Green Arches *Anaplectoides prasina*
Broad-bordered White Underwing *Anarta melanopa*
Light Knot Grass *Acronicta menyanthidis*
Scarce Dagger *Acronicta auricoma*

## PRIVET *Ligustrum* Pl. 26

**Geometridae**
March Moth *Alsophila aescularia*
Yellow-barred Brindle *Acasis viretata*
Lilac Beauty *Apeira syringaria*
Scalloped Oak *Crocallis elinguaria*
Swallow-tailed Moth *Ourapteryx sambucaria*
Orange Moth *Angerona prunaria*
Brindled Beauty *Lycia hirtaria*
Waved Umber *Menophra abruptaria*
Willow Beauty *Peribatodes rhomboidaria*

**Sphingidae**
Privet Hawk-moth *Sphinx ligustri*

**Noctuidae**
Flame Brocade *Trigonophora flammea*

## PLANTAIN *Plantago* Pl. 27

**Hepialidae**
Common Swift *Hepialus lupulinus*

**Nymphalidae**
†Marsh Fritillary *Eurodryas aurinia*
*False Heath Fritillary *Melitaea diamina*
*Spotted Fritillary *Melitaea didyma*
*Knapweed Fritillary *Melitaea phoebe*
Glanville Fritillary *Melitaea cinxia*
Heath Fritillary *Mellicta athalia*

**Geometridae**
Sub-angled Wave *Scopula nigropunctata*

**Arctiidae**
Wood Tiger *Parasemia plantaginis*
Muslin Moth *Diaphora mendica*

**Ctenuchidae**
*Nine-spotted *Syntomis phegea*

**Noctuidae**
Garden Dart *Euxoa nigricans*
Heart and Dart *Agrotis exclamationis*
Flame *Axylia putris*
Pearly Underwing *Peridroma saucia*
Barred Chestnut *Diarsia dahlii*
Setaceous Hebrew Character *Xestia c-nigrum*
Six-striped Rustic *Xestia sexstrigata*
Square-spot Rustic *Xestia xanthographa*
Dot Moth *Melanchra persicariae*
Clay *Mythimna ferrago*
Black Rustic *Aporophyla nigra*
Feathered Ranunculus *Eumichtis lichenea*
Sweet Gale Moth *Acronicta euphorbiae*
Knot Grass *Acronicta rumicis*
Small Angle Shades *Euplexia lucipara*
Rosy Rustic *Hydraecia micacea*
Rustic *Hoplodrina blanda*

## HONEYSUCKLE *Lonicera* Pl. 28

**Nymphalidae**
White Admiral *Ladoga camilla*

**Geometridae**
Streamer *Anticlea derivata*
Early Tooth-striped *Trichopteryx carpinata*
Lilac Beauty *Apeira syringaria*
Scalloped Oak *Crocallis elinguaria*
Orange Moth *Angerona prunaria*
Mottled Umber *Erannis defoliaria*
Mottled Beauty *Alcis repandata*

**Sphingidae**
Broad-bordered Bee Hawk-moth *Hemaris fuciformis*

**Arctiidae**
Buff Ermine *Spilosoma luteum*

**Noctuidae**
Twin-spotted Quaker *Orthosia munda*
Early Grey *Xylocampa areola*
Angle Shades *Phlogophora meticulosa*
Plain Golden Y *Autographa jota*
Gold Spangle *Autographa bractea*

## DANDELION *Taraxacum* Pl. 29

**Hepialidae**
Ghost Moth *Hepialus humuli*

**Geometridae**
Small Fan-footed Wave *Idaea biselata*
Riband Wave *Idaea aversata*
Plain Wave *Idaea straminata*
Yellow Shell *Camptogramma bilineata*
**Gnophos glaucinarius*

**Arctiidae**
Wood Tiger *Parasemia plantaginis*
Garden Tiger *Arctia caja*
Cream-spot Tiger *Arctia villica*
Clouded Buff *Diacrisia sannio*
White Ermine *Spilosoma lubricipeda*
Buff Ermine *Spilosoma lutea*
Muslin Moth *Diaphora mendica*
Ruby Tiger *Phragmatobia fuliginosa*
Jersey Tiger *Euplagia quadripunctaria*

**Ctenuchidae**
*Nine-spotted *Syntomis phegea*

**Noctuidae**
Shuttle-shaped Dart *Agrotis puta*
Large Yellow Underwing *Noctua pronuba*
Stout Dart *Spaelotis ravida*
Triple-spotted Clay *Xestia ditrapezium*
Gothic *Naenia typica*
Red Chestnut *Cerastis rubricosa*
Hebrew Character *Orthosia gothica*
Clay *Mythimna ferrago*
Beaded Chestnut *Agrochola lychnidis*
Mottled Rustic *Caradrina morpheus*
Gold Spangle *Autographa bractea*

## GRASSES Pls 31 & 32

### Hepialidae
Ghost Moth *Hepialus humuli*
Common Swift *Hepialus lupulinus*

### Hesperiidae
Chequered Skipper *Carterocephalus palaemon*
Small Skipper *Thymelicus sylvestris*
Lulworth Skipper *Thymelicus acteon*
Silver-spotted Skipper *Hesperia comma*
Large Skipper *Ochlodes venata*

### Satyridae
Speckled Wood *Pararge aegeria*
Wall *Lasiommata megera*
Mountain Ringlet *Erebia epiphron*
Scotch Argus *Erebia aethiops*
Marbled White *Melanargia galathea*
Grayling *Hipparchia semele*
*Woodland Grayling *Hipparchia fagi*
Gatekeeper *Pyronia tithonus*
Meadow Brown *Maniola jurtina*
Small Heath *Coenonympha pamphilus*
Large Heath *Coenonympha tullia*
Ringlet *Aphantopus hyperantus*

### Lasiocampidae
Grass Eggar *Lasiocampa trifolii*
Drinker *Philudoria potatoria*

### Geometridae
Shaded Broad-bar *Scotopteryx chenopodiata*
Yellow Shell *Camptogramma bilineata*

### Noctuidae
Northern Rustic *Standfussiana lucernea*
Large Yellow Underwing *Noctua pronuba*
Lesser Yellow Underwing *Noctua comes*
Square-spot Rustic *Xestia xanthographa*
Feathered Ear *Pachetra sagittigera*
Antler Moth *Cerapteryx graminis*
Clay *Mythimna ferrago*
Common Wainscot *Mythimna pallens*
Shoulder-striped Wainscot *Mythimna comma*
Black Rustic *Aporophyla nigra*
Red Sword-grass *Xylena vetusta*
Dark Brocade *Mniotype adusta*
Beaded Chestnut *Agrochola lychnidis*
Dark Arches *Apamea monoglypha*
Cloaked Minor *Mesoligia furuncula*
Common Rustic *Mesapamea secalis*
Flounced Rustic *Luperina testacea*
Haworth's Minor *Celaena haworthii*
Marbled White Spot *Protodeltote pygarga*

## SPECIES POLYPHAGOUS ON DECIDUOUS TREES AND SHRUBS

### Cossidae
Leopard Moth *Zeuzera pyrina*
Goat Moth *Cossus cossus*

### Lasiocampidae
December Moth *Poecilocampa populi*
†Small Eggar *Eriogaster lanestris*
Lackey *Malacosoma neustria*

### Geometridae
March Moth *Alsophila aescularia*
Common Emerald *Hemithea aestivaria*
November Moth *Epirrita dilutata*
Winter Moth *Operophtera brumata*
Common Pug *Eupithecia vulgata*
Double-striped Pug *Gymnoscelis rufifasciata*
Large Thorn *Ennomos autumnaria*
August Thorn *Ennomos quercinaria*
Canary-shouldered Thorn *Ennomos alniaria*
Early Thorn *Selenia dentaria*
Lunar Thorn *Selenia lunularia*
Purple Thorn *Selenia tetralunaria*
Scalloped Hazel *Odontopera bidentata*
Scalloped Oak *Crocallis elinguaria*
Swallow-tailed Moth *Ourapteryx sambucaria*
Feathered Thorn *Colotois pennaria*
Orange Moth *Angerona prunaria*
Pale Brindled Beauty *Apocheima pilosaria*
Brindled Beauty *Lycia hirtaria*
Oak Beauty *Biston strataria*
Peppered Moth *Biston betularia*
Scarce Umber *Agriopis aurantiaria*
Dotted Border *Agriopis marginaria*
Mottled Umber *Erannis defoliaria*
Willow Beauty *Peribatodes rhomboidaria*
Mottled Beauty *Alcis repandata*
†Pale Oak Beauty *Serraca punctinalis*
†Clouded Silver *Lomographa temerata*
Light Emerald *Campaea margaritata*

### Notodontidae
Buff-tip *Phalera bucephala*

### Lymantriidae
Vapourer *Orgyia antiqua*
Pale Tussock *Calliteara pudibunda*
†Black Arches *Lymantria monacha*
*Gypsy Moth *Lymantria dispar*

### Arctiidae
Garden Tiger *Arctia caja*
*Fall Webworm *Hyphantria cunea*
Buff Ermine *Spilosoma lutea*

**Noctuidae**
Broom Moth *Ceramica pisi*
Hebrew Character *Orthosia gothica*
Sprawler *Brachionycha sphinx*
Satellite *Eupsilia transversa*
Alder Moth *Acronicta alni*
Grey Dagger *Acronicta psi*
Dun-bar *Cosmia trapezina*

## SPECIES POLYPHAGOUS ON LOW-GROWING HERBACEOUS PLANTS

**Hepialidae**
Ghost Moth *Hepialus humuli*
Common Swift *Hepialus lupulinus*

**Geometridae**
Common Emerald *Hemithea aestivaria*
Plain Wave *Idaea straminata*
Gem *Orthonama obstipata*
Yellow Shell *Camptogramma bilineata*
Lime-speck Pug *Eupithecia centaureata*
Wormwood Pug *Eupithecia absinthiata*
Common Pug *Eupithecia vulgata*
V-Pug *Chloroclystis v-ata*
Double-striped Pug *Gymnoscelis rufifasciata*

**Arctiidae**
Garden Tiger *Arctia caja*
Cream-spot Tiger *Arctia villica*
**Rhyparia purpurata*
White Ermine *Spilosoma lubricipeda*
Buff Ermine *Spilosoma lutea*
Muslin Moth *Diaphora mendica*
Jersey Tiger *Euplagia quadripunctaria*

**Noctuidae**
Garden Dart *Euxoa nigricans*
Turnip Moth *Agrotis segetum*
Heart and Dart *Agrotis exclamationis*
Flame *Axylia putris*
Large Yellow Underwing *Noctua pronuba*
Lesser Broad-bordered Yellow Underwing *Noctua janthina*
Pearly Underwing *Peridroma saucia*
Gothic *Naenia typica*
Cabbage Moth *Mamestra brassicae*
Dot Moth *Melanchra persicariae*
Bright-line Brown-eye *Lacanobia oleracea*
Broom Moth *Ceramica pisi*
Hebrew Character *Orthosia gothica*
Red Sword-grass *Xylena vetusta*
Sword-grass *Xylena exsoleta*
Knot Grass *Acronicta rumicis*
Old Lady *Mormo maura*
Angle Shades *Phlogophora meticulosa*
Mottled Rustic *Caradrina morpheus*
†Scarce Bordered Straw *Heliothis armigera*
Silver Y *Autographa gamma*

# General Index

Figures in **bold** denote plate numbers


Abdomen, 11, 129
*abietaria Eupithecia*, 91, **1**
*abietis Dasychira*, 204, **1**
*Abraxas*, 100
*Abrostola*, 266
*abruptaria Menophra*, 111, **26**
*absinthiata Eupithecia*, 92, **28**
*absinthii Cucullia*, 237, **28**
*Acanthobrahmaea*, 67
*Acasis*, 99
*aceris Acronicta*, 249, **33**
*Acherontia*, 117
*Achlya*, 72
*Acronicta*, 248–52
*acteon Thymelicus*, 31, **32**
*adippe Argynnis*, 52, **23**
Adonis Blue, 46, **21**
*Adscita*, 25
*adusta Mniotype*, 243, **5**
*aegeria Pararge*, 57, **31**
*aescularia Alsophila*, 73, **16**
*aestivaria Hemithea*, 75, **14**
*aethiops Erebia*, 58, **31**
*agathina Xestia*, 225, **24**
*agestis Aricia*, 45, **23**
*Aglais*, 51
*aglaja Argynnis*, 54, **23**
*Aglia*, 65
*Agriopis*, 110
*Agriotes*, **34**
*Agrius*, 116
*Agrochola*, 245, 246
*Agrotis*, 215–17
*albicillata Mesoleuca*, 83, **15**
*albipunctata Cyclophora*, 76, **4**
*alceae Carcharodus*, 32, **22**
*Alcis*, 111
Alder Kitten, 123, **5**
Alder Moth, 249, **5**
*Aleucis*, 114
*alexanor Papilio*, 35, **24**
*algae Archanara*, 259, **30**
*Allophyes*, 243
*alni Acronicta*, 249, **5**
*alniaria Ennomos*, 104, **5**
*alpicola Xestia*, 222, **25**
*alpina Apocheima*, 108, **28**
*Alsophila*, 73
*alternaria Semiothisa*, 101, **18**
*Amphimallon*, **34**
*Amphipyra*, 252, 253
Anal claspers, 11, 129
*Anaplectoides*, 226
*Anarta*, 226, 227
*anceps Peridea*, 125, **33**
*Angerona*, 108
Angle Shades, 254, **22**
*annulata Cyclophora*, 76, **8**
Annulet, 115, **14**
Antennae, 11, 129
*Anthocharis*, 40
*Anticlea*, 83
*antiopa Nymphalis*, 51, **2**
*antiqua Orgyia*, 203, **14**
Antler Moth, 232, **31**
*Apamea*, 255
*Apanteles*, 14, 200
*Apatura*, 49, 50
*Apeira*, 103
*Aphantopus*, 60
*Apocheima*, 108
*Apoda*, 27
*apollinus Archon*, 34, **9**
Apollo, 33, **13**
*apollo Parnassius*, 33, **13**
*Apopestes*, 268
*Aporia*, 38
*Aporophyla*, 240

*aprilina Dichonia*, 243, **6**
*Araschnia*, 53
*Archanara*, 258, 259
Archer's Dart, 215, **26**
*Archiearis*, 73
*Archon*, 34
*Arctia*, 208, 209
Arctiidae, 207
*Arctornis*, 205
*areola Xylocampa*, 242, **28**
*Arge*, **34**
*argiades Everes*, 44, **21**
*argiolus Celastrina*, 47, **8**
*argus Plebejus*, 44, **19**
*Argynnis*, 54, 55
*Aricia*, 45
*arion Maculinea*, 47, **26**
*armigera Heliothis*, 261, **33**
*artaxerxes Aricia*, 45, **23**
*asella Heterogenea*, 28, **7**
Ash Pug, 98, **8**
Ashworth's Rustic, 224, **10**
*ashworthii Xestia*, 224, **10**
*Aspitates*, 115
*assimilata Eupithecia*, 93, **22**
*asteris Cucullia*, 238, **28**
*atalanta Vanessa*, 50, **9**
*aterrima Phymatocera*, **34**
*Atethmia*, 247
*athalia Mellicta*, 56, **27**
*atomaria Ematurga*, 113, **24**
*atriplicis Trachea*, 254, **11**
*atropos Acherontia*, 117, **27**
August Thorn, 104, **6**
*aurago Xanthia*, 247, **8**
*aurantiaria Agriopis*, 110, **4**
*auricoma Acronicta*, 250, **15**
*aurinia Eurodryas*, 55, **28**
*australis Colias*, 37, **19**
*Autographa*, 265, 266
*autumnaria Ennomos*, 104, **4**
*aversata Idaea*, 78, **16**
*Axylia*, 217

Bacteria, 15, 200
*badiata Anticlea*, 83, **14**
Barred Chestnut, 222, **10**
Barred Hook-tip, 69, **7**
Barred Sallow, 247, **8**
Barred Yellow, 85, **14**
Bath White, 39, **13**
*batis Thyatira*, 70, **15**
Beaded Chestnut, 246, **12**
Beating Tray, 17
Beautiful Brocade, 229, **5**
Beautiful Carpet, 83, **15**
Beautiful Hook-tip, 269, **32**
Beautiful Yellow Underwing, 226, **24**
Bedstraw Hawk-moth, 120, **26**
Beetles, **34**
*belia Anthocharis*, 40, **12**
*bellargus Lysandra*, 46, **21**
*Bembecia*, 29, 30
*berbera Amphipyra*, 253, **6**
Berger's Clouded Yellow, 37, **19**
*betulae Thecla*, 41, **18**
*betularia Biston*, 109, **6**
*bicruris Hadena*, 232, **11**
*bicuspis Furcula*, 123, **5**
*bidentata Odontopera*, 106, **18**
*bifida Furcula*, 124, **3**
Bilberry Pug, 97, **25**
*bilineata Camptogramma*, 82, **10**
*binaria Drepana*, 68, **6**
*bipunctaria Scotopteryx*, 80, **21**
Birch Mocha, 76, **4**
Birch Sawfly, **34**
Bird's Wing, 253, **9**
*biselata Idaea*, 77, **15**
*Biston*, 109
Black Arches, 206, **1**
Black Hairstreak, 42, **18**
Black Rustic, 240, **10**
Black-veined White, 38, **17**
Blair's Shoulder-knot, 241, **1**
*blanda Hoplodrina*, 260, **11**
Blood-vein, 76, **10**
Blossom Underwing, 233, **6**
Bordered Beauty, 103, **2**
Bordered Sallow, 261, **20**
Bordered Straw, 262, **20**
Bordered White, 113, **1**
*Brachionycha*, 240
Braconidae, 14
*bractea Autographa*, 266, **28**
Brahmaeidae, 67
*brassicae Mamestra*, 228, **13**
*brassicae Pieris*, 38, **13**
Brick, 245, **7**
Bright-line Brown-eye, 230, **11**
Brimstone, 38, **22**
Brimstone Moth, 103, **17**
Brindled Beauty, 109, **7**
Brindled Ochre, 240, **24**
*Brithys*, 233
Broad-bordered Bee Hawk-moth, 119, **28**
Broad-bordered White Underwing, 227, **25**
Broad-bordered Yellow Underwing, 219, **17**
Broom Moth, 230, **32**
Broom Tip, 98, **19**
Brown Argus, 45, **23**
Brown Hairstreak, 41, **18**
Brown-spot Pinion, 246, **14**
Brown-tail, 204, **18**
*brumata Operophtera*, 89, **16**
*brunnea Diarsia*, 222, **15**
Brussels Lace, 112, **32**
*bucephala Phalera*, 122, **5**
Buff Arches, 71, **15**
Buff Ermine, 210, **15**
Buff-tip, 122, **5**
Bulrush Wainscot, 258, **30**
*Bupalus*, 113
Burnet Companion, 267, **21**
Burnet Moth, 25
Burnished Brass, 264, **9**

*c-album Polygonia*, 52, **9**
*c-nigrum Xestia*, 223, **11**
Cabbage Moth, 228, **13**
*caeruleocephala Diloba*, 128, **16**
*caja Arctia*, 208, **10**
*callidice Pontia*, 40, **12**
*Callimorpha*, 212
*Callistege*, 267
*Calliteara*, 204
*Callophrys*, 41
*callunae L. quercus ssp.*, 63
*Calosoma*, 201
Camberwell Beauty, 51, **2**
*cambrica Venusia*, 98, **16**
*camilla Ladoga*, 49, **28**
Camouflage, 15
*Campaea*, 114
Campion, 231, **11**
*Camptogramma*, 82
Canary-shouldered Thorn, 104, **5**
Cannibalism, 19
*captiuncula Photedes*, 256, **30**
*capucina Ptilodon*, 126, **4**
*Caradrina*, 260
*carbonaria Semiothisa*, 102, **19**
*Carcharodus*, 32
*cardamines Anthocharis*, 40, **12**
*cardui Cynthia*, 50, **29**
*carpinata Trichopteryx*, 99, **5**
*Carterocephalus*, 30
*castaneae Phragmataecia*, 24, **30**
*Catocala*, 267
*Celaena*, 258
*Celastrina*, 47
*centaureata Eupithecia*, 92, **28**
*centrago Atethmia*, 247, **8**
Centre-barred Sallow, 247, **8**
*Ceramica*, 230
*Cerapteryx*, 232
cerasi Fabricius, Orthosia 243, 6
*Cerastis*, 226
*Cerura*, 122
Chafer, **34**
Chalk Carpet, 80, **21**
Chalkhill Blue, 46, **21**
Chamomile Shark, 238, **28**
*chamomillae Cucullia*, 238, **28**
*Charaxes*, 48
*chenopodiata Scotopteryx*, 81, **20**
Chequered Skipper, 30, **32**
*Chesias*, 97, 98
Chestnut, 245, **6**
Chinese Character, 70, **17**
*Chloroclysta*, 85
*Chloroclystis*, 96, 97
Chocolate-tip, 128, **3**
Chrysalis, 13
*chrysidiformis Bembecia*, 30, **10**
*chrysitis Diachrysia*, 264, **9**
*chryson Diachrysia*, 264, **28**
*chrysoprasaria Hemistola*, 75, **12**
*chrysorrhoea Euproctis*, 204, **18**
*Cidaria*, 85
*Cilix*, 70
*Cimbex*, **34**
Cinnabar, 212, **29**
*cinxia Melitaea*, 56, **27**
*circellaris Agrochola*, 245, **7**
*citrago Xanthia*, 247, **8**
*citrata Chloroclysta*, 85, **25**
Claspers, 11
*clathrata Semiothisa*, 101, **21**
*clavaria Larentia*, 82, **22**
Clay, 236, **11**
*Cleorodes*, 112
Click Beetle, **34**
Cloaked Minor, 256, **31**
Cloaked Pug, 91, **1**
*clorana Earias*, 262, **2**
*Clossiana*, 53, 54
*Clostera*, 128
Clouded Apollo, 34, **12**
Clouded Border, 100, **2**
Clouded Buff, 209, **10**
Clouded Drab, 235, **16**
Clouded Magpie, 100, **7**
Clouded Silver, 113, **18**
Clouded Yellow, 37, **20**
*Coccinella*, **34**
Cocoon, 13
*Coenobia*, 259
*coenobita Panthea*, 263, **1**
*Coenonympha*, 60
*coenosa Laelia*, 202, **30**
Coleoptera, **34**
*Colias*, 36, 37
*Colocasia*, 264
*Colotois*, 107
*comes Noctua*, 219, **31**
*comitata Pelurga*, 83, **11**
Comma, 52, **9**
*comma Hesperia*, 31, **31**

*comma Mythimna*, 237, **31**
Common Blue, 45, **20**
Common Emerald, 75, **14**
Common Footman, 207, **32**
Common Heath, 113, **24**
Common Lutestring, 71, **5**
Common Marbled Carpet, 85, **25**
Common Pug, 93, **15**
Common Quaker, 234, **6**
Common Rustic, 256, **30**
Common Swift, 23, **27**
Common Wainscot, 236, **31**
*confusa Hadena*, 231, **11**
*confusalis Nola*, 214, **16**
*Conistra*, 245
Conservation, 21
*contigua Lancanobia*, 229, **5**
*contiguaria Idaea*, 78, **25**
*convolvuli Agrius*, 116, **26**
Convolvulus Hawk-moth, 116, **26**
Copper Underwing, 252, **6**
*cordigera Anarta*, 227, **25**
*Cordyceps*, 14
*coridon Lysandra*, 46, **21**
*coryli Colocasia*, 264, **5**
*Cosmia*, 255
Cossidae, 24
*Cossus*, 24
*cossus Cossus*, 24, **8**
Coxcomb Prominent, 126, **4**
*craccae Lygephila*, 268, **20**
Cranefly, **34**
*crataegi Aporia*, 38, **17**
*crataegi Trichiura*, 61, **17**
Cream-bordered Green Pea, 262, **2**
Cream-spot Tiger, 209, **29**
Crescent, 258, **30**
Crimson Speckled, 208, **26**
*crini Brithys*, 233, **30**
*Crocallis*, 107
*croceus Colias*, 37, **20**
Crochets, 11
*Croesus*, **34**
*cruda Orthosia*, 233, **14**
*Cryphia*, 252
Ctenuchidae, 213
*cucullatella Nola*, 214, **17**
*Cucullia*, 237–9
*cucullina Ptilodontella*, 127, **8**
Cudweed, 239, **28**
*cultraria Drepana*, 69, **7**
*cunea Hyphantria*, 210, **33**
*Cupido*, 43
Currant Clearwing, 29, **22**
Currant Pug, 93, **22**
*curtula Clostera*, 128, **3**
*Cyaniris*, 46
*Cyclophora*, 76
*Cynthia*, 50
Cypress Pug, 95, **1**

*dahlii Diarsia*, 222, **10**
*daplidice Pontia*, 39, **13**
Dark Arches, 255, **32**
Dark Brocade, 243, **5**
Dark Dagger, 250, **16**
Dark Green Fritillary, 54, **23**
Dark Marbled Carpet, 85, **25**
Dark Spectacle, 266, **9**
Dark Spinach, 83, **11**
Dark Tussock, 203, **19**
Dark Umber, 88, **22**
*Dasychira*, 204
*Dasypolia*, 240
Death's Head Hawk-moth, 117, **27**
*debiliata Chloroclystis*, 97, **25**
December Moth, 61, **3**
*defoliaria Erannis*, 110, **5**
*Deilephila*, 121
*Dendrolimus*, 64
*dentaria Selenia*, 105, **4**
*depuncta Eugnorisma*, 217, **10**
*derivata Anticlea*, 83, **14**
*dia Clossiana*, 54, **23**
*Diachrysia*, 264
*Diacrisia*, 209
*diamina Melitaea*, 55, **27**
*Diaphora*, 211
*Diarsia*, 221, 222
*Dicallomera*, 203
*Dichonia*, 243
*didyma Melitaea*, 55, **27**
*didymata Perizoma*, 90, **25**
*Diloba*, 128
Dilobidae, 128
*dilutata Epirrita*, 88, **7**
*dimidiata Idaea*, 78, **24**
Dingy Footman, 207, **32**
Dingy Skipper, 32, **21**
*Diprion*, **34**
Diptera, **34**
*Discestra*, 227
*dispar Lycaena*, 43, **10**
*dispar Lymantria*, 206, **18**
*distinctaria Eupithecia*, 94, **26**
*distinctata Aleucis*, 114, **18**
*ditrapezium Xestia*, 223, **15**
*dolabraria Plagodis*, 102, **2**
*domestica Cryphia*, 252, **32**
*dominula Callimorpha*, 212, **26**
Dot Moth, 229, **27**
Dotted Border, 110, **5**
Dotted Chestnut, 245, **18**
Double Square-spot, 223, **17**
Double-striped Pug, 97, **17**
Drab Looper, 98, **22**
*Drepana*, 68, 69
Drepanidae, 68
Drinker, 64, **32**
*dromedarius Notodonta*, 124, **4**
*dubitata Triphosa*, 88, **18**
Duke of Burgundy Fritillary, 48, **25**
Dun-bar, 255, **7**
*duplaris Ochropacha*, 71, **5**
Dusky Thorn, 105, **8**
*Dypterygia*, 253
*dysodea Hecatera*, 231, **29**

*Earias*, 262
Early Grey, 242, **28**
Early Moth, 114, **17**
Early Thorn, 105, **4**
Early Tooth-striped, 99, **5**
*Ecliptopera*, 84
Egg, 12
*Eilema*, 207
*Elaphria*, 260
Elephant Hawk-moth, 121, **23**
*Eligmodonta*, 125
*elinguaria Crocallis*, 107, **18**
*elpenor Deilephila*, 121, **23**
*Ematurga*, 113
Emperor Moth, 65, **24**
Endromidae, 67
*Endromis*, 67
*Ennomos*, 104–5
*Entephria*, 82
*Epione*, 103
*epiphron Erebia*, 57, **32**
*Epirrhoe*, 81
*Epirrita*, 88, 89
*Erebia*, 57, 58
*Eriogaster*, 62
*erosaria Ennomos*, 105, **8**
*Erynnis*, 32
Essex Emerald, 74, **28**
*Euchloe*, 40
*Euclidia*, 267
*Eugnorisma*, 217
*Eugraphe*, 220
*Eulithis*, 84
*Eumichtis*, 244
*euphorbiae Acronicta*, 251, **5**
*euphorbiae Hyles*, 120, **22**
*euphrosyne Clossiana*, 53, **23**
*Eupithecia*, 90–6
*Euplagia*, 212
*Euplexia*, 254
*Euproctis*, 204, 205
*Eupsilia*, 244
*Eurodryas*, 55
*europaea Acanthobrahmaea*, 67, **18**
European Map, 53, **9**
*Eustroma*, 86
*Euxoa*, 215
*Everes*, 44
*exclamationis Agrotis*, 216, **13**
*exsoleta Xylena*, 242, **20**
*exulans* Zygaena, 25, **25**
Eyed Hawk-moth, 118, **2**

*fagana Pseudoips*, 263, **6**
*fagata Operophtera*, 89, **4**
*fagi Hipparchia*, 59, **32**
*fagi Stauropus*, 124, **7**
*Falcaria*, 68
*falcataria Drepana*, 69, **4**
Fall Webworm, 210, **33**
False Apollo, 34, **9**
False Heath Fritillary, 55, **27**
*fascelina Dicallomera*, 203, **19**
Feathered Ear, 228, **31**
Feathered Ranunculus, 244, **13**
Feathered Thorn, 107, **2**
*femoratus Cimbex*, **34**
Fern, 87, **12**
*ferrago Mythimna*, 236, **11**
Festoon, 27, **6**
Fiery Clearwing, 30, **10**
Figure of Eight, 128, **16**
Figure of Eighty, 71, **3**
*filigrammaria Epirrita*, 89, **25**
*filipendulae Zygaena*, 26, **21**
*fimbriata Noctua*, 219, **17**
*firmata Thera*, 86, **1**
Five-spot Burnet, 26, **21**
Flame, 217, **26**
Flame Brocade, 244, **12**
Flame Wainscot, 237, **30**
*flammea Panolis*, 232, **1**
*flammea Senta*, 237, **30**
*flammea Trigonophora*, 244, **12**
*flavago Gortyna*, 257, **27**
*flavicinctata Entephria*, 82, **14**
*flavicornis Achlya*, 72, **4**
*flexula Laspeyria*, 269, **32**
Flounced Rustic, 257, **33**
*fluctuata Xanthorhoe*, 80, **13**
Forester, 25, **10**
Four Spotted, 268, **26**
Fox Moth, 63, **24**
Foxglove Pug, 91, **27**
Frass, 17
*fraxinata Eupithecia*, 95, **8**
Freyer's Dappled White, 40, **13**
Frosted Green, 72, **6**
Frosted Orange, 257, **27**
Frosted Yellow, 102, **19**

*fuciformis Hemaris*, 119, **28**
*fuliginosa Phragmatobia*, 211, **29**
*fulvata Cidaria*, 85, **14**
*furcata Hydriomena*, 86, **5**
*Furcula*, 122–4
*furcula Furcula*, 123, **2**
*furuncula Mesoligia*, 256, **31**
*fuscantaria Ennomos*, 105, **8**

*galathea Melanargia*, 58, **32**
*galiata Epirrhoe*, 81, **26**
*galii Hyles*, 120, **26**
Galium Carpet, 81, **26**
*gamma Autographa*, 265, **13**
Garden Carpet, 80, **13**
Garden Dart, 215, **10**
Garden Tiger, 208, **10**
*Gastropacha*, 65
Gatekeeper, 59, **31**
Gem, 79, **9**
*Geometra*, 74
Geometridae, 73
Ghost Moth, 23, **29**
*gilvaria Aspitates*, 115, **16**
Glanville Fritillary, 56, **27**
*glaucata Cilix*, 70, **17**
*glaucinaria Gnophos*, 115, 13
*glomeratus Apanteles*, 14
*glyphica Euclidia*, 267, **121**
*gnaphalii Cucullia*, 239, **28**
*gnoma Pheosia*, 126, **4**
*Gnophos*, 115
Goat Moth, 24, **8**
Gold Spangle, 266, **28**
Golden Plusia, 265, **12**
Golden-rod Pug, 95, **28**
*Gonepteryx*, 38
Gooseberry sawfly, **34**
*goossensiata Eupithecia*, 93, **24**
*Gortyna*, 257
Gothic, 225, **16**
*gothica Orthosia*, 235, **29**
*gracilis Orthosia*, 234, **23**
*Graellsia*, 66
*graminis Cerapteryx*, 232, **31**
Grass Eggar, 62, **21**
Grass Emerald, 74, **19**
Grass Wave, 116, **19**
Grayling, 59, **32**
Great Oak Beauty, 112, **6**
Great Peacock, 66, **33**
Great Prominent, 125, **33**
Green Arches, 226, **15**
Green Hairstreak, 41, **19**
Green Pug, 96, **16**
Green Silver-lines, 263, **6**
Green-brindled Crescent, 243, **17**
Green-veined White, 39, **13**
Grey Arches, 228, **15**
Grey Carpet, 98, **12**
Grey Dagger, 250, **16**
*griseata Lithostege*, 98, **12**
*griseata Timandra*, 76, **10**
*griseola Eilema*, 207, **32**
Grizzled Skipper, 33, **15**
*grossulariata Abraxas*, 100, **17**
*Gymnoscelis*, 97
*Gynaephora*, 203
Gypsy Moth, 206, **18**

*Habrosyne*, 71
*Hadena*, 231, 232
*halterata Lobophora*, 99, **3**
*Hamearis*, 48
*harpagula Sabra*, 69, **8**
*Harpyia*, 125, **33**
Hartig's Brahmaea, 67, **18**
Haworth's Minor, 258, **30**
Haworth's Pug, 90, **12**
*haworthiata Eupithecia*, 90, **12**
*haworthii Celaena*, 258, **30**
Heart and Dart, 216, **13**
Heath Fritillary, 56, **27**
Heath Rustic, 225, **24**
Hebrew Character, 235, **29**
*Hecatera*, 231
Hedge Brown, 59, **31**
*Heliothis*, 261, 262
*Hemaris*, 119
*Hemistola*, 75
*Hemithea*, 75
Hepialidae, 23
*Hepialus*, 23
Herald, 268, **2**
*Hesperia*, 31
Hesperiidae, 30
*Heterogenea*, 28
Heterogynidae, 28
*Heterogynis*, 28
High Brown Fritillary, 52, **23**
*Hipparchia*, 59
*hirtaria Lycia*, 109, **7**
Holly Blue, 47, **8**
Hop Dog, 204
*Hoplodrina*, 260
*Horisme*, 87
Hoverfly, **34**
Humming-bird Hawk-moth, 120, **26**
*humuli Hepialus*, 23, **29**
*hyale Colias*, 36, **21**
*Hydraecia*, 257
*Hydriomena*, 86
*Hyles*, 120, 121
*Hyloicus*, 118
*Hypena*, 269
*hyperantus Aphantopus*, 60, **31**
*Hyphantria*, 210
*Hypomecis*, 112
*Hyppa*, 255

*icarus Polyommatus*, 45, **20**
Ichneumon, 14
Ichneumonidae, 14
*icteritia Xanthia*, 248, **2**
*Idaea*, 77–9
*ilia Apatura*, 50, **3**
*ilicifolia Phyllodesma*, 64, **25**
*Inachis*, 52
*incerta Orthosia*, 235, **16**
Ingrailed Clay, 221, **10**
Instar, 12
*io Inachis*, 52, **9**
*Iphiclides*, 35
*iris Apatura*, 49, **2**
Iron Prominent, 124, **4**
*isabellae Graellsia*, 66, **1**
*Isturgia*, 102

*jacobaeae Tyria*, 212, **29**
*janthina Noctua*, 219, **17**
*jasius Charaxes*, 48, **25**
Jersey Tiger, 212, **29**
*Jodis*, 75
*jota Autographa*, 265, **26**
July Highflyer, 86, **5**
Juniper Carpet, 86, **1**
Juniper Pug, 95, **25**
*juniperata Thera*, 86, **1**
*jurtina Maniola*, 60, **31**

Kentish Glory, 67, **4**
Kew Arches, 233, **30**
Knapweed Fritillary, 56, **29**
Knot Grass, 252, **33**

Labial palps, 11
Labium, 11, 129
Labrum, 11, 129
*lacertinaria Falcaria*, 68, **4**
Lackey, 62, **16**
*lactearia Jodis*, 75, **4**
*lactucae Cucullia*, 238, **29**
*Ladoga*, 49
Ladybird, **34**
*Laelia*, 202
*Lancanobia*, 229, 230
*lanestris Eriogaster*, 62, **17**
*Laothoe*, 119
Lappet, 65, **17**
Larch Pug, 96, **1**
*Larentia*, 82
Large Blue, 47, **26**
Large Copper, 43, **10**
Large Dark Prominent, 125, **3**
Large Emerald, 74, **4**
Large Skipper, 32, **32**
Large Thorn, 104, **4**
Large Tortoiseshell, 51, **7**
Large Wainscot, 259, **30**
Large White, 38, **13**
Large Yellow Underwing, 218, **29**
*lariciata Eupithecia*, 96, **1**
*Lasiocampa*, 62, 63
Lasiocampidae, 61
*Lasiommata*, 57
*Laspeyria*, 269
*lathonia Argynnis*, 54, 23
Latticed Heath, 101, **21**
Lead Belle, 81, **19**
Least Black Arches, 214, **16**
Least Minor, 256, **30**
Leather jacket, **34**
*leautieri Lithophane*, 241, **1**
*legatella Chesias*, 97, **19**
Leopard Moth, 24, **16**
*leporina Acronicta*, 249, **4**
*Leptidea*, 36
Lesser Broad-bordered Yellow Underwing, 219, **17**
Lesser Purple Emperor, 50, **3**
Lesser Swallow Prominent, 126, **4**
Lesser Yellow Underwing, 219, **31**
Lettuce Shark, 238, **29**
*Leucoma*, 205
*leucostigma Celaena*, 258, **30**
*levana Araschnia*, 52, **9**
*libatrix Scoliopteryx*, 268, **2**
*lichenaria Cleorodes*, 112, **32**
*lichenea Eumichtis*, 244, **13**
Light Brocade, 230, **19**
Light Emerald, 114, **7**
Light Knot Grass, 250, **5**
Light Orange Underwing, 73, **3**
*ligustri Sphinx*, 117, **26**
Lilac Beauty, 103, **26**
*limacodes Apoda*, 27, **6**
Limacodidae, 27
*limbaria Isturgia*, 102, **19**
Lime Hawk-moth, 118, **8**
Lime-speck Pug, 92, **28**
*Limenitis*, 49
*linariata Eupithecia*, 91, **27**
Ling Pug, 93, **24**
*Lithophane*, 241
*Lithostege*, 98
Little Emerald, 75, **4**
*litura Agrochola*, 246, **14**
*Lobophora*, 99
Lobster, 124, **7**
*Lomaspilis*, 100
*Lomographa*, 113

*lonicerae Zygaena*, 26, **21**
Looper caterpillars, 16
*lubricipeda Spilosoma*, 210, **29**
*lucernea Standfussiana*, 218, **13**
*lucina Hamearis*, 48, **25**
*lucipara Euplexia*, 254, **27**
*luctuosa Tyta*, 268, **26**
Lulworth Skipper, 31, **32**
Lunar Thorn, 106, **18**
*lunularia Selenia*, 106, **18**
*Luperina*, 257
*lupulinus Hepialus*, 23, **27**
*lurideola Eilema*, 207, **32**
*luteolata Opisthograptis*, 103, **17**
*lutea Spilosoma*, 210, 15
*lutosa Rhizedra*, 259, **30**
*Lycaena*, 43
Lycaenidae, 41
*lychnidis Agrochola*, 246, **12**
Lychnis, 232, **11**
*lychnitis Cucullia*, 239, **27**
*Lycia*, 109
*Lycophotia*, 221
*Lygephila*, 268
*Lymantria*, 206
Lymantriidae, 202
Lysandra, 46

*machaon Papilio*, 35, **24**
*Macroglossum*, 120
*Macrothylacia*, 63, **24**
*Maculinea*, 47
Magpie Moth, 100, **17**
*Malacosoma*, 62
Mallow, 82, **22**
Mallow Skipper, 32, **22**
*malvae Pyrgus*, 33, **15**
*Mamestra*, 228
Mandibles, 11, 129
*Maniola*, 60
Maple Prominent, 127, **8**
Marbled Beauty, 252, **32**
Marbled Clover, 261, **20**
Marbled Coronet, 231, **11**
Marbled White, 58, **32**
Marbled White Spot, 262, **31**
March Moth, 73, **16**
*margaritata Campaea*, 114, **7**
*marginaria Agriopis*, 110, **5**
*marginata Lomaspilis*, 100, **2**
Marsh Carpet, 90, **12**
Marsh Fritillary, 55, **28**
Marsh Pug, 92, **11**
*maura Mormo*, 253, **33**
Maxillary palps, 11
Mazarine Blue, 46, **20**
Meadow Brown, 60, **31**
*megacephala Acronicta*, 248, **3**
*megera Lasiommata*, 57, **31**
*Melanargia*, 58
*Melanchra*, 229
*melanopa Anarta*, 227, **25**
*Melanthia*, 87
*Melitaea*, 55, 56
*Mellicta*, 56
*mendica Diaphora*, 211, **10**
*mendica Diarsia*, 221, **10**
*Menophra*, 111
*menyanthidis Acronicta*, 250, **5**
Merveille du Jour, 234, **6**
*Mesapamea*, 256
*Mesoleuca*, 83
*Mesoligia*, 256
*meticulosa Phlogophora*, 254, **22**
*mi Callistege*, 267, **21**
*micacea Hydraecia*, 257, **27**
*milhauseri Harpyia*, 125, **33**
Miller, 249, **4**
*Mimas*, 118
*minimus Cupido*, 43, **20**
*miniosa Orthosia*, 233, **6**
*Mniotype*, 243
*Minoa*, 98
*mnemosyne Parnassius*, 34, **12**
Mocha, 76, **8**
*monacha Lymantria*, 206, **1**
*moneta Polychrysia*, 265, **12**
*monoglypha Apamea*, 255, **32**
Moorland Clouded Yellow, 36, **25**
*Mormo*, 253
Morocco Orange-tip, 40, **12**
*morpheus Caradrina*, 260, **29**
Mother Shipton, 267, **21**
Mottled Beauty, 111, **7**
Mottled Rustic, 260, **29**
Mottled Umber, 110, **5**
Moulting, 12
Mountain Clouded Yellow, 37, **20**
Mountain Ringlet, 57, **32**
*mucronata Scotopteryx*, 81, **19**
Mullein Moth, 239, **27**
*munda Orthosia*, 235, **7**
*mundana Nudaria*, 207, **32**
*munitata Xanthorhoe*, 80, **9**
*murinata Minoa*, 98, **22**
Muslin Footman, 207, **32**
Muslin Moth, 211, **10**
*myopaeformis Synanthedon*, 29, **16**
*myrtilli Anarta*, 226, **24**
*Mythimna*, 236, 237

*Naenia*, 225
*napi Pieris*, 39, **13**
Narrow-bordered Bee Hawk-moth, 119, **28**
Narrow-bordered Five-spot Burnet, 26, **21**
*nebulosa Polia*, 228, **15**
*Nematus*, **34**
Netted Carpet, 86, **22**
Netted Mountain Carpet, 102, **19**
*neustria Malacosoma*, 62, **16**
*nigra Aporophyla*, 240, **10**
*nigricans Euxoa*, 215, **10**
*nigropunctata Scopula*, 77, **12**
Nine-spotted, 213, **29**
*Noctua*, 218, 219
Noctuidae, 215
*Nola*, 214
Nolidae, 214
*Nonagria*, 258
Northern Brown Argus, 45, **23**
Northern Dart, 222, **25**
Northern Drab, 234, **14**
Northern Rustic, 218, **13**
Northern Spinach, 84, **25**
Northern Winter Moth, 89, **4**
*notata Semiothisa*, 101, **4**
*notha Archiearis*, 73, **3**
*Notodonta*, 124, 125
Notodontidae, 122
November Moth, 88, **7**
*Nudaria*, 207
*nupta Catocala*, 267, **2**
Nut-tree Tussock, 264, **5**
Nutmeg, 227, **11**
*Nycteola*, 263
Nymphalidae, 48
*Nymphalis*, 51

Oak Beauty, 109, **6**
Oak Eggar, 63, **15**
Oak Hook-tip, 68, **6**
Oak Nycteoline, 263, **6**
Oak Processionary, 201, 6
*obfuscata Gnophos*, 115, 19
*obscurata Gnophos*, 115, 14
*obstipata Orthonama*, 79, **9**
*ocellaris Xanthia*, 248, **3**
*ocellata Smerinthus*, 118, **2**
Ocelli, 11, 129
*Ochlodes*, 32
*Ochropacha*, 71
*ochropus Arge*, **34**
*ocularis Tethea*, 71, **3**
*Odontopera*, 106
Old Lady, 253, **33**
*oleracea Lacanobia*, 230, **11**
*Operophtera*, 89, 225
*opima Orthosia*, 234, **14**
*Opisthograptis*, 103
*or Tethea*, 71, **3**
Orache Moth, 254, **11**
Orange Moth, 108, **18**
Orange Sallow, 247, **8**
Orange-tip, 40, **12**
*Orgyia*, 202, 203
*Orthonama*, 79
*Orthosia*, 233–5
Osmeterium, 12
*Ourapteryx*, 107
*oxyacanthae Allophyes*, 243, **17**

*Pachetra*, 228
Painted Lady, 50, **29**
*palaemon Carterocephalus*, 30, **32**
*palaeno Colias*, 36, **25**
Pale Brindled Beauty, 108, **18**
Pale Clouded Yellow, 36, **21**
Pale Eggar, 61, **17**
Pale Oak Beauty, 112, **6**
Pale Prominent, 127, **3**
Pale Tussock, 204, **9**
Pale-lemon Sallow, 248, **3**
*pallens Mythimna*, 236, **31**
*palpina Pterostoma*, 127, **3**
*pamphilus Coenonympha*, 60, **31**
*Panolis*, 232
*Panthea*, 263
*paphia Argynnis*, 55, **23**
*Papilio*, 35
*papilionaria Geometra*, 74, **4**
Papilionidae, 33
*Pararge*, 57
*Parasemia*, 208
*Parnassius*, 33, 34
*pavonia Saturnia*, 65, **24**
Peach Blossom, 70, **15**
Peacock, 52, **9**
Peacock Moth, 101, **4**
Peak White, 40, **12**
Pearl-bordered Fritillary, 53, **23**
Pearly Underwing, 221, **13**
Pebble Hook-tip, 69, **4**
Pebble Prominent, 125, **2**
*peltigera Heliothis*, 262, **20**
*Pelurga*, 83
*penella Heterogynis*, 28, **19**
*pennaria Colotois*, 107, **2**
Peppered Moth, 109, **6**
*Perconia*, 116
*Peribatodes*, 111
*Peridea*, 125
*Peridroma*, 221
*Perizoma*, 90
*persicariae Melanchra*, 229, **27**
*Phalera*, 122
*phegea Syntomis*, 213, **29**
*Pheosia*, 126
*phicomone Colias*, 37, **20**
*Philereme*, 88
*Philudoria*, 64

*phlaes Lycaena*, 43, **10**
*Phlogophora*, 254
*phoebe Melitaea*, 56, **29**
*phoebus Parnassius*, 34, **14**
*phoeniceata Eupithecia*, 95, **1**
*Photedes*, 256
*Phragmataecia*, 24
*Phragmatobia*, 211
*Phyllodesma*, 64
*Phymatocera*, **34**
Pieridae, 36
*Pieris*, 38, 39
*pilosaria Apocheima*, 108, **18**
Pimpinel Pug, 94, **24**
*pimpinellata Eupithecia*, 94, **24**
Pinacula, 12
*pinastri Hyloicus*, 118, **1**
Pine Beauty, 232, **1**
Pine Carpet, 86, **1**
Pine Hawk-moth, 118, **1**
Pine Processionary, 201, **1**
Pine Sawfly, **34**
Pine-tree Lappet, 64, **1**
*pini Dendrolimus*, 64, **1**
*pini Diprion*, **34**
*piniaria Bupalus*, 113, **1**
*pisi Ceramica*, 230, **32**
*pityocampa Thaumetopoea*, 201, **1**
*Plagodis*, 102
Plain Clay, 217, **10**
Plain Golden Y, 265, **26**
Plain Pug, 94, **11**
Plain Wave, 79, **15**
*plantaginis Parasemia*, 208, **27**
*Plebejus*, 44
Plumed Prominent, 127, **8**
*plumigera Ptilophora*, 127, **8**
*podalirius Iphiclides*, 36, **18**
*Poecilocampa*, 61
*Polia*, 228
*polychloros Nymphalis*, 51, **7**
*Polychrysia*, 265
*Polygonia*, 52
*Polyommatus*, 45
*Polyploca*, 72
*polyxena Zerynthia*, 34, **9**
*Pontia*, 39, 40
Poplar Admiral, 49, **3**
Poplar Grey, 248, **3**
Poplar Hawk-moth, 119, **3**
Poplar Kitten, 124, **3**
Poplar Lutestring, 71, **3**
*populata Eulithis*, 84, **25**
*populi Laothoe*, 119, **3**
*populi Limenitis*, 49, **3**
*populi Poecilocampa*, 61, **3**
*porcellus Deilephila*, 121, **23**
*porphyrea Lycophotia*, 221, **24**
*potatoria Philudoria*, 64, **32**
Powdered Quaker, 234, **23**
*prasina Anaplectoides*, 226, **15**
Predators, 14
Pretty Chalk Carpet, 87, **12**
*primaria Theria*, 114, **17**
Privet Hawk-moth, 117, **26**
*proboscidalis Hypena*, 269, **9**
*procellata Melanthia*, 87, **12**
*processionea Thaumetopoea*, 201, **6**
Prolegs, 11, 129
*pronuba Noctua*, 218, **29**
*Protodeltote*, 262, 31
*pruinata Pseudoterpna*, 74, **19**
*prunaria Angerona*, 108, **18**
*pruni Strymonidia*, 42, **18**
*Pseudoips*, 263
*Pseudoterpna*, 74
*psi Acronicta*, 250, **16**
*Pterostoma*, 127
*Ptilodon*, 126
*Ptilodontella*, 127
*Ptilophora*, 127
*pudibunda Calliteara*, 204, **9**
*pulchella Utetheisa*, 208, **26**
*pulchellata Eupithecia*, 91, **27**
*punctinalis Serraca*, 112, **6**
Pupa, 12
Purple Clay, 222, **15**
Purple Emperor, 49, **2**
Purple Hairstreak, 42, **6**
Purple Thorn, 106, **5**
*purpuralis Zygaena*, 27, **26**
*purpurata Rhyparia*, 210, **19**
*pusillata Eupithecia*, 95, **1**
Puss Moth, 122, **2**
*puta Agrotis*, 216, **9**
*putris Axylia*, 217, **26**
*pygarga Protodeltote*, 262, 31
*pygmaeata Eupithecia*, 92, **11**
*pyramidea Amphipyra*, 252, 253, **6**
*Pyrgus*, 33
*pyri Saturnia*, 66, **33**
*pyrina Zeuzera*, 24, **16**
*pyritoides Habrosyne*, 71, **15**
*Pyronia*, 59
*Pyrrhia*, 261

*quadripunctaria Euplagia*, 212, **29**
Queen of Spain Fritillary, 54, **23**
*quercifolia Gastropacha*, 65, **17**
*quercinaria Ennomos*, 104, **6**
*quercus Lasiocampa*, 63, **15**
*quercus Quercusia*, 42, **6**
*Quercusia*, 42

*rapae Pieris*, 39, **13**
*ravida Spaelotis*, 220, **10**
*recens Orgyia*, 202, **2**
*rectangulata Chloroclystis*, 96, **16**
*rectilinea Hyppa*, 255, **15**
Red Admiral, 50, **9**
Red Carpet, 80, **9**
Red Chestnut, 226, **29**
Red Sword-grass, 242, **9**
Red Underwing, 267, **2**
Red-belted Clearwing, 29, **16**
Reed Leopard, 24, **30**
Reed Tussock, 202, **30**
*repandaria Epione*, 103
*repandata Alcis*, 111, **7**
*reticulata Eustroma*, 86, 22
*revayana Nycteola*, 263, **6**
*rhamni Gonepteryx*, 38, **22**
*Rhizedra*, 259
*Rhodometra*, 79
*rhomboidaria Peribatodes*, 111, **17**
*Rhyparia*, 210
Riband Wave, 78, **16**
*ribesii Nematus*, **34**
*ridens Polyploca*, 72, **6**
Ringlet, 60, **31**
Riodinidae, 48
*ripae Agrotis*, 217, **11**
*rivularis Hadena*, 231, **11**
*roboraria Hypomecis*, 112, 6
Rose Sawfly, **34**
Rosy Marbled, 260, **16**
Rosy Marsh Moth, 220, **33**
Rosy Rustic, 257, **27**
*rubi Callophrys*, 41, **19**
*rubi Macrothylacia*, 63, **24**
*rubiginata Scopula*, 77, **21**
*rubiginea Conistra*, 245, **18**
*rubricosa Cerastis*, 226, **29**
Ruby Tiger, 211, **29**
*rufa Coenobia*, 259, **30**
*rufata Chesias*, 98, **19**
*rufifasciata Gymnoscelis*, 97, **17**
*rumicis Acronicta*, 252, **33**
*rumina Zerynthia*, 34, **9**
Rush Wainscot, 259, **30**
Rustic, 260, **11**

*Sabra*, 69
*sacraria Rhodometra*, 79, **9**
*sagittata Perizoma*, 90, **12**
*sagittigera Pachetra*, 228, **31**
*salicis Leucoma*, 205, **33**
Sallow, 248, **2**
Sallow Kitten, 123, **2**
*sambucaria Ourapteryx*, 107, **23**
Sand Dart, 217, **11**
*sannio Diacrisia*, 209, **10**
Satellite, 244, **7**
*Saturnia*, 65, 66
Saturniidae, 65
Satyridae, 57
*saucia Peridroma*, 221, **13**
Sawfly, 11, **34**
*scabriuscula Dypterygia*, 253, **9**
Scalloped Hazel, 106, **18**
Scalloped Hook-tip, 68, **4**
Scalloped Oak, 107, **18**
Scarce Blackneck, 268, **20**
Scarce Bordered Straw, 261, **33**
Scarce Burnished Brass, 264, **28**
Scarce Dagger, 251, **15**
Scarce Hook-tip, 69, **8**
Scarce Swallowtail, 35, **18**
Scarce Umber, 110, **4**
Scarce Vapourer, 202, **2**
Scarlet Tiger, 212, **26**
*Scoliopteryx*, 268
*scopigera Bembecia*, 29, **20**
*Scopula*, 77
Scorched Wing, 102, **2**
Scotch Annulet, 115, **19**
Scotch Argus, 58, **31**
Scotch Burnet, 25, **25**
*Scotopteryx*, 80, 81
*scrophulariae Cucullia*, 239, **27**
*secalis Mesapamea*, 256, **30**
*segetum Agrotis*, 216, **10**
*selene Clossiana*, 53, **23**
*Selenia*, 105, 106
*selenitica Gynaephora*, 203, **20**
*semele Hipparchia*, 59, **32**
Semi-looper, 215
*semiargus Cyaniris*, 46, **20**
*semibrunnea Lithophane*, 241, **8**
*Semiothisa*, 101, 102
*Senta*, 237
September Thorn, 105, **8**
*septentrionalis Croesus*, **34**
Seraphim, 99, **3**
*Serraca*, 112
Setaceous Hebrew Character, 223, **11**
Seven-spot Ladybird, **34**
*sexstrigata Xestia*, 224, **15**
Shaded Broad-bar, 81, **20**
Sharp-angled Peacock, 101, **18**
Short-cloaked Moth, 214, **17**
Short-tailed Blue, 44, **21**
Shoulder Stripe, 83, **14**
Shoulder-striped Wainscot, 237, **31**
Shuttle-shaped Dart, 216, **9**
*silaceata Ecliptopera*, 84, **23**
Silk, 11
Silver Y, 265, **13**
Silver-spotted Skipper, 31, **31**
Silver-studded Blue, 44, **19**
Silver-washed Fritillary, 55, **23**

*similis Euproctis*, 205, **17**
*simpliciata Eupithecia*, 94, **11**
*simplonia Euchloe*, 40, **13**
*sinapis Leptidea*, 36, **20**
Single-dotted Wave, 78, **24**
Six-belted Clearwing, 29, **20**
Six-spot Burnet, 26, **21**
Six-striped Rustic, 224, **15**
Sleeve, 20
Sloe Carpet, 114, **18**
Small Angle Shades, 254, **27**
Small Apollo, 34, **14**
Small Autumnal Moth, 89, **25**
Small Blue, 43, **20**
Small Copper, 43, **10**
Small Dark Yellow Underwing, 227, **25**
Small Eggar, 62, **17**
Small Elephant Hawk-moth, 121, **23**
Small Emerald, 75, **12**
Small Fan-footed Wave, 77, **15**
Small Heath, 60, **31**
Small Lappet, 64, **25**
Small Pearl-bordered Fritillary, 53, **23**
Small Phoenix, 84, **23**
Small Quaker, 233, **14**
Small Ranunculus, 231, **29**
Small Rufous, 259, **30**
Small Skipper, 31, **31**
Small Tortoiseshell, 51, **9**
Small Waved Umber, 87, **12**
Small White, 39, **13**
*smaragdaria Thetidia*, 74, **28**
*Smerinthus*, 118
Snout, 269, **9**
Solomon's Seal Sawfly, **34**
*solstitialis Amphimallon*, **34**
Southern Festoon, 34, **9**
Southern Swallowtail, 35, **24**
*Spaelotis*, 220
Spanish Festoon, 34, **9**
Spanish Moon Moth, 66, **1**
*sparganii Archanara*, 258, **30**
Speckled Wood, 57, **31**
Spectacle, 266, **9**
*spectrum Apopestes*, 268, **33**
Sphingidae, 116
*Sphinx*, 117
*sphinx Brachionycha*, 240, **7**
*Spilosoma*, 210, 211
Spinneret, 11, 129
Spiracles, 11, 129
Spiracular line, 11, 129
Spotted Fritillary, 55, **27**
Sprawler, 240, **7**
Spurge Hawk-moth, 120, **22**
Square-spot Rustic, 224, **11**
*Standfussiana*, 218
Star-wort, 238, **28**
*statices Adscita*, 25, **10**
*Stauropus*, 124
*stellatarum Macroglossum*, 120, **26**
Stick caterpillar, 16
Stout Dart, 220, **10**
*straminata Idaea*, 79, **15**
*strataria Biston*, 109, **6**
Straw Belle, 115, **16**
Streak, 97, **19**
Streamer, 83, **14**
*strigillaria Perconia*, 116, **19**
Striped Lychnis, 329, **27**
*Strymonidia*, 42
Sub-angled Wave, 77, **12**
*subrosea Eugraphe*, 220, **33**
Summer Chafer, **34**

Svensson's Copper Underwing, 253, **6**
Swallow Prominent, 126, **3**
Swallow-tailed Moth, 107, **23**
Swallowtail, 35, **24**
Sweep net, 18
Sweet Gale Moth, 251, **5**
Sword-grass, 242, **20**
Sycamore, 249, **33**
*sylvata Abraxas*, 100, **7**
*sylvestris Thymelicus*, 31, 31
*Symphyta*, **34**
*Synanthedon*, 29
*Syntomis*, 213
*syringaria Apeira*, 103, **26**
*Syrphus*, **34**

Tachinidae, 14, 200
*tages Erynnis*, 32, **21**
*tau Aglia*, 65, **7**
Tau Emperor, 65, **7**
Tawny Pinion, 241, **8**
Tawny Prominent, 125, **33**
Tawny Wave, 77, **21**
*temerata Lomographa*, 113, **18**
*templi Dasypolia*, 240, **24**
*tersata Horisme*, 87, **12**
*testacea Luperina*, 257, **33**
*Tethea*, 71
*tetralunaria Selenia*, 106, **5**
*Thaumetopoea*, 201
Thaumetopoeidae, 201
*Thecla*, 41
*Thera*, 86
*Theria*, 114
*Thetidia*, 74
Thoracic legs, 11, 129
Thorax, 11, 129
*Thyatira*, 70
Thyatiridae, 70
Thyme Pug, 94, **26**
*Thymelicus*, 31
*tiliae Mimas*, 118, **8**
*Timandra*, 76
*Tipula*, **34**
*tipuliformis Synanthedon*, 29, **22**
Tissue, 88, **18**
*tithonus Pyronia*, 59, **31**
*tityus Hemaris*, 119, **28**
Toadflax Pug, 91, **27**
*torva Notodonta*, 125, **3**
*Trachea*, 254
Tracheae, 11
*transalpina Zygaena*, 27, **19**
Transparent Burnet, 27, **26**
*transversa Eupsilia*, 244, **7**
*transversata Philereme*, 88, **22**
*trapezina Cosmia*, 255, **7**
*tremula Pheosia*, 126, **3**
Triangle, 28, **7**
*triangulum Xestia*, 223, **17**
*Trichiura*, 61
*Trichopteryx*, 99
*tridens Acronicta*, 250, **16**
*trifolii Discestra*, 227, **11**
*trifolii Lasiocampa*, 62, **21**
*trifolii Zygaena*, 26, **21**
*trigemina Abrostola*, 226, **9**
*Trigonophora*, 244
*Triphosa*, 88
*triplasia Abrostola*, 266, **9**
Triple-spotted Clay, 223, **15**
*tripunctaria Eupithecia*, 94, **24**
True Lover's Knot, 221, **24**
*truncata Chloroclysta*, 85, **25**
*tullia Coenonympha*, 60, **30**
Turnip Moth, 216, **10**
Twin-spot Carpet, 90, **25**
Twin-spotted Quaker, 235, **7**

Two-tailed Pasha, 48, **25**
Two-winged Flies, **34**
*typhae Nonagria*, 258, **30**
*typica Naenia*, 225, **16**
*Tyria*, 212
*Tyta*, 268

*umbra Pyrrhia*, 261, **20**
*urticae Aglais*, 51, **9**
*urticae Spilosoma*, 211, **26**
*Utetheisa*, 208

*v-ata Chloroclystis*, 96, **12**
V-Moth, 102, **22**
V-Pug, 96, **12**
*vaccinii Conistra*, 245, **6**
*Vanessa*, 50
Vapourer, 203, **14**
Vegetable caterpillar, 14
*venata Ochlodes*, 32, **32**
*Venusia*, 98
*venustula Elaphria*, 260, **16**
*verbasci Cucullia*, 239, **27**
*versicolora Endromis*, 67, **4**
*vespertilio Hyles*, 121, **23**
Vestal, 79, **9**
*vestigialis Agrotis*, 215, **26**
*vetusta Xylena*, 242, **9**
*villica Arctia*, 209, **29**
*vinula Cerura*, 122, **2**
Violet Fritillary, 54, **23**
*viretata Acasis*, 99, **23**
*virgaureata Eupithecia*, 95, **28**
*viriplaca Heliothis*, 261, **20**
Virus, 15, 200
*vitalbata Horisme*, 87, **12**
*vulgata Eupithecia*, 93, **15**

*w-album Strymonidia*, 42, **7**
*w-latinum Lacanobia*, 230, **19**
Wall, 57, **31**
Warning coloration, 16
Water Betony, 239, **27**
Water Ermine, 211, **26**
*wauaria Semiothisa*, 102, **22**
Waved Umber, 111, **26**
Weaver's Fritillary, 54, **23**
Weaver's Wave, 78, **27**
Webb's Wainscot, 258, **30**
Welsh Wave, 98, **16**
White Admiral, 49, **28**
White Ermine, 210, **29**
White Letter Hairstreak, 42, 7
White Satin, 205, **33**
White-spotted Pug, 94, **24**
Willow Beauty, 111, **17**
Winter Moth, 89, **16**
Wireworms, **34**
Wood White, 36, **20**
Woodland Grayling, 59, **32**
Wormwood, 237, **28**
Wormwood Pug, 92, **28**

*Xanthia*, 247, 248
*xanthographa Xestia*, 224, **11**
*Xanthorhoe*, 80
*Xestia*, 222–5
*Xylena*, 242

Yellow Horned, 72, **4**
Yellow Shell, 82, **10**
Yellow-barred Brindle, 99, **23**
Yellow-ringed Carpet, 82, **14**
Yellow-tail, 205, **17**

*Zerynthia*, 34
*Zeuzera*, 24
*ziczac Eligmodonta*, 125, **2**
*Zygaena*, 25–7
Zygaenidae, 25

# Foodplant Index

Figures in **bold** denote plate numbers

*Abies*, 64, 113, 204, 233, 263, **1**
*Acer*, 76, 127–8, 245, 247, 249, 264, **8**, **33**
*Achillea*, 74, 92, 109, 116, 212
*Aconitum*, 265
*Aesculus*, 249
*Agropyron*, 57, 64, 236, 255, **32**, **33**
*Agrostis*, 60
*Aira*, **32**
*Alcea*, 82
*Alchemilla*, 80, 85, 261, **14**
Alder, 68, 69, 72, 74–6, 99, 101, 103–5, 118, 123, 124, 249, 250, **5**
Alder buckthorn, 38, 47, 88, 243
Alison, 40
*Alliaria*, 39, 40, **13**
*Allium*, 228
*Alnus*, 68, 69, 72, 74–6, 99, 101, 103–6, 118, 123, 124, 243, 249, 250, **5**, **34**
Alpine bearberry, 102, 223, 227, 255, **25**
Alpine lady's mantle, 80, 85
*Althaea*, 32
*Alyssum*, 40
*Ammophila*, 63
*Andromeda*, 220
*Anemone*, 90, 229
Angelica, 94, 240
*Angelica*, 35, 94, 240
Annual meadow grass, 57, 225, 228, 236, **31**
Annual mercury, 120
*Anthemis*, 79, 238
*Anthriscus*, 78, **24**
*Anthyllis*, 30, 44, 46, **20**
Apple, 29, 38, 62, 65, 66, 70, 73, 89, 90, 97, 103, 109, 118, 119, 201, 210, 214, 225, 235, 245, 250, **16**
*Arabis*, 39
*Arbutus*, 49, **25**
*Arctium*, 50, 223, 256
*Arctostaphylos*, 102, 223, 227, 255, **25**
*Aristolochia*, 34, **9**
*Armeria*, 115, 244
*Armoracia*, 80, **13**
*Artemisia*, 30, 74, 75, 92, 237, **28**
Ash, 67, 95, 105, 106, 117, 119, 241, 244, 246, 247, 252, **8**
Aspen, 49–51, 71, 73, 99, 100, 118, 119, 123–8, 235, **3**
*Aster*, 238
*Astragalus*, 27
*Atriplex*, 76, 84, 94, 228, 230, 254, **11**

*Barbarea*, 41
Bedstraw, 79, 119–22, 226
Beech, 28, 42, 65, 69, 74, 90, 100, 110, 114, 124, 125, 214, 240, 244, 247, 263, 264, **7**
Bell heather, 44, 113, 115, 116, 221, 225, 226, **24**
*Bellis*, 80, 109, **28**
Bent-grass, 60
*Beta*, 215, 216, 228, **11**
*Betula*, 42, 51, 61, 62, 65, 66, 68, 69, 72, 74–6, 85, 89, 90, 99, 101, 102, 104–12, 114, 118, 119, 123–7, 204, 219, 222, 224, 228, 229, 233, 234, 244, 245, 249–51, 253–5, 263, 264, **4**, **34**
Bilberry, 25, 36, 41, 53, 62–4, 66, 76, 79, 84, 85, 87, 89, 90, 93, 97, 111, 114, 221–3, 226, 227, 251, **25**
Birch, 42, 51, 61, 62, 65, 66, 75, 76, 89, 118, 119, 123–7, 204, 222, 224, 228, 229, 233, 234, 250, 251, 253–5, 263, 264, **34**
Bird cherry, 88, 113, **18**
Birdsfoot, 63, **21**
Birdsfoot trefoil, 26, 27, 30, 32, 36, 41, 44, 45, 80, 116, **21**
Birthwort, 34, **9**
*Biscutella*, 40, 41, **12**
Bistort, 115
Biting stonecrop, 82, 218, 244
Bitter vetchling, 36
Black knapweed, 92, **29**
Black medick, 101, 116, 267, **21**
Black poplar, 71, 100, 103, 248, 249, **3**
Blackcurrant, 29, 93, 102
Blackthorn, 35, 38, 42, 43, 63, 65, 66, 70, 75, 89, 99, 100, 101, 103–10, 113, 114, 201, 205, 206, 212, 214, 219, 220, 224, 225, 234, 235, 243, 244, 245, 250, 253, **18**, **33**
Bladder campion, 232, 243, **11**
Blue moor-grass, 58
Bog myrtle, 113, 206, 209, 220, 229, 234, 243, 251, **5**, **33**
Bog rosemary, 220
Bogbean, 121
Borage, 208, **26**
*Borago*, 208, **26**
*Brachypodium*, 30–32, 59, 228, 262, **32**
Bracken, 211, 222, 229, 230, 254, **32**
Bramble, 33, 41, 54, 62, 63, 66, 70, 71, 77, 79, 83, 93, 204, 212, 220, 221–4, 226, 228, 230, 234, 246, 251, 252, 254, 255, 260, **15**
Branched bur-reed, 202
*Brassica*, 38, 39, 80, 216, 221, 229, 244, 265, **13**
Broad-leaved dock, **10**
Broad-leaved willow herb, 84
*Bromus*, 30
Broom, 28, 41, 44, 63, 74, 81, 97, 98, 102, 108, 116, 203, 230, 244, 261, 268, **19**, **33**
Buckler mustard, 40, 41, **12**
Buckthorn, 38, 41, 88, **22**
*Buddleia*, 240
Bulbous corydalis, **12**
Bulrush, 259, **30**
Bur chervil, 78
Bur-reed, 259
Burdock, 50, 223, 256
Burnet rose, 83, 85
Burnet saxifrage, 78, 94, **24**
Buttercup, 246

Cabbage, 38, 39, 80, 221, 229, 265, **13**
*Cakile*, 217
*Calendula*, 262
*Calluna*, 62, 63, 66, 78, 85, 87, 89, 93, 97, 100, 111, 113, 115, 116, 203, 209, 219–21, 223, 225, 226, 241, 251, **24**
*Campanula*, 218, 224
Campion, 262
Candytuft, 41
*Cardamine*, 39, 40
*Carduus*, 50, 252, 257
*Carex*, 60, 242, 256, **30**
Carnation, 261
Carnation grass, **30**
*Carpinus*, 76, 110, 252, 264, **5**
Carrot, 216
Cat's tail, 58, **32**
Catchfly, 119
Cedar, 201
*Cedrus*, 201
*Centaurea*, 55, 56, 92, **29**
*Cerastium*, 92
*Chaerophyllum*, 90
*Chamaecyparis*, 96, 241, **1**
*Chamaemelum*, 238
Chamomile, 79, 238
*Chamomilla*, 238
Charlock, 39, 40, 216
*Cheiranthus*, 80
*Chenopodium*, 84, 94, 216, 217, 228, 230, 254, **11**
Cherry, 35, 51, 73, 210
Chickweed, 76, 78–80, 82, 90, 211, 215, 216, 218–20, 223, 224, 225, 226, 236, 241, 246, 254, 260, **11**
*Chrysanthemum*, 261, **33**
Cinquefoil, 33, 75
*Circaea*, 84
*Cirsium*, 50, 252, 257, **29**
*Cladium*, 202, 258
*Clematis*, 75, 77, 87, 88, 91, 96, 97, 108, **12**
Clover, 26, 37, 45, 46, 77, 80, 81, 101, 109, 215, 221, 236, 262, 265, 267, **21**
Cock's-foot, 32, 57, 58, 64, 219, 228, 236, 237, 255, 256, **31**
Comfrey, 212, **26**
Common cow-wheat, 55, 56, **27**
Common figwort, **27**
Common mallow, 82, **22**
Common meadow-rue, 90, **12**
Common orache, 76, 84, 94, **11**
Common reed, 202, 237, 259
Common rock-rose, 45, 208, 224, **23**
Common sorrel, 25, **10**
Common storksbill, 45
Common toadflax, 91, **27**
*Convolvulus*, 79, 117, 268, **26**
Corn chamomile, 238

*Cornus*, 47, 99, 223
*Coronilla*, 27, 32, 36, 37, 46, **19**
Corydalis, 34, **12**
*Corydalis*, 34, **12**
*Corylus*, 62, 72, 74, 87, 89, 100, 110, 111, 118, 122, 124, 127, 220, 223, 224, 229, 233, 263, 264, **5**
Cotton-grass, 60, 258, **30**
Couch-grass, 57, 64, 236, 255, **32**, **33**
Cow parsley, 78, **24**
Cowberry, 25, 84, 223, **25**
Cowslip, 48, 218, **25**
Cranesbill, 45
*Crataegus*, 29, 35, 38, 61–3, 65, 66, 70, 73, 75, 76, 85, 89, 90, 93, 97, 100, 103–8, 110, 111, 114, 201, 202, 204, 205, 214, 219, 220, 224, 225, 228, 233, 236, 240, 241, 243, 246, 250, 252, 253, 255, **17**
Creeping cinquefoil, 115, 116, **16**
Creeping sallow, 63, 224
Creeping thistle, **29**
Creeping willow, 206, 223
*Crepis*, 231, 262
Cross-leaved heath, 113, 115, 221, 225
Crowberry, 25, 78, 227, **25**
Crown vetch, 27, 37, **19**
Cruciferae, 36
Cuckoo flower, 39, 40
Cupressus, 96, 241
Currant, 100, **34**
Cut-sedge, 258
*Cynoglossum*, 217, 234
Cypress spurge, **22**
*Cytisus*, 28, 41, 44, 63, 74, 81, 97, 98, 102, 108, 116, 203, 230, 244, 261, 268, **19**, **33**

*Dactylis*, 32, 57, 58, 64, 219, 228, 236, 237, 255, 256, **31**
Daisy, 80, 109, **28**
Dandelion, 77–9, 82, 115, 208, 209, 211–13, 217, 218, 220, 223, 225, 226, 236, 246, 260, 266, **29**
Dark mullein, 239, **27**
*Daucus*, 35, 216
Dead-nettle, 213, 219, 220, 246, 264–6
Delphinium, 265, **12**
*Delphinium*, 265, **12**
*Deschampsia*, 241, 256
*Descurainia*, 98, **12**
Devilsbit scabious, 55, 119, **28**
Dewberry, 83
*Dianthus*, 232, 261
*Digitalis*, 56, 91, 219, 257, **27**
*Dipsacus*, 119
Dock, 30, 43, 75, 76, 78, 79, 82, 209, 211, 212, 215–21, 223–6, 228–30, 236, 237, 241, 246, 252–4, 257, 260, **10**, **33**
Dog rose, 83, 85, **14**
Dog violet, 52, 53, 55, **23**
Dog's mercury, 254, **22**
Dogwood, 47, 99, 223
Douglas fir, 64
Dwarf treacle mustard, 40
Dyer's greenweed, 28, 115, 230, 234, **19**

Early hair grass, **32**
Elder, 94, 104, 117, 229
Elm, 51, 52, 89, 104, 108, 109, 111, 114, 118, 122, 204, 206, 220, 235, 244, 255, **7**
*Empetrum*, 25, 78, 223, 227, **25**
Enchanter's nightshade, 84
English elm, 42
*Epilobium*, 84, 120–22, 241, **23**
*Equisetum*, 257
*Erica*, 44, 62, 63, 66, 78, 93, 113, 115, 116, 209, 221, 225, 226, **24**
*Eriophorum*, 60, 258, **30**
*Erodium*, 45
*Eryngium*, 32
*Erysimum*, 40, 98, **16**
*Euonymus*, 47, 100
*Eupatorium*, 79, 92, 96, 264, **28**
*Euphorbia*, 99, 120, **22**
European larch, 96, 113, 263, **1**
Evening primrose, 121

*Fagus*, 28, 42, 65, 69, 74, 90, 100, 110, 114, 124, 125, 214, 240, 244, 247, 263, 264, **7**
False-brome, 59
Fat hen, 84, 94, 216, 217, **11**
Fennel, 35
Fescue, 59
*Festuca*, 31, 58, 59, 218, 256, **31**
Feverfew, 238
Fiddle dock, **10**
Field bindweed, 79, 117, 268, **26**
Field maple, 76, 127, 128, 247, 249, 264, **8**
Field mouse-ear, 92
Field scabious, 55, 119
Figwort, 239, 240, **27**
*Filipendula*, 66, 234, 236, 246
Fir, 233
Flixweed, 98, **12**
*Foeniculum*, 35
Forgetmenot, 208
Foxglove, 56, 91, 219, 257, **27**
*Fragaria*, 33, 82, 83, 85, 115, **15**
*Frangula*, 38, 47, 88
*Fraxinus*, 67, 95, 105, 117, 119, 241, 244, 245, 247, 252, **8**
*Fuchsia*, 120, 121
Funeral cypress, 241

*Galeopsis*, 264
*Galium*, 78, 79, 81, 119–22, 215, 217, 224, 226, **26**
Garden marigold, 262
Garden pansy, 53
Garlic mustard, 39, 40, **13**
*Genista*, 28, 74, 115, 230, 234, 261, 268, **19**
*Geranium*, 45, 115
Germander, 115
*Geum*, 78, **16**
Glaucous sedge, 256
Globe flower, 265
Goat willow, 49, 84, 99, 101, 243, 248, 249, **2**
Golden rod, 92–6, 212, 229, 238, 239, **28**
Good King Henry, 84
Gooseberry, 29, 100, 102, **34**
Goosefoot, 228, 230, 254
Gorse, 41, 44, 47, 74, 81, 97, 116, 203, 209, **19**
Great fern-sedge, 202
Great mullein, **27**
Great reedmace, 258, 259, **30**
Great woodrush, 222
Greater birdsfoot trefoil, 26
Greater knapweed, 55
Greater stitchwort, 92, **11**
Greenweed, 261
Grey sallow, 49, 84, 248, **2**
Grey willow, 101
Groundsel, 74, 79, 80, 208, 213, 223, 226, 246, 266
Guelder rose, 99, 117

Hairy greenweed, 268
Hairy woodrush, 256, **30**
*Halimione*, 217
Harebell, 218, 224
Hawksbeard, 262
Hawkweed, 56, 209
Hawthorn, 29, 35, 38, 61–3, 65, 66, 70, 73, 75, 76, 85, 89, 90, 93, 97, 100, 103–8, 110, 111, 114, 201, 202, 204, 205, 214, 219, 220, 224, 225, 228, 233, 236, 240, 241, 243, 246, 250, 252, 253, 255, **17**
Hazel, 62, 72, 74, 87, 89, 100, 110, 111, 118, 122, 124, 127, 220, 223, 224, 229, 233, 263, 264, **5**
Heath, 63, 93
Heath bedstraw, 81
Heath false-brome, 31, **32**
Heather, 62, 63, 66, 78, 85, 87, 89, 93, 97, 100, 111, 113, 115, 116, 203, 209, 219–21, 223, 225, 227, 241, 251, **24**
*Hedera*, 47, 99, 107, 111, 253, **23**
Hedge bedstraw, 78, 81, 120, 215, 217, 224, **26**
Hedge mustard, 39, 40, 80, **12**
Hedge woundwort, 265, **26**
*Helianthemum*, 41, 45, 115, 208, 224, **23**
Hemp agrimony, 79, 92, 96, 264, **28**
Hemp-nettle, 264
Henbane, 261
*Heracleum*, 94, 215, 240, **24**
Herb bennet, 78
*Hibiscus*, 32
*Hieracium*, 56, 209, 238
*Hippocrepis*, 27, 30, 37, 46, **21**
*Hippophae*, 95, 205
Hogweed, 94, 215, 240, **24**
*Holcus*, 30, 59, **31**
Holly, 47, 97, 99, **8**
Hollyhock, 82
Honewort, **24**
Honeysuckle, 49, 83, 99, 103, 107, 110, 119, 235, 242, 266, **28**
*Honkenya*, 261
Hop, 50, 52, 204, 235, 266, **9**
Hornbeam, 76, 110, 252, 264, **5**
Horse chestnut, 249
Horse-radish, 80, **13**
Horseshoe vetch, 27, 30, 37, 46, **21**
Horsetail, 257
Houndstongue, 217, 234
Houseleek, 33
*Humulus*, 50, 52, 93, 204, 235, 252, 266, **9**
*Hyoscyamus*, 261

*Iberis*, 41
*Ilex*, 47, 97, 99, **8**
*Impatiens*, 86, **22**
*Iris*, 211, 242, 258, 259, **30**
Ivy, 47, 99, 107, 111, 253, **23**

Jointed rush, 259, **30**
*Juglans*, 201
*Juncus*, 232, 258, 259, **30**
Juniper, 86, 95, 241, **1**
*Juniperus*, 86, 95, 241, **1**

*Knautia*, 55, 119
Kidney vetch, 30, 44, 46, **20**
Knapweed, 56
Knotgrass, 76–9, 116, 217, 221, 226, 228, 230, 243, 253, 260, **9**

Labrador tea, 220
*Laburnum*, 74
*Lactuca*, 221, 231, 238, 265, **29**
Lady's bedstraw, 78, 81, 120, 215, **26**
Lady's mantle, 80, 261, **14**
*Lamium*, 213, 219, 220, 223, 246, 264–6
Larch, 230, **1**
*Larix*, 96, 113, 230, 263, **1**
*Lathyrus*, 203, **20**
Lawson's cypress, 96, 241, **1**
*Lecidea*, 252
*Ledum*, 220
Leguminosae, 41
Lesser celandine, 90, 244, **12**
Lesser meadow-rue, 90
Lesser reedmace, 256, 259
Lettuce, 221, 231, 238, 265, **29**
Lichen, 112, 207, 208, 214, 252, 269, **32**
*Ligustrum*, 67, 73, 99, 103, 105, 107, 111, 117, 241, 244, **26**
Lilac, 103, 111, 117
Lime, 42, 65, 104, 105, 108, 109, 118, 122, 206, 247, 253, **8**
*Linaria*, 56, 91, 262, **27**
*Lonicera*, 49, 83, 99, 103, 107, 111, 119, 235, 242, 266, **28**
Loosestrife, 79, 121
*Lotus*, 26, 27, 30, 32, 36, 41, 44, 45, 77, 80, 116, **21**
Lousewort, 211
Lucerne, 36, 37, 63, 267, **21**
*Luzula*, 222, 256, **30**
*Lychnis*, 119, 231, 232, **11**
*Lycopersicon*, 261
*Lysimacha*, 79, 211, 234, **26**
*Lythrum*, 66, 96, 121, 122, 234, **23**

Maize, 261
Mallow, 32, 50, **22**
*Malus*, 29, 38, 62, 65, 66, 70, 73, 89, 90, 97, 103, 109, 118, 119, 201, 210, 214, 225, 235, 245, 250, **16**
*Malva*, 32, 50, 82, **22**
Maple, 245
Marjoram, 77
Marram grass, 63
Mat-grass, 58, 232, **32**
*Matricaria*, 238, **28**
Meadow buttercup, 87, **12**
Meadow fescue, 256, **31**
Meadow grass, 60
Meadow saxifrage, 82
Meadow vetchling, 36, 203, **20**
Meadowsweet, 66, 234, 236, 246
*Medicago*, 36, 37, 44, 63, 101, 116, 267, **21**
Medick, 44
Mediterranean cypress, 96
*Melampyrum*, 55, 56, **27**
Melilot, 46, 267, **20**
*Melilotus*, 46, 267, **20**
*Mentha*, 211
*Menyanthes*, 121
*Mercurialis*, 120, 254, **22**
Mignonette, 40
Milk-parsley, 35, **24**
Milk-vetch, 27
Mint, 211
*Molinia*, 30, 58, 232, 262, **31**
Monkshood, 265
Monterey cypress, 96, 241
Moss, 207
Mossy saxifrage, 82
Mountain houseleek, 34
Mouse-ear hawkweed, 238
Mugwort, 75, 237
Mullein, 239, 240, **27**
Mustard, 39
*Myosotis*, 208
*Myrica*, 113, 206, 209, 220, 229, 234, 243, **5**

*Nardus*, 58, 232, **32**
Nasturtium, 38, 39
Navelwort, 78
Nettle, 212, 229, 230, 254, 260, 264–6, 269, **9**
Northern bilberry, 36, 220
Norway spruce, 91, 113, 118, 204, **1**

Oak, 28, 42, 61–3, 65, 68, 72, 75, 76, 89, 102, 104–10, 112, 114, 122, 124–6, 201, 202, 204–6, 214, 229, 233, 235, 236, **6**, **33**
*Oenothera*, 121
Onion, 228
*Onobrychis*, 203
*Ononis*, 45, 82, 261, 262, **20**
Orache, 228, 229, 254
*Origanum*, 77
*Ornithopus*, 63, **21**
Orpine, 100
Osier, 263, **1**

*Pancratium*, 233, **30**
*Parietaria*, 50
Parsnip, 216
*Pastinaca*, 94, 216
Pea, 265
Pear, 29, 51, 66, 70, 89, 97, 109, 210, 214, 250, **16**
*Pedicularis*, 211
Pellitory of the wall, 50
*Peltigera*, 207
Petty whin, 74, 115, **19**
*Peucedanum*, 35, **24**
*Phleum*, 31, 58, **32**
*Phragmites*, 24, 202, 237, 259, **30**
*Physcia*, 269
*Picea*, 64, 91, 113, 118, 204, 206, 233, **1**
*Pimpinella*, 78, 94, **24**
Pine, 64, 66, 91, 201, 206, 233, 263, **1**, **34**
*Pinus*, 64, 66, 86, 91, 113, 118, 201, 206, 233, 263, **1**, **34**
*Pisum*, 265
*Plantago*, 55, 56, 77, 208, 211, 213, 215–17, 221–5, 229, 236, 241, 244, 251, 252, 254, 256, 260, **27**
Plantain, 55, 56, 77, 208, 211, 213, 215–17, 221–5, 229, 236, 241, 251, 252, 254, 256, 260, **27**
Plum, 38, 70, 73, 109, 114, 205, 210, 214, 241, 267
*Poa*, 57, 60, 225, 228, 236, **31**
*Polygonatum*, **34**
*Polygonum*, 76–9, 115, 116, 217, 221, 226, 228, 230, 243, 253, 260, **9**
Poplar, 28, 49–51, 61, 66, 71, 72, 87, 108, 118, 119, 123–8, 205, 206, 245, 246, 249, 267, 269, **3**
*Populus*, 28, 49, 50, 51, 61, 66, 71–3, 87, 99, 100, 103, 108, 118, 119, 123–8, 205, 206, 235, 245, 246, 248, 249, 267, 269, **3**
Potato, 117, 257, **27**
*Potentilla*, 33, 75, 115, 116, 260, **16**
*Prenanthes*, 238
Prickly saltwort, 217, **11**
Primrose, 48, 78, 90, 218–21, 223–6
*Primula*, 48, 78, 90, 218–21, 223–6, **25**
Privet, 67, 73, 99, 103, 105, 107, 111, 117, 241, 244, **26**
*Prunus*, 35, 38, 42, 43, 51, 62, 65, 66, 70, 75, 76, 88, 89, 97, 100, 101, 103–5, 106–10, 113, 114, 201, 205, 206, 212, 214, 219, 220, 224, 225, 234, 235, 241, 243, 244, 250, 253, 267, **18**, **33**
*Pseudotsuga*, 64
*Pteridium*, 211, 222, 229, 230, **32**
*Ptychotis*, 35
Purple lettuce, 238
Purple loosestrife, 66, 96, 122, 234, **23**
Purple moor-grass, 30, 58, 232, 262, **31**
Purple saxifrage, 82
*Pyrus*, 29, 51, 66, 70, 89, 97, 109, 210, 214, 250, **16**

*Quercus*, 28, 42, 61–3, 65, 68, 72, 75, 76, 89, 102, 104–9, 112, 114, 122, 124–6, 201, 202, 204–6, 214, 229, 233, 235, 236, 240, 243–6, 249–55, 263, **6**, **33**

Ragged robin, 231, 232, **11**
Ragwort, 79, 92, 93, 95, 213, 234, 224, **29**
*Ranunculus*, 87, 90, 244, 246, **12**
Rape, 80
*Raphanus*, 41
Raspberry, 33, 83, 251, 255, **15**
Red campion. 90, 232
Red clover, **21**
Redcurrant, 29, 93, 102, 111, **22**
Redshank, 79, 230
Reed, 24, **30**
Reedmace, 259
*Reseda*, 38–40, **13**
Rest-harrow, 45, 82, 261, 262, **20**
*Rhamnus*, 38, 41, 88, **22**
*Rheum*, 257
Rhubarb, 257
*Rhynchospora*, 60, **30**
Ribbed melilot, **20**
*Ribes*, 29, 93, 100, 102, 111, **22**, **34**
Ribwort plantain, 56, 224, **27**
Rock cress, 39
Rock-rose, 41, 115
Rocket, 41
*Rosa*, 73, 75, 85, 109, 110, 233, 234, 246, 250, **14**, **34**
Rose, 73, 75, 109, 110, 233, 234, 246, 250, **34**
Rosebay willow herb, 84, **23**
Rough chervil, 90
Rowan, 29, 70, 98, 99, **16**
*Rubia*, 120
*Rubus*, 33, 41, 54, 62, 63, 66, 70, 71, 77, 79, 83, 93, 204, 212, 220–24, 226, 228, 230, 234, 246, 251, 252, 254, 255, 261, **11**

*Rumex*, 25, 30, 43, 75, 76, 78, 79, 82, 209, 211, 212, 215–26, 228–30, 236, 237, 241, 246, 252–4, 256, 260, **10**, **33**
Rush, 232, 258

Sainfoin, 203
Salad burnet, 115, 224, **14**
*Salix*, 49–52, 62–6, 71, 84, 85, 87, 99, 100–103, 105–110, 112, 118, 119, 122–8, 202, 204–6, 219, 220, 222–6, 228–30, 233–6, 240, 243, 245–7, 249–55, 263, 267, 269, **2**, **33**
Sallow, 50, 51, 62–6, 71, 85, 87, 100, 102, 103, 105–8, 110, 112, 118, 122–8, 202, 204–6, 219, 220, 222–6, 228–30, 233–6, 240, 245, 246, 249, 251–5, 269, **2**, **33**
*Salsola*, 217, **11**
*Sambucus*, 94, 107, 117, 229
*Sanguisorba*, 115, 224, **14**
*Saxifraga*, 34, 80, 82, 218, **14**
Saxifrage, 34, 80
*Scabiosa*, 213
Scabious, 213
Scented mayweed, 238
Scentless mayweed, 238, **28**
*Scirpus*, 232, 258, 259, **30**
Scorpion vetch, 32, 36, 46
Scots pine, 86, 113, 118, **1**
*Scrophularia*, 224, 239, 240, **27**
Sea aster, 238
Sea beet, 228, **11**
Sea buckthorn, 95, 205
Sea campion, 231, 232
Sea daffodil, 233, **30**
Sea plantain, 244, **27**
Sea purslane, 217
Sea rocket, 217
Sea sandwort, 261
Sea wormwood, 74, **28**
Seablite, 217
Sedge, 60, 242
*Sedum*, 33, 82, 100, 115, 218, 244, **13**
*Sempervivum*, 33, 34
*Senecio*, 74, 79, 80, 92, 93, 95, 208, 213, 223, 226, 234, 244, 246, 262, 266, **29**
*Seseli*, 35
*Sesleria*, 58
Sheep's fescue, 31, 58, 218, **31**
Sheep's sorrel, 25, 218, 224, **10**
Shining cranesbill, 115
*Silene*, 90, 231, 232, 243, 262, **11**
Silver birch, 68, 69, 72, 74, 76, 85, 89, 90, 99, 101, 102, 104–12, 114, 219, 222, 244, 245, 249, **4**
Silver fir, 64, 113, 204, 263, **1**
*Sinapis*, 39, 40, 216
*Sisymbrium*, 39–41, 80, **12**
Sitka spruce, 64
Slender false-brome, 30, 32, 228, 262, **32**
Small-leaved lime, 69, **8**
Smooth hawksbeard, 231
Snowberry, 47, 119
Soft rush, 259
*Solanum*, 117, 257, **27**
*Solidago*, 92–6, 212, 229, 238, 239, **28**
Solomon's seal, **34**
*Sonchus*, 220, 225, 231, 238
*Sorbus*, 29, 70, 98, 99, **16**
Sorrel, 30, 43, 76, 218, 241, 253
Sow-thistle, 220, 225, 231, 238
*Sparganium*, 202, 259
Speedwell, 55, 56
Spindle, 47
Spruce, 91, 206, 233, 263
Spurge, 120
Square-stemmed willowherb, 241
*Stachys*, 77, 257, 265, **26**
*Stellaria*, 76, 78–80, 82, 90, 92, 211, 215, 216, 218–20, 223–6, 236, 241, 246, 254, 260, **11**
Sticky groundsel, 262
Stinging nettle, 50–53
Stinking chamomile, 238
Stinking goosefoot, 84
Stitchwort, 215
Stonecrop, 33, 115, **13**
Strawberry, 82, 83, 85
Strawberry tree, 49, **25**
*Suaeda*, 217
*Succisa*, 55, 119, **28**
Sugar beet, 215, 216
Sweet violet, 219, **23**
Sweet William, 232
Sycamore, 76, 127, 128, 249, **33**
*Symphoricarpos*, 47, 119
*Symphytum*, 212, **26**
*Syringa*, 103, 111, 117

Tall fescue, 256
*Tanacetum*, 74, 238
Tansy, 74
*Taraxacum*, 77–9, 82, 115, 208, 209, 211–13, 217, 218, 220, 223, 225, 226, 236, 246, 260, 266, **29**
*Taxus*, 206, **1**
Teasel, 119
*Teucrium*, 56, 90, 115
*Thalictrum*, 90, **12**
Thistle, 50, 252, 257, **29**
Thrift, 115, 244
Thyme, 77, 115
Thyme-leaved speedwell, 116
*Thymus*, 27, 47, 77, 94, 115, 116, 224, **26**
*Tilia*, 42, 65, 69, 104, 105, 108, 109, 118, 122, 206, 247, 253, **8**
Timothy grass, 31
Toadflax, 56, 262
Tomato, 261
Tormentil, 260
Touch-me-not balsam, 86, **22**
Travellers joy, 75, 77, 87, 88, 91, 96, 108, **12**
Treacle mustard, 98
Trefoil, 26, 77
*Trifolium*, 26, 37, 45, 46, 77, 80, 81, 101, 109, 215, 221, 236, 262, 265, 267, **21**
*Trinia*, 35, **24**
*Trollius*, 265
*Tropaeolum*, 38, 39
True bulrush, **30**
Tuberous pea, 36, **20**
Tufted hair-grass, 241, 256
Turnip, 216, **13**

*Typha*, 258, 259, **30**

*Ulex*, 41, 44, 47, 74, 81, 97, 116, 203, 209, **19**
*Ulmus*, 42, 51, 52, 89, 100, 104, 108, 109, 111, 114, 118, 122, 204, 206, 220, 235, 245, 246, 255, **7**
*Umbelicus*, 78
*Urtica*, 50–53, 212, 229, 230, 254, 260, 264, 266, 269, **9**

*Vaccinium*, 25, 36, 41, 53, 62–4, 66, 76, 79, 84, 85, 87, 89, 90, 93, 97, 111, 114, 220–23, 226, 251, **25**
*Verbascum*, 239, 240, **27**
*Veronica*, 55, 56, 116
Vetch, 26, 36, 37, 81, **20**
*Vicia*, 26, 36, 37, 81, 268, **20**
*Viburnum*, 99, 117
Vine, 121
*Viola*, 52–5, 79, 219, **23**
Violet, 54, 79
*Vitis*, 121

Wallflower, 80
Walnut, 201
Water avens, 78, **16**
Water dock, 43, 211, **10**
Water figwort, 224
White beak-sedge, 60, **30**
White campion, 232
White dead-nettle, 223
White mullein, 239
White sallow, **2**
Wild apple, 107
Wild cabbage, 244
Wild carrot, 35
Wild hop, 93
Wild madder, 120
Wild mignonette, 38, 39, **13**
Wild parsnip, 94
Wild plum, 106–8, 110, 113, 245, 250, **18**
Wild radish, 41
Wild strawberry, 33, 115, **15**
Wild thyme, 27, 47, 94, 116, 224, **26**
Willow, 50–52, 100, 103, 109, 118, 119, 123, 125, 127, 128, 202, 267, **2**
Willowherb, 120–22
Winter cress, 41
Wood anemone, 90
Wood meadow grass, 228, 236
Wood sage, 56, 90
Wood spurge, 99, **22**
Wood vetch, 268, **20**
Wormwood, 92, 237, **28**
Woundwort, 77, 257
Wych elm, 42, 100, 246, 7

*Xanthoria*, 269

Yarrow, 74, 92, 109, 116, 212
Yellow iris, 211, 242, 258, 259, **30**
Yellow loosestrife, 211, 234, **26**
Yellow saxifrage, 34, 80, 82, 218, **14**
Yew, 206, **1**
Yorkshire fog, 31, **31**

*Zea*, 261

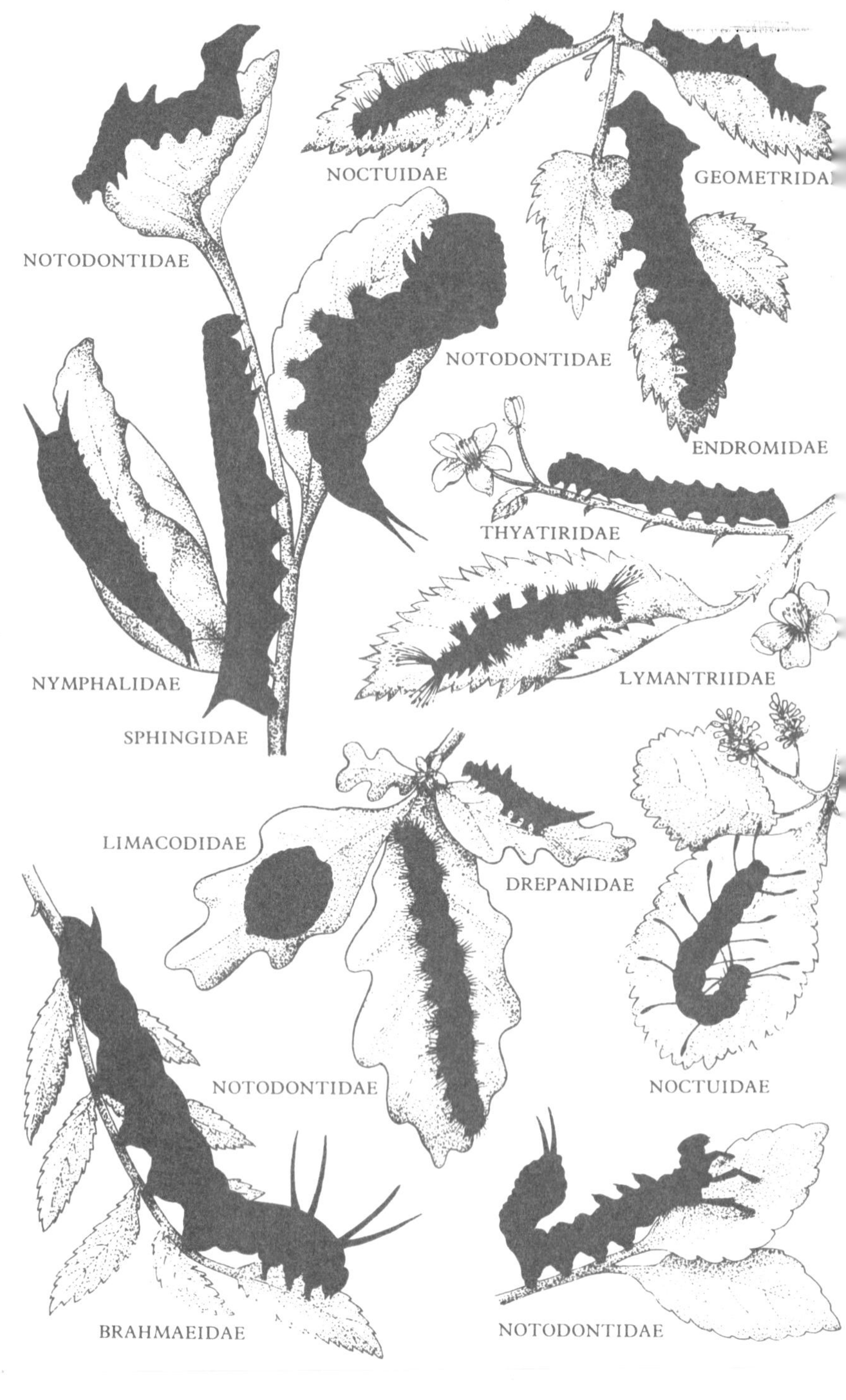
NOTODONTIDAE
NOCTUIDAE
GEOMETRIDAE
NOTODONTIDAE
ENDROMIDAE
THYATIRIDAE
LYMANTRIIDAE
NYMPHALIDAE
SPHINGIDAE
LIMACODIDAE
DREPANIDAE
NOTODONTIDAE
NOCTUIDAE
BRAHMAEIDAE
NOTODONTIDAE